Clinical Social Work

BEYOND GENERALIST PRACTICE WITH INDIVIDUALS, GROUPS, AND FAMILIES

LAMBERT MAGUIRE
University of Pittsburgh

BROOKS/COLE

THOMSON LEARNING

Australia • Canada • Mexico • Singapore • Spain • United Kingdom • United States

Dedicated to Barbara, Amy, and Mandy.

BROOKS/COLE

✳ ™

THOMSON LEARNING

Executive Acquisitions Editor: *Lisa Gebo*
Manuscript Editor: *Jeanne Patterson*
Assistant Editor: *Alma Dea Michelena*
Permissions Editor: *Sue Ewing*
Marketing Team: *Carolyn Concilla,*
  Megan Hansen, Tami Strang
Cover Design: *Roger Knox*

Print Buyer: *Vena Dyer*
Editorial Assistant: *Sheila Walsh*
Typesetting: *Shepherd, Inc.*
Project Editor: *Laurel Jackson*
Printing and Binding: *Webcom Ltd.*
Production Service: *Shepherd, Inc.*

For more information about this or any other Brooks/Cole product, contact:
BROOKS/COLE
511 Forest Lodge Road
Pacific Grove, CA 93950 USA
www.brookscole.com
1-800-423-0563 (Thomson Learning Academic Resource Center)

For permission to use material from this work, contact us by
www.thomsonrights.com
fax: 1-800-730-2215
phone: 1-800-730-2214

Printed in Canada

10 9 8 7 6 5 4 3 2 1

Library of Congress Cataloging-in-Publication Data

Maguire, Lambert.
   Clinical social work : beyond generalist practice with individuals, groups, and families / Lambert Maguire.—1st ed.
     p. cm.
   Includes bibliographical references and index.
   ISBN 0-534-57583-8 (alk. paper)
   1. Psychiatric social work. I. Title.

HV689 .M33 2001
362.2'.0425—dc21

2001035726

Brief Contents

Contents

Part Two

SYSTEMS-BASED APPROACHES   65

Chapter 3

Systems Interventions with Individuals   66

Chapter 4

Case Management   94

Chapter 5

Group Interventions   120

Chapter 6

Family Systems Interventions   *158*

Part Three

ADVANCED TECHNIQUES WITH INDIVIDUALS   185

Chapter 7

Psychodynamic Interventions   186

Chapter 8

Behavioral Interventions   *221*

Chapter 9

Chapter 10

Brief Interventions   277

Chapter 11

Putting It All Together: Documentation, Assessments, and Treatment Plans   295

Preface

Clinical social work is changing at a rapid pace, and this book describes and integrates those changes. Clinical practice or advanced social work has shifted to a broad generalist orientation, and practitioners are required to apply very advanced techniques. Research establishes the most efficient and effective approaches with an emphasis on brevity. In addition, social workers are recognizing and planfully dealing with the obvious fact that certain populations are at greater risk than others and that diversity of race, religion, culture, sexual orientation, and other factors require new skills that necessitate the questioning of social workers' personal and professional values and ethics. Empowerment and a strengths perspective, which support the development of innate abilities and recognize differences in a positive manner, are also helping social workers increase the individual client's capacity to learn to use his or her own systems constructively. Managed care has also affected the way clinical social workers practice. These issues, which are redefining practice, are described at length in this text.

Clinical social work is generalist in its base, but it is a type of advanced practice. It currently includes a variety of systems-based interventions that use advanced generalist as well as ecologically based frameworks, family and group systems, and an eclectic integration of cognitive, behavioral, and psychodynamic methods. The goal of this textbook is to describe clearly the underlying theories and basic techniques of each approach in the context of this rapidly changing field.

Although this text is oriented toward an advanced level of practice, some undergraduates may also relate to the material in this book if they have a solid foundation in the theory of each of the major types of treatment, some interviewing skills, and a basic knowledge regarding the forming of therapeutic relationships. This text should also be useful to experienced social workers who need updated information about current interventions that have been particularly affected by the recent dramatic shifts in social service agencies and health and mental health settings.

This book is oriented toward direct clinical practice or micro- and mezzo-levels that include work with individuals, groups, and families. Social workers using this book may call themselves clinical social workers, caseworkers, case managers, clinicians, therapists, counselors, family or group workers, or psychotherapists. Their titles may vary in this vast and rapidly changing field, but the values, ethics, knowledge base, and many of the skills draw social workers together.

Now, at the beginning of the 21st century, the definition of *clinical social worker* has shifted among some social workers toward a realization that practitioners must go beyond the generalist orientation while maintaining it as a base. This orientation mirrors that of other helping professions in recognizing that individuals are affected by a wide variety of systems including social, political, economic, psychological, and biological systems, as well as by early developmental influences. To genuinely help individuals, practitioners must be broad based and aware of how these multiple systems and forces combine and interact in causing the types of difficulties encountered by social workers' clients. The revised definition of clinical social work practice says that the same generalist problem-solving approach can be applied in all social service settings. However, advanced levels of practice require a much higher level of knowledge and expertise than is generally described within a generalist perspective.

Clinical social workers practice in a complex environment that disallows the narrower focus of past practice. A high level of specialized knowledge and skills is required to deal with the complex demands of clients. This current perspective says that clinical social work practice is a systems-based approach that integrates empirically validated methods and eclectic frameworks. Practice builds on a broad-based systems orientation to understanding and solving problems but also integrates the advanced behavioral, cognitive, and psychodynamic techniques that are supported by research and required of higher-level professionals in today's demanding and competitive market.

The more "high-powered" specific clinical interventions that are designed for particular problems or diagnoses are essential. For instance, a large body of research indicates that cognitive interventions should be used with depression (Beck, 1996), just as behavioral approaches are most appropriate for phobias or when insight is limited. Behavioral approaches are also typically used for many institutionalized patients and for rather localized disorders such as tantrums, tics, bedwetting, or even violent outbursts (Lambert & Bergin, 1994). Furthermore, complex problems that are primarily a function of deep, ingrained life problems or a result of long-term parental abuse or neglect frequently necessitate insight and techniques that use or at least recognize the transference phenomenon or rely upon uncovering repressed or subconscious issues. It is essential that advanced social workers have the knowledge and ability to use such specialized techniques, even in managed care settings or when brevity is a prerequisite.

Clinical social work is a type of advanced practice that goes beyond generalist. A basic generalist approach does not sufficiently build on the strength of these specific advanced interventions. This text is based in the premise that clinical social work practice is a practical process of problem solving that requires a high level of knowledge and advanced techniques.

This text is designed for social work practitioners and students who struggle daily with the serious issues of how best to help their clients. It is a cliché to say that social work practice is an art and a science, but in reality, practitioners need the creativity, insight, and sensitivity of an artist as well as the skills of a scientist. This delicate balance practitioners can achieve by developing the knowledge and ability to use research concerning human behavior. This text recognizes that clinical social workers are advanced practitioners who require a high level of empirically based clinical skills that they can apply to a wide variety of client's needs.

Any text that describes current advanced social work or clinical practice must be based in solid research, sensitive to the reality of multiple causes and a wide variety of systems (including groups and families), and clear in its description of highly advanced techniques with individuals (Thyer & Wodarski, 1998). This text attempts to delineate these requisites. It is a textbook on clinical social work practice that covers the empirically validated, widely practiced major methods currently used in advanced social work, such as the broader systems-based generalist, ecological, and case management approaches and their strong emphasis on groups and families. Beyond that, this text clearly describes advanced knowledge and techniques based on psychodynamic, behavioral, cognitive, and various brief interventions.

Part One contains two chapters that define contemporary clinical social work practice. It begins with a chapter that describes the state of contemporary practice and factors that influence clinical social work, such as managed care, research, and the need for a generalist base while recognizing that both brevity and highly advanced skills are essential. Furthermore, these demands must be met in a fashion that is both ethical and sensitive to the unique values of the profession and to the diverse populations that social workers serve (see Chapter 1).

Chapter 2 explains how clinical social work practice begins with a generalist practice perspective that is based in a systems approach and a biopsychosocial understanding of human behavior. Chapter 2 also examines the basic major theories of current clinical practice and provides general guidelines to help students to understand research in choosing and combining approaches and techniques based on the large, complex empirical evidence and research in both the process and outcome of social work practice.

The theoretical foundation described is broad-based and eclectic and recognizes that clinical social work emanates from theories, which in turn posit the origin of biopsychosocial problems in several ways. Part One of this text recognizes that the problems of social work clients result from by a combination of psychological, social, and biological forces. Subsequently, social workers intervene with their clients based on their ability to understand and use a complex, and multifaceted knowledge base. Chapter 2 recognizes the need for an integrated and cohesive approach to advanced social work that builds upon the basic generalist skills.

Part Two consists of four chapters that reflect the systems-based orientation of clinical social work. These chapters describe systems interventions with individuals (Chapter 3), case management (Chapter 4), group interventions (Chapter 5), and family interventions (Chapter 6).

Part Three consists of five chapters that describe the major, essential theoretical approaches and methods used in advanced social work practice with individuals. Those approaches include psychodynamic (Chapter 7), behavioral (Chapter 8), and cognitive interventions (Chapter 9). Chapter 10 describes brief interventions that typically rely on one or more of those major theories. Chapter 11 summarizes and concretely describes the process of organizing and documenting assessments and clinical interventions in a treatment plan.

Acknowledgments

I would like to thank the following students who helped with research or with editing this book: David Bandler, Sarah E. Bledsoe, Carol Brooks, Ann Ruffalo, Elizabeth Stork, and my daughter Amy Maguire. I am also indebted to my many supportive colleagues at the University of Pittsburgh, particularly Dean David Epperson, Michael Patchner (now the dean at the University of Indiana), Valire Carr, Christina Newhill, Betty Blythe (now at Boston College), Ray Engel, Hide Yamatani, and Wynne Korr. I also appreciate the support provided to me by Carol Anderson and my colleagues at the NIMH Mental Health Services Research Center, where I serve as an associate director.

My thanks also to the following reviewers for their insightful comments and suggestions: Kevin Corcoran, Portland State University; Ronald Feldman, Columbia University; David Fike, Barry University; Bruce Friedman, Michigan State University; Grafton Hull, University of Utah; Bogart Leashore, Hunter College, CUNY; Katherine Shank, Northwestern University School of Law; and Joseph Walsh, Virginia Commonwealth University.

Brooks/Cole and Lisa Gebo have been unwavering in their support and encouragement. They have provided accurate and useful feedback and direction throughout the years that this text has been developing. I could not have asked for a better or more supportive publisher.

I am also indebted to my mentors at the University of Chicago's School of Social Service Administration and at the University of Michigan. This eclectic group of scholars included Helen Harris Perlman and Arthur Schwartz during my master's degree program and Tony Tripodi, Robert Vinter, Rosemary Sarri, and John Tropman during my doctoral program in Ann Arbor.

Finally, I thank the many clients I have seen over the last 25 years of my own clinical practice. I hope I have helped them as much as they have helped me in the process of understanding effective clinical social work.

DEFINING CONTEMPORARY PRACTICE

OVERVIEW OF CONTEMPORARY PRACTICE

Clinical social work has changed significantly in the last decade. New research and continuous changes in society have resulted in the development of a service delivery system that is radically different from that of the past. In this chapter, the task of defining clinical social work is preceded by a look at some of those changes.

Social workers practice in a rapidly changing society. Government policy continues to shift the responsibility for programs from the federal level to the states, which in turn often shift them down to cities, towns, or counties. The immediate future suggests a mixed economy for the provision of services that will include government, for-profit, nonprofit, and voluntary organizations all competing for the same sources of funds. In addition to these trends, Austin (1997) anticipates for the future

> continued increase in ethnic/cultural population diversity in the United States; the increasing number and longevity of older adults; increased diversity in family structures; increased polarization of public attitudes along both gender and ethnic lines; redefinition of the primary causes of chronic and severe mental illness as being biological rather than psychological; a two-tiered labor force with limited crossover from unskilled and semiskilled nontechnical jobs to skilled, technical, managerial and professional jobs. (p. 402)

An additional issue or trend no doubt includes increased globalization. However, globalization does not affect practice quite as much as the other trends and issues.

As clinical social workers move beyond basic generalist practice, they are expected to be able to work independently with a higher level of expertise and responsibility. What exactly does that mean? It means that in addition to their knowledge of generalist practice, advanced practitioners differ from generalists by the fact that they are expected to perform at a higher level in reference to major contemporary issues that significantly define and affect practice.

If a dozen experienced social workers and practice researchers were asked to list and describe the major issues and trends in contemporary practice, they probably would develop 12 different lists. In this first chapter, an attempt is made to describe the context of clinical practice and the central issues and trends challenging clinical practitioners today.

There are at least eight issues and trends that define contemporary and developing clinical social work practice:

1. *Systems-based approaches* such as the generalist and ecological approaches are used more, with an additional utilization of case management and informal support systems, as well as family and group methods.

2. *Advanced-practice techniques* are also the norm. Social workers are required to be highly skilled practitioners who integrate a vast and eclectic knowledge of methods and techniques to supplement their generalist perspective.

3. *Research* is relied upon extensively as the basis for all practice. Postmodernism and empiricism are debated widely (Thyer & Wodarski, 1998). These issues concern such diverse topics as the methodological preferences of qualitative versus quantitative methods; the sociopolitical issue of feminism and male-dominated research; and the philosophical question concerning free will as opposed to determinism in behavior. Another research issue involves the question of whether social work should use various lists of "problem statements" or the diagnostic categories defined in the *Diagnostic and Statistical Manual of Mental Disorders, Fourth Edition,* text revision, (American Psychiatric Association, 2000) or use a social work categorization method such as the "person in environment" (PIE) model (Karls & Wandrei, 1994). Perhaps a field as wide and diverse as social work actually requires multiple, separate "languages," each of which has been developed out of different traditions and cultures. Although the setting of the practice often determines the appropriate language or classification, some still question whether the field should push for its own classification set (PIE) or defer, at least in medical or psychiatric settings, to the generally accepted diagnoses of *DSM-IV-TR.*

4. *Brevity* in interventions is essential, and concerns arise regarding the legitimate need to keep costs down while still providing the best quality of care. Even though a half-century of research suggests that long-term, insight-oriented approaches are not only less efficient but also less effective than many short-term methods (Bergin & Garfield, 1994), the current push toward brevity is motivated by insurance and profit-oriented bottom lines of health and human service organizations, not necessarily by best practice.

5. *Diversity*—including a sensitivity to the wide range of cultural, ethnic, racial, sexual, and gender differences that exist among our clients—is a focal concern. Practitioners at an advanced or clinical level have to be knowledgeable of and sensitive to the important differences in behavior, attitudes, and emotions of diverse client groups. A clinical social worker

or advanced clinician must go beyond basic stereotypes and gain an appropriate understanding of the client's unique perspective to achieve a successful outcome. Race, gender, age, religion, sexual orientation, education and other background characteristics all must be considered in helping the unique individuals we serve.

6. *Ethics and values* are essential factors in practice, particularly in relation to issues of social and economic justice for populations at risk. A clear understanding of appropriate individual and professional standards of behavior and ethical norms is needed in the many difficult situations social workers encounter. It is often the clinical social worker who must be the arbiter between individual rights and societal needs, between parental rights and the needs of individual children, or between those with money and power and those without it and dependent on the ethics and values of their social worker.

7. *Empowerment and the strengths perspective* are major components of virtually all methods of helping. Contemporary practitioners recognize that most successful outcomes happen only when clients use their own capacities and take the lead in making changes for themselves.

8. *Managed care* has mandated new and different ways of intervening. Costs, benefits, and the services defined as allowable all affect practice methods and services; practitioners need to work with the system, changing it where necessary and improving it whenever possible.

It is not enough for a clinical social worker simply to be aware of contemporary practice issues since those issues will undoubtedly change. An advanced practitioner must be a leader who anticipates the future while dealing with current issues with a high level of knowledge and expertise. A generalist will be affected by these issues, but a clinical or advanced practitioner actually effects changes to benefit individuals, groups, families, communities, and society.

SYSTEMS-BASED APPROACHES

The history of the social work field is characterized by sensitivity to the interactions between people and their environments. Social workers are trained to view their clients as individuals who continuously interact with different significant systems. These systems include the family, the community, the work environment, and a wide variety of other social systems that affect and are affected by clients. Social workers study human behavior and the social environment, which help us to understand how biological, psychological, cultural, economic, and political factors impact individuals, families, and communities.

The early history of social work in settlement houses and workers' philanthropic efforts exemplify how social work has always been sensitive to the effects of relocation; economic hardship; cultural, racial, and ethnic insensitivity; and unemployment. Even in the subsequent phase of the profession's development—from the 1920s through the 1950s—when social workers drew from the new science of psychoanalysis for practice knowledge, social work developed its own social variation. By the mid 1950s, when social services and mental health fields were being challenged on the basis of research to become even more sensitive to social and environmental forces, leaders in the field such as Helen Harris Perlman (1957) and Florence Hollis (1964) were developing the problem-solving approach and the psychosocial model, respectively.

The emphasis in social work education and practice on group dynamics and family systems also points to an ongoing focus on interactional, holistic, and broad-based systemic approaches to helping. This "ecological approach" includes not only Carel Germain's masterful works (Germain, 1991; Germain & Gitterman, 1996) but also other systems-oriented social work practitioners such as Hartman, who focuses on the interactional dynamics between individuals and their family systems (Hartman & Laird, 1983; Hartman, 1978), groups (Rose, 1990), or general social support systems (Maguire, 1991).

This ecological approach epitomizes *advanced* generalist practice since it begins where basic generalist practice ends. The broad-based systemic, or ecological, approach is the profession's most distinguishing characteristic in contemporary practice. Furthermore, advanced practitioners differ from generalists in that advanced practitioners understand and utilize the social environment and ecology of the client's system at a more complex level. The advanced-practice ecological approach and variations such as Mattaini's ecological systems approach (1995a; 1995b; 1997) are described in this book in Chapter 3. They are the basis and underlying elements for advanced practice and all of the specialized techniques and models that follow.

Clinical social workers modified their psychoanalytic approaches in the 1940s and, especially, in the 1950s as more ego psychological approaches were developed. For instance, practitioners such as Florence Hollis (1964) in social work established approaches that carried a balance between the social forces that impact upon feelings and behavior and the inner workings of the psyche. These psychosocial and ego-oriented casework approaches grew and developed, and a concurrent revolution in the treatment of mental health problems was seen in the development of new, psychotherapeutic, strengths-focused interventions—as opposed to the traditional psychoanalytic model.

The decade of the 1950s was a turning point in modern clinical social work in that two radically distinct modes of intervention emerged to challenge the psychodynamic approach. Behavior modification and a Rogerian or client-centered approach developed at that time within the helping professions as a response to the clear need for interventionist alternatives. Rogerian or client-centered social work differed from psychoanalytic approaches in its strong emphasis upon the individual's innate strength and capacity for self-actualization. The opinions of behaviorally oriented social workers also differed significantly from the traditional, medically oriented viewpoints. Behaviorists believed problems were caused by inappropriate learned responses to stimuli in the environment. Departure from the traditional models allowed clinical social workers to explore the strengths and healthy capacities that people either innately had or could be taught to develop by modifying their behavior.

Furthermore, the groundbreaking research of Hans Eysenck (1952) and, later, of Joel Fischer (1973) pointed out the limitations—if not outright failures—of traditional, insight-oriented, long-term therapy for a wide variety of client or patient populations. Several major, federally supported panels have also subsequently reinforced the fact that long-term, insight-oriented therapy as practiced in the 1950s and before was both inefficient and ineffective and that alternatives—especially those that empowered people to use the community, family, and individual resources and, particularly, self-help—must be further developed (President's Commission on Mental Health, 1978).

Self-help groups, community support systems, social networks, and family systems were used increasingly in the 1960s and 1970s in social services and mental health systems to help patients make the adjustment from large, inpatient state hospitals back into their home communities. This practice, which was mandated by the Community Mental Health Centers Act of 1963, was almost invariably hailed initially as a progressive, efficient, cost-effective, and humane way to empower people and build on their strengths but was eventually criticized for "dumping" people into the communities (Gerhart, 1990). In too many instances, the funds never transferred from inpatient to outpatient facilities and the initial hopes and plans of the 1963 Community Mental Health Centers Act were never fully put into practice. The trend toward deinstitutionalization and using the least-restrictive environment, such as the community, continues today for our clients with severe problems; but the most effective programs rely on people helping themselves.

The decades of the 1960s and 1970s also saw an increased focus on community organizing and macrosystem change in social work practice. In fact, there was even some backlash against clinical social workers who preferred to work directly with individuals, families, or small groups rather than larger systems. The profession became more immersed in understanding the system and attacking social inequities and injustices, particularly racism and poverty.

Contemporary clinical social work's emphasis upon systems—advanced techniques as well as generalist methods and an ecological approach— is therefore the result of recent history. When research in the 1950s through the 1970s found that clinical social work focused too much upon internal and unconscious psychodynamics rather than upon the social environment, leaders such as Helen Harris Perlman developed the problem-solving method

(1957) and, later, William Reid and Laura Epstein developed the task-centered approach (1972, 1977). These approaches, along with Florence Hollis's psychosocial approach (Hollis 1964), were impressive, unique social work adaptations that bridged traditional therapy and the advanced and ecologically oriented systems approaches of today.

The term *holistic* comes to mind in describing what many clinical social workers are currently doing. In contemporary practice, advanced social workers are required to recognize the validity of various etiological perspectives because the concept of any singular etiology for most severe mental health problems is no longer well accepted. Clinical social workers recognize that biological and biochemical forces are clearly affected by social and psychological forces and learned behaviors and emotions. They all interact in various ways. While the debate will no doubt continue for generations to come regarding the relative weight or impact of one causal force over another, few in clinical social work would be willing to suggest that they are not all factors in causing or at least in maintaining many severe emotional disorders. It is essential therefore that clinical social workers rely upon skills that are both advanced and generalist.

ADVANCED-PRACTICE TECHNIQUES

Social workers practice in a wide variety of settings, but they invariably are required to integrate the best possible interventions from a diverse skills base of several models and techniques for a given problem and client. Clinical practice requires an eclectic background in which practitioners know the techniques of several models and apply them propitiously on the basis of clinical research and solid empirical evidence.

At a recent statewide conference of evaluators of programs and services in mental health and social services, the keynote speaker criticized the audience of evaluators and researchers by accusing them and, subsequently, the thousands of service providers throughout the state of essentially being incompetents who must know by now exactly what to do for clients but refuse to do it to protect their jobs. The speaker was the director of the state department of human services and a highly regarded economist hired to "reform the system" and make it more responsive and efficient.

At one point, she said to this audience, "You can't tell me that after dozens of years of clinical research and evaluation of what works and what doesn't work, you people, who are supposed to be experts, don't even know what to do to help your clients efficiently?" This audience was composed of clinical social workers and researchers who had devoted years of their careers to the cause of answering the seemingly simple question of what to do for clients. They were all surprised, shocked, and angered by this accusation, but it also encouraged many to once again confront the seemingly unanswerable.

The ideal method of choosing an appropriate intervention is the use of valid clinical outcome research that uses well-controlled comparative analysis with clearly defined client populations and equally specific definitions of the intervention methods. If social workers could simply refer to the clinical literature or, even better, a standard reference book that would state clearly what type of treatment to use for a given problem or diagnosis, then clinical practice would be infinitely more effective and efficient. Why has this not happened?

Advanced practice and clinical social work are different now than in the past. In current social work settings, the utilization of the advanced mix of behavioral, cognitive, and psychodynamic techniques is more likely to be added onto a generalist or broad-based interventionist foundation. Clinical social workers thus begin virtually all interventions from a generalist perspective but then often add appropriate advanced techniques from their eclectic repertoire of models to assure efficient and effective outcomes. Social workers need to be able to "mix and match" approaches (Meyer & Palleja, 1995). Our client needs are diverse, and many valid approaches exist within the field to address those needs.

This move toward eclecticism was initially well articulated by Joel Fischer in 1978 in *Effective Casework Practice: An Eclectic Approach,* which challenged social workers to break away from their compartmentalized and acrimoniously competing mode of viewing practice in terms of loyalty to either behavioral *or* psychodynamic *or* other methods. Fischer encouraged social workers to be eclectic and base their choices of strategies on research, not on inappropriate and counterproductive identifications with any one method. Up until now, this type of research, based upon eclecticism, has been the norm in the field and the standard in most current social work textbooks, although many prefer the term *differential* to distinguish it from the occasionally disjointed concept of eclecticism (Turner, 1986, 1996; Zastrow, 1999; Greene & Ephros, 1991; Meyer & Mattaini, 1995).

One problem with eclecticism is that it is difficult, if not impossible, for a clinician to develop and maintain a high level of expertise in multiple models. Social work educators often grapple with the "depth versus breadth" quandary, having to balance and weigh the level of knowledge necessary to teach in each type of intervention. An alternative to eclecticism is preparing clinical social workers extremely well in one particular approach (such as ecological or cognitive or psychodynamic) and applying that model to all appropriate clients. That approach, although quite common up until the mid-1970s, is not considered realistic in present practice, which recognizes the need to fit the client's problem and unique needs to the specific method that will yield the most effective outcome.

RESEARCH

Research is central to clinical practice. After this introduction to research, the history is examined, followed by: Methodological Concerns: Some Questions; Methodological Concerns: Some Answers; Postmodernism and Empiricism; and Problem Statements, Diagnoses, or Person in Environment (PIE): Finding a Common Language.

Introduction

> Truly effective psychosocial interventions have been developed and can be used on a widespread scale . . . and contingencies being imposed by managed care companies, insurance carriers, and governmental agencies are hastening the integration of research into practice and practice into research. (Thyer, Isaac, & Larkin, 1997, p. 315)

The ultimate responsibility for defining the "best" advanced techniques for social workers rests with social workers. David Austin, who chaired the NIMH Task Force on Social Work Research, has noted that the questions are being addressed but not by social work clinicians who are oriented to the here-and-now practical problems of social work (1992). He points out that, beginning in the 1960s, much of the policy research related to poverty and income has been done at public policy schools. In health care financing, economists have defined the role of social workers in terms of diagnostically related groups (DRGs), which diminishes and alters the role of the field in those health settings by focusing on purely medical diagnostic groupings rather than recognizing their social context. In relation to school systems, the field of education has often taken the lead in examining the interface of social workers with the community.

Finally, much of the mental health clinical research has been dominated throughout the 1990s by biological and pharmaceutical researchers even though social workers now constitute the majority of professionals in mental health services. As a result, much of the research deals with medication doses and effects, with clinical social workers often very generally described or combined with a vague notion of therapy along with nurses, physicians, or aides.

So the question of advanced techniques and their effectiveness is responded to by others. As any researcher knows, the way the question is asked defines and limits the response range; so, by leaving this research in the hands of non–social workers, we have not only been left with some useless data, but we have passively colluded in allowing our questions and concerns to be redefined and altered to meet the needs of those who know nothing about current clinical social work practice.

Thus, when a health economist asks the question, "How effective is practice?" he or she defines *effectiveness* as the speed of getting patients placed or referred to aftercare resources. A public policy analyst answers that same question in terms of the efficiency of providing the welfare check or placing a client in a job. The researcher from the field of education may answer the effectiveness question in terms of how quickly the school social worker called the parents to inform them of their child's truancy, or how quickly the social worker scheduled an appointment to talk to the psychologist for testing. Such research does very little to answer the pressing question of effectiveness of our services, because it is often the wrong question asked by researchers who are not social workers.

For many years, the major research-related question in clinical social work was, are our interventions effective? Several researchers in the 1950s and well into the 1980s were still asking this question. Now practice research is moving in the direction of asking, Which particular type of treatment works best with a particular client under a specific set of circumstances? Some authors have attempted to answer that question (Seligman, 1990; Thyer & Wodarski, 1998; Bergin & Garfield, 1994) or have recommended specific treatment plans appropriate for specific behavioral problems (Jongsma & Peterson, 1999). However, a practical and honest answer is that social workers and related professionals still struggle with developing a consensus relative to defining specific treatment methods for specific types of clients. Social workers need to be informed researchers and consumers of current, rigorous research. This is an ongoing process that requires social workers to critically develop, read, assess, and implement new and developing techniques in practice.

In conclusion, it can be said that the task of defining and using the most effective advanced methods of clinical social work was a major issue in the 20th century and continues to be a major issue in the 21st century. In the next section, a description of the history of research in clinical social work practice is presented.

History

Historically, the family or community constructively dealt with most welfare or social service functions whereas the treatment of people with mental illness or psychological disturbances often consisted of harsh and primitive treatment in some countries, benign neglect in others, and fairly enlightened concern in yet others. Various cultures historically have relied on different types of research or empirical evidence to support their interventions. Treatment flowed from a logical belief in the cause of the problem or etiology of the disorder.

Anthropologists tell us that in many cultures—particularly in Africa and among Native Americans—marital, family, and even individual problems frequently were handled within the small village or community, which consisted primarily of extended family and clans. When such communities were constructive, they no doubt served as social *support systems* and prevented minor problems from becoming major disorders; but, if the individual was viewed as possessed by the devil or a spirit, he or she would be seen by a *specialist,* such as a shaman, doctor, or spiritualist knowledgeable in the causes and treatments of such problems. These individuals were highly regarded in their communities because, as we would define it today, they were the experts or professionals and they knew the research or had some empirical evidence that their interventions would yield successful outcomes.

In the European and American traditions of the 18th and 19th centuries, there were also, of course, enlightened asylums and hospitals that used the best available research and techniques such as baths, rest, relaxation, and even opportunities for long discussions and walks. However, it was primarily the family or community that would manage the care and feeding of the individual.

At the dawn of the 20th century, Jane Addams and Charlotte Towle pioneered case studies that described methods and results in social work practice, but their capacity to evaluate scientifically that which they had created was not yet developed. They used case study descriptions of the process along with subjective assessments of the outcome.

Pioneers in the field of clinical social work frequently wrote insightful and moving descriptions of their cases and intervention efforts, but modern research methods and the actual evaluation of mental health and social services did not begin until the early part of the 20th century when the Berlin Psychoanalytic Institute began compiling records (Waskow & Parloff, 1975). These records were case descriptions of the process of treatment with subjective appraisals of client change. Since clinical social work by the 1920s and 1930s was predominantly psychoanalytic and more rigorous and quantitative methods of clinical research were not yet developed, the evaluations tended to be interesting and descriptive but imprecise and lacking in valid measurement.

This method did not change significantly until the 1950s with those who challenged the long-term, increasingly expensive psychodynamic orientation of the field and argued for the use of the scientific method—or, at least, measurable and observable phenomena—as a test of effectiveness. Humanistic and client-centered social workers joined in soon thereafter, upsetting the psychodynamic traditionalists. The client-centered social workers used relatively sophisticated quantitative methods to support their assertions that certain specific, trainable skills and techniques such as empathy, genuineness and warmth, and unconditional positive regard contributed to successful outcomes. They further suggested that their research proved that these were the necessary and sufficient qualities needed to effect successful treatment outcomes. The clinical research wars were just beginning.

The notion of the subconscious and concepts such as the Oedipus complex and penis envy were further challenged by the influence of the behaviorists in the 1960s and 1970s. The behaviorists could show clearly superior results of symptom reduction in clients who were depressed and phobic as well as dramatically quicker behavioral improvements for very disturbed patients, such as those with schizophrenia and autism.

On another front, research began supporting an increased use of *support systems* (Caplan, 1974), while major, government-sponsored research projects validated the need for *community, family, and individual support systems* (Joint Commission on Mental Illness and Health, 1961; Gurin, Veroff, & Feld, 1960) or *social networks* (Maguire, 1983, 1991).

Empirically based practitioners and clinical researchers continued their efforts in the 1970s with government-mandated requirements to evaluate mental health services. This wholesale effort began the development of new generations of social workers who not only were interested in social and community support systems but also intervened on the basis of methodologically rigorous research. A combination of political, social, and economic resources interacted with a growing frustration, which culminated in the realization among social work practice researchers that research *must* form the basis for practice. Even though it has limitations as the absolute basis for defining practice, research is essential in informing and guiding practitioners. Contemporary social work practitioners need to engage themselves in the ongoing process of research in practice, constantly questioning and looking for answers.

Methodological Concerns: Some Questions

Contemporary clinical social workers support the view that practice should be based on research and clear, objective assessments of effectiveness or the relative success of outcomes of intervention. However, there are many practical methodological questions that must be addressed before research can realistically guide social work practice. For instance, "*Where* should social work practice take place; *what* precisely should be focused upon; and *how* do social workers intervene, based upon those results?"

Clinical research must take place in clinical settings, not in laboratories. Many of the research methods that are necessary in social sciences—such as control groups; randomization; and static, clearly defined immutable conditions—are either difficult to establish in social work practice settings or their establishment for clinical research purposes is unethical (Tripodi, 1994). In other instances, research protocol so alters the typical, rational intervention process that the results no longer realistically represent actual results in treatment. A balance between traditional controls and sensitivity to the fluidity of social service agencies needs to be maintained.

The other basic methodological question, "*What* is the most effective social work interventionist method?" is simply not being asked as often. Social work practice research has taken a rather dramatic turn since the 1970s. There is a recognition that there is no single approach that works well for all clients regardless of presenting problem, personality, race, gender, and psychological mindedness (Thyer & Wodarski, 1998). Social workers now realize that the questions that must drive practice research are different from those questions asked even a few years ago:

> Questions today are being asked at the micro level: What works with this type of care? rather than at the macro level: What is the nature of human personality? This trend has been dictated partly by consumer, government, and insurance company pressures for evidence of prompt efficacy and partly by the failure of macro theories to yield definable practices that are clinically and empirically tenable. (Bergin & Garfield, 1994, pp. 821–822)

Clinical research has shifted to answering these questions, which are far more complex and multifaceted but which are finally able to yield less equivocal results. Qualitative methods and ethnographic approaches are widely regarded as appropriate methods for analyzing complex interactions; whereas, in the past, they had been viewed as "too subjective." Now, social workers need to rely upon examining numerous outcome studies that look at a variety of treatment modalities and populations. There is no single, definitive study one can rely upon to conclusively answer, "What works best?" However, a variety of studies can answer a lot of questions and give practitioners very clear direction.

Finally, the methodological question, "*How* should social work practice intervene?" is being answered. More recent researchers have learned that the focus must be narrowed to establishing precisely which problem can be alleviated with a specific type of intervention (Reid & Hanrahan, 1981; Sheldon, 1986; Thyer & Wodarski, 1998). This higher degree of specificity informs clinicians far better (Fischer, 1978). In short, it does social workers no good to be informed that, overall, general interventions of 30 years ago seemed to have been of no more help to clients than no intervention at all when applied across a wide range of general and vaguely defined problems.

Clinical social workers have an even more demanding task methodologically than do those in other helping professions because of their broader base of knowledge, skills, and client problems. For instance, a social work researcher in England was concerned recently about the relative paucity of solid research on the effectiveness of social work practice compared to medical intervention. She decided to ask her medical practice research colleagues at Oxford University to help her design a research strategy for a fairly typical social work example. She gave them the example of single mothers on public assistance who had varying degrees of social and community support, symptoms of depression that varied from very mild to rather severe, low self-esteem, and inadequate capabilities to provide care for their children. When this social work researcher asked her highly experienced medical research colleagues to help her evaluate the effectiveness of her intervention, which included short- and long-term help and varying aspects of practical support, counseling, supervision, behavioral programs, and group work, she was told to "forget it" and that even attempting such complex, broad-based research could only hurt her professional reputation (Cheetham, 1992).

Methodological Concerns: Some Answers

Clinical social workers must engage in practice research. In a broad-based field such as social work, narrowing and clearly defining the focus of research are difficult but essential. Even the case example from England is, in fact, quite doable. The question itself simply needs to be redefined into smaller, more specific, concrete, and, preferably, even measurable terms. So the question, "Does broad-based general social work intervention have an effect on its clients?" can be answered by any of three responses:

"No—and one can look at much of the research of the 1970s and before to support that answer."

"Maybe, but I don't really have a good idea of what the answer is or where to find it" (which is, unfortunately, another understandable response for many current clinicians, due to the complexity and range of relevant variables).

"Yes, but the question has to be more clearly defined in terms of what specific clinical social work intervention is being referred to, with what specific problem and client population."

As clinical researchers in social work practice continue to refine and improve their methodology, some of their methodological criteria become directly translated into practice principles (Thyer & Wodarski, 1998). Corcoran and Videka-Sherman (1992) have argued on the basis of research that the most effective practice is that which is structured. More specifically, they point to the research conclusions of Wood (1978), which coincide with Wells's (1992) empirically based standards for effective, planned short-term treatment. The general consensus of these research-based proponents of clinical social work is that effective "quality practice" requires the following:

1. A clear description of the presenting problem
2. A clear statement of the plan of practice intervention
3. Objective descriptions of factors that create, maintain, or encourage the problem's existence
4. Clearly defined, workable goals
5. The development of a mutually agreed upon contract

It is noteworthy that these requirements are the same type of guidelines given to clinical researchers. Clarity, objectivity, and consensual agreement regarding terms are essential in both practice and research.

Another methodological concern that affects the use of research in social work practice is the "true believer" mentality (Kendall & Butcher, 1982). A *True believer* maintains the following characteristics in clinical research:

Selective attention and inattention. The clinical researcher pays attention to data that are congruent with his or her own belief system and ignores or deemphasizes results that conflict with that belief system.

Data distortion and creation. The findings are unclear or ambiguous, so the researcher construes them as somehow being supportive of his or her belief system.

Confirmatory set. The pervasive bias of the researcher is that all data are confirming; this bias becomes even more pronounced when the results are more equivocal.

Discreditory defensiveness. The clinical researcher is confronted with data that disagree with his or her belief system, so the researcher minimizes or denies the significance of the anomalous data or claims that the data in question are deviant or abnormal.

Expedient reasoning. The clinical researcher uses *less-demanding* standards for evaluating evidence that supports his or her beliefs and uses *more stringent* standards for evaluating research that contradicts his or her beliefs.

Certainty and closure. The clinical researcher has become closeminded to considering alternatives, even to examining the basis for his or her beliefs or to considering variations of it.

Memory dysfunction. The researcher tends to remember data and results that support personal beliefs and tends to forget results that are not supportive of those beliefs.

Pervasive exemplars and tacit submergence. The researcher has the capacity to bring forth numerous, seemingly pervasive, examples of studies that agree with his or her belief and gradually views that belief as axiomatic and seemingly self-evident to all.

System saving. The clinical researcher mildly alters or modifies aspects of a belief purely for the purpose of proving the belief's validity. This is usually done in the face of mounting evidence that the belief is simply incorrect and should be discarded.

The need for clinical research and clear empirical bases for social work practice must be continued, and these methodological issues need to be constantly addressed. The process of conducting the research, questioning the results, debating alternatives, and varying the designs and the interventions all have considerable merit simply by keeping social workers involved, up-to-date, and noncomplacent. The practice research issue is analogous to marital and family social work intervention. The social worker knows from the beginning that he or she will never come to one simple immutable answer to the problem, but he or she can significantly improve the situation by engaging in the process. By challenging the couple or family to try new ways of interacting, to open up communication, or to objectively reanalyze whatever works or does not work, the dynamics invariably improve (Thyer & Wodarski, 1998).

The skepticism of the past has given way to a far more positive acceptance of clinical research results among social work practitioners. There is a growing acceptance that research methods in clinical social work interventions simply need to become more sophisticated for development of clear treatment plans for specific presenting problems (Jongsma & Peterson, 1999). Some suggest single-subject research designs as the best method for developing knowledge in social work practice (Tripodi, 1994); and ethnographic approaches are now widely used. In the past, when there were limited clinical intervention strategies and even more limited research capabilities or even interests, the interventions were probably less effective. Current practitioners have been and will no doubt continue to be taught an increasingly differential or eclectic approach to practice wherein they are expected to apply the most effective intervention for a particular client and problem based upon the results of research. Tremendous strides have been made in the last 20 years, and even greater use of knowledge and research can be anticipated in the future.

The quest for a single "right" approach to social work has long been forgotten. Clinical social workers proceeded in the 20th century through stages of accepting, then rejecting, a wide variety of interventions, coming to the 21st century with the recognition that clinical social workers must all be generalists with additional advanced knowledge of many types of intervention. The honing and fine-tuning of this process begins with a generalist, broad, systemic orientation followed by research-based efforts in matching approaches to client needs. This imperfect yet vastly improved process is the foundation for current clinical social work practice.

Postmodernism and Empiricism

Other answers to the continuously vexing methodological questions are being found in recent redefinitions of essential concepts such as *empiricism* and *effectiveness*. Empiricism as a basis for social work practice or even research has become an important topic. The *Social Work Dictionary* (Barker, 1995) defines *empirically based practice* as: "A type of *intervention* in which the professional social worker uses research as a practice and problem-solving tool; collects data systematically to monitor the intervention; specifies problems, techniques, and outcomes in measureable terms; and systematically evaluates the effectiveness of the intervention used" (p. 119).

Traditionally, *empiricism* refers to the use of objective facts; reality; or proven, research-based outcomes as the basis for practice. An empirically based social worker is one who views methodologically rigorous clinical research as the appropriate source of data for choosing the particular model of intervention needed to yield the most effective and efficient outcomes for his or her clients. Knowledge of research methods and designs and an attitude that supports using objective evidence concerning practice are required of contemporary social workers.

However, the concept of empiricism has been challenged by those who support a *postmodernist* approach to clinical social work practice (Hartman, 1991; Pardeck, Murphy, & Choi, 1994). This perspective views empiricism as being too constrictive for social workers in that it is linguistically biased. Post-modernists suggest that each community defines normalcy through its own perspective. Language is too much a function of the predominant culture to be used as the so-called empirical, objective, or scientific basis for working with diverse communities that have their own, different perspectives for defining "reality."

Yet another philosophical competitor to empiricism among cognitive and behaviorally oriented clinical social workers is *constructivism* (Thyer & Wodarski, 1998; Mahoney, 1991). Constructivists contend that the seemingly scientific approach of empiricism, with its reliance upon objective facts and reality, fails to recognize the way people think. In reality, people process and thus bias information on the basis of their own environments and histories. Reality is *constructed* in unique ways through various steps and processes that must be considered when intervening with individual clients. This under-standable concern is particularly evident when examining the early (some-times referred to as "radical") behaviorists who had a particularly disturbing, mechanistic, and deterministic stimulus-response (S-R) formula for all human behavior (Skinner, 1974). When simply contrasted with the pure stimulus-response (S-R) framework of early behaviorists, the constructivists' more com-plex mediational model (S-O-R), which says that all stimuli must be processed and thus modified by the organism before it responds, makes a great deal more sense to social workers. From a social work perspective wherein the unique cultural issues as well as race, gender, age, orientation, and social con-ditions are all crucial to understanding and subsequently ameliorating the problem, the constructivists are certainly a "better fit" among the behaviorally oriented models. Empiricism and the scientific method are being reexamined by social workers.

Finally, *effectiveness* is also being reconsidered. It is the term for describ-ing the best or most successful *intervention* or treatment *outcomes* as estab-lished on the basis of factual evidence and research. Effectiveness is estab-lished operationally for social workers through the application of research designs with treatment populations or social work clients. It involves compar-ing results relative to each other, typically on the basis of some quantitative (or occasionally qualitative) measure of the outcome of various interventions with the same treatment population. The issue of outcome scores serving as the basis for practice has been a somewhat elusive goal in social work and other helping professions, although tremendous strides have been taken toward this goal (Blythe & Tripodi, 1989). Those efforts as well as the still existent impediments are described in detail in subsequent sections of this and the next chapter.

Problem Statements, Diagnoses, or Person in Environment (PIE): Finding a Common Language

Social work is a field that historically has drawn from many other fields and currently interacts extensively with a variety of professions. While there are advantages to this, there are also disadvantages. One negative from a research perspective is that social work has no single, consistent, widely used terminology or vocabulary. Although the person-in-environment or PIE system is a good attempt for "describing, classifying, and coding the problems of social functioning of the adult clients of social workers" (Karls & Wandrei, 1995, p. 1818), it is far from being accepted universally.

Epidemiology bears witness to the fact that social workers see a tremendously diverse range of people and their problems. The problems of social work clients include depression, marital conflict, school phobia, stress related to employment, schizophrenia, a lack of housing, physical impairments that cause one to be overly aggressive or angry, unresolved issues from an abused childhood, or any problems of the human condition from a seemingly infinite list. Social workers deal with all of them.

Clinical social work does not have its own uniformly accepted or consistent list of valid and reliable presenting problems. Even if the more purely defined social services such as welfare payments, housing, jobs, and treatments for physical problems within hospital settings are excluded, clinical social workers frequently are confronted with a requirement to know the *DSM-IV-TR* (2000) plus myriad lists of presenting problems some agencies prefer as tools in evaluating their goals.

Consequently, clinical social workers presently use four different types of lists, nomenclature, or categories that make interventionist research difficult to compile or to be utilized by the majority of social workers. The first type of list, which is independently developed and used in many social service agencies, consists of the many possible presenting problems. Today, very few agencies maintain their own, internally generated lists of problems. However, there are several models of "typical" presenting problems that agencies can choose.

The second list is the *DSM-IV-TR* (2000) which is utilized primarily in mental health settings. Due to the dominance of psychiatry in mental health, this list of diagnoses and descriptions of symptoms is supported by insurance companies and other third-party providers of payments and reimbursements. It lacks the social-environmental perspective central to social work but has improved significantly over the years as it has become more behaviorally specific and less oriented toward psychodynamics.

Third, the different treatment clinicians have developed their own terms, or jargon, that are directly related to the manner in which they conceptualize the problem. Social workers who practice either cognitive, psychodynamic, or behavioral perspectives use essentially different "languages" to describe the same client's problem. Certain construct-bound or theoretically defined terms are used in settings in which social workers intervene with clients who have complex problems. Thus, a psychodynamically oriented social worker may describe a client's problems in terms of repressed feelings or unresolved Oedipal tendencies; a cognitively oriented social worker would describe the same client in terms of his or her faulty schema; a behaviorally oriented social worker may prefer using terms describing intermittent reinforcement patterns of dysfunctional behaviors.

The fourth list or language used by clinical social workers is the previously mentioned person-in-environment system of coding, listing, or categorizing. The implications of not having a consistent and universally utilized language or terminology are considered very important by some:

> For social work to gain parity with professions like medicine/psychiatry, law, and the ministry, it must adopt a nomenclature for identifying its area of expertise. The future of PIE is linked to the willingness of social work practitioners, administrators, and educators to learn and implement a new way of identifying client problems. (Karls & Wandrei, 1995, pp. 1825–1826)

Social work is a profession with a rich history, a broad base of populations served, an eclectic and varied acceptance of practice orientations and interventions, and a commitment toward diversity. It is a profession that is sensitive to the importance of recognizing and building upon the strengths that diverse populations have to offer. Although there is no common social work language or coding system that is consistently and universally utilized, the field has the advantage of maintaining its needed rich breadth and diversity for the future. Research appears to be moving more in the direction of interdisciplinary research and understandings of multifaceted, complex human behaviors. Perhaps the fluidity, openness, and diversity that has been a tradition in social work will be of benefit to the profession in the future as it continues to grow, change, learn from, and teach the many sciences and professions with which it interacts.

Validity and *reliability* are important issues for practitioners to understand. Social workers who use research as the basis for practice recognize that the validity of the diagnosis or presenting problem is essential. *Validity* refers to the assumption that a diagnosis is accurate. Historically, this has been a problem in clinical research. The rate of schizophrenia, for instance, varies widely across different countries, thus leading to inaccurate research along the lines of establishing the genetic, biochemical, or sociocultural factors that may have caused such different rates. The inaccurate rates existed because researchers were misled because the mental health professionals defined schizophrenia differently in such countries as Japan and Great Britain. The difference was in how people defined and understood the diagnosis, not in the incorrectly assumed differences among populations or cultures (Garfield & Bergin, 1986).

The *reliability* of the diagnosis refers to the agreement among clinical social workers in assigning a name or *label* to the problem. If ten social workers view the same person and nine of them agree that the person has a bipolar disorder or is depressed, then there is a 90% reliability rate. If only 30% of them agree on the diagnosis, then there is a low rate of reliability, which is unacceptable. For research purposes, this is extremely important because if the clinical research is focused upon establishing the effectiveness of interventions with a specific diagnosis and the diagnosis is inaccurate, then the results of the research are useless and possibly even misleading. Social work researchers in the mental health field have been aware of this need for reliable diagnoses for many years and have supported psychiatry's efforts to make the *DSM* clearer, more behaviorally specific, and operational for diagnoses. The *DSM-IV-TR* (2000) no longer uses relatively vague, presumed or subconscious motivations or dynamics to define diagnoses. This has significantly improved the validity and reliability for disorders, thus partially minimizing the past problems of relying on research that was unknowingly misleading clinicians.

BREVITY

Brief interventions are now essential in direct social work practice. Because of cost constraints and managed care, "with their emphasis on intensive, short-term interventions for a wide range of mental illness condition" (Austin, 1997, p. 405), practice methods are changing. In fact, many agencies and funding sources, both public and private, frequently require that services be completed within a limited number of sessions, ranging from 4 to 20 within a year. Fortunately, there are several brief models of social work intervention that have been developed in recent years that manage to help clients within those limited time frames with the same or even better outcomes than the much longer interventions of the past. Chapter 10 of this book is devoted to such brief interventions.

Brevity implies efficiency. To be efficient, a social worker must intervene in a thorough and sensitive manner while being careful to protect and preserve limited psychological and material resources. Those limited resources include those of the client, the social worker, and the social service setting. Social workers today are required to be aware of how they use finite and limited funds, time, energy, and resources. Efficiency involves the maximum utilization of necessary resources while carefully minimizing unnecessary, extraneous efforts that may be wasteful or duplicative. Efforts toward efficiency are central in the profession's *case management* approaches (see Chapter 4), which incorporate aspects of the generalist perspective (see Chapter 3). Both approaches share concern for coordinating available resources and supports for the purposes of developing or strengthening potentially therapeutic or rehabilitative systems based on the client's problems, needs, and capacity to grow and develop. Both generalists and case managers are coordinators of resources. Their tasks involve minimizing duplication and waste in service intervention. Furthermore, case managers and generalists strengthen and empower clients to develop their own internal resources to deal with future concerns.

DIVERSITY

The United States is rich in its diversity. Its mix of races, religions, cultures, sexual orientations, political beliefs, and social orientations, combined with freedoms of press and speech, are perhaps the defining characteristics of this country. With increased globalization and population migrations throughout the world, other countries may look to the United States as a model for both what to do and what not to do in terms of harmoniously integrating diverse peoples. The United States can provide examples of both success and failure in its history.

This country continues to deal with a history of slavery and racism that is a source of divisiveness in the United States. While a very large and growing segment of the African American population is in the economic middle or upper class, there is also a large and nearly intractable population of people who are poor, underserved, and neglected minorities of color who are increasingly marginalized. These include recent immigrants from Central and South America, Asia, Africa, and parts of Eastern Europe, as well as families who have been here for generations.

Certain populations such as minorities of color; gays; immigrants; and people who are poor, homeless, and victimized individuals with chronic severe social and psychological problems have many individuals with special needs. The social work profession has long recognized the fact that social, psychological, political, and economic reality differs markedly in this society as a result of race, age, gender, ethnic background, sexual orientation, and a wide variety of other cultural and demographic traits.

A recognition of the strengths and contributions of each culture, religion, race, sexual orientation, and point of view is becoming a mainstay of social work. The social work profession is the profession that is most closely identified with helping and working with these diverse, underserved populations. Social workers must be sensitive to and understanding of the rich cultural

backgrounds, histories, and subsequent points of view of these diverse populations. In fact, interventions without such knowledge and sensitivity are
unlikely to succeed.

Further research is needed to examine how different populations respond
to different interventions. The work that has been done in this area has been
highly useful (McGoldrick, Giordano, & Pearce, 1996) in providing general
guidelines for establishing which racial or ethnic groups seem to respond better to specific types of treatment. There is also a large body of research that
examines the issue of matching client and practitioner on the basis of race and
gender, although meta-analyses indicate that the findings tend to be somewhat
ambiguous (Bergin & Garfield, 1994).

One of the primary tools that social workers may now rely upon is epidemiology. *Epidemiology* is the research method that tracks and monitors the incidence of a problem or disease within designated populations. For social workers, it is the basis or foundation for differential practice since it is an objective
tool for understanding diversity. Social work practice has increasingly recognized
that diverse populations not only have a varying incidence of certain problems
and disorders but also respond differently to different interventions. Some of
the greatest gains in recent years have been in understanding and, therefore, in
treating men and women differently. Occasionally, a scholarly yet popular book,
such as Deborah Tannen's (1990) *You Just Don't Understand: Women and Men
in Conversation,* has led to a greater awareness of the differences between men
and women in communication patterns, priorities, and goals.

Solid research continues to be needed to further develop bases for both
understanding and treating people with diverse backgrounds, particularly
related to gender and sexual orientation. For instance, the incidence of violent
sexual behavior is significantly higher for males than females, and the incidence of attention-deficit hyperactivity disorder (AD/HD) is also significantly
higher for young males than for young females. Females by comparison have
much higher rates of depression and eating disorders than males. Such epidemiological knowledge helps social workers by potentially informing them of
underlying dynamics and subsequent interventions. Furthermore, if a social
worker knows of higher rates of infant mortality among adolescent mothers,
the worker should be sensitized to the possibility of likely underlying structural causes such as lack of prenatal care, transportation, money, or information about pregnancy. Resources such as the *Social Work Almanac* (Ginsberg,
1995), second edition, are useful as the basis of interventions.

The importance of tracking types of services by race and diagnoses cannot
be underestimated as the delivery system moves into managed care. For
instance, inner-city African American black males with long-term mental
health problems tend to be among the most disadvantaged in job skills, enti-
tlements, and insurance. Tracking suggests that this population is also denied

access to any hospitals except state facilities that frequently lack the resources to aggressively treat them (Belcher, 1992; Belcher, DeForge, Thompson, & Myers, 1995). Social workers have accepted economic constraints as a legitimate concern throughout the history of the social work profession. However, as the service delivery system increasingly dictates the type of service provided on the basis of economic conditions and the client's type of coverage, it is also structurally "locking in" lower-quality or, at least, lower-cost services to those already struggling. Race has been a factor in obtaining access to Social Security Income and Social Security Disability, so populations already at risk of social injustice are further disadvantaged through exclusion from higher-cost and sometimes more aggressive forms of intervention (GAO, 1992, cited in Belcher et al., 1995).

Objectivity and careful epidemiological analyses on issues of diversity lead to a greater understanding of the etiology or causes of the problems of clients. However, these analyses must be used appropriately. For instance, the arrest rates for African American inner-city youth are much higher than are the arrest rates for rural or White youth. Does this mean that African American youth are inherently more violent? No. It only means what it says: rates of arrest are higher. Such information can be used to shed light on the causes and thus the subsequent treatment of such problems. Once such epidemiological data are disseminated and assessed, the social worker's task becomes one of finding the causes for the higher incidence, which may lead the social worker to assess data on employment opportunities, racism, school dropout rates, academic preparedness, and other factors.

There was a time during the politically charged 1970s and 1980s when some social work researchers avoided conducting major research relevant to race and gender (Wilson, 1987). This was unfortunate since it left the research environment open only to those who did not share the value base or ethics of the social work profession. That situation has changed dramatically in recent years; and, ideally, even more research efforts will be devoted in the future to race and gender studies. For instance, the issue of trying to match clients on the basis of race or gender requires considerably more attention.

During my three years of living and working on the Pine Ridge Reservation in South Dakota, there was no clearly discernible pattern based strictly on race. In fact, whereas many clients preferred talking to fellow Native Americans for help, others preferred seeing White staff who generally had the advantage of better education and credentials but who were more likely chosen because of a *lack* of affinity. In this isolated rural community, not only did everyone know everyone else, they were probably related. So the less-connected White professionals were trusted with secrets that reservation members feared would be shared with family or friends if they confided in someone who was born and raised on the reservation.

Clients come to treatment with a wide range of characteristics. These diverse characteristics can be organized into discrete categories or variables. The variables that are relevant in understanding both the cause and subsequent treatment for the client typically include the client's presenting problem or diagnosis; age; race; religion; education; living arrangement or marital status; and a social, family, and development history. Epidemiologists examine each of these variables and can establish the incidence or prevalence rates for given problems for each of these variables.

How does this relate to social work practice? Advanced social workers are the preeminent professionals in understanding diversity in an effort to achieve social justice and equity. To effectively treat clients from diverse backgrounds, social workers must understand how the clients' backgrounds and characteristics may be related to their present problems. Social workers must, therefore, ask themselves about the nature of the relationship between the presenting problems and the diverse characteristics of the clients. Whether in relation to individual clients, populations served, or the field in general, social workers must constantly ask such questions as

Is there a relationship between age and violence?

Why are men more likely to be the perpetrators of violence than women?

Why are African American clients more likely to be unemployed than Whites?

Why do women have higher rates of eating disorders than men?

Why do women indicate higher rates of suicidal ideation and attempts, yet men actually kill themselves at higher rates?

Why do African American females have different types of eating disorders than their White counterparts?

Why do young White males have higher rates of diagnosis of attention-deficit/hyperactivity disorder but lower rates of learning disorders than their African American counterparts?

The list of questions could go on indefinitely, and many of them define the uniqueness of the social work field. Clinical social work deals with the disadvantaged populations and clients; it is only by clearly, discretely, objectively, and unambiguously defining and understanding the factors that put these populations and clients at a disadvantage that social workers can help. The seemingly mundane data sets that categorize client populations on the basis of race, gender, and other demographic variables form the basis for much of the orientation of the field. Clinical social workers cannot say they are sensitive to issues of diversity if they are ignorant of the types of problems that affect their clients. This can only lead to doing a disservice to those clients.

Another issue of diversity concerning advanced or clinical social workers in interpreting results is that social workers need to be cautious in using this data and avoid stereotyping or presuming the existence of a disorder just because the client falls into a certain category. For instance, the diagnosis of hysteria has existed since the time of Hippocrates, but he defined it as a female disorder that was related to a "wandering uterus." Some feel that this type of bias still exists today when a few doctors discount the symptoms of women as being purely hysterical or label the elderly as *senile* rather than disoriented as a result of hearing loss or adverse reactions to prescribed medications.

Case 1.1 presents a group of clinical social workers struggling with some of the issues described in this section.

Case 1.1: Gender, Depression, Suicide, and Marriage
Jeanne Benet, MSW, the Director of Cayahoga Social Services, left an urgent e-mail message for her three senior staff members, telling them to meet her in 48 hours. They were to brainstorm and come up with the beginning of a proposal for developing a treatment program for suicide prevention. The state suddenly had money in this area, and if they could respond with a good proposal documenting their knowledge of and effectiveness in treating this problem, they could receive funding.

"Well, according to Regier and others [1988], the total number of people suffering from any affective disorder at any given time in the United States is between 9.6 million and 13.7 million. Persons ages 24 to 44 are at the highest risk for depression, and those over 65 have the lowest rate. Individuals who are separated or divorced are 2.2 times more likely to have a major depressive episode than married individuals, although there is evidence that marital discord also puts individuals at risk. Of particular interest to social workers is the fact that there is no significant difference on the basis of race or ethnicity or even high or low socioeconomic status. Also, NIMH indicates that 80–90% of persons today with a major depressive disorder can be treated successfully, even though only one of three actually seeks treatment," said Jeanne as she began the brainstorming session.

"Yes. I read that same study, and it went on to indicate that suicide attempts have been found in only 1% of the population with no lifetime history of mental disorder, with the rate rising to an alarming 24% of the bipolar disordered clients having attempts, 18% of those with major depression, and 17% of those with dysthymia," added Sally, reminding them that the proposal was for suicide treatment and prevention, not for depression or other disorders.

"You're right, Sally. We need to be more specific in relation to which populations actually commit suicide," said Bill in support of Sally. "Actually, that study that Jeanne shared with us went on to say that, in each age category, married people have lower rates of suicide and young widowed males have exceptionally high rates, although rates for never married males are consistently lower than for widowed or divorced males. The suicide rates for adult males declined rapidly with age so that, by age 45 or older, the rates for widowed and divorced males are approximately the same."

"But our agency has to make a case for our unique abilities. According to our agency demographics, nearly 80% of our clients are single women. A study by Smith, Mercy, and Conn [1988] says that women differ from men in their suicide rates in that divorced females have consistently higher rates than the widowed. Both widowed and divorced people have approximately three times the suicide rate of married individuals. When women do commit suicide, it is usually during midlife whether they are divorced, married, never married, or widowed. The general belief is that married people are at a significantly lower risk of suicide than unmarried people for three reasons: the social networks of married people integrates them into a more supportive system than the nonmarried; those who marry may be healthier from a psychological as well as physical point of view initially; and the experience of loss for the widowed or divorced, rather than any intrinsic positives of marriage per se, may account for the differences."

"Really? That's interesting," added Bill. "But when I went to that training at Western Psychiatric in Pittsburgh [Western Psychiatric Institute & Clinic, 1990], they said that males are the patients who actually kill themselves, not females. In fact, they said that for every marital status group, White males have the highest rates of suicide followed by African American males, White females, then African American females. A total of 15% of patients with a history of severe depression eventually complete suicide. Those at highest risk for completion include, of course, those with a previous history of psychiatric illness, particularly affective disorders, and those with previous attempts. One to two percent of attempters complete the act each year over a 10-year period. Social factors that increase the likelihood include imitation; availability of lethal weapons; loss or loosening of social ties; and the previous mentioned aspects of age, marital status, and race."

"Well, we don't see as many adult males in this agency as some programs do, but we see quite a few adolescent boys diagnosed with major depression and boys who have had previous suicide attempts. That WPIC monograph says that they are at the highest risk for suicide while, for girls, the diagnosis of major depression increases the risk considerably," said Sally.

"We're all forgetting about our work with AA. Did you all know that this agency provides a meeting place for 150 AA members a week?" said Bill. "For alcoholics, the rate of suicide has been placed as high as 15%, but this figure is suspect with more precise analyses putting the figure at 0.2% to 11% and with the risk increasing dramatically as a function of later symptoms of the disease itself. Of completed suicides, studies in the WPIC monograph [1990] indicate a range of from 15% to 31% who were alcoholics, and only 40% of those alcoholic suicide completers had been under medical or psychiatric care in the year prior to their suicide. Some of the same risk factors as for others exist for alcoholic suicidal individuals such as an affective disorder, disruption of close personal relationships, and a history of previous attempts, but with poor failing health, job change, and high intelligence being additional risk factors. Our agency does see quite a few alcoholics; we just don't track them very well. Also, maybe we could try to improve or somehow formalize our relationship with all of those AA groups that we sponsor."

"Okay," said Jeanne as she stood up to leave. "You've all done a good job in collecting some initial data on gender, age, race, marital status, diagnoses, and their relationship or impact upon suicide rates. Let's develop this proposal so we can improve our services here."

Epidemiological data help clinical social workers track *where* clients are being served in addition to *who* is being served. For instance, state hospital populations were dramatically diminished as seriously emotionally disturbed patients were placed back into the community during the last few decades, a practice that was accelerated by the Community Mental Health Centers Act of 1963. Also, the advent of powerful anti-psychotic medication, antidepressants, and psychotropic medications improved the living conditions in psychiatric facilities while moving their residents into communities (Kiesler & Sibulkin, 1987).

ETHICS AND VALUES

Ethical considerations are becoming increasingly important in social work practice. The Council on Social Work Education (CSWE, 2001) is clear in requiring schools of social work to build into their curriculum a basis for evaluating and teaching ethical behavior based upon social work values. According to the *Social Work Dictionary* (Barker, 1995), *ethics* refers to a "system of moral principles and perceptions about right versus wrong and the resulting philosophy of conduct that is practiced," whereas *values* refers to "customs, standards of conduct, and principles considered desirable by a culture, a group of people, or an individual."

In a profession such as social work, absolute answers relevant to "right or wrong" can be problematic. Is it ethical to encourage a young, single, practicing Catholic to have an abortion? Is it ethical to agree to limit the treatment of a traumatized adolescent boy who was sexually abused for years by an older sibling just because his insurance will only pay for six sessions per year? Is it ethical to deny treatment to the life partner of a lesbian client whose HMO does not recognize same-sex couples? Is it ethical to report a family to the child protective authorities or even the police when it is learned that the family disciplines their children with harsh physical punishment, or when the parents neglect a young daughter so that their son can go to a National Rifle Association (NRA) weekend outing? What if the values, traditions, and norms of behavior of a client differ from that of the social worker or commonly accepted moral norms?

These ethical dilemmas are a common issue in social work practice. Fortunately, both the National Association of Social Workers and the Council on Social Work Education defined certain values that can be utilized as a guide in making ethical decisions (Zastrow, 1999). According to the *Social Work Dictionary* (Barker, 1995), there are ten overall values for social workers:

1. Commitment to the primary importance of the individual in society
2. Respect for the confidentiality of relationships with clients
3. Commitment to social change to meet socially recognized needs
4. Willingness to keep personal feelings and needs separate from professional relationships
5. Willingness to transmit knowledge and skills to others
6. Respect for individual and group differences

7. Commitment to develop clients' ability to help themselves
8. Willingness to persist in efforts on behalf of clients in spite of frustrations
9. Commitment to social justice and the economic, physical, and mental well-being of all members of society
10. Commitment to a high standard of personal and professional conduct

The Council on Social Work Education's *Educational Policy and Accreditation Standards* or EPAS (CSWE, 2001), which defines academic standards and requirements for accrediting schools of social work, specifically requires that values and ethics content must be provided to students so that they graduate with the knowledge and skills to enable them to

1. Identify and articulate one's own personal values and their development.
2. Identify and analyze ethical dilemmas and the ways in which these dilemmas affect the quality of services.
3. Evaluate ethical methods of decision making and engage in an ethical decision-making process.
4. Assume accountability for ethical practice.
5. Develop, demonstrate, and promote the values of the profession.

The CSWE specifies that curricular content should include an educational experience that provides students with the opportunity to be aware of personal values, to analyze how values shape practice, and to recognize and address conflicting values as well as ethical dilemmas in a variety of settings. The CSWE further cites the National Association of Social Workers *Code of Ethics* as an important resource.

EMPOWERMENT AND THE STRENGTHS PERSPECTIVE

The NASW's and the CSWE's sets of values also support the trend in recent practice to encourage clients to utilize their own potentials as well as social systems to empower themselves. *Empowerment* involves supporting and strengthening the natural capacities and resources of clients while encouraging autonomy. It stands in contrast to (a) the *psychopathology model,* which views certain social-emotional problems as sickness or disease; and (b) the *victim model,* which views clients as weak or helpless in response to circumstances that they are powerless to defend themselves against. The encouragement of empowerment also directly challenges some past helping strategies that allowed dependency to develop.

The responsibility for change must remain with the client. Clients need to be encouraged to see their personal inner strength to truly change, grow, and maintain such changes after the treatment is completed. In fact, a value among recent social workers has been referred to as a *strengths perspective,* which essentially says that social work practice must shift more toward recognizing the client's own positive resources as well as that of his or her social system (Rapp, 1998). The client is now perceived by practitioners as a very active partner in the helping process. The client's strength, knowledge, skills, and resources are highly valued and extensively utilized during the intervention.

MANAGED CARE

The issues of efficiency and cost-containment are viewed with mixed reactions by many in clinical social work. Those practitioners who are trained in traditional psychotherapy based upon long-term approaches find the push for managed care with its emphasis on cost-containment and brevity an anathema to their practice. It is viewed by some as simply a push for cheaper and quicker services, regardless of outcome. For many practitioners, clinical social work and individual treatment involve a complex, involved and highly personal process that sometimes requires a reworking of major issues that began in the client's childhood. Treatment involves a process of gradually helping the client to work through his or her defenses to develop insight into the powerful unconscious experiences that had previously been repressed. There are many in the field of social work who believe that managed care is overly reliant on providing only low-cost and quick results, regardless of long-term unresolved concerns.

This managed care orientation to practice is changing the way social workers practice. As David Austin, the former chair of the NIMH Task Force on Social Work Research stated,

> The most dramatic changes in the institutional structure for human services for the immediate future are occurring in the provision of health care and mental health care services through "managed care" systems—that is through the commercialization of health and mental health services. Nonprofit organizations are competing with "for-profit" organizations for participation in health care/mental health care networks that may be put together by insurance companies, mega health care/hospital corporations like Columbia HCA, large employers, existing nonprofit health care providers, or by individual entrepreneurial professionals, including social workers. (Austin, 1997, p. 400)

Managed care is not a clearly defined term, nor is there agreement upon its key characteristics. However, Hoyt (1995) describes eight features of managed behavioral health care: specific problem solving; rapid response and early intervention; clear definition of patient and therapist responsibilities, with an emphasis on patient competencies, resources, and involvement; time used flexibly and creatively; interdisciplinary cooperation; multiple formats and modalities; intermittent treatment or "family practitioner" model; and results orientation and accountability (p. 6–7).

Many clinical social workers have embraced the need for efficiency and effectiveness for three reasons: (a) insurance companies and government sources require it; (b) it is unethical to treat clients in any way other than that which is the quickest and therefore most humane approach; and (c) now the social work profession has improved its clinical knowledge base concerning what is truly effective and has the ability to apply techniques that were either unknown or untested in the past.

Effective interventions are those that produce the desired outcome; *brief* or *efficient interventions* are those that can be implemented without undue effort or unnecessary amounts of time. Interventions can be effective without being efficient (e.g., long-term, vague therapy that slowly but successfully resolves the problem) or efficient without being effective (e.g., treatment that is quick and highly focused but leaves the client with only partial resolution of the problem and related issues) (Thomas, 1984).

The future will no doubt see increased cost-containment pressure coming from insurance companies and government providers. However, this pressure comes from a long and logical history. The decade of the 1950s witnessed several challenging research results that encouraged practitioners to question the effectiveness of their approaches. The 1960s witnessed an increase in community mental health, social systems, and family involvement in the process of therapy and rehabilitation as means of making intervention more effective and longer in duration. The 1970s saw a focus on evaluation of services and accountability with the government requiring that publicly funded programs set aside funds to evaluate the effectiveness of their services. The 1980s witnessed a tremendous increase in costs in spite of a variety of efforts to contain costs; it also witnessed the acceptance of eclecticism and more holistic approaches. The 1990s saw more pressure for the field of social work to become efficient and to use the available research to further develop cost-effective interventions. The early 21st century is witnessing a continuance of the efforts toward effective yet brief interventions.

The near foreseeable future for clinical social work should be one in which the profession and its training and research institutes and universities continue to search for the "best" interventions for different types of presenting problems. Cost-containment and requirements to meet insurance or government regulations alone cannot and should not be the primary driving forces behind change. However, health care costs currently comprise a large portion of the economy of this country, so it is necessary to examine ways to control these costs.

Economics and the need for retaining the cost of services are essential factors in providing social services. Financial resources have been increasingly scrutinized in health, mental health, and social services because of the need to reduce their escalating costs. While economic factors alone should never be the basis for a decision regarding the quality of care, social workers increasingly recognize the importance of appropriately allocating finite resources in a manner that will ensure that all clients are adequately served. Economic factors are also increasingly shaping types of services used. An article in *The Journal of Mental Health Administration* states unequivocally what most clinical social workers already know: "Hospitals in the private sector are clearly making the decision to admit or not admit patients based on potential reimbursement" (Belcher, DeForge, Thompson, & Myers, 1995, p. 384).

Economic concerns are also closely related to efficiency and effectiveness in that costs are minimized by utilizing interventions that can ultimately achieve the most successful outcomes in the shortest period of time or by using fewer needed resources. Managed care systems are often very much oriented toward economics and saving money. However, the ethical value base of the social work profession clearly supports the fact that economic considerations cannot override client needs. The goals of maintaining low costs and achieving high levels of needed care must be continuously monitored by clinical social workers.

SUMMARY

Clinical social work for advanced-level or MSW-level practitioners is a constantly changing and evolving endeavor. There are trends toward wider systems interventions that necessitate a background in systems theory as well as a biopsychosocial orientation to viewing people. At the same time, the field of clinical social work requires practitioners to have a high level of expertise in the specific intervention methods that research supports. In spite of debates concerning research methods and qualitative or quantitive designs, advanced-level practitioners are expected to be engaged in some way in evaluating their interventions. Different terminologies are used in this broad field reflecting the fact that clinical social workers practice in social service agencies, mental health clinics, and family and children's programs. Within these settings, different terms are used: *presenting problem* in some settings, *diagnoses* in many mental health programs, and a description of the *person in environment* in other social service settings.

Interventions are briefer now than ever before. This trend, which has existed for many years, began as a reaction to long-term insight-oriented therapy but is now being supported by managed care's orientation to cut costs and avoid unnecessary services or duplication of services. Furthermore, as society becomes even more diverse, clinical social workers will be expected to have a greater sensitivity to and awareness of cultural differences and the impact of these differences on responses to treatment. It is not sufficient to apply a basic generalist approach to all clients. Important, complex but sometimes subtle differences exist among clients based upon their age, gender, sexual orientation, race, ethnic background, and the unique interaction of characteristics that define each person.

The ethical codes of conduct as defined by the NASW, the CSWE, and other social workers guide practitioners in their use of interventions that are appropriate and sensitive to the background of the client, while recognizing their uniqueness and individuality. The strengths and capacities of the client's system are invariably involved in any intervention. Dependency is minimized, and clients are now the partners or even the leaders in their interventions. Managed care has supported most of these trends, particularly the research basis of practice, broad systems approaches, higher skill levels, and brevity.

BEYOND GENERALIST

Clinical Social Work Practice

GENERALIST AND SPECIALIST: COMBINING THE BEST

Clinical social work practice evolves, changing and adapting to the needs of society on the basis of new research and improved interventionist strategies. Such changes are inevitable and challenging. New knowledge and research necessitate the development of new practice skills; yet, integrating this knowledge and their related interventions in a field as broad as social work can be difficult. At present, clinical social work practice adheres to a broad-based systems orientation and adds specialized advanced techniques where research supports such practice; that is, clinical social work practice begins with a generalist orientation and moves forward. Social workers employ interventions that are broad and encompass a practical, problem-solving approach in additional to utilizing advanced skills whenever needed. Practice is based on a *biopsychosocial foundation* that recognizes that virtually all problems that require social work intervention are caused by some combination of biological, psychological, and social factors, as well as learned behavior.

The generalist-practice orientation of clinical social work serves well as a basic framework for resolving most of these issues. By its nature, it is inclusive and integrative in its capacity to understand human behavior in the social environment. Furthermore, contemporary practice—with its orientation toward managed care; brevity; and research-based, cost-effective strategies—requires a broad generalist base. Narrow "specialist" approaches are discouraged, at least in terms of a societal or public health orientation to what society needs. As clinical social work becomes more of a systems-oriented field, it must also maintain, further develop, and integrate the specialized advanced methods of clinical practice. How can social workers balance the broad needs of society with the equally pressing need to utilize the most effective "high-powered" clinical strategies available? The latter part of the 20th century was rich in developing effective strategies to help families and individuals function more successfully in society. How can clinical social workers coming from a broad generalist base integrate the advanced techniques needed to treat the many complex and difficult problems seen in practice in the 21st-century?

It is *not* necessary to choose between being a generalist or a specialist. In fact, clinical social work practice is ideally a hybrid, a product of taking a broad-based systems foundation and a generalist approach and then adding the best possible available advanced skills when required. Clinical social work is a type of advanced social work practice that builds from a broad base and then integrates specialized, advanced techniques to maximize the likelihood of successful outcomes.

For some, the difference between a generalist and an advanced practitioner who uses specialized techniques is based on the practioner's level of education. Maria O'Neil McMahon (1996), who has written extensively on clarifying distinctions between generalist and advanced practice, suggests that while all baccalaureate-level social workers need a generalist approach to practice, the MSW degree must prepare the "advanced practitioner . . . a person who has the foundation knowledge, values, and skills of the generalist and advanced knowledge and skill for working with a particular population, problem, or area of practice, who may use a traditional or a specialized method or methods" (p. 38). Furthermore, McMahon suggests that while all beginning-level BSWs need to be "ecological generalists,"

> The beginning generalist, however, is not expected to have developed in his or her generalist education the knowledge and skills for worker focused interventions. The beginning generalist, therefore, is not eclectic when it comes to choosing specialized methods. To practice with these approaches, the entry-level generalist would need further education and supervised experience. (p. 339)

Basic generalist approaches are sufficiently *client focused* and *problem focused;* but, to be an advanced practitioner, one must also be *worker focused* (McMahon, 1996). This third level distinguishes advanced practitioners from BSW generalists and requires that the advanced worker take a major role in taking responsibility for goal accomplishment. He or she must utilize specialized interventions. "Behavior modification, class advocacy, Gestalt therapy, psychoanalysis, psychotherapy, and social planning may be among the models of this group" (p. 338).

HISTORY

In the early 1900s, the social work field was rather generalist, using a broad-based philanthropic approach to helping the poor and disadvantaged. It then became more psychoanalytic, an approach that was seen at the time as more scientific and professional, although the profession maintained its identity by maintaining its focus on social forces and the disadvantaged.

This began to change again in the 1950s as Florence Hollis and other social workers spelled out the profession's unique psychosocial orientation to helping (Hollis, 1964). Rogerian approaches and behavioral techniques developed at that time as well, particularly in the mental health arena; but the profession applied such approaches from a social-environmental perspective and adapted them to the poor, minorities, and other disadvantaged populations. The profession has always had its unique ways of applying new practice methods. "Social workers do not practice personality or behavioral theory directly; rather, their practice is strained through the available social work defined approaches that rest on professional purposes, values and ethical contexts, and service structures" (Meyer & Palleja, 1995, p. 108).

Beginning with studies at the Berlin Psychoanalytic Institute in the early years of the 20th century, research had mixed results over the last century regarding the outcomes of therapeutic interventions (Walborn, 1996). Some of that research was methodologically weak by current standards, and some studies were tainted by the researchers' efforts to prove the effectiveness of one approach over another. While that massive body of research has provided some direction in comparing overall effectiveness (Bergin & Garfield, 1994), it has as yet yielded no clear "winner." Clinical research has shown, if nothing else, that no one intervention model is more effective than all others for a wide range of problems.

During the 1950s and 1960s, clinical social workers began using many new methods, particularly behavioral and Rogerian variations, as a response to traditional psychoanalytically based approaches. Clinical social workers used these methods and modified them to fit their social-environmental orientation and their profession's values and ethics, which often differed markedly from other professions. However, considerable hostility existed among the varying factions within social work as well as between social work and other professions. As accountability and evaluation became more common and required, social workers began to use the resultant data to help them choose effective models of intervention for different client problems (Jayaratne, 1978).

Psychosocially oriented clinical social workers throughout the 1960s and 1970s became even more socially and environmentally oriented in their techniques as they began to recognize the need to deal with the everyday reality of problems in their clients' environments. At the same time, behaviorally oriented clinical social workers—who historically had prided themselves on their objective and systematic application of techniques—were encouraged to develop some rapport with clients and to be aware of their environments and past histories (Schwartz, 1982).

Over time, more behaviorally oriented clinical social workers began attending to psychosocially oriented colleagues whose nods of approval were viewed by them as indications of positive social reinforcement. At the same time, the psychodynamically oriented clinical social workers pointed out that some behavioral successes were the result of positive transference. In short, the "therapy wars" subsided as the need for integration of methods became apparent. Clinical social workers recognized that, realistically, advanced practitioners could not know the 400 or so supposedly separate models of intervention (Kazdin, 1986); but they needed to know those specific models that yielded the best outcomes for their clients' problems.

At this point in the evolving history of clinical social work, advanced practitioners must be able to utilize an advanced and eclectic repertoire of knowledge and skills while shifting away from longer-term interventions. People in the profession can anticipate an increased use of systems-based methods such as an advanced-level approach combined with a generalist approach or an ecological approach and case management models (Woodside & McClam, 1998) with a greater inclusion of group and family systems interventions. Furthermore, clinical social workers will need to include a mix of cognitive (Granvold, 1994), ecological (Mattaini, 1997; Germain & Gitterman, 1996), and many other structured (Corcoran, 1992) and brief (Ell, 1996; Wells, 1994; Epstein, 1992) interventions in their eclectic and empirically based repertoire of techniques and models.

DEFINING CLINICAL SOCIAL WORK PRACTICE

Clinical social work practice is a systems-based approach that integrates advanced systems methods with empirically validated techniques and an eclectic framework:

- It is *advanced* in that it applies a higher level of knowledge, skills, and expertise required in professional social work settings. This level of practice requires a sophisticated knowledge base and repertoire of the appropriate behavioral, cognitive, psychodynamic, problem-solving, and other developing methods required to resolve complex psychosocial problems.
- It is *systems based* in that it recognizes the effects of the interacting social environment and particularly the need to increase social supports and decrease sources of stress and negative forces in the client's system.
- It is *integrative* in its use of methods that build upon a broad base, which then narrows in strategy and blends the required advanced methods into a logical, consistent, and coherent intervention. The

ultimate intervention is, therefore, the culmination of a consistent strategy that builds from broad to specific methods in a logical sequence.

- It is *empirical* in its utilization of rigorous practice research as a basis for practice. The final intervention uses the specific methods that the objective facts suggest will lead to a successful outcome, given the client's own perspective and cultural needs and characteristics.
- It is *eclectic* in that it utilizes a variety of major, validated theories and subsequent interventionist methods drawn from commonly accepted human behavioral perspectives.

There are at least two major (and an unlimited number of minor) alternative viewpoints to defining what it is to be a highly skilled clinical social worker. Some use the terms *eclectic practitioner* or *advanced generalist*. The term *advanced generalist* is used by some to describe advanced social work practice (McMahon, 1996). The term *eclectic practitioner,* while fairly accurate in describing contemporary professional clinical social work, has become overly redefined in recent years and is already strongly identified as a descriptor for professions such as clinical psychology, counseling, nursing, rehabilitation and vocational work, and psychiatry. Over the years, scholars have added terms such as *systematic* (Hepworth & Larson, 1993), *technical* (Lazarus, 1981), and *differential* (Turner, 1986) to explain eclecticism.

Developing a professional identity and defining what clinical social workers are and do has been complicated over the years by the fact that many advanced-practice social workers identify strongly with their chosen area of practice. Thus, there are clinical social workers who identify themselves both personally and professionally as family therapists, behaviorists, psychodynamically oriented practitioners, cognitive therapists, Rogerians, or one or several of other "identities." Some agencies encourage and even require this type of identification. For instance, many child welfare agencies, private practices, and virtually all psychoanalytic institutes employ clinical social workers who identify themselves as psychodynamic psychotherapists rather than social workers. Similarly, agencies such as residential facilities for adolescents or group homes for court-ordered adults are typically behavioral, and the clinical social workers employed there often consider themselves behavioral therapists.

> To make judicious choices and to implement chosen interventions skillfully requires knowledge of numerous practice theories and techniques and a rigorous approach to selecting those that are most appropriate for a given client. Systematic eclecticism . . . is such a rigorous approach to practice. A systematic eclectic practitioner adheres exclusively to no single theory but rather applies models and theories that best match a given problem situation and accords highest priorities to techniques that have been empirically demonstrated to be effective and efficient. Systematic eclecticism is thus most demanding, requiring the practitioner to keep abreast of emerging theories and research findings. In our judgment, this approach to practice holds the highest promise of being efficacious

with a broad range of clients and problems. (Hepworth & Larson, 1993, pp. 17–18)

However, an eclectic approach is far from universally accepted in the field of clinical social work. In fact, Carol Meyer (1983) is very critical of practitioners who "adopt a mix and match attitude: a pinch of problem solving here; a dash of psychosocial theory there; a sprinkling of behavioral, life model, and task-centered practice; and the net result—confusion instead of coherence" (p. 731). She even concludes that "Eclecticism appears to be a popular way to avoid the use of theory" (p. 732). Much of her criticism of eclectics is based upon her observation that a clear, consistent theoretical framework and approach have merit over a rather haphazard and theoretically muddled series of changing interventions, which is certainly true.

History has indirectly added to the eclectic nature of contemporary clinical social work. In the past, the term *psychotherapist,* or *therapist,* was viewed by some as referring to the "real, genuine practice" of insight-oriented, psychoanalytically based clinical social work intervention. To many, it is still the treatment of choice for mental health problems whenever the problem is viewed as having originated in childhood or whenever an individual is repressing or denying something that is obvious to others. For others, the long-term therapies have lost their scientific legitimacy (Specht & Courtney, 1994). The relatively poor outcomes of insight-oriented social work interventions have made some clinical social workers distance themselves from that orientation and move completely toward a generalist, ecological, or other case management style with the utilization of behavioral or cognitive approaches when required.

Eclecticism is reinforced in current clinical social work because those practitioners within social services and mental health have grown to accept the biological basis of severe disorders and, increasingly, the less-severe disorders and personality characteristics. While there is a growing debate concerning the use of medications to alter personalities and their use as a substitute rather than a complement to treatment in managed care, psychopharmacology is certainly viewed as one of the mix of eclectic interventions (Bentley & Walsh, 2001; Kramer, 1993).

Research rather than ideology has become the basis for training and subsequent interventions for advanced practice. The arguments of various helping professions and previously warring factions within social work that acrimoniously disagreed concerning interventions and theoretical approaches have subsided. Currently, better-trained practice students (i.e., trained in more rigorous, less biased methodologies) and less ideologically biased recent graduates are more accepting of a blending of techniques.

Generalist texts suggest that generalist practice is sufficient for most basic interventions (McMahon, 1996; Kirst-Ashman & Hull, 1993). However, advanced social work practice builds on that same systems-oriented base

(Meyer & Mattaini, 1995) and includes an eclectic mix of empirically validated methods (Mattaini, 1995b).

BIOPSYCHOSOCIAL BASIS FOR HUMAN BEHAVIOR

The Council on Social Work Education (CSWE), which is the educational accrediting body for schools of social work, has mandated that social work curricula deal with the theories and research in social, behavioral, and biological sciences (CSWE, 2001). Curricula must do so in a way that interrelates and connects these areas and that illustrates divergencies. The CSWE requires that schools have content that deals with biological, psychological, social, and cultural systems and how these various systems change and affect people throughout their life cycles. Of most importance to practitioners, the Council also requires that the relevance of each of the theoretical frameworks be related to practice and that social workers be well trained in working with issues of diversity, social and economic justice, values and ethics, and populations at risk.

When viewed in toto and particularly in the context of a requirement from an accrediting agency, the task seems daunting if not impossibly cumbersome. Curricula are expected to cover the theory and practice application of the wide range of generally unrelated perspectives. But, in spite of all of this, as Carel Germain (1991) said, "It is neither necessary nor sufficient, for example, that social workers become experts in sociology, psychology, anthropology, political science, economics, biology or other behavioral and life sciences. Rather, social workers need to understand and apply relevant concepts and findings from various disciplines and bodies of thought that will provide a base for professional decisions and actions as filtered through the lense of social work purpose, values and ethics" (p. 56).

Different techniques derived from various theoretical models are more effective than others. In their exhaustive review and meta-analysis of virtually all of the methodologically rigorous outcome studies of the last two decades, Lambert and Bergin (1994) concluded that "Behavioral and cognitive methods appear to add a significant increment of efficacy with respect to a number of difficult problems (e.g., panic, phobias, and compulsion) and to provide useful methods with a number of non-neurotic problems with which traditional therapies have shown little effectiveness (e.g., childhood aggression, psychotic behavior, and health related behaviors)" (p. 181). Furthermore, an increasing body of evidence points to specific diagnoses, such as depression, as being more effectively treated by cognitive techniques than by any other (Granvold, 1994; Burns, 1980).

Social workers lead the way in examining the "person-in-environment," (Karls & Wandrei, 1994), which necessitates a here-and-now focus that is sensitive to a wide variety of social forces. Social workers are required to be aware of the social, political, and economic forces that particularly affect women, minorities, and the disadvantaged. It is essential that social workers be capable of addressing the needs of a schoolchild who is depressed because the child's mother has lost her job, as well as being able to work with the mother herself whose perception of the problem is radically different from her child's. Even in this simple scenario, one could envision a need for case management, career counseling or placement, cognitive therapy and supportive group counseling of the mother and/or the child, advice on economic concerns, social support system development, and possibly antidepressant medication if these social and economic conditions do not soon improve.

No single theory adequately explains human behavior except those that rely upon a broad systemic orientation (Germain, 1991). For instance, pure psychodynamic practitioners believe in the primacy of early developmental experiences, particularly bonding and the child's relationship and interactions with the mother. Historically, psychodynamic practitioners even blamed the mothers of children with autism or schizophrenia as being causal in the subsequent disorders of the child, suggesting that there was a profound early trauma and rejection. Now psychodynamic practitioners accept the fact of genetic and biological predisposers as prerequisites for such severe disorders but integrate that knowledge with a focus on positive relationships in early years as a means of diminishing the likely negative biological effects.

The purely biologically based psychiatrist or nurse is also less frequently seen in current practice because of a wider acceptance of the biopsychosocial origin of so many problems. In the past, they may have told families that the prescribed antipsychotic or antidepressant medication alone was sufficient to treat the patient with bipolar or delusional episodes. Today, a patient in such psychiatric settings is likely to be referred to a social worker who teaches the patient to consciously recognize the onset of certain symptoms (Bentley & Walsh, 2001). The social worker also helps the client to develop a social support system and develop insight into how their behavior affects family dynamics and current interpersonal relationships (Maguire, 1991). Furthermore, the social worker may educate the client so that he or she can monitor the physical and psychological effects of his or her medication.

In a similar fashion, the behaviorist who successfully conditions the mother to stop her "crying behavior" over her child who died years before can hardly be called successful in spite of having achieved the goal of symptom eradication. The underlying loss and grief needs to be explored, and repressed feelings of guilt or anger need to be addressed in a slow, insight-oriented approach. Again, an eclectic and broader view of the nature of the causes and treatments of social, emotional, and psychological problems seems to be indicated.

With the exception of certain purists in each camp, clinical social workers today are sensitive to the fact that there are clear biological, social, psychological, environmental, and learned causes of behavior and/or problems. Since any effective intervention has to be based upon understanding and attacking the problem at its root cause, it is essential for advanced clinicians to understand the theories of causation as well as the treatments that logically flow from them.

Thus, it is necessary for the clinical social worker to know some psychodynamic approaches when dealing with problems that have their origin in early, repressed childhood trauma. On the other hand, if the problem originated in maladaptive learned responses to stimuli in the environment that are no longer present or a threat, then the client needs to modify his or her behavior to become more adaptive. If the social environment or stressors are causing the difficulty, then the environment or coping response needs to change. If the cause of the problematic behavior is in biological form—as is the case with schizophrenia, bipolar disorders, most severe depressions, and some hyperactivity and learning disorders—then the client needs medication as well as counseling to help him or her effectively cope with the medical problem. Advanced practitioners need not be experts in each area, but they do need to be broadly trained enough to use the "best" approach or combination of approaches.

Most social work textbooks currently in use support eclectic, research-based viewpoints among practitioners. For instance, a leading text in human behavior and the social environment says, "This text will give particular attention to concepts of learning and cognitive theories, and the viewpoints of the schools of psychoanalytic and humanistic psychology. . . . The practitioner employs a number of theories to devise the strategies of intervention most likely to succeed in dealing with client's problems . . ." (Specht & Craig, 1987, p. 5). Another preeminent social work textbook states, "For a long time the profession suffered from a dearth of theory. This was replaced by an almost complete dependence on psychoanalytic thinking, now being replaced by a broad based commitment to the wide range of systems discussed in this book. . . . [T]his diversity has strengthened our understanding of the importance of tested theory and demonstrated the pitfalls in a practice that is either devoid of theory or overdependent on a single theory" (Turner, 1986, p. 2).

Current research indicates that most types of severe disorders that clinical social workers deal with are viewed as having their etiology or, at least, maintenance in several areas. Clinical researchers generally find that severe disorders such as schizophrenia, bipolar disorders, clinical depression, and even many personality disorders have some biological origin. However, recurrent episodes can be diminished in frequency and severity through a variety of nonbiochemical interventions such as psychotherapy or developing social support systems or somehow teaching patients to change their responses to certain situations or stimuli that have previously led them into overreaction, sometimes of psychotic proportions.

Advanced practitioners, therefore, need to understand systems theory and generalist practice as well as the eclectic research-based methods used currently in practice. This cannot be done in a "watered-down" sense wherein they know relatively little relevant to many areas. Rather, they need to have extensive knowledge of some methods that are relevant to the client populations they serve and at least enough knowledge about other methods of practice so that they know when and how to seek assistance or consultation.

PRACTICE PERSPECTIVES

Advanced-level clinical practitioners need to have knowledge and skills in both broad-based systems methods and in advanced methods. The broad-based systems methods include: the *generalist*, the *ecological approach, case management*, and *family and group systems interventions*. These are all described in Part Two of this book. Although there are literally hundreds of different models (Kazdin, 1986) and an infinite variety of current techniques, the three perspectives that form the basis for the most widely used advanced methods include *psychodynamic, behavioral*, and *cognitive*. The biological perspective and medical interventions are briefly described in this chapter since some knowledge of its relevance to most major disorders is needed, but it is not described in depth. Instead, a chapter on *brief interventions* is included. These are all described in Part Three of this book, along with a concluding chapter that describes the required treatment plans and documentation for the most commonly accepted methods (see Chapter 11).

There are many reasonable and acceptable alternative models for looking at advanced practice. The most likely would be to simply define advanced practice as *advanced generalist* (McMahon, 1996) or as *ecological* (Germain & Gitterman, 1996; Mattaini, 1997), particularly since both already include and integrate many of the advanced techniques from psychodynamic, behavioral, cognitive, and other research-supported methods. Advanced social work practice incorporates the advanced techniques, so they are defined and developed separately in this text to allow for the necessary depth in practice skills.

There are several perspectives that currently exert a major influence on advanced social work practice (see Table 2.1). In social work practice, the major underlying theory is *systems theory. Systems theory* is the basis for such *systems interventions* as the advanced generalist, ecological, case management, and family and group approaches. Advanced practice also uses *psychoanalytic* and *developmental theory*, which is the basis for *psychodynamic interventions; learning theory*, which leads to *behavioral interventions; cogni-*

TABLE 2.1	ADVANCED SOCIAL WORK PRACTICE PERSPECTIVES

Theory	Applied Treatment Orientations
Systems Theory	Advanced generalist
	Ecological
	Case management
	Family interventions
	Group interventions
Psychoanalytic/Developmental	Psychodynamic and psychosocial
Learning Theory	Behavioral interventions
Cognitive	Cognitive and constructivist

tive theory, which is the basis for *cognitive* and *constructivist interventions;* and the *biological perspective,* which is recognized as a major determinant of behavior even though its subsequent application, the *medical model,* is not directly practiced by most social workers. Each perspective attempts to explain the origin and nature of disordered behavior. Surprisingly, there is some consensus in advanced-practice texts and recent agreement in social work practice that the foundation for practice includes systems, cognitive, behavioral, and psychoanalytic theoretical bases (Brandell, 1997). These theories, in turn, influence the development of particular applied treatment orientations as outlined in Table 2.1 and discussed subsequently. This table lists the major theories and their most commonly applied treatment orientations. There are literally hundreds of variations used in advanced practice.

Clinical social workers are the preeminent professionals in the use of systems theory, which requires a social systems or ecological interventionist response. Most clinical social workers are also well versed in either psychoanalytic/developmental theory, cognitive, or behavioral theories. The area in which clinical social workers typically have the least expertise is the biological model that requires a medical or somatotherapeutic response such as psychopharmacological intervention (Bentley & Walsh, 2001).

Systems Theory

Systems theory focuses upon aspects of relationships between people and their environments. This theory posits that individuals are constantly interacting with other individuals in social systems that may include family systems, groups, institutions, court systems, or even larger political and economic forces. When one acts upon the system, one affects change in the system which, in turn, may affect the individual. For instance, families are sometimes known to target one individual as the "problem" and often that family member, in turn, acts out the problems of the entire family. When that individual is successfully treated, the dysfunctional family system is invariably thrown into disarray and is forced to deal with its problems without projecting or displacing the problem onto the one designated "disturbed" member. Systems-oriented family therapy is used to help family members recognize that each member affects the other and that it would be better for each of them to deal directly with individual problems but in the context of needing to live with, help, and support each other to help himself or herself.

Systems interventions are closely aligned with the social work ethos, which includes the belief that factors such as poverty, racism, sexism, or homelessness affect individuals psychologically. Interventions confirm that an objective, rational awareness of such social forces is useful and should be a conscious factor in effecting positive change for individuals as they interact in their respective systems.

Treatment involves encouraging understanding, adaptation, coping, and integration with the environment or the system. Factors such as catharsis, "working through the problem," and insight are not particularly valued compared to their primacy in psychodynamic approaches. Whenever factors such as stress develop, approaches that alleviate the effects of stress or enhance constructive responses are encouraged. These involve encouraging and instructing clients how to become involved actively and appropriately with others. Therapists may also work to reestablish the social network within which the individual has functioned. This can involve the therapist's direct intervention as an advocate, expediter, or facilitator; or efforts are made toward restructuring a support system. Frequently, therapists use self-help or support groups, church groups, or even sports teams as transitional social systems. Clients are encouraged to break patterns of harmful or self-destructive interactions and are helped to develop positive relationships with supportive individuals and systems (Maguire, 1991). Case 2.1 is an example of a systems-based social work intervention.

Case 2.1: Systems-Based Intervention

Cindy Atherton is a 23-year-old single mother of two boys, ages 1 and 3. She has been drinking heavily for two years ever since her husband abandoned her and left her pregnant and in debt. She realizes she needs help but came to Catholic Social Services with a request for child care help for her one-year-old, who is not developing in the same way as her older child and who looks "strange." The clinical social worker, Ms. Jensen, immediately recognized the facial characteristics and delayed developmental patterns of the infant as being consistent with fetal alcohol syndrome. She also smelled alcohol on Cindy's breath, detected a slurred speech, and assessed that Cindy was overwhelmed and lacking in financial, social, and familial supports.

Ms. Jensen agreed to get the baby into free child care but first referred Cindy to a pediatrician who specialized in fetal alcohol syndrome. She also asked Cindy more about herself and listened for a half hour as Cindy described her struggles with money, her anger toward her ex-husband whose debts she was dealing with, her feelings of being "worthless" as a mother, her lack of friends or any social life, and her fear that she was becoming a "drunk with a retarded baby because I couldn't control my drinking."

"You know, Cindy, you really do seem to be trying your best, but sometimes we need help from others," said Ms. Jensen. Ms. Jensen then helped Cindy draw a diagram of her social network, with a detailed follow-up describing all past, present, and future sources of help or support. After two sessions assessing the strengths and deficits in her support system, Cindy and Ms. Jensen began developing a list of organizations, family, and friends who might help.

A lawyer was found who specialized in finding and collecting money from "deadbeat" fathers. The pediatrician supported the diagnosis of fetal alcohol syndrome for the infant, and Cindy agreed to join a treatment group at the agency for young female alcoholics. She also met with Ms. Jensen every other week to talk about efforts to rebuild friendships with a variety of individuals and about organizations that helped her with child care, finances, and socialization opportunities.

Psychodynamic and Developmental Theory

Psychodynamic and developmental theory posits that there was some trauma or difficulty during a stage of psychological development (i.e., during the oral, anal, phallic, latency, or genital stage). While social environment is considered, the emphasis is still placed upon intrapsychic factors. This perspective suggests that the source of most psychological problem lies within an individual and can be alleviated or changed by changing some aspect of personality, particularly by breaking through defenses and resistance that keep the conflicted problem at a subconscious level.

The relevance of this perspective has been in question for many years; in fact, it has been in decline as an accepted approach for over 40 years. Clinical social workers as well as psychologists, psychiatrists, counselors, and clinical nurses are less likely to be trained in its applications than in the past. It has been criticized as being ineffective and inefficient in its outcomes, old fashioned and sexist in its theory, and far too slow and costly in today's managed care environment. Its adherents in clinical social work are viewed by some as culturally and politically insensitive or somewhat irrelevant. So why is it still described in virtually every book on human behavior and the majority of practice books? The answer is that, in spite of its many drawbacks, there is simply no way of treating many of the problems clinical social workers must address without knowing and understanding the effects of early childhood influences within some orderly and consistent frame of reference. The essential psychodynamic and developmental theory says that childhood, and particularly the interactions a developing child has with his or her own parents, is a major factor in subsequent growth, behavior, attitudes, and personality. While learning theory, systems theory, cognitive theory, and biology all deal with and offer some basis for understanding the effects of childhood and family on subsequent personality and behavior, none of the other theories is as focused or developed in that particular area.

The future of traditional psychodynamic interventions is unclear in clinical social work and managed care environments. Psychoanalytic theory, particularly related to psychosexual development for women, has long been repudiated. Traditional psychodynamic techniques—such as working through repressed material through free association, symbolic interpretations of dreams and behaviors, and the "blank screen" style of psychodynamic social workers—are described in Chapter 7. These techniques are used only in situations in which the effects of early childhood trauma need to be consciously addressed to treat a significant current problem. A basic understanding of psychodynamic and developmental theory, as well as knowledge of certain techniques, still remains important for clinical or advanced practice.

Psychodynamic interventions in current practice are far more brief; directive; and object-, reality-, or ego-oriented than in the past. The clinical social worker helps the client work toward greater self-understanding through new insights that result from a clarification of the psychological meaning of emotions and feelings. Therapeutic change often happens through insight. For instance, a client may realize that his or her passive-aggressive personality stems from being raised by an aggressive, hostile mother or that the client's overachieving is really based upon insecurity related to parental rejection. A clinical social worker using the psychodynamic approach with a depressed, anxious young woman who has been a high achiever would help the client gradually realize that certain repressed memories from earlier development are affecting her current feelings and behavior. With this insight comes better understanding and, ultimately, feelings and actions differently based on these new understandings. The clinical social worker also recognizes and even encourages transference, a process whereby the client relates to the therapist as if the therapist were the mother or father. By re-working some of those earlier pathological dynamics in a positive manner, the client can change and grow. Case 2.2 is an example of a psychodynamically based social work intervention.

Case 2.2: Psychodynamically Based Intervention
John is a 12-year-old boy who was brought to Family and Children's Social Services because of rather sudden poor school performance, violent and self-destructive acting out, depression, and suicidal ideation subsequent to his father's death in a car accident the previous year. His clinical social worker, Bill Jones, is well versed in systems, behavioral, and cognitive interventions but chose to deal with John psychodynamically after the first session.

John very reluctantly walked in to Mr. Jones's office. John had been crying in the waiting room, which added to this young man's feelings of anger and humiliation at being forced to come here by his mother. The boy wanted his mother to leave, and, since a fairly detailed intake and psychosocial history had already been gathered from her, Mr. Jones agreed to talk alone with John. After a minute of John staring at his feet as he tried to hold back tears, Mr. Jones softly said, "John, I'm very sorry about your father. I know how much you loved him."

John lost all composure and began to sob openly but still did not look up, and finally said, "Yeah, well, how come I killed him?"

Mr. Jones was surprised but did not express it as he asked, "Can you tell me more, John? I'm not sure what you mean."

"Dad was coming to get me from baseball practice. I was mad at him because he wasn't at practice like usual. I told him to hurry up and get here. I waited for almost an hour, and I told a friend my father was a jerk for not picking me up. I didn't know he was killed on the way over," John sobbed.

Even though the accident had happened over a year before, John had never before mentioned his own feelings of guilt and blame in his father's death. The thought of being responsible for it had only recently occurred to John at a more conscious level. Mr. Jones looked and acted a bit like John's father, and the quick and obvious transference was immediately recognized as an opportunity to help John successfully work through his previously repressed feelings of guilt and blame.

In the following months, Mr. Jones encouraged John to talk about his feelings of loss as well as his misguided belief that he had caused his father's death. On several occasions, they went to a nearby field and played catch, just as John had so often done with his father. The repressed feelings of guilt were discussed at length. A reoccurring nightmare in which John was driving the car that killed his father was also discussed. Mr. Jones interpreted that as another subconscious indication of John's feeling responsible for his father's death.

Sessions continued weekly for six months, with the last six sessions being devoted to the issue of termination and loss as they ended treatment. Mr. Jones indicated in his closing case record that his own positive countertransference toward John had no doubt facilitated the treatment. However, the primary dynamics were the quick and positive transference John felt toward Mr. Jones, which he supported, thus allowing John to consciously analyze his repressed feelings of guilt over "killing" his beloved father. The unresolved loss and guilt had been the bases for John's fights, violence, school failures, and suicidal tendencies. He had been trying to punish himself or even end his life rather than consciously recognize his misguided belief that he killed his father.

Learning Theory

From the learning theory perspective, "abnormal behavior" reflects a learned but persistent and maladaptive response acquired in anxiety-generating situations. The response is maladaptive because the response still persists even though no realistic or objective threat exists. Overt symptoms are regarded as the proper focus of treatment since it is reasoned that they symptoms represent the problem and are not secondary manifestations of either disease or unconscious conflict.

Behavioral interventions are based in this theory, and treatment often involves developing schedules that weaken maladaptive responses and reinforce more adaptive behavior (e.g., desensitization, condition-avoidance, and the use of positive and negative reinforcement, as well as aversive conditioning, extinction, flooding or saturation).

Clinical social workers who accept the premise that mental health problems originate in the maladaptive learning situation treat their clients' disorders by changing the response patterns. This is true in behavior modification. (See Chapter 8: Behavioral Interventions.) Case 2.3 is an example of a behavioral intervention.

Case 2.3: Behavioral Intervention

Jim was a salesman, age 24, who was depressed because his germ phobia kept him from having any close contact with a potential partner. His condition had worsened in recent years, and, the more he worried about it, the worse his symptoms became. He was so embarrassed about this behavior that he kept it secret, and no one even knew he suffered from this problem. He came in to see Sally, the social worker at the mental health clinic, only after he read an article in the newspaper that said that such problems were common and treatable.

Sally and Jim developed a gradual, incremental plan in which Jim began by simply concentrating upon a mildly anxiety-producing scene while combining imaging, focusing, and various deep relaxation techniques to control his fears (see the behavior-modification chapter for an explanation of these techniques). Through a gradual process of working toward his desired goal of touching and kissing a person he had long wanted to date, his phobic behavior was stopped; and his anxiety and depression, which were secondary to the social effects of the phobia, also lifted.

Cognitive Theory

Cognitive theory differs from learning theory, and, subsequently, behavior modification in several ways. Cognitive theory states that the problem originates in faulty cognitions or understandings that naturally lead to inappropriate or dysfunctional responses, behaviors, attitudes, or feelings on the part of individuals. Cognitive theorists believe individuals develop patterns of thinking in which they gradually see the world as good or bad, black or white. Particularly when under stress, clients are incapable of making appropriate behavioral decisions because they cannot analyze the data or evidence in a flexible, useful way. Thus, mildly rude or negligent behavior on the part of family, friends, or colleagues is seen as a major insult under emotional duress. Subsequently, the individual thinks and feels that he or she has to respond in a similar manner. This can lead to a pattern of inappropriate and extreme emotions or responses.

Cognitive interventions involve challenging or confronting the client when he or she verbalizes certain assumptions that are, in fact, distorted or false. For instance, a depressed individual typically views the environment as either all good or all bad. This is frequently layered with perfectionistic self-demands that never can be realistically met. Therefore the client believes or thinks that, since he or she only received a "C" on a test, he or she must be "stupid" or a complete fool who will be judged as such by "everyone." Or, a young, overwhelmed mother angrily slaps her infant, thus "proving" that she is a "horrible abusive mother" just as her own mother was toward her.

Such extreme and pervasive thought patterns significantly affect one's self-perceptions, images, emotions, and subsequent behaviors. Cognitive interventions, therefore, involve techniques that encourage the client to realistically "re-think" such self-beliefs, while looking at alternative and more objective and realistic explanations. For instance, a cognitive intervention might involve homework assignments using a three-column sheet. In Column 1, the client writes an objective statement of some behavior demonstrated by another; in Column 2, the client writes his or her "automatic response" to that behavior; and, in column 3, the client writes a more realistic response. So, Column 1 might say: "Coworker Alice did not say hello to me in the elevator." Column 2 would describe the client's automatic, patterned thought, which is, "Alice hates me and thinks I am stupid." Column 3 would contain an alternative belief or thought such as, "Alice did not see me and says nothing to anyone at work until after her morning coffee. I have no reason to think she dislikes me or thinks of me as stupid." (See Chapter 9: Cognitive Interventions.) Case 2.4 is an example of a cognitive intervention.

Case 2.4: Cognitive Intervention

Ginny was a 16-year-old Korean American student who was referred to Family Services because her mother found and read her daughter's diary, which contained multiple suicidal references and obvious feelings of self-hatred. Ginny tearfully confided to Joyce, her social worker at the Eastern Area Community Center, that she felt completely worthless, lonely, unattractive, and stupid.

Joyce listened attentively, occasionally asking for clarification, and then summarized back to Ginny the essence of what she had said in equally bleak and extreme terms. Ginny paused, seemingly embarrassed, and then politely rephrased Joyce's summary in more positive terms.

Joyce was supportive and empathic but gently confronted Ginny with the fact that she really was only trying to understand the situation and restate what Ginny had originally stated: "I don't have a single friend and everybody hates me . . . and I'm the ugliest girl in school."

A discussion ensued in which Joyce encouraged and modeled a more realistic, factual, and balanced self-description that included Ginny's multiple strengths and capabilities, as well as recognizing areas where she could make some changes in her behavior and attitude. As Ginny became increasingly realistic and, thus, positive in her thoughts, attitudes, and moods, she also increased her capacity to talk openly about them rather than keeping them "inside" where they tended to fester and become less realistic without the needed "reality check" about which Joyce and Ginny had joked.

It was difficult for Joyce to stop herself from quickly reassuring Ginny that her thoughts were virtually all unwarranted. However, she knew that this perfectionistic and mildly withdrawn young woman would not have cognitively accepted or believed early positive feedback. Instead, Ginny needed to personally develop the cognitive skills so that in the future she would recognize her past patterns of negativity and self-criticism and correct those thoughts with more accurate ones.

Biological Theory

Biological theory is based on the evidence that severely disturbed behavior is determined mainly by physical and organic processes and brain functioning. From the biological perspective, deviant behavior is viewed as a psychiatric disorder or as a disease. Neurobiologists believe that abnormal behaviors and psychiatric disorders are the result of faulty pathophysiological processes and neurochemistry. A biological or physiological defect is a necessary condition for "mental illness," and psychiatric symptoms occur when persons with such inherited defects are faced with adverse circumstances that bring out their weaknesses. The nervous systems of these individuals make them more vulnerable to the negative effects of social stress.

Medical interventions generally follow the classical medical theory of disease that is focused upon pathology. Clinicians, usually physicians, use medications and a variety of drugs or electroconvulsive therapy or surgery. Verbal approaches are minimal and usually very direct, that is, tell the patient explicitly that he or she has an illness and explain what is needed to cure it. This perspective is widely accepted for severe disorders such as schizophrenia, bipolar disorders, major depression, and chronic drug and alcohol abuse. It is very different from the psychoanalytic perspective that rarely tells patients the precise nature of their problems since they believe the origins of the problem are usually not consciously known, at least initially, by the patient.

The biological perspective requires treatment to be medical or somatotherapeutic. In short, the cause of the disorder is biological; therefore, the subsequent treatment must also be biological, which primarily includes medications to treat the pathological or dysfunctional chemistry of the individual patient's brain (Bentley & Walsh, 2001).

Social work practice does not include directly dispensing medication or other strictly medical interventions, but it has become much more holistic—an orientation that recognizes the interaction of physical and psychological balances. For instance, one of the first issues social workers address with anxious, depressed, overwhelmed clients is the client's eating and sleeping patterns. Building a healthy lifestyle that includes exercise as well as increased social interactions and active collaborations with physicians and nurses by the worker and client is standard procedure now.

There is currently a realization that the consensual agreement upon the causes or the etiology of much of human behavior and, particularly, "mental illness" are unresolved and possibly unresolvable issues, at least in a narrow or definitive sense. This reality is evident even in psychiatry, which is much narrower in the types of problems it encounters than social work. In the *DSM-IV-TR* (2000), as well as related guides, there is an explicit recognition that earlier editions had been overly anchored in specific theories (particularly psychodynamic), and such orientations are no longer as widely accepted.

The field of psychiatry is moving away from diagnostic classifications based on any single theoretical base. It is returning to its historical roots, and current classifications now prefer "a menu or signs and symptoms; any assumption of etiology has vanished. . . . This descriptive approach does not invalidate previous concepts but rather cautions against determining etiology too easily" (Othmer & Othmer, 1989, p. 3). Instead, the trend is toward classifications based upon empirically verifiable factors such as family history and epidemiology. It accepts etiological perspectives that are compatible with biological as well as psychological and social perspectives.

This approach is widely accepted now by most, but certainly not all, clinical social workers. However, the clinical social worker who is still treating schizophrenia as if the problem were based on double-binding communication patterns or insufficient bonding with a maternal figure in the first few days of life or because of any variety of repressed or unresolved problems of a psychodynamic origin is reasonably at risk for a lawsuit. To treat acute psychotic disorders or bipolar disorders from any perspective other than at least partially through psychopharmacological intervention is inappropriate since the evidence is so overwhelming that these disorders originate and are consistently affected by biochemical and genetic forces.

Most medical interventions are performed by physicians. Only licensed medical doctors can prescribe medication or perform psychosurgery. This is certainly rational since the education and training in the biological model forms the basis for such interventions and social work education generally does not emphasize this model. However, knowledge of the significance of medical interventions and psychopharmacology is essential for social workers who treat severe disorders (Bentley & Walsh, 2001).

Psychoses, major depression, bipolar disorders, and severe anxiety disorders are all successfully treated with appropriate medications and social work intervention. Neither psychopharmacological intervention nor social work treatment intervention alone is adequate. Both must be used together to treat major mental health disorders. The type of medication, dosage, and frequency often involve detailed knowledge of biochemistry and pharmacology. It is the clinical social worker's task to make appropriate medical referrals and to engage the client in treatment or case management (Moseley & Deweaver, 1998).

Knowledge of the basis of this model and good, interactive, mutually respectful collegial relationships with physicians tend to lead to the best client care. Unlike the other perspectives and related interventions, there are no chapters in this book on this perspective since social workers do not carry out medical interventions directly, even though current practice requires a recognition of this perspective in the cause and treatment of many severe psychological problems. However, many MSW programs now require prerequisite courses in human biology and emphasize holistic approaches that emphasize proper diet, exercise, sleep, and the importance of a healthy body.

CHOOSING INTERVENTIONS

Advanced-level practitioners are capable of independent practice. They decide how to treat their clients, applying whatever approach they believe to be the most effective. But how is that choice made? How do clinical social workers know if the approach chosen is a good match for the client? What factors influence those choices? Are there models and suggestions for making specific choices? The remainder of this chapter examines the issues of *matching client and worker, factors influencing choices,* and *guidelines for choosing interventions.*

Matching Client and Worker

It is essential that clinical practitioners separate and independently assess attributes of both the therapist and the client; this includes an evaluation of environment, life events, attitudes, and behaviors of both, as well as the type of treatment considered. The voluminous research in various aspects of this endeavor has helped considerably (Bergin & Garfield, 1994a; Hill, 1989). As clinical research has become more methodologically rigorous and specific in purpose and design, its utility to practitioners has improved. At times, however, independent clinicians can be overwhelmed in the search for what really works best for their clients.

In a meta-analysis of such research, Beutler, Crago, and Arizmindi (1986) attempted to distinguish between internal and external characteristics and therapy-specific versus extratherapy characteristics. Extratherapy characteristics have more of an unplanned effect in comparison to therapy-specific characteristics, which include factors designed by the clinician's approach or training to consciously produce change, such as the clinician's decision to use behavioral desensitization. An extratherapy factor might be the rehiring of a client who was depressed over the loss of a job or the independent decision on the part of a client to leave an abusive partner. Therapy-specific attributes are assumed to be under the clinician's control, whereas the extratherapy characteristics are not controlled by the clinician.

Their assessments of the most methodologically rigorous research indicate the following results for matching practitioners and clients:

- *Age* differences can present a problem for some clients. Survey research indicates some preference by older clients for more mature clinicians, or at least not being matched with young therapists, although a high-status young therapist or otherwise high-credibility clinician may be acceptable even if relatively young. Young clients, by contrast, prefer relatively youthful clinicians.

- *Gender* is an area that has received a great deal of attention in more recent years. Again, the results of the various studies yield differing results in purely factoring out gender since experience, environmental factors, and diverse populations differ tremendously. However, the consensus is that gender does exert a modest effect on the selection of patients, the nature of therapy, and outcomes. In general, it appears that similar gender dyads are more helpful than opposite-gender pairings in treatment. Some studies particularly note that female clients responded more positively to female therapists.

- *Ethnicity and race* have also been studied extensively. Perhaps the most noteworthy finding has been that it is the race of the *researcher* that seems to account for results. Beutler, Craig, and Arizmindi (1986) cite research that suggests that researchers of Caucasian descent generally indicated that race or matching race is not a factor in outcomes whereas researchers of African American descent concluded that race is a factor. Research does modestly support the viewpoint that dropout rates may be minimized by matching ethnic background, but outcome results show no clear difference. Being sensitive to racial, ethnic, and cultural factors and differences is viewed as essential in any social work intervention (Feit, Cuevas, & Hann-Dowdy, 1998) even though the effects on outcomes are inconclusive.

- *Socioeconomic status* (SES) is less clear, partially because of the difficulty in separating the issues of current SES and income, education, and professional status as opposed to historical background and issues of culture and class. Results in this area are inconclusive.

- *Personality* patterns are also inconclusive. Some studies do suggest that dissimilarity in personality or cognitive styles may be the best match. A related issue is that of therapy for the therapists. Historically, the process of psychotherapy for clinicians had a great deal of support, particularly in psychoanalytic circles. However, current research simply does not support the viewpoint that clinicians who have undergone therapy or analysis themselves develop into more effective therapists.

- *Attitudes and values* are difficult to factor out, or identify, in therapy since they change for individuals, and they can change in the interactional process of therapy. In terms of patient selection, there is little evidence that clients seek out therapists of similar values with the exception of clients who are particularly religious. Once in therapy, a rather consistent finding is that clients begin to accept the therapist's belief system concerning morals, religion, and more general concepts. Some research indicates that it is preferable for the therapist to accept the client's values and to provide treatment that is consistent with the beliefs and values of the client to maximize outcomes.

- *Relationship attitudes* have historically been affected by the various studies on Rogerian or client-centered therapy conducted throughout the late 1950s and 1960s. Therapists trained at that time were told that the one consistent clinical research finding was that the therapist attitudes of empathy, genuineness and warmth, or unconditional positive regard were the "necessary and sufficient" qualities for achieving positive outcomes with clients. Subsequent research indicated that these qualities were not as useful when included in non-Rogerian therapy. This area of research is also dominated by weaker designs that tend to be naturalistic or correctional. However, one fairly consistent finding is that patients who perceive of their therapists as having a positive facilitative attitude are likely to have better results than clients who do not perceive of their therapists in this way.

  It is noteworthy that, contrary to earlier findings, some clients actually respond poorly to empathy and support. The notion of the worker's attitude being the sine qua non of successful therapy is inadequate; more than just the relationship is involved. There is a need for further study that examines the complex, dynamic, interactive process of the clinician and the client.

- *Social influence* attributes have been adopted from social psychologists in the clinical research arena. These attributes include expertness, trustworthiness, attraction, credibility, and persuasiveness. Perceived expertness has been seen to be a rather consistent positive finding in controlled studies in which the client has been manipulated and told that certain clinicians have greater expertise than others. Persuasiveness and credibility have similarly positive findings in several studies.

- *Therapist expectation* has been found to exert a positive influence on outcome, although some studies refute this finding. The general consensus is that, even when the client is initially incongruent with the clinician in terms of expectations of outcome, he or she can often be persuaded to become more positive in expectations of results, and this change in the client can translate into beneficial effects.

Factors Influencing Choice

Among the major factors that influence choice of interventions are education and training, values and ethics, and experience. This section is followed by guidelines for choosing an appropriate model of intervention.

Education and Training   The choice of the type of intervention is invariably partially defined by the practitioner's training and theoretical orientation. For instance, if the practitioner's academic background and training viewed depression from the biological model as being caused by a dysfunction of the neurotransmitter system as well as being correlated with various biological and physiobiological anomalies or even as a response to some medications, then the worker would first refer a depressed client to a medical doctor or psychiatrist for appropriate medications. A worker who was psychodynamically trained would view the problem as the result of aggression turned inward or of object loss with resultant loss of self-esteem based on an inability to achieve the ego ideal. A behaviorally oriented social worker would see depression as a problem of learned helplessness in response to aversive social and economic stimuli or as a lack of past reinforcements when attempting to accomplish positive goals in the environment. A systems-oriented worker may view depression as originating in a loss of role or status within the social system or community.

A worker whose training and education were primarily from an existential perspective would see a client's depression as a crisis related to an inability to find meaning in life during transitions in life stages or because of major alterations in life's circumstances. A cognitively educated worker may view depression as being found in patterns of thinking in which a client self-blames—even when he or she is not directly involved—because of a pervasive overall negative view of life, the environment, and the future.

Some practitioners were even educated in a unified approach to understanding the etiology of problems that combines virtually all of these theories into the concept of loss of "social *zeitgebers*"—persons, social demands, or tasks that set the biological clock; that is, the various psychosocial and biological theories are combined into one that looks at the disruption of social rhythms (Ehlers, Frank, & Kupfer, 1988). While this approximates the ideal, even it is too narrow in current academic and practice preparation for clinical social workers.

It is unrealistic to expect clinical social workers to be experts in all of the currently accepted theories of social work, mental health, and psychosocial treatment or counseling. At best, all that can be realistically hoped for is for advanced-practice clinical social workers to be sufficiently well versed in a variety of orientations to apply the appropriate intervention strategy themselves or, when necessary, to refer to a practitioner who can more expertly use the needed intervention. Ultimately, all clinicians use some combination of research, guess work, knowledge, and science in choosing and applying intervention (Bromley, 1986). Professionals need to recognize that the client's best interests must remain the priority, and, as such, practitioners must be open to all explanatory evidence.

In the past, education in some instances referred to the dominant model of intervention used at the university and/or clinical placement and field internship for the student. Over the years, certain schools of social work had been viewed as being more behaviorally oriented (University of Michigan in the 1970s and 1980s), psychoanalytically oriented (Smith), or systems-oriented (University of Pittsburgh). Although none of these generalizations were totally accurate and, in fact, each school usually had faculty who taught approaches other than the dominant one, there was some likelihood that students would be immersed in one approach more than another. Graduates of Smith had solid backgrounds in psychoanalytic applications of social work practice and would therefore tend to use it predominantly in their practice; just as Michigan graduates would be more likely to use behavioral approaches; and those graduating from Pittsburgh would use systems approaches, sometimes regardless of the client's needs or circumstances. Practitioners used what they knew best, and their training predisposed them to utilize the same methods for all clients. Students and, ultimately, clinical social workers were held captive to some extent by their sources of training. Today, no school of social work would be accredited if it failed to offer a wide array of systems-based, empirically validated, advanced methods.

Values and Ethics   Values play a tremendous role in choosing interventions. They are central to intervention of any sort. The values considered by clinicians include ethics, rights of the client, confidentiality, client choices and self-determination, the role of family and society, and how interventions affect such systems. Ethics themselves include issues such as the clinician's behavior, attitudes, and feelings toward the client. The degree of sharing and intimacy between clinician and client is an aspect of this, as is the degree of confrontation. Some clinicians question the ethics of the highly confrontive clinicians who encourage "tough love" for parents who punish and demand certain behaviors on the part of their children. Certain group tactics, such as putting a person in the middle of the group and encouraging all members to attack any defensive behavior and/or denial, are now considered ethically questionable. The techniques that some view as therapeutic are seen by others as abusive.

Related ethical issues concern physical contact. Some clinicians view any physical contact as potentially harmful, whereas others see it as a natural way of expressing support and concern. Cultural differences are significant here.

Thus, clinical social workers have justified hugging or even kissing certain clients under certain conditions because the social workers felt that it was ethically or culturally condoned. The problem often lies in the clinician's insensitivity to the client's culture, where such behavior may be viewed as offensive, inappropriate, or sexually forward.

In choosing appropriate interventions and specific techniques with clients, the value base of the client takes precedence over that of the clinician. The clinician may view holding hands or hugging as being therapeutic and healthy for the client, but such action must be carefully checked in relation to the client's personal history and cultural style before presuming it is therapeutic.

Ethical issues have become critical to practitioners in recent years, partly due to increased litigation but also due to an increased awareness of racial and cultural diversity. Inner-city children raised on the streets of large cities do not use the same middle-class vocabulary of most social work clinicians. Those social workers who value polite discussion, the absence of swearing, and the complete condemnation of violence, whether physical or verbal, quickly find themselves out of place with many of their clients. Our universities and training institutes rarely appropriately address the fact that many of our clients do not share our values. It may be appropriate for us to discourage violence or even certain types of verbalizations in group sessions, but it is not appropriate for us to assume that the middle-class values that are deemed as the norm within our profession are always appropriate or useful for our clients. Such presumptions can distance practitioners from their clients.

Experience   Experience entails both the learning that one develops concerning life and oneself over the years as well as the resultant perspective on life. This experience gained through the interactive experience with others can be therapeutically focused, for instance, in group sessions in which such interpersonal learning is one of the most significant and pervasive therapeutic factors.

Clinical social workers have a long history of valuing their own life experiences and even entering personal therapy, particularly among psychoanalytically trained clinicians, to gain a better understanding of those experiences. There is some question concerning whether such analysis translates into the development of better clinicians (Bergin & Garfield, 1994a). However, there is little debate about the fact that a higher degree of self-awareness, insight, and enlightenment helps clinicians to be aware of the forces that may impact their interventions. For instance, the conscious recognition that certain personality traits are personally difficult for clinicians is useful. If a clinical social worker personally has or had a parent who is or was an alcoholic and if that social worker has strong personally biased reactions to alcoholic clients, then he or she either should not accept them as clients or should consciously deal with and control the countertransference issues.

Life experience and the conscious use of the interpersonal learning that clinicians have had can affect their choice of therapeutic interventions. The clinical social worker who grew up in a highly chaotic, neglectful, or abusive family environment or who grew up in an extremely rigid, authoritarian, ultraconservative family will no doubt have certain personal attitudes toward issues of control, self-determination, and empowerment. Such attitudes cannot be judged as good or bad, but they do need to be consciously recognized as life-experience factors that strongly affect our *weltanschauung* (view of the world); and, more importantly, they predispose workers toward certain types of interventions.

The clinical social worker who was raised in an open, liberal family in which children were encouraged to make their own decisions would possibly be comfortable with a Rogerian, client-centered approach, which highly values self-determination and the capacity of clients to ultimately make decisions that are right for them. The degree to which the life experience is acceptable, comfortable, or internally consistent to the social worker will have a considerable effect on such choices, whether the worker agrees or disagrees with his or her own family of origin's value system. Such life experiences are ultimately translated into internalized values systems that, in turn, predispose workers' choices of clinical interventions.

Guidelines for Choosing Interventions

The issue of choosing an intervention has become a major concern to practitioners. Fortunately, several have offered guidelines for this choice. Hepworth and Larsen (1993), whose entire approach to practice "is systematic eclecticism practiced under the umbrella of ecological systems theory" (p. 18), suggest several criteria for choosing:

- Choose interventions that are supported by strong empirical research.
- If two interventions have both been proven to be effective, the intervention that produces results with the least expenditure of time, money, and effort is the more efficient and is preferable to the other.
- Choose interventions and techniques subsumed under clearly dilineated theories. Theories with clear, concrete applications to practice are preferable to abstract theories with poorly defined applications.
- Choose ethically based interventions.
- Choose only those interventions for which the practitioner has the requisite training and skills.

The issue of choosing appropriate interventions for social work has existed for as long as the field itself. Jane Addams and her colleagues at Hull House had to develop a profession to serve the tremendously diverse needs of the large numbers of immigrants and other poor people in the later part of the

19th century. They used "scientific philanthropy" as the basis for developing appropriate interventions. Mary Richmond later attempted to organize and, thus, further professionalize social work in her seminal *Social Diagnosis* (1917), which was perhaps the first major attempt to pick and choose appropriate theoretical models and then apply them to social work practice.

Early social workers based their work on either Freud, Rank, Skinner, or the neo-Freudians and adapted them to different populations and settings within social work agencies. Current social work practitioners develop methods of intervention based upon theories and research from more recent clinicians who are not necessarily social workers but whose knowledge and research continue to add to the eclectic repertoire. The social work profession is rich in a history of borrowing and using an extremely broad base of knowledge and research. Workers rely on sociology, economics, psychology, history, political science, and even business to develop their own hybrid of practice.

While the profession in some respects is becoming more generalist, ecological, or systems-oriented, it is also very eclectic. There appears to be a move toward empirically supported behavioral approaches and cognitive interventions and away from longer-term, insight-oriented approaches (Thyer & Wodarski, 1998). Corcoran, for instance, develops a strong case for such interventions in *Structuring Change* (1992) but also includes a chapter advocating a feminist perspective for depression (Van Den Bergh, 1992) and a variety of short-term intervention approaches that are partially based on communication and interpersonal theories (Wells, 1992). Other suggestions for choosing interventions are highly affected by orientations toward either families or group systems. With these many possible choices, some have argued, at least since the 1970s, that the "best" approach by far is that which is empirically validated (Thyer & Wodarski, 1998; Corcoran & Fischer, 2000; Ivanoff, Blythe, & Briar, 1987).

Some would reasonably suggest that a holistic theory of biological, social, and psychological basis is simply too broad and generalist to be ultimately narrowed into a coherent practice approach. Holistic theories become operationalized as simply broad-based, nonspecific interventions and, as such, cannot be used (at least as the basis) for analyzing different clinical approaches (Meyer, 1983).

Another social work scholar who has edited several of the leading textbooks in clinical practice (Turner, 1996) has suggested that practicians continue to recognize that theory is important and central to practice, that many different theories of practice have validity, and that no one theory can be used for the many varied clients seen by practitioners.

This present state of multiple interlocking theories that often influence each other is far better than the beginning days of practice when there was little to no theory for the field. It is also far better than when the field relied solely on psychoanalytic theory. In fact, Turner (1986) views the field as having reached a time when the major theories, many of which developed in the

1950s and 1960s as a reaction to the psychoanalytic dominance, can all strengthen the field:

> This diversity has strengthened our understanding of the importance of tested theory and demonstrated the pitfalls in a practice that is either devoid of theory or overdependent on a single theory. As a first step in understanding their differential use, the field must know something about each system. Only from this basis can we begin to identify more clearly the relative and differential use of each, and also assess how this type of intersystem comparison contributes or takes away from ongoing progress to strengthen the knowledge base of practice. (p. 2)

Using clinical research as the basis for choosing interventions is arguably the best objective means of choice. The research-based social worker is seemingly the ideal that has been established in the field of clinical practice. Furthermore, several excellent texts have been written to guide clinicians in the process of empirically studying and measuring their own interventions (Blythe & Tripodi, 1989; Corcoran & Fischer, 2000) and those of others (Gambrill, 1990).

However, the types of problems presented to clinical social workers are often highly complex and idiosyncratic. The choice of an intervention can be decided only in the context of the client's unique history and predisposition. Contemporary social workers accept research as a primary factor in deciding how to proceed with a particular client; but then they must evaluate such data in light of the broader cultural, political, economic, and social circumstances relevant to that client. For instance, a social worker in a family-planning agency would likely consider discussing both abortion and suicide when treating young, frightened adolescents with unwanted pregnancies. However, most research ignores the important religious and cultural considerations which are very relevant for young women of Latino descent. (See Box 2.1 for a discussion of multimodal therapy.)

Gambrill's (1990) excellent book *Critical Thinking in Clinical Practice* discusses in depth the association between defining the causes of a client's problem and making the ultimate choices regarding the appropriate intervention. Gambrill points out that, even though a great deal of information may be collected to help to make decisions, ultimately only a limited amount of that information is used to actually make the decision. Furthermore, describing the influence of preconceptions, she points out that practice theories are often the basis for both highlighting certain types of information and ignoring—sometimes with hazardous results—certain other types of data that are inconsistent with or contrary to the clinician's preconceived notions of practice. For instance, ecologically oriented clinicians are very careful in examining life changes, relationships, or stress; whereas biologically oriented practitioners focus upon changes in medication or other medical symptoms. Such practice is inevitable; but, by limiting the causal focus to the information that is somehow relevant to preconceived theories, clinicians inevitably miss equally appropriate and often more accurate and useful explanations from other practice theories. Gambrill suggests an objective assessment of the research while keeping open a wide variety of interventionist options.

Balanced clinical evidence for most social workers refers to an expectation that their choices of interventionist techniques will be formed by their knowledge of research. Efforts to develop models that methodically direct clinicians into making empirically supported choices have merit but may ultimately

2.1 *Multimodal Therapy*

Research-based clinicians have developed detailed systems for choosing interventions. One of the better-known systems builds into its eclectic model a recognition that one generally needs to utilize several modalities with the same client but that it can be done in a logical, consistent manner. That system is called *multimodal therapy* (Lazarus, 1981).

Multimodal therapy (Lazarus, 1981) recognizes the multiple causes of mental health problems and emphasizes the need to consider a wide variety of factors in understanding the causes and, subsequently, the treatments of many problems. Multimodal therapy refers to the *seven modalities* and their acronym, *BASIC ID*. It posits a biochemical/neurophysiological basis as a starting point. It then suggests that our personalities are a function of our *behaviors, affective processes, sensations, images, cognitions, interpersonal relationships,* and *biological functions* (although the author uses the word *drugs* instead of *biological functions* to get the acronym BASIC ID) or *identity,* which represents the basic human personality.

In multimodal therapy, there is—typically, but not always—a chain of events beginning with sensations that lead to cognitions, followed by imagery, then behavior, and finally interpersonal repercussions. All of this is based on—biochemical/neurophysiological research. This chain of events can begin with any modality. For instance, a panic attack could begin when a person imagines or focuses upon a frightening event, which could then lead to a sensation such as dizziness, and so on.

Multimodel therapy uses many techniques and approaches together. Using the acronym of *BASIC ID* as the basis for understanding an individual and his or her problems, Lazarus typically outlines the relevant problems and subsequent techniques in the following way:

(continued)

Modality	Problems	Proposed Techniques
Behavior	Compulsive checking (stove, doors, etc.)	Self-monitoring; response prevention
Affect	Bottles up, blows up; anxiety attacks	Assertiveness training; calming self-statements; slow abdominal breathing
Sensation	Tension; premature ejaculation (seldom exceeded two minutes of coital stimulation)	Relaxation training; threshold training
Imagery	Pictures of ridicule as a child and as an adolescent	Desensitization
Cognition	*Shoulds,* internal self-demands, self-downing, perfectionism	Cognitive restructuring
Interpersonal	Competitive most of the time; too involved with power and control	Friendship training; relationship building
Drugs	Valium—5 mg. daily; Darvon for headaches; Lomotil for colitis	Teach relaxation skills; attempt phasing out of medication

Source: Lazarus, 1981, pp. 148–149.

serve more heuristic than practical clinical purposes. Empiricism has limits; the most obvious one is the complexity of the individual in interaction with his or her environment.

A final suggestion, which is developed in more depth in Chapter 11, indicates that the mainstream methods described in this book are well accepted by other clinical social workers, agencies, insurance companies, and other funding sources (Brandell, 1997). Furthermore, there are reasonably clear, widely accepted documentation methods currently utilized that can be applied to virtually all clinical social work treatment plans and standard case records. It is appropriate to know these methods as well as the methods of recording and planning treatment with these approaches.

Contemporary social workers are influenced by their educations, values, ethics, life experiences, and research. A conscious balance of all of these factors, with an emphasis on constantly improving one's skills and keeping current with practice research, is generally the most accepted method of working with clients and choosing appropriate interventions.

SUMMARY

Clinical social work is an advanced, systems-based approach that integrates empirically validated methods and an eclectic framework. Practitioners now utilize a systems model as the basis for interventions, utilizing a variety of advanced behavioral, cognitive, psychodynamic, biological, and broad-based systemic techniques to guide them. This biopsychosocial orientation is based on a recognition that past models, as well as any one of the methods alone, are too narrow to adequately treat many of the concerns currently seen.

Research in matching clients and workers on the basis of age, gender, race, and a variety of other variables has had somewhat ambiguous results, although there are useful guidelines in choosing interventions. Researchers tend to conclude that a broad-based systems approach that relies on research and critical use of advanced, specialized techniques is appropriate. Furthermore, although clinicians are all influenced by their educations, values, ethics, life experiences, and knowledge of research, a certain balanced and objective awareness of all of these factors legitimately comes into the process making solid clinical choices.

PART two

SYSTEMS-BASED APPROACHES

SYSTEMS INTERVENTIONS WITH INDIVIDUALS

At this point in its evolution, clinical social work is viewed by many as a systems-based profession that takes a generalist approach to working with people. However, the definition of *systems* may vary from practitioner to practitioner, and the types of intervention that are defined as "systems-oriented" may vary widely. Kirst-Ashman and Hull (1993) emphasize that a systems model provides the framework for generalist practice. They define a system as "a set of elements which forms an orderly, interrelated, and functional whole. . . . The set of elements must be orderly. The elements must be arranged in some pattern which is not simply random" (p. 4).

In its broadest sense, a systems orientation to social work practice includes any intervention that utilizes a broad-based coordinated approach that recognizes multiple diverse needs of clients. In this context, the term *system* is not limited to only the notion of individual, family, group, community, or national or global contexts (Meyer & Mattaini, 1995). Perhaps the best examples of this systems orientation include Germain and Gitterman's (1996) life model or ecological approach, the "newer" psychosocial interventions as opposed to the older approaches that tended to be more psychoanalytic (Woods & Robinson, 1996), and many others that use systems theory as the basis for a variety of models (Friedman, 1997). Thus, virtually all case managers are applying a systems approach because their work typically includes assessing the varied psychological, social, economic, and other problems of their clients and then coordinating the necessary services required to meet those needs and solve the problems.

Family therapists are systems-oriented in that they view and treat the family as a system of interacting individuals whose needs and goals may bring them into conflict with each other as a function of either incompatible or differing needs or as the result of faulty communication or imbalances within the family system. The systems-oriented family therapist's goal may be developing clear communication and recognition on the part of each family member that the family is a unit or system whose members' behaviors and attitudes need to be addressed and brought into a balanced or homeostatic state in which each person helps the other achieve his or her goals through mutual support.

Group workers are inherently systems-oriented in that their goal is also one of enabling individual members of a system to learn how to grow, change, and understand themselves and their behavior by interacting with other individuals within a group with similar needs. The task of the group social worker is to coordinate and use the group's dynamics as a tool in facilitating the process of mutual support, exploration, confrontation, shared insights, and feedback. Again, the social worker is the coordinator and developer of a system of interacting individuals with diverse needs and behaviors. The group social worker's tasks are to assess those needs, deficits, problems, resources, and strengths and turn the group system into a constructive, supportive, and therapeutic tool.

The history and orientation of the field of social work place social work practitioners at a historical advantage relative to other helping professions. These professionals have always known how and why to use broad-based systems interventions. Social workers have invariably focused upon the complex interaction between people and their social systems. A social worker's extensive training and sensitivity to human behavior in the social environment orient him or her to immediately consider the client or individual, couple or family in terms of the client's social system. The social system will no doubt continue to be the appropriate unit of both analysis and intervention within managed care or virtually any type of recent or developing interventionism because such broad generalist approaches are appropriate in light of the evidence of multicausality.

In today's complex and stressful society, there is a growing consensus that the best and most cost-effective interventions are those that utilize the natural support system. Traditional interventions, which actually isolated the "patient" or client by treating them individually with an orientation toward re-working earlier developmentally based problems were limited in their success because such interventions did not integrate the tremendously important system of family and friends. In fact, the family and community systems were viewed too often as adversaries or as causal, negative influences on the client rather than as sources of actual or potential strength (Rapp, 1998). This same system, which could have been therapeutic, often ultimately worked *against* the social worker. In extreme instances in which hospitalization was required, the level of anger, shame, guilt, and feelings of rejection on the part of the client's social system unfortunately established a foundation for distancing between the client and his or her system.

Current clinicians in social work are well aware of the vast research that shows in many different ways that one's "mental health" or even self-image or functionality is intimately intertwined with one's social system. The broad concept of functionality or "mental health" can be operationally defined for research and practical purposes in a variety of ways. A functionally healthy person can be operationally defined as one who currently exhibits no overt symptoms as listed in the *DSM-IV-TR* (2000); or, he or she can be defined as one who performs his or her roles adequately as a worker, husband, wife, father, mother, student, or teacher. A functional or mentally healthy person could alternatively be defined as one who has high scores on various tests of self-esteem or self-actualization; or, a mentally healthy person could be defined as a community leader who has received various community, professional, or civic awards for outstanding service to others. Coulton (1995) has described using such decidedly middle-class and often culturally biased indicators as income, education, or capacity to get and maintain a job. The one common factor with all of these diverse yet commonly used operational definitions is the belief that one must have a capacity to interact with, develop, and maintain a social system.

Conversely, virtually any broad-based definition of a low functioning, dysfunctional, or "mentally ill" individual includes an incapacity to engage with or positively maintain healthy interpersonal relations with a system of family or friends. The presenting clients of social workers are almost invariably those with dysfunctional or nonexistent social systems. Typical examples might include

- Depressed mothers who feel overwhelmed and undersupported
- Alcoholics with no family or friends except their network of equally dysfunctional and depressed fellow alcoholics
- Teenagers who have become suicidal because they have no friends; or, more likely, because a peer, boyfriend, or girlfriend rejected them
- Couples who are breaking up because neither feels the other cares
- Aging adults whose families rarely see them and who feel worthless because their closest friends have died
- Physically incapacitated or handicapped individuals whose mobility is limited and who, therefore, stop interacting with their former system so that they will not be a "burden"

As already stated, the factor that virtually all social work clients have in common is that they have poor, dysfunctional, or nonexistent social systems. The initial task of the social worker is to assess the presenting problem in the context of the client's social system. Then the social worker develops that system using the pre-existing informal system of family and friends to their greatest realistic level. Finally, the social worker develops, coordinates, and manages new, effective, and efficient systems of needed formal and professional resources.

The social work profession has become defined as one that utilizes the system of its clients. This is done through a broad, generalist approach that includes advanced-practice and generalist methods, the ecological approach, case management, and group and family systems interventions. There are dozens of levels and variations of systems-based interventions, but all of these have in common the realization that supportive, therapeutic, healthy, and sensitive systems are the sine qua non of functionality or mental health.

SYSTEMS THEORY

The generalist practitioner uses a systems perspective and operates from a person-in-environment or an ecological model. Advanced applications are derived from Germain and Gitterman's (1980, 1996) ecological perspective or a similar balanced ecological core (Allen-Meares, 1987; Johnson, 1986; Landon, 1995; Sheafor, Horejsi, & Horejsi, 1991; Whittaker, Shinke, & Gilchrist, 1986; Zastrow, 1999). Although social work practitioners have done an impressive job of developing approaches and techniques that apply systems theory to broad-based practice, systems theory itself can be rather abstract and complex.

To have a clear understanding of systems theory it is important to define commonly used terms in the theory. A *system* is any unit that has definable boundaries and interacting parts. These parts can be *physical* (e.g., money, housing, molecules, or organic material); *social* (e.g., a system of family, friends, neighbors and coworkers); *economic* (e.g., factors relevant to banking, finance, budgeting, and investments); or any of a veritable infinite number of interacting and connected concepts, physical entities, ideologies, and theories.

Perhaps the system most relevant to social workers is a *social system*. (Maguire, 1991) Talcott Parsons is credited by many for developing a general social systems theory referred to as the *functionalist action* or *Grand Theory* of systems, although his work was preceded by Herbert Spencer. Parsons's four-function model (Parsons & Bales, 1955) was a theory for analyzing virtually all aspects of social systems. He saw four schemes as essential components in understanding social systems. These four schemes, which are frequently abbreviated with the letters *L, I, G,* and *A,* are

> *L* for latent pattern maintenance or the need for all systems to have a
> regular pattern, which serves as a guide
> *I* for integration, which refers to the need for systems to keep their parts
> together
> *G* for goal attainment, which refers to a system's requirement to seek
> and attain some output and achievement
> *A* for adaptation, which suggests a system's need to physically support
> itself in a material environment

Parsons's systems theory also dichotomized his perspective by suggesting a need to view systems from an *internal/external* as well as a *means/ends* view.

Parsons's framework was an early and abstract method, but it was consistent and logical (although conflict theorists, social phenomenologists, and others in the 1950s would not even agree with that). Within social work practice,

Gordon Hearn (1958, 1969, 1979) is generally recognized as the individual who adapted and developed the orientation for this field. In more recent years, many models of practice based in systems theory have developed, most notably within family systems approaches (Walsh, 1997), the ecological model (Germain & Gitterman, 1996), generalist case management (Woodside & McClam, 1998), and advanced generalist models focusing upon social support systems (Maguire, 1991).

The concepts that are particularly relevant to advanced-practice social workers include the following:

- *Open systems* interact with their environments and change as a result of that process.
- *Closed systems* have impermeable boundaries and do not interact with the outside.
- *Boundaries* refer to the limits or borders of a system and serve as the basis for establishing what is inside or outside of a specific system.
- *Energy* refers to the process that maintains the cycle of activity through exchange with the external world or from internal sources.
- *Entropy* and *negentropy* are opposites of the same process. *Entropy* describes situations in which a system exports more energy than it imports (gradually ending in decay), and *negentropy* is the more growth-oriented term for systems that import more energy than they consume.
- *Homeostasis* refers to balance and the tendency for any system to have a need to "right itself" or return to a comfortable state of equilibrium. Homeostatic balance is not static but changes or self-regulates as a response to changing conditions in the environment.
- *Feedback* is the process typically found in open systems whereby the system accepts and uses information as the basis for change.

Social work students are required to study human behavior in the social environment (HBSE). These courses set the stage for social work practice and provide social workers with a framework or guide to viewing the human condition. Most HBSE courses stress the fact that as social workers, their perspective is one that envisions individuals as being interactive with multiple diverse systems. These systems include at a minimum *families* and *communities* in addition to the larger *societal* and the *cultural milieu* in which individuals exist. Human behavior, which includes what one does as well as how one feels and thinks, is strongly affected by forces in this social environment (Germain, 1991; Greene & Ephros, 1995; Zastrow, 1999).

There is a tremendous range of all-encompassing dynamics even within the four previously mentioned systems of family, community, society, and culture. For instance, the family dynamics include not only an individual's history, early childhood experiences, and the effects of varying parenting styles but also current influences. Individuals are strongly affected by the level of stress or support received within their marriages and in relation to the concerns or problems of their children. As adults, individuals are also affected by the ups and downs of their aging parents, experiencing joy or sorrow along with their parents in their successes and failures. Aunts, uncles, grandparents, and cousins may also affect individuals by deliberate intent or simply by virtue of the fact that, within their close personal relationships, compassion and mutual identification tend to support a sharing of the joys and sorrows of fellow family members.

Community systems affect individuals in relation to the level of crime, the quality of the schools, the cleanliness of the air or streets, or the health of the local economy or job market (Baum & Twiss, 1996). The community within which one lives can also be interpreted as a group. Communities can include, for example, fellow social workers, therapists, bowlers, or baseball fans. If a community's baseball team has a dismal season and loses nearly all of its games, the fans may be saddened, become angry, or lose interest in the sport. If the social work community is granted licensure and the status and pay rise dramatically, moods of the members of that social work community are elevated and, perhaps, the members identify more and begin to interact more with this community.

Societal systems affect individuals in a broader but often intense way. For instance, if society shifts toward racist attitudes or blaming the poor as lazy rather than lacking opportunity, then the societal goals of social workers are negatively affected and social workers may become doubtful or hopeless for the future of society. Society is affected by a variety of global, economic, and political forces that can affect individuals both directly and indirectly. The historical ups and downs of government policies as they affect immigration, jobs, schools, crime, and the environment all give reason for hope and positive anticipation for the future or fear of a degradation of the quality of life for all of those who live in this society. Social work is a profession that supports efforts toward equity and social justice in this diverse society. If those goals are undermined by government policy that stigmatizes the poor, elderly, immigrants, or any members of the populations with whom social workers interact, this adversely impacts upon society as a whole and the social work profession.

Cultural dynamics and pressure have an impact upon an individual's belief systems, orientations toward those who differ culturally from the norm, and even manners of interaction. Personality characteristics are partially culturally derived, and the Anglo Saxon or Central European styles of interaction that dominate middle-class America can often be misunderstood by the more reserved styles of Asians and some others. African Americans as well as Jews, Irish, and Italians in this country have all been affected by urban experiences and pressures; and they, in turn, have greatly affected the tone, style, and even language of urban America and the entire American culture (McGoldrick, Giordano, & Pearce, 1996).

REASONS FOR GREATER USE OF SYSTEMS

The social work profession is not alone in shifting toward broader-based, more inclusive systemic or generalist approaches to services. There appears to be a greater realization now that narrow, unidimensional interventions are insufficient with the majority of problems presented to social workers and other helping professionals.

Social workers are asked to help clients who are negatively affected by a wide range of adverse forces such as a lack of employment or education, health problems related to housing or sanitation, and the ever-constant need to adapt and cope with the pressures of today's rapidly changing society. Social workers are asked to have an impact upon multiple systems that often appear to be unrelated to each other. While social workers have limited resources, their clients have even less.

A systems-based approach to practice seemingly meets the needs for greater efficiency and effectiveness in these times of limited resources. Social work approaches have to be inexpensive to *contain costs.* Effective, empirically supported *research* has to be the basis for practice. Approaches need to be *culturally compatible,* so that services are provided in useful, understandable, and sensitive ways to varying populations. Services must be *managed* or well coordinated with other resources to avoid unnecessary duplication. Finally, services and interventions must be *empowering* for the client so that he or she can independently deal with similar concerns in the future. These five factors are the reasons that social work and related fields are becoming increasingly systems oriented.

Cost Containment

Cost containment has been a consistent factor in social work, and systems-oriented practitioners consciously recognize the need to contain costs and incorporate that need into their orientation. Economic and political forces currently do not support an extensive increase in expenditures for the disadvantaged or poor or those with long-term psychosocial or mental health problems (Gerhart, 1990). Consequently, social workers are developing ways to keep costs to a minimum.

There are two reasons that a systems approach to social work is cost-effective. First, by utilizing family, friends, and the natural helping resources of the informal system, fewer of the more expensive professional resources are needed. Systems-oriented workers sensitize people to the often dormant resources available to them through those who are already closest to them. In fact, the argument has been made that it is an inefficient use of time and money for social workers to take so much time to develop and form a trusting relationship with a client when so many other preexisting and infinitely stronger relationships already exist with potentially helpful parents, spouses, and even neighbors and coworkers. Behaviorists have shown how the effects of behavioral interventions can be significantly magnified by training parents and teachers who are already part of a child's system (Tharp & Wetzel, 1969). Family systems therapists make a clear economic argument by demonstrating how the therapeutic effects of social networks—a natural system—ultimately reduce costs (Rueveni, 1979).

The second cost-containment argument is based in the concept of *prevention.* While the concept of prevention historically has been plagued with the seemingly impossible methodological problem of validating itself by proving it can save money in the future, preventive efforts certainly have logical merit. By helping a natural system develop itself into a therapeutic, supportive, or rehabilitative helping resource, professional systems interventionists put into place an entity that should preclude the need for continued professional involvement. Systems-oriented social workers sensitize, train, and educate the social systems of target clients. This prevents the likelihood that these same professional services will be needed in the future since the social system available to the client will know better what to do to help the client.

Research Validation

Research validation is essential for systems-based approaches. The research that supports a systems approach is highly varied. The approach itself is not as well validated as is its basis in the areas of social systems or support systems (Maguire, 1991). In fact, some of the rationale for systems approaches is derived from the extremely rich research, which essentially shows that people who are involved closely with others in meaningful relationships and in constructive activities are less likely to have significant interpersonal or psychological problems.

Longitudinal studies of the effects of unemployment on men clearly showed the moderating effects of social support systems (Gore, 1978, 1981). Susan Gore surveyed men before a factory was to close as well as at intervals after the factory closing. She had a very detailed and broad survey of issues dealing with both physical and psychological health. Her survey results indicated a correlation between the strength of the social support system and the men's responses. Those workers who had support from family or friends managed to cope more successfully than those who were socially isolated. In fact, these social systems seemingly protected the workers from possible heart disease and even elevated cholesterol levels as well as the more obvious psychological problems of depression, drugs, alcohol abuse, and family disintegration.

Support systems are also helpful in seemingly purely health-related issues such as pregnancy and childbirth. One study found that women who have supportive systems of husbands, family, or even close friends are statistically less likely to have complications related to childbirth (Nuckolls, Cassell, & Kaplan, 1972).

Social support systems have also been found to protect individuals from stress. Using the Holmes and Rahe Scale, which has been used extensively in research examining life stressors and social support, Dean and Linn (1977) found consistently high correlations between positive support systems of family and friends and low scores on depression, suicide, psychiatric disorders, and even heart disease and leukemia. Individuals who lacked such systems invariably had a higher incidence of problems in all areas.

Large-scale surveys have historically found similar results. The classic surveys done at Yale called the Midtown Manhattan Study (Srole, Langer, Michael, Opler, & Rennie, 1962), which predated the work at the University of Michigan's Institute of Social Research (Campbell, Converse, & Rogers, 1976), found not only that individuals who are socially isolated suffer far higher rates of psychiatric as well as physical disorders and morbidity rates but also that they are less likely to gain as much satisfaction from their roles or lives. Men and women who derive satisfaction from their work and family tended also to have lower rates of depression and family problems. Those who are not involved with others socially are at a much higher risk than those who interact with systems of family and friends.

Two studies that provide support for systems approaches looked extensively at the sizes of and interactional patterns of social networks (Pattison, Francisco, Wood, Frazier, & Crowder, 1975; Tolsdorf, 1976). Both studies found that the networks and support systems of more disturbed individuals such as those with schizophrenia tended to be very small and that the support was unidirectional; that is, the small network almost invariably consisting of family helped the schizophrenic, but the network was rarely helped in turn. At the other end of the mental health continuum, those highly functional, fulfilled, or more self-actualized individuals tended to have large and highly interactive systems of family and friends who were continuously constructively engaged. Middle ranges of individuals—who were either defined as neurotic or at least somewhere in between the high- and low-functioning individuals—tended to have systems that were smaller than those of the high-functioning individuals but larger than those of schizophrenics.

Research on support systems and social systems is large, diverse, and almost overwhelming. Researchers in social work, as well as in sociology, public health, psychiatric epidemiology, and social psychology, all study this area extensively; but the question must rightfully be raised as to whether this type of systems research actually validates systems interventions. Although the various systems approaches per se have not been extensively subjected to rigorous, methodologically controlled, clinical outcome studies, the extraordinarily rich related areas have been extensively researched (Biegel, McCardle, & Mendelson, 1985). Research in social support and systems in general would lead to the conclusion that the planned and ordered manipulation or development of a supportive system through networking interventions, case management, ecological approaches, or general system development is indeed very well validated (Maguire, 1991). The entire social systems orientation is based on the notion that successful intervention relies upon understanding and utilizing the social system and the environment of the client in a therapeutic or supportive way.

Cultural Sensitivity

Cultural sensitivity is inherent in systems approaches. The approach relies heavily on using the positive and most constructive elements of the client's own social support system, which is composed of their family, friends, and other elements of the natural social system. Typically, such elements share the same culture if for no other reason than biology.

The concept of the *dual perspective* (Greene, 1991; Bush, Norton, Sanders, & Solomon, 1983; Miller, 1981) is helpful for social workers in that it gives systems-oriented practitioners a frame of reference for working with minorities. A dual perspective establishes a clear way of describing the relationship between individuals in the broadening context of their families, friends, culture, and, finally, the larger dominant culture of society. Chestang (1972), for instance, focuses upon the two systems of (a) the dominant or sustaining culture and (b) the nurturing system or immediate social environment consisting of family and friends. The importance of this perspective is that it recognizes the reality of difficulties inherent in a diverse, multicultural society with frequently different, if not outright contradictory, orientations.

The Native American society demonstrates the need for this dual perspective very well (Lewis, 1980). In that culture, the family is invariably the first contact when help is needed. Next comes the extended family or clan, or what the Sioux call the *tiospaye,* which may involve several related families. If the problem is still not resolved, religious or spiritual leaders are asked for help. However, this writer's experience with the Sioux was that primarily the traditional, typically rural families use this source but the more urbanized, middle-class members do not. The more urban Native Americans petition the tribal council for various types of help and support, with the formal system of social workers or other professionals being utilized only when all other more culturally compatible systems have been tried (Maguire,1983).

Individuals typically go first to family and friends for most social, emotional, and even minor health problems before seeking help in the formal system. Minority members whose cultural perspectives may vary widely from that of highly trained White professionals are often reluctant to seek help (Yamatani, Maguire, Rogers, & O'Kennedy, 1996). In fact, there is a clear difference in the way many African Americans view the formal system of help. Polls during the O. J. Simpson trial and the previous trial of Rodney King indicated that many African Americans viewed police and courts with far more suspicion than White Americans. African Americans were more likely to see the police and courts as potentially unfair systems of oppression than were Whites, who viewed them as sources of help. Such perceptions, as well as experiences, alter the patterns of how, when, and, particularly, where people go for help.

The systems approach clearly recognizes that interventions must be geared to the *individual's* specific social system, which includes primarily family and friends who typically share the cultural perspective of the client. This *informal system* is the "first line of defense," that is, the social system that is seen as the first system to go to for help (Yamatani et al., 1996). It reflects the client's *culture*, which is an essential factor in understanding service delivery.

Managed Care Orientation

Managed care orientation refers to the compatibility of the broad-based systems perspective with current social service, health, and mental health organizational requirements. Although a significant factor in managed care is the cost-containment issue, managed care also refers to the very legitimate concern for coordination of services. In past service-delivery systems, there was occasional duplication, overlap, and waste of limited resources. The term *managed* suggests a rational design that incorporates all of the diverse needs of the client with the resources of his or her system.

Managed care further suggests proactive plans that approach client problems in a manner that planfully utilizes all necessary and available systems but no more than necessary. *Efficiency* is a key word of managed care and an important factor in resource coordination and case management. The more efficiently the social worker can coordinate resources by tightening communication and developing linkages between the client and his or her system, the better the level of managed care.

Management and managed care still have a strong profit motive and business orientation that understandably concern some social workers. However, there is much to be learned in a cross-fertilization of business management and social work. Management of resources is the basic goal of both business and social work. In business, those resources are economic. In social work, the resources are human. In both fields, the professional develops a careful plan to coordinate all available resources while pulling in other needed resources whenever realistically possible. The goal of both social work and business management is to maximize the efficient utilization of resources so that the client is left "better off," or in a position to function at a higher economic or psychosocial level. A problem arises for social workers in managed care when the profit motive of managed care takes precedence over the social worker's goal of helping clients regardless of financial costs.

Empowerment

Empowerment, a practice perspective that supports the client's own strengths, has been increasingly viewed as a needed focus in social work practice (Rapp, 1998). Traditionally, the social work profession has relied on stressing the importance of teaching clients how to develop their own resources, which is the essential definition of empowerment.

The historical roots of social work included the realization that the client's own social system of family and friends needed to be strengthened in its linkage to the individual so that that individual could become the master of his or her own fate. While current social workers look askance at the upper-middle-class exhortations of their forebearers who preached the moral superiority of the work ethic and religion as the way to "improve oneself," such admonitions were meant to encourage individual responsibility, even if misguided by some standards of today. Individuals were encouraged to take action for themselves and their families rather than becoming dependent upon the government or philanthropy.

Current social work practice similarly fosters empowerment as the basis for long-term, independent "success." Empowerment today suggests strengthening the client's "self-connection" or realization that by doing and acting on one's own behalf, one can achieve his or her defined life goals more effectively and efficiently. With help in examining and defining purposeful independent goals, a client serves not only his or her self-interests but also those of society.

The current American political and sociocultural climate appears less willing than in the past to support individuals who are unable to take individual actions to function independently without the financial, social, or psychological assistance of professional help. Social workers are frequently the first "line of defense" for those who are the least able to defend themselves in the Darwinian capitalism that defines some government policy and even popular perceptions. In this climate, current practitioners need to be advocates and political activists, but social workers must also help empower clients by supporting them to strengthen themselves through drawing on their own resources and connecting to other available resources.

This rise in the need to empower clients is, unfortunately, reactive and even defensive at one level. However, at a positive and constructive level, it meets legitimate social work practice goals, such as the need for self-determination, the need to analyze oneself and define purpose and need on the basis of that analysis, and the need to reach self-defined goals that give meaning and purpose to existence based upon one's own culturally varied criteria.

SYSTEMS PERSPECTIVE

The social work profession is one that intervenes with its clients from a perspective that says that, to effectively help, the social worker must first make a broad-based assessment of the client's needs and problems, taking into consideration the multiple systems that affect the client. Once an assessment is made, an intervention plan is developed that has as its purpose the effective coordination of constructive forces and the diminishment of destructive forces that affect the individual. All social work practice essentially says that intervention must rely upon the recognition that multiple diverse forces interact with an individual and sometimes cause pain or dysfunctional behavior. Systems-based interventions say precisely the same thing—that a variety of diverse interacting forces or systems are causal in the development of psychosocial problems. Consequently, the only appropriate, effective, and therapeutic interventionist response is one that assesses and responds in a manner that constructively engages and uses those forces (Hepworth & Larson, 1993; Meyer & Mattaini, 1995).

However, social work practice exists within the context of a variety of social service, health, and mental health settings. As such, practitioners are presented with varying difficult and complex problems that require their personal additional repertoire of advanced and specialized techniques. Social workers who work in broad-based service programs can and should use a broad-based or generalist systems approach. However, advanced-practice social workers who practice in family, children, or community-based social service agencies; hospitals; or mental health settings additionally need an interventionist skills base that draws upon the research in psychotherapy outcomes. This research supports behavioral, cognitive, psychodynamic, or family or group treatment techniques that have been proven to be more effective than broad-based systems interventions (Lambert & Bergin, 1994).

Contemporary advanced-level social work practitioners, therefore, need to be knowledgeable of the broader systems orientation as a basis for practice. The advanced skills and techniques required for narrower and more specialized client problems are also addressed from Chapter 7 to the end of this text.

Systems interventions are those social work models that specifically use a *systems* orientation—one that is based on integrating and utilizing multiple coordinated resources. These systems interventions include case management, network intervention, system development, the family and group systems social work models, and the ecological perspective. Since case management (Chapter 4), group interventions (Chapter 5), and family systems interventions (Chapter 6) are all major and essential components of current systems-based social work practice, each of them is addressed in separate chapters.

Clinical social work practice is seen as currently requiring a broad, generalist approach, which invariably integrates systems into its interventions at a complex and sophisticated level. The challenge becomes balancing and integrating broad, generalist perspectives and orientations in a manner that recognizes the difficult and complex problems of many clients of clinical social workers. These complex problems often cannot be resolved with overly broad methods. They require a sophisticated knowledge of the theories and techniques of behavioral, cognitive, and psychodynamic approaches somehow integrated with and based in a systems-oriented, generalist perspective, which McMahon (1996) views as "a base or foundation for advanced practice in selected concentrations" (p. 23).

GENERALIST PRACTICE

The *Social Work Dictionary* (Barker, 1995) defines a *generalist* as "A social work practitioner whose knowledge and skills encompass a broad spectrum and who assesses problems and their solutions comprehensively. The generalist often coordinates the efforts of specialists by facilitating communication between them, thereby fostering continuity of care" (p. 147).

The *Encyclopedia of Social Work* (Landon, 1995) states, "There is no agreed-on definition of generalist practice. . . . There is some agreement on common characteristics, but rationales differ. . . . There appears to be definitional agreement on the centrality of the multimethod and multilevel approach, based on an eclectic choice of theory base and the necessity for incorporating the dual vision of the profession on private issues and social justice concerns. Differences lie in emphases placed on the use of the planned change process, the ecosystem base, and the various central philosophical concepts such as empowerment; the centrality of context; and the definition of specific knowledge and skills needed, which depend a great deal on the theoretical stance of those who write the definitions" (Landon, 1995, pp. 1102–1103).

Historically, the generalist approach has been viewed as the major approach for baccalaureate-level social workers who operate within a systems and person-in-environment (PIE) perspective. The Council on Social Work Education (2001) has required that master's-level practitioners be trained as generalists as well, even though it has been viewed as more "entry level" by most authors (Brieland, Costin, & Atherton, 1985). There is agreement on the fact that social workers are frequently asked to intervene as change agents by using a broad spectrum of approaches with individuals, families, groups, and communities. There is also agreement that the old divisions of casework, group work, and community organization are no longer sufficient (Zastrow, 1999).

In the rapidly changing fields of social services, health, mental health, and social welfare, a broad-based generalist perspective is essential. A professional in any of these varied arenas is often considered the *problem solver.* A hospital social worker may be asked to conduct bereavement counseling, locate an appropriate nursing home, secure financial aid for a single teenage mother, and provide therapy to a suicidal emergency patient all in the same day. Even those agencies called *social service agencies* typically encompass family counseling, advocacy efforts for recently evicted clients, job finding, running both treatment and support groups, and a range of linking and referral efforts at the micro and macro community and interagency levels. Being a generalist is not a choice or any singular approach for most social workers; it is an essential fact of their professional experience.

The generalist approach has no single developer or author. As previously stated, there is not even agreement in its definition. However, there are several representative models of systems-based approaches in the social work literature. *Generalist practice* as developed by McMahon (1996) is described in some detail and serves as a representative of that approach. Equally well-regarded approaches, such as the *generalist intervention model (GIM)* (Kirst-Ashman & Hull, 1993) or the *generic problem-solving approach* (Bloom, 1990), are also briefly described at the end of this section.

The *generalist practice* developed by McMahon (1996) says that "The theoretical perspective pervasive throughout generalist practice combines general systems, social systems, and ecological theories" (p. 25). She makes a distinction between the generalist perspective and generalist practice, indicating that the first is what a social worker brings to a problem-person situation and the latter refers to what that worker does. Furthermore, the five characteristics of generalist practice are (a) an ecological perspective, (b) a problem focus, (c) a multilevel approach, (d) an open selection of theories and interventions, and (e) a problem-solving process.

An *ecological perspective* is essential to generalist practice because it "enhances one's view of person in environment by emphasing the interactions and transactions that take place among the various 'parts' and at the boundary at which the person and environment interface" (McMahon, 1996, p. 25). The ecological perspective looks at how organisms fit in their environment, so generalist social workers must examine this fit between client and environment to see how it contributes to the problem.

Generalist practice uses a *problem focus.* A *problem* is defined as "an issue, need, question, or difficulty" (McMahon, 1996, p. 30). Once the problem is clearly defined, the social worker selects an appropriate intervention that is deemed to be the most effective for that specific problem and ultimate goal.

The third element of generalist practice is its *multilevel approach,* which refers to the fact that the worker must be prepared to deal with a wide variety of clients with a wide range of problems and levels of difficulty. Generalists may work with individuals, groups, neighborhoods, or any other system. The levels of practice include *micro, mezzo,* and *macro.* "Micro is individual work with clients. Mezzo is working with groups. Macro is working with a community, organization, institution, or society" (McMahon, 1996, p. 30).

The fourth element of generalist practice in this model is an *open selection of theories and interventions.* Generalists do not stick to any one particular theory or intervention but, rather, decide upon the intervention based upon the nature of the problem. If a worker encounters a problem that cannot be dealt with most effectively with a beginning generalist approach, the worker makes a referral to an advanced worker. The advanced worker is one who has capabilities in the specialized skills and techniques necessary to treat more difficult and complex problems.

Finally, a *problem-solving process* is essential. This process is called the *General Method.* "The General Method is a problem solving process that is built on the holistic base of knowledge, values, and skills and it is carried out within the context of the generalist perspective. This means that throughout the process and during each of its stages, the worker focuses on identifiable problems, brings an ecological-systems theoretical framework, selects openly from a range of theories and interventions, and readily practices at different levels" (McMahon, 1996, p. 37).

In McMahon's general method of social work practice, she describes six stages: (a) engagement, (b) data collection, (c) assessment, (d) intervention, (e) evaluation, and (f) termination. These stages are not necessarily followed in order. In fact, they may go on simultaneously or even in reverse order and return to a previous stage.

In the *engagement* stage, the worker determines not only what the problem is and how the client views the problem but also how related systems view the problem. Goals are also identified in this stage by the client, the worker, referring agencies, or other systems that are directly related to the identified problem. The worker explores specifics of the problem in the *data collection* stage; prioritizing the problems and developing an effective plan to address and alleviate the problems are done during the *assessment* stage.

The *intervention* stage is a shared attempt by the worker and the client to achieve the goals agreed upon while carrying out the plan. During the *evaluation,* the worker and the client determine whether the specific goals have been met. They also examine whether it was the intervention or extraneous factors in the social environment or elsewhere that led to the goal achievement. While reviewing their contract, unachieved goals are looked at to determine whether there might be another way to accomplish them.

At *termination,* the worker and the client determine whether there is a need for further services. Either the case is closed or, in some instances, a referral for more advanced interventions may be agreed upon.

McMahon (1996) makes a clear distinction between the beginning generalist practitioner and the advanced generalist. "The beginning generalist social worker should be able to effectively handle most problems that are of little severity if the client has obvious strengths and coping capacities" (p. 40). Often a beginning generalist is able to intervene in more severe problems if the client has a great deal of support from other systems and some positive strengths.

The advanced generalist is someone with an MSW who not only possesses the foundation, knowledge and skills of the generalist and can use the General Method, but can also demonstrate traditional or specialized methods with a particular population (McMahon, 1996). McMahon describes graphically where an advanced-level worker and a beginning-level generalist part. Basically, whenever the severity of the problem is high and the strengths of the client system are low, an advanced-level social worker is needed. If the severity is low and the strengths of the client system are high, then a beginning generalist, using the General Method, is appropriate. A problem or need is of "little severity" when it has recently emerged, when it has limited scope, and when it has little life or death magnitude. The client is said to have low strengths when he/she has limited coping skills, motivation, and resources.

In this generalist model, all methods can be categorized as either client-focused, problem-focused, or worker-focused. When using client-focused interventions, the worker assumes a limited role, giving support mainly through listening and reassuring the clients of their potential for coping with difficulties. The client is mainly responsible for directly dealing with the problem. Developmental counseling is an example of this focus.

Problem-focused interventions are more worker-involved: Here the client and the worker become like a team and work together, sharing control and always focusing on the identified problem (McMahon, 1996, p. 337). In a worker focused intervention, such as behavior modification, the worker is responsible for planning, coaching and structuring for the client (McMahon, 1996).

Holism is also a central component of this model. *Holism* "refers to a totality in perspective, with sensitivity to all of the parts or levels that constitute the whole and to their interdependence and relatedness" (McMahon, 1996, p. 3). Holism is an approach for viewing the whole person, including the environment that surrounds and influences that individual. The goal of holism is to understand the client as a whole and to understand the factors influencing him or her without losing sight of their relation to the client.

In treatment, the focus is not so much on a single isolated problem but, rather, is on the client in the context of his or her entire environment of family, social milieu, economics, and other forces and systems. The notion of working within a treatment team is central to holism, which encourages interagency and interorganizational work. The integration of multiple human services is viewed very positively as an efficient manner of applying holistic principles to the generalist practice approach.

The *generalist intervention model (GIM)* is characterized by four features. First, it is based on certain knowledge, skills, and values espoused by the profession. Second, it involves micro, mezzo, and macro systems as targets of change in its problem-solving approach. Third, the GIM says that nearly any problem can be addressed through a wide number of perspectives. Fourth, GIM uses a flexible problem-solving method. The six stages in this model's problem-solving method are (a) assessment, (b) planning, (c) intervention, (d) evaluation, (e) termination, and (f) follow up (Kirst-Ashman & Hull, 1993).

The *generic problem-solving approach* is another generalist variation. Seven stages are identified in its problem-solving approach: (a) identify problems and strengths in the client/situation, (b) identify alternative theories about causal factors, (c) identify goals and objectives, (d) make decisions and contracts, (e) implement and evaluate the plan of action, (f) change interventions as needed, and (g) follow up (Bloom, 1997). In introducing this model, Bloom stated that it is ". . . a distillation of a common approach used by case workers, group workers, community workers, and many other helping professionals, as an ordinary and reasonable analysis of problems and strengths so as to deal with the client's concerns. The problem solving approach fits no particular case situation perfectly, but it will be a useful beginning guide for almost every situation" (pp. 101–102).

CSWE Guidelines

The Council on Social Work Education's proposed curriculum policy guidelines (CSWE, 2001) identify various skills, content areas, and knowledge bases required in social work practice. These are introduced in the following sections.

Defining Issues, Problems, Resources, and Assets   This first phase of social work practice is crucial since it is the beginning of the process and therefore establishes a direction. Social workers have long been aware of the complexity of such a seemingly mundane task. "Defining the problem" or "defining issues" or "resources" or "assets" is subject to three factors. First, the *context or setting* makes a difference since the "problem" or "issue" is defined differently in various social work settings. If the setting is a psychiatric unit, a mental health setting, or a private practice, the task is really that of establishing a diagnosis using the *DSM-IV-TR* (2000). If the setting is a typical social work agency oriented toward helping families and children, the social worker might implement the person-in-environment (PIE) system (Karls & Wandrei, 1994). Or, if the social worker is in a large public social service agency or a large social work department in a national health system such as the Veteran's

Administration (VA), he or she would probably use a "problem" statement, which may even require a relevant task and a statement of the anticipated goal used in some managed care settings.

The second factor in defining the problem/issue concerns the *treatment orientation*. A behaviorally oriented social worker defines the "problem" in precise, observable, and preferably quantifiable terms. The insight-oriented social worker may see the same person but define the "problem" as being primarily one of unresolved trauma related to abuse during childhood. Each orientation has its own set of terms and varying theoretical bases that significantly alter the course of the intervention (see Chapter 2).

The third factor related to defining the problem/issue concerns the *client/worker perspective,* or whether the social worker essentially takes the client's definition of the "problem" at face value or interprets and redefines the "issue" in terms of what the social worker's experience may tell him or her. For instance, in this writer's 25 years of practice experience, there has never been a single couple who has requested marital or family treatment who agreed on the definition of the "issue." Couples require help in defining the issue by slowly pulling facts that they initially view as being very different from their separate perspectives.

Typically, when abuse or intimidation has occurred within most heterosexual couples, the man sees the problem as his wife or partner "forcing" him to behave as he does. The woman in such abusive relationships often accepts far more self-blame than is warranted but does recognize that the abuse is unacceptable. She often needs help recognizing that such abuse is never her "fault," and the "issue" in an abusive relationship may need to be redefined. That allows the focus of treatment to be more appropriately redefined. The goals of the intervention then become developing the woman's assertiveness, independence, and self-esteem and getting the man to recognize the inappropriateness and danger of his abuse or intimidation. Although neither partner initially would have defined such concerns as the "problem"—and the tremendous importance of recognizing and respecting client statements of the problem cannot be undermined—there are times when the social worker's perspective legitimately differs from the client's.

Defining the problem/issue is, however, an achievable task within a generalist approach. Virtually all social work perspectives stress the importance of clarity and keeping the issues relatively concrete so that one ultimately can evaluate whether the "issue" has been successfully treated. Furthermore, the number and complexity of the issues or problem statements must be addressed. Too many vague, complex, or multifaceted problems lead to confusion and inefficiency. Where necessary, complex and multifaceted problems need to be redefined and clarified into terms that are comprehensible to the social worker and the client alike. These problem statements need to be defined in terms that ultimately lend themselves to workable tasks and achievable goals.

Resources and assets are positive and potentially therapeutic strengths that the client brings into treatment. The social worker must assess those strengths and integrate them into the intervention. Social workers have enthusiastically utilized this *strengths perspective* as a tool in empowering clients and increasing treatment effectiveness.

Collecting and Assessing Information   In this second guideline, the CSWE recommends that social workers gather facts and information relevant to the issue or problem. An emphasis is placed upon clear and objective data, although the generalist perspective recognizes that the three factors related to defining issues—the context or setting, the treatment orientation, and the client/worker perspective—partially shape the type and nature of the data.

The generalist approach is broad-based; as such, the types of data collected may include relevant background and demographics such as age, education, income, race and ethnic background, work history, family and individual case histories, and a clear picture of the relevant social and environmental factors that precipitated, maintained, motivated, or reinforced the occurrence of the issue or problem. The data may be quite detailed, particularly when there are significant family or social history issues. For instance, abusive parents whose families of origin were also abusive need to include some detail regarding their own abuse. Similarly, where there is marital conflict, the social worker needs to include some description of the marriages of the parents of the clients to see what types of models the clients viewed in their early years. Clients who present problems related to assault or rape who may have previous histories of victimization similarly need their social worker to be very sensitive to their past experiences and how the previous trauma will impact upon current intervention.

Planning for Services   The third guideline involves developing a clear working plan and an agreement with the client to take some action to alleviate the issue. This often takes the form of a written treatment plan or contract, very similar to a legally binding agreement, in which both the client (or clients) and the social worker agree to do some specific tasks that will directly affect their agreed-upon problem and issue statement. Treatment plans are described in the last chapter of this book. The entire, formal treatment plan may not necessarily be a joint product developed by the worker and the client. However, the general plan for treatment does need to be discussed at length, and a written contract or clear plan is useful.

Formal, written treatment contracts that clearly define the problems, plan of action, and even desired goals are used in some behavioral as well as task-centered social work approaches. Formal treatment contracts have at least four distinct advantages. First, they precisely and clearly define the agreed-upon problem. This is extremely helpful in that it minimizes the likelihood that the involved parties will later disagree with the problem as stated and, thus, the subsequent tasks and goals. This is important because one of the biggest problems in treatment historically has been the tendency to "drift" into other problems, often eventuating into a vague, meandering, never-ending path to desired outcomes or termination.

Second, the formality of the contract, particularly when written and signed by both the client and the social worker, lends a weight or a binding legal orientation to the agreement. It is a promise, agreement, and binding contract to seriously act upon the problem.

A third advantage of a formal treatment contract is that the contract is a document that can be referred to later if or when disputes arise regarding the "real" problem or what each person accepted or agreed to do. This can therefore settle disputes before they begin, often avoiding the common problem in treatment in which one party quits treatment or does not follow through with commitments because he or she believed the problem or assigned tasks were different.

The fourth advantage of a formal treatment contract is that it effectively guides all parties toward a treatment goal by articulating the proposed and agreed-upon plan of action. Keeping this goal "in sight" from the very earliest phases of treatment increases the likelihood of achieving it. Every session and every action are geared toward that plan and the contract designed to reach that goal. (Contracts are further discussed in this book in the chapter on behavioral interventions.) In fact, many agencies require some level of mutual agreement or contracting as a standard initial phase of treatment. There are contract forms specifying the problem statement, task requirements for both the client and the social worker, and clearly defined outcomes or goals with dates for achieving those goals.

Identifying Evidence-Based Alternative Interventions   Even the best of plans requires flexibility and alterations. No one can foresee certain problems that inevitably develop. The teacher who was initially so helpful may go on a sabbatical; or the school psychologist may insist upon changing a goal; or the depressed adolescent client may have hidden a drug abuse problem from the social worker that, when discovered, necessitates a complete reworking of the contract. These are not failures. They are simply realistic alterations due to the changes and vagaries of life. At their initial meeting with clients, social workers should discuss alternatives and the need for flexibility in the contract. The client and the practitioner must even presume that some changes, refinements, and even significant alterations in problem statements, tasks, plans, and goals are inevitable. It is, however, the social worker's ongoing task to keep a plan on target, that is, keep treatment moving effectively and efficiently forward but altering some plans when necessary to achieve the treatment goals.

Some managed care organizations are still learning to adapt to the necessary flexibility of generalist social work practice. Ideally, administrative and clinical concerns coincide in their need to shift and change occasionally as a way of more effectively addressing the client's problems. Administrative impediments to change—typically in the form of rigid initial treatment plans that do not allow for change, adaptation, and improvement of treatment through using alternatives— can definitely undermine goal achievement. Social workers are often challenged in practice to maintain that essential balance between staying clear and "on target" while remaining flexible enough to improve and even shift problems and goals when it is in the best interest of the client.

Selecting and Implementing Appropriate Courses of Action   Generalist social work involves a clear, consistent, and agreed-upon course of action. All parties begin with the same understanding of the problem and then work together as a team to take the "best" route to achieving closure and the successful amelioration of that problem or issue. Treatment, therefore, entails discussion of various strategies, including discussion of needed resources and additional partners in the plan. Plans and discussion include the pros and cons of involving other social workers, teachers, doctors, counselors, or programs and agencies. Decisions need to be made regarding how others would help and precisely what they could do to achieve the plan and its goal.

What additional "cost" is related to bringing in others? This "cost" could be financial, psychological, or social, such as a "cost" in giving up independence or a growing sense of autonomy or self-esteem. Objective and rational analyses of the various actions or contemplated partners are themselves very helpful and therapeutic actions. This is the same type of *problem solving* that must be developed by the client to achieve independence and autonomy once this particular set of problems has been set aside. The goal of treatment is not only the resolution of the immediate problem but also the education of the client in learning to develop the needed skills that will allow him or her to better deal with the same or similar problems in the future.

A problem frequently encountered by less experienced social workers, as well as those pressured to quickly "fix" a problem, is that of developing the plan without the client or with insufficient input from the client. This often has the effect of slowing down or completely halting the therapeutic progress. In fact, the client may have better knowledge of the wide courses of action available. All available types of client systems should be explored. If the client is not active, informed, and highly involved in the development and utilization of the plan, problems invariably ensue.

Applying Evidence-Based Knowledge and Technological Advances
Computers are available in virtually every large program. They allow clinicians
to maintain better clinical records and to keep abreast of new developments in
the causes and treatments of psychosocial problems. Case records are now
routinely computerized, allowing social workers to have quick access to data
relevant to client progress.

Clinical social workers can easily develop graphs that chart client behaviors, and the Web allows clinicians and clients the ability to identify helpful
books for bibliotherapy. Community resources are also easily accessed in most
communities, and clinicians empower clients by supporting clients in their
efforts to access and use resources and ideas found through computer
searches.

**Using Appropriate Research to Monitor and Evaluate Program-
matic and Clinical Outcomes**   Current generalist practice requires ongoing and objective appraisal and monitoring (Mattaini, 1997). It is helpful to
specify dates and concrete goals to be achieved at various intervals as a means
of facilitating the process of monitoring progress toward plan completion. Single-subject research methods, which typically involve time series analyses or
some form of multiple assessments after establishing an initial behavioral
baseline (Tripodi, 1994), are recommended. Alternatively, objective discussion
of progress or lack of progress, using one of the many clinical outcome instruments (Corcoran & Fisher, 2000), could be utilized.

Behaviorally based measures, which stress measurable and concrete goals,
tasks, and outcomes, facilitate this monitoring process and have the additional
benefits of helping to keep the intervention on a straight path. Behaviorally
based measures reinforce each successive and successful achievement by the
fact of their completion. This monitoring helps both client and worker to move
forward without deviating into any of the many possible tangential concerns
that slow or confuse goal achievement.

All social work practitioners need to educate themselves in new advances
and techniques. This field has witnessed tremendous change in recent years;
and, while some of the change has been structural, administrative, or political
in its origin and effects, much has related to practice. Some of these new
changes include advances in using groups for AIDS patients, which has added
to the growing research in how the emotions impact the immune system. The
psychopharmacological interventions in the treatment of obsessive-compulsive
disorders and phobias are very recent developments that displaced previously
unsuccessful psychological efforts. Change has come about through research in
cognitive and behavioral interventions with depressed clients. There is evidence that such interventions actually have an effect on chemicals in the brain,
thus adding to the rapidly growing appreciation for more holistic approaches.

The last two decades have witnessed a major shift in social work practice in which medication has gone from being viewed with suspicion or even hostility to the recognition that medication can and must be used in conjunction with generalist practice for many severe disorders.

Using Supervision and Consultation to Improve Practice Effectiveness

For students, the field placement provides the greatest opportunity they may ever have for clinical supervision. Field instructors are typically very experienced clinicians who accept responsibility for guiding the developing clinician. When the supervisory relationship is open, honest, and supportive of the development of knowledge and skills, then this method of learning is probably the most effective method available for skill acquisition.

Supervision and case consultation are also a necessary part of the ongoing process of improving practice effectiveness. Clinical social workers are human. They possess biases and perspectives that impact upon the treatment process in a variety of ways. Many of these biases are positive and constructive and further the treatment process. However, even the most experienced clinicians can improve their effectiveness by consulting with supervisors or colleagues who may offer new, different, and perhaps even better ideas regarding treatment.

Using Communication Skills Differentially Across Systems   Social workers interact with many systems. They work with the social system of clients, the neighborhoods of clients and colleagues, the political systems that develop policies, and the economic systems that support society. Clinical social workers need to know how, when, and where to communicate needs, demands, recommendations, and ideas.

Social workers may spend the morning teaching adolescents and the afternoon lobbying state legislators. The highly varied systems with which social workers interact require very different communication skills. In a single day, social workers may edit newsletters for a client group, teach colleagues in a classroom, demonstrate a treatment method to a new student, and write letters to the local editor.

Providing Leadership to Promote Social and Economic Justice

Social workers are leaders. Leadership requires skill. To be effective leaders, social workers need to develop skills in analyzing, developing, and advocating change. Social and economic justice are the foundations for an adequate quality of life in a just society. Treatment skills and clinical knowledge are necessary and important. However, social workers are invariably advocates and leaders who challenge those who oppress, undermine, or ignore the problems and needs of their clients.

In many instances, clinical social workers teach clients to protect and defend their rights. Clinicians model behavior that serves to empower clients so that they will never be harmed or disadvantaged in future interactions with systems that have an impact upon them or their families or communities.

Life Model and the Ecological Approach

The systems approach that has been the most clearly articulated and defined is undoubtedly Carel Germain and Alex Gitterman's *ecological approach* or *life model of practice* (Germain & Gitterman, 1980, 1996; Germain, 1991). The ecological perspective is a holistic approach that views people in the context of their environments. It states that individuals are in a state of continuous exchange, interaction, and reciprocal influence with their environments. People change their environments and are also changed by environmental forces. This environment consists of biological, psychological, cultural, emotional, and social forces, which must be understood and utilized in helping individuals to adapt or "fit" into their own systems. This intervention is not a passive attempt at adaptation or coping but, rather, an active, constructive, conscious, and deliberate effort to understand and subsequently use these diverse influences in a therapeutic or otherwise constructive fashion.

This approach is particularly appropriate in issues related to cultural differences. It states that one's perspective is dominated by his or her cultural values, assumptions, biases, traditions, and heritage. Ecological fit necessitates a sensitive awareness of the client's culture and background. "Because it emphasizes the interdependence of organism and environment, ecology is especially suitable as a *metaphor* for social work, given our historic commitment to the person-environment fit" (Germain & Gitterman, 1996, p. 5).

This model works through initial, ongoing, and ending stages, even in one session or in short-term therapy. It focuses upon (a) difficult life transitions and traumatic events; (b) poverty, oppression, and harshness of social and physical environments; and (c) dysfunctional interpersonal processes in families and groups or between the practitioner and the people served. Germain and Gitterman's revised model (1996) replaced the previous term of *problems in living* with a preferred *life-stressor—stress-coping* paradigm to avoid the implication that the client is deficient and to capitalize instead upon the strengths perspective.

The ecological model emphasizes the environment as well as the life-stressor–stress-coping paradigm and the unlimited variations of transitions and events that confront individuals. The life model social worker needs to be sensitive to the influence of the community, organizations, and even legislative issues on people's life stressors. In this model, both the social reform movement and clinical practice combine to help the individual or community meet their needs. Practice requires knowledge of the likely intended as well as the unintended effects of programs, events, policies, and interventions.

Germain and Gitterman added three concepts (1996) to their original four (1980). These seven concepts are the basis for the *person:environment* relationships that form ecological, life-modeled practice. In the revised model, the authors prefer a colon to repair the conceptually fractured relationship suggested by the hyphenated *person-environment* term. The seven concepts central to the revised ecological approach are introduced and discussed in the subsequent sections.

Person: Environment Exchange   This first concept describes the fluid and multidirectional interactions among people; their personalities, behavior, level of functioning, and goals; and demands of their environments. A good fit results in positive growth and released potential of people and communities and, consequently, a vibrant environment. A poor fit leads to impaired functioning and a damaged environment that does not support growth.

Varied Levels of Fit   This second concept refers to the *fit* that occurs in person:environment exchanges. The goal in the ecological approach is to improve the level of fit through helping individuals adapt or fit into their environments. *Adaptedness* occurs when the environment offers the resources and opportunities needed to promote people's biopsychosocial functioning. *Adaptation* is the change individuals go through to improve the level of fit with their environment. These are growth-oriented terms in that they require a recognition that the human species has taken cultural evolution to the point that allows us to tolerate toxic conditions such as overpopulation and pollution.

Life Stressors That Threaten Fit and Coping   Life stressors, the third concept, produce a negative exchange in the person:environment fit. This is often caused by an external life stressor bringing about internal stress reactions. Anxiety, which is often labeled as stress, is one of many possible reactions to life stressors. People can learn to adapt to life stressors in ways other than being anxious.

New jobs, marriages, and a variety of other normal transitions are often difficult transitions. Stress can be quite severe in instances of death, accidents, and disasters. How the individual *views* the stressor, or the meaning the individual assigns it, affects the person:environment fit as well as coping strategies. A *primary appraisal* is performed to assess whether the stressor is benign, dangerous, or unimportant. This appraisal varies considerably from one individual to another based upon their backgrounds and previous interactions and experiences with similar stressors in their environments.

A *challenge,* or eustress, is a life event that one feels capable of overcoming, even if a great deal of energy needs to be expended. A *stressor,* or distress, is an event that overwhelms the coping capabilities of an individual; or, at least, they feel incapable of effectively adapting to the threatening event or trauma.

Human Relatedness, Competence, Self-Esteem, and Self-Direction
These elements of the fourth concept are the result of past and present experiences in the environment, which are all interrelated. *Relatedness* is based on attachment theory, which states that attachment behaviors are genetic and necessary for survival of the species. Infants use attachment to grow and survive, but research in psychoneuroimmunology suggests that a lack of attachment is not only socially debilitating but also physically threatening.

Vulnerability to Oppression, Abuse, and Social/Technological Pollution   Germain and Gitterman (1996) note that the latter half of the 20th century was marked by an increase of corporate financial abuse as well as an increase in the use of power to dominate different organizations, governments, nationalities, socioeconomic levels, and ethnic and racial groups. More groups appear to be systematically oppressed, leaving more people as victims of oppression. Social workers are encouraged to turn this disempowerment, the fifth concept, around and help clients overcome abuse.

Healthy and Unhealthy Habitats and Niches   This sixth concept refers to the physical environments in which an individual lives—*habitat*—and to the level or status a person has in that environment—*niche*. Different cultures afford different levels of status to people. For instance, some Asian cultures view their elders as having positions of esteem, whereas many Western cultures do not. The relative value of money, physical appearances, or various types of status based upon power differentials have significant differences of meaning placed upon them. Wherever there is stigma attached to individuals, that value must be examined based upon the individual's culturally derived viewpoint:

> Because dominant groups discriminate on the basis of personal and collective characteristics such as color, gender, sexual orientation, socioeconomic status, physical or mental condition, many people are forced to occupy niches that limit their opportunity, rights, and aspirations. Dominant groups coercively use power to oppress and disempower vulnerable populations, creating and maintaining such social pollutions as poverty, chronic unemployment, lack of affordable housing, inadequate health care and schools, institutionalized racism and sexism, homophobia, and barriers to community participation by those with physical or mental disabilities. (Gitterman, 1996, p. 393)

Life Course   This seventh concept refers to the unique developmental pathways of people. Diverse human experiences, histories, cultures, and viewpoints invariably lead to differing understandings of the environment. Birth cohort studies, which recognize that people born at the same time are affected by certain common histories, add to our understandings of people. For instance, the baby boomers, who grew up in the growing economies of the 1950s and 1960s, are very different from their parents, who experienced economic hardship and the effects of World War II.

Children growing up today have a very different outlook on jobs, marriages, and community stability than their grandparents. Young adults today see job change as a healthy norm, whereas it was a considerable source of stress for previous generations. Social workers need to consider not only the different *historical times* experienced by individuals but also how that individual uniquely processed those forces of social, political, or economic change.

SUMMARY

Social work practice relies upon systems theory and a generalist approach as a basis. Systems theory recognizes that human behavior is the result of a variety of interacting forces in the environment. Although complex or severe problems and needs of clients often necessitate the use of advanced methods such as psychodynamic, behavioral, or cognitive methods, the overall use of broad-based systems models is increasingly integrated into these as advanced social work practice. Systems-based approaches are used extensively in contemporary practice because they contain costs; they have research validation, cultural sensitivity, and a managed care orientation; and they empower clients by building on their strengths.

There is a wide variety of excellent generalist-practice models, including one representative model by McMahon (1996). This generalist-practice model is characterized by an ecological perspective, a problem focus, a multilevel approach, an open selection of interventions and theories, and a problem-solving process.

The CSWE practice guidelines (2001) suggest that students understand and develop ten skills in understanding the practice process: define issues, collect and assess data, plan, identify alternative interventions, select and implement appropriate courses of action, apply evidence-based knowledge, use appropriate research to monitor and evaluate outcomes, use supervision to improve effectiveness, use a wide range of communication skills, and promote social and economic justice.

The life model and ecological approach (Germain & Gitterman, 1996) was described as perhaps the most clearly articulated systems-based model of social work intervention. Its conceptual framework views individuals as being in an exchange relationship with their environments. Some individuals fit and adapt to their environments, whereas others may be overwhelmed by life stressors. Human relatedness, self-esteem, and competence are all related to the notion of fit within one's habitat or environment. Some groups are vulnerable to oppression, abuse, and social/technological pollution, often because their niche in society is denigrated. The ecological approach suggests that human development is a nonuniform path that interacts with a wide variety of environmental forces that need to be understood and appreciated by social workers.

CASE MANAGEMENT

Managing a client's needs, as opposed to treating clients, is rapidly becoming the primary service provided by social workers. Although case management has been a significant tool in the repertoire of social workers for many years, it was not until the early to mid-1990s that it became the primary task of so many in this field. The reason for this shift is related to the wide-ranging effects of managed care, its emphasis on cost-containment, and the fact that many traditional approaches were very time-consuming and, thus, expensive (Woodside & McClam, 1998).

In recent years, case management has evolved from being perceived as a rather simple, low-status, semiadministrative chore for bachelor-level staff to being seen as a complex, demanding, and advanced skill for only the most experienced and knowledgeable social workers. There is more recognition that clear expertise is required (Moseley & Deweaver, 1998). The newer, advanced case-management approaches emphasize a high level of professionalism. Case managers are now required to be highly skilled managers who know of available resources as well as how to link the client with those needed resources (Gerhart, 1990).

There is, however, some concern that managed care's preference for case management, with its historical place among baccalaureate-level or even untrained high-school graduates, is an effort to "de-professionalize" and therefore cut costs, particularly where long-term or severe problems exist. Practitioners who had previously proudly referred to themselves as professional social workers and received the pay and status commensurate with that high level of expertise are now being referred to as *case managers* by insurance companies and large agencies. The pay, status, and even authority to properly perform the often demanding job of coordinating and linking multiple resources is potentially diminished in this environment.

Case management has its historical roots in the mental health arena, particularly with long-term or (previously referred to as) chronic patients. Up until the 1970s, social workers were encouraged to apply the same psychotherapeutic techniques to schizophrenics and other severely disturbed clients that they used with higher-functioning clients. This seemed fair and rational, since the social worker's code of ethics requires provision of the best type of services, regardless of the client's race, religion, age, or presenting problem or diagnosis. Social workers had relatively little success with this population of clients until the advent of the community mental health movement of the 1960s and 1970s and the voluminous research supported by the National Institutes of Mental Health (NIMH), which clearly validated the use and coordination of support systems in the community and a renewed reliance on linking with both the formal and informal system of help (President's Commission on Mental Health, 1978).

Some severe disorders or problems in the health and mental health arenas cannot be eradicated or "cured." They need to be managed so that their symptoms do not have too negative an effect on the lives and functioning of clients and their families. Goals do not involve curing the problem or pathology or psychopathology as the traditional medical model would suggest; rather, goals involve supporting clients to maximize their potential strengths socially, physically, psychologically, and economically so that they can lead as productive and fulfilling lives as possible, given their limitations (Rapp, 1998; Rapp & Chamberlin, 1985).

Case management evolved in social work as a practical response by this ever-innovative profession to help clients get the most out of life, given that neither they nor their helping social workers had unlimited resources. So, throughout the 1960s and 1970s, there was a shift away from therapy for severe or long-term problems and toward management and stabilization (Gerhart, 1990). Case managers were given greater status and legitimacy as a result of the NIMH Community Support Program and were seen as key players in service provision in the four-volume *Task Panel Reports* by the President's Commission on Mental Health (1978). It has not been true until just the last few years that social work has accepted this approach as an equal and, increasingly, major role in the profession. In fact, during the mid 1990s when managed care and health maintenance organizations were dramatically altering the types of services offered by social workers, case management rather suddenly transformed in image from a low-status, marginal service to the major, essential service provided by social workers in a wide variety of settings (Woodside & McClam, 1998).

THE MODELS

Case-management models have two rather different and distinct approaches. The two models are the *traditional long-term* and the *managed care short-term* approaches.

Traditional Long-Term Model

The *traditional long-term* model of case management is the older, mainstream approach that grew out of a recognition that there are certain long-term or "chronic" health or mental health problems that will exist throughout one's life that cannot be successfully treated or "cured." The alternative is to manage them, that is, to provide the needed minimal resources to allow the individual to function at his or her best level, recognizing that the problem will always exist. Thus, various intractable problems, from chronic schizophrenia and significant intellectual deficits to health problems such as severe, lifelong diabetes, epilepsy, or paralysis, were given *traditional* case management.

Rothman's (1992) social work book on case management says: "Given that clients in case management have severe impairments that are chronically debilitating, it is no wonder that a multifaceted diagnosis is undertaken. . . . [C]lients are dependent on support over long periods of time; hence concerted effort at ongoing monitoring is essential to this service mode" (p. 14).

The *traditional* model is well suited for the three common types of social work cases that follow:

> LOUISE: *Louise is a 54-year-old African American single homeless woman. She has been diagnosed with schizophrenia since age 23 and has been hospitalized dozens of times, once for three years in a state hospital from 1968 to 1971. At that time, she was deinstitutionalized and sent into a low-income community, which had six halfway houses. Although she did engage in partial hospitalization programs and vocational training and support, she has not ever been able to sustain employment due to her unusual affect and occasional periods of delusions.*
>
> JOEY: *Joey is a 12-year-old who was abandoned at birth at the county hospital by his mother who was addicted to crack cocaine. He was two months premature and weighed exactly five pounds at birth. In spite of seven operations for a variety of disorders, his physical, social, and academic development have been extremely below average and his IQ, which has been tested on two occasions, has been found to be 62, which has precluded his involvement in the mainstream school system.*
>
> VIRGINIA: *Virginia is an 82-year-old woman with Alzheimer's, severe arthritis, and partial blindness as a result of deteriorating diabetes. She was recently placed into a nursing home by her 60-year-old daughter after the daughter suffered a stroke and could no longer care for her mother. All of Virginia's conditions are deteriorating, although her heart is strong; and there are no immediate life-threatening problems as long as she has proper care.*

All three of these cases are excellent candidates for *traditional long-term case management*. Why? There are four reasons: (a) multiple causality, (b) poor prognosis, (c) long-term needs, and (d) a need for coordination.

Multiple Causality   Clients who have a variety of problems and disorders—any one of which would require intervention—are candidates for traditional long-term case management due to *multiple causality*. The causes may be separate and distinct, but they also typically interact and are cumulative. For instance, many clients will have a variety of economic, psychological, physical, and social problems, each with their own dynamics.

> *Louise has schizophrenia (both a physical and psychological problem), economic problems related to the unstable nature of her condition, and housing problems, which exacerbate the social support system deficits. Joey has multiple physical problems that also affect his intellectual capabilities, which, in turn, limit his academic potential and, therefore, his finances. Virginia has multiple physical problems that directly affect housing and, therefore, social options. Her care will also be very expensive.*

Poor Prognosis   Unlikely or impossible eventuality in complete amelioration of a disorder such that the anticipated best outcome of intervention is only diminishing the effects or symptoms is considered to have a *poor prognosis*. There is no cure for major birth disorders, organic brain damage or dementia, amputations, or certain psychotic disorders and personality disorders. The effects or symptoms can, however, be significantly diminished through effective intervention.

> *Louise will always have schizophrenia; but, with appropriate intervention, she may never have another acutely psychotic episode. Joey's physical and intellectual capabilities may remain below average even with the best of management due to profoundly negative factors during his fetal development. However, effective case management will significantly improve his capabilities, even to the point where he may ultimately live a very normal, independently functioning life. Virginia's Alzheimer's and partial blindness will remain for the rest of her life. Fortunately, the symptoms or effects can be diminished to the point where they might have only a minor impact on her life.*

Long-Term Needs   When the client's problems will require years or literally the rest of the client's life to continuously deal with the problem and its effects, he or she is considered to have *long-term needs*. There is no brief intervention that will permanently stop the effects of certain problems. The case-management model used will involve intervention on an "as needed" basis and/or some type of ongoing monitoring with services and supports provided continuously but at a less-intense level.

Louise's history suggests the future possibility of ongoing efforts to provide her with lifelong supports in protected and supportive environments. She may need economic, social, vocational, and residential services for the remainder of her life. Joey may also have to be supported in a special academic and therapeutic environment. However, given his young age, an intensive case-management approach, with a focus on teaching academic and social skills, could significantly diminish the need for care in later life. Ideally, he could develop and learn independent-living skills at his early age and potentially need minimal help or no help at all as an adult. Virginia's problems are primarily physical and assessed as being deteriorative in nature. Symptoms and effects can be stopped and even reversed, but her frail condition will probably require some degree of ongoing support for the rest of her life.

Need for Coordination   When a service intervention plan is needed that organizes services so that the varied types of needed help are provided in a nonduplicative manner that complements and supports other services, *coordination* is often the key to effective case management. The holistic, biopsychosocial approach that is the framework for case management recognizes that each of the varying systems that impact on the individual client needs to be addressed and integrated.

Louise's long case record will likely show evidence of her severe episodes being preceded by significant stress. Her history is probably one in which she was hospitalized and delusional only when she had been evicted, living on the street, out of medications, and devoid of social supports. By coordinating needed housing, medication, and a supportive and therapeutic environment, an effective case manager may be able to help keep Louise symptom-free and living independently and happy. Joey's case manager will need to keep a special school environment in contact with the various doctors and therapists who help him. If these varied systems work together, his growth and development will be helped significantly. Virginia also needs doctors talking with nurses and social workers and rehabilitation therapists. Each of these professionals can help by supporting the varied efforts. For instance, a speech therapist might also encourage Virginia to speak to others in a support group for stroke victims. The case manager/social worker may help her develop a system for keeping track of her medications while timing it with social activities and exercise schedules developed by a rehabilitation therapist.

Managed Care Short-Term Model

The second model of case management, referred to as the *managed care short-term* model, focuses primarily on coordination and linking of resources so that they support each other in a nonduplicative and synergistic fashion. In this model, treatment or therapy may be included as part of the "mix," but the focus is on analyzing the presenting problem in a broad context and then efficiently solving the problem by coordinating needed social, emotional, financial, medical, and therapeutic resources in an organized plan of action. This model is aggressive and relatively brief.

Three common case examples typical of the *managed care short-term* model of case management are the following:

TOM: *Tom is a 16-year-old White male who has recently deteriorated in his school and socialization. He is the only child of Helen, who has raised Tom alone since his birth. Helen's boyfriend for the last three years recently left them, and she is depressed and beginning to drink excessively. She has also found traces of marijuana in Tom's room but has not confronted him for fear that he would leave home. Tom's only interest is in occasionally playing basketball, and his former coach at school has called the home several times inquiring about Tom.*

TANYA: *Tanya is a 19-year-old single African American female high-school graduate with a two-year-old daughter who performs below average developmentally. Tanya is pregnant again and has recently experienced panic attacks as well as an inability to sleep. She admits that she is extremely anxious and occasionally cries "for no reason." Her boyfriend is only marginally committed to her and says that he wants her to abort the child, particularly since he feels that her daughter is already "messed up" and the next child may be the same. Her employer of nearly two years is supportive but says that if she does not get help, she will have to let Tanya go.*

GINNY: *She is a 43-year-old White recently divorced female with four children who range in age from 22 to 11. She is receiving assistance from the state and a small sum "under the table" from her ex-husband, who has been in and out of prison several times and has never had a regular job. She often takes him back even though their relationship has a long history of physical and mental abuse toward her and the children. He wants to return to them, and Ginny is ambivalent. She is afraid of him, given his abusive past, but claims that he is basically a decent man. She also indicates an overwhelming feeling of loneliness and a desperate need to have someone help her with the children and her bills.*

What do the preceding three cases have in common? In each case, there are multiple causes and a need for coordination but not necessarily a poor prognosis or long-term needs. This managed care short-term model is also both *time-limited* and *intensive*. In the past, these three cases would not have been considered for case management in most professional social service agencies. Now, at least within managed care settings, these are rather typical.

Multiple Causality   Why are these cases typical? First, *multiple causes* are evident.

> *Tom has school performance problems, his mother Helen is depressed and possibly alcoholic, he has a drug abuse problem, and his mother is unsure of how to help him. Tanya has a daughter who needs to be both physically and psychologically evaluated, and she needs both prenatal care and counseling to address her depression and relationship concerns. Ginny is overwhelmed socially and financially and is desperate for someone to help her.*

Need for Coordinated Care   Secondly, the managed care short-term model of case management is appropriate because there is a clear need for *coordinated care* and the linking of resources.

> *Tom has a coach who is willing and available. Tanya has an employer who will help and encourage her, as long as she seeks assistance. Ginny's support, in the form of a partner with a history of abuse, is not a positive resource; and she will need help to develop alternatives, beginning with her case manager, who can at least initially serve as a major source of support.*

Time-Limited   Third, and this is where it essentially differs from the traditional model, the managed care model is *time-limited*, unlike the other model, which requires both a poor prognosis and long-term needs. In the managed care model, the focus is on assessing the multiple causes, coordinating and linking resources, and doing it in a time-limited fashion.

> *Tom, Tanya, and Ginny can be told that the case management intervention will last for only a few sessions. While their concerns are serious and could become lifelong, it is also possible that effective and immediate care could provide them with new, lifelong skills that will allow them to deal with similar concerns independently in the future. This expectation needs to be addressed planfully and possibly written into a contract. The time-limited expectation within short-term case management reinforces the clients' individual strengths by supporting the fact that they can overcome these problems by using the skills taught to them in the case management process. A psychoeducational and instructive approach is needed. Tom, Tanya, and Ginny will essentially be told, "We will work together for a number of sessions with the purpose of learning and developing coping skills for now and the future. You have the capacity to change, grow, and independently deal with these issues if they start to develop again in the future."*

Intensive   Finally, this model is *intensive* or aggressive in its utilization of a wide and exhaustive list of resources "up-front"—at the beginning of the intervention. By dealing very thoroughly with virtually all of the client's presenting concerns in a highly organized planned manner, the belief is that there will be long-term gain. In this model, the belief is that by broadly and holistically confronting such diverse needs as health problems, parenting, social and interpersonal difficulties, and economic issues all at once or in a coordinated, thorough, but intense, time frame, the client should be able to function more independently for a longer period of time.

> *Tom and his mother Helen have drug and alcohol problems as well as a mix of depression, social, and academic concerns. These problems interact negatively. The more they use drugs, the more socially isolated, academically deficient, and depressed they become. Focusing on any one problem would undoubtedly help, but attempts at simultaneous impact with all of the interrelated problems may be even more efficient and effective. Tanya could also be helped by getting her to see that her panic attacks and her sleep disorder are related to her concerns about her daughter and her current pregnancy. She needs to reduce these various stressors, while increasing social and economic supports, perhaps by the case manager reinforcing her potential strength. Ginny's problems also are interrelated. Her poor self-esteem is directly related to her dependence on an unreliable and violent partner. She needs help in asserting her independence so that she can begin to independently improve her economic condition, thus also protecting and supporting her children. By improving her own economic and social conditions, her insecurity and loneliness will diminish. Her felt "need" to rely on someone who is in fact a source of stress, not support, must be addressed to help her avoid such negative relationships in the future.*

Generalist Model versus Specialist Model

There are several other models of case managers (Levine & Fleming, 1985; Rothman, 1992). For instance, there is the *generalist* model versus the *specialist* model. In the *generalist* model, the case manager is required to individually provide all aspects of care for the client. Whether the manager is a social worker, nurse, rehabilitation therapist, or general counselor, he or she needs to be able to provide a wide variety of services. These may include individual therapy, vocational guidance, developing guidelines for better nutrition and exercise, and discussing past problems. There are relatively few problems in coordinating or linking resources since everything is performed by this generalist case manager. The other distinct advantage is that the client has only one person to deal with and, thus, avoids the difficulty of developing adequate working relationships or conflicting advice that can develop when too many people are working with the same client. However, the obvious problem of insufficient expertise is apparent. No single individual can expertly perform all of these duties. The *generalist* case manager is often required to possess the knowledge and skills of a physician, psychologist, and lawyer on behalf of the same client, and that range of expertise is simply not realistic.

There is also a *specialist (team)* model (Levine & Fleming, 1985; Rothman, 1992) in which a group of practitioners divides the tasks needed among themselves and works closely together to coordinate client needs. The advantage here is that the client relates to a consistent group of clinicians who, in turn, work closely together, using their own expertise to complement each other. So, the various team members specialize in defined tasks and provide all of those needed services to individuals, therefore combining in-depth skills as well as broad-based services. If the coordination or teamwork is efficient, this is certainly a reasonable model.

Referral Model versus Primary Therapist Model

Case management has had some difficulty in developing due to a lack of agreement concerning its parameters. The types of service provided under different models cover a wide range. This is epitomized in the *referral* model versus the *primary therapist* model. At one extreme is a *referral* model, which limits case managers to a simple, mechanistic, and bureaucratic role of simply gathering basic facts and then referring the client to a list of professionals who will then provide the various needed services. Under this model, the social worker never sees the client again and provides no direct service.

At the other end of the continuum is the *primary therapist* model. In this model, the social worker accepts basically the same role of a traditional therapist, with the recognition that certain specialized or marginal services are to be provided by others. Typically, those others include teachers, doctors, welfare workers, and health specialists. However, the primary task of providing treatment remains with the social worker whose role is essentially no different than a traditional therapist, with the exception of more overtly and planfully accepting the role of secondary helpers in aiding with support or complementary services.

Mixed Model

A very similar model, called the *mixed model*, relies primarily on a *single therapist* who treats the client but also accepts some management responsibilities, which contrasts with the other end of the continuum in which the case manager is a *broker of services* and has no treatment tasks at all but simply refers and coordinates needed services (Rapp & Chamberlain, 1985; Johnson & Rubin, 1983). At present, most case managers are somewhere in between those two extremes.

PRIMARY ROLES

Although the specific roles and tasks of case managers are highly defined by the agency, client problems, resources available, and setting, most do focus on six primary roles as case managers: (a) resource coordinators, (b) direct-service providers, (c) planners, (d) monitors, (e) supporters, and (f) evaluators.

Resource coordinators link and combine needed aids and services with clients in a manner that provides them with their primary, necessary supports. Detailed planning of strengths and availability of resources is first conducted so that all gaps in needs are met without overlapping or duplicating help. Then the case manager strengthens the connections and patterns of interaction among the various systems so that they effectively and efficiently meet all of the necessary needs. Without adequate coordination, duplication of services or even instances of undermining of services can develop. Coordination assures that all systems are working together to achieve the same goals in a manner that complements and reinforces each unit within the helping system.

Direct-service providers intervene with clients by serving as therapists, counselors, helpers, or primary agents in giving the clients their needed services. Whether the social worker provides therapy, money, or information, service is directly provided. Models vary in the degree to which direct services are provided, but most case managers give some direct service as well as resources such as support, information, or physical aids.

Planners work with clients by helping them assess strengths and presenting problems, then developing a strategy to meet specific relevant goals and designing tasks to be carried out by the client to achieve those goals. Planning for change necessitates a degree of objective professionalism. Previous, negative patterns of habitual behavior need to be addressed realistically as the worker helps the client incorporate new behaviors and insights into plans for the future. Obstacles to goal achievement are thoroughly discussed in the context of looking at new strategies that will work successfully and that can be integrated into new coping behaviors for the future.

Monitors assess progress or lack of progress in achieving goals, meeting needs, completing relevant tasks, providing resources, and completing outcomes. The social worker serves as a role model who can balance a high level of caring and concern with an equally high level of clear, realistic analysis. Monitoring requires occasionally reappraising or changing plans and objectives. As clients grow, learn, and change during the course of the case-management process, they may need help staying on a gradual and sequential plan of action.

Supporters encourage and reinforce behaviors and task accomplishments that are designed to meet needs and develop resources. As new behaviors are attempted, clients may need to be supported and encouraged in these initial attempts. The client who has spent a lifetime passively resenting but allowing abuse or discrimination will need help the first few times he or she stands up for personal rights. Assertiveness is a learned behavior for many, and initial attempts may be ineffective or even embarrassing for clients. Clients need to be supported in their change process for it to continue, and occasional setbacks and failed attempts should be anticipated and expected. When they happen, the client and social worker simply examine the behavior or series of events, learn from them, and develop a new strategy. Maintaining ongoing support for a positive but realistic and flexible plan is essential.

Evaluators provide feedback to clients relevant to their goal achievement and identify additional or different resources or services that may be needed. If there has been sufficient monitoring and supporting of the change process throughout the intervention, then the evaluation is essentially a summary and review. The evaluation task involves objectively assessing what worked or did not work effectively, with a realization that the behaviors and insights are now available internally. The client can be reminded of his or her accomplishments as well as being helped to examine whatever behaviors from the past or present did not help toward the planned achievement of goals.

THE STAGES

Books on case management have rather clearly described the approach and its history, rationale, and methods. These authors have typically described several stages wherein the social worker does an initial assessment; then does planning with the client, linking of needed resources, monitoring the process, and occasional advocacy to assure that resources are provided; and then a termination phase (Rapp, 1998; Rothman, 1992, & Sullivan, 1981).

Although some describe as few as three stages (Woodside & McClam, 1998) and others describe as many as eight (Rothman, 1992), there is some agreement in describing the process and tasks involved in the stages of case management:

- Stage 1: Initial assessment: Defining the problem and the strengths
- Stage 2: Planning
- Stage 3: Linking and coordinating
- Stage 4: Monitoring and supporting
- Stage 5: Summarizing, evaluating, reinforcing, crediting, and closing

Stage 1: Initial Assessment: Defining the Problem and the Strengths

This intake process involves gathering relevant data and history concerning (a) the presenting problem, (b) factors that led to the problem, (c) past attempts to ameliorate the problem, (d) the client's present and past social support system, and (e) potential resources for help. Some agencies require developmental or psychosocial histories, and all require standard demographic data. Frequently, social workers request or develop ecograms of the family or diagrams of the social network (Maguire, 1991) as tools in quickly and concretely examining potential support systems.

The initial stage is important because it sets the tone for the intervention while laying the foundation for the relationship between the client and the worker. The social worker's attitude should be accepting and warm while also being objective and organized. The first session or two should focus on defining and understanding the reasons the client came in for help. A clear understanding of the specific behaviors, feelings, and reactions is needed. A supportive discussion of the development of the problem or issue is essential, with the social worker supportively probing for an understanding of how the client responded both behaviorally and emotionally. Was the client's response typically helpful or not? Did he or she do anything to increase or decrease the frequency of the problematic behavior in the past? What is keeping the problem alive? What has worked or might possibly work in the future to stop the problem from reoccurring? Are there individuals or other actual or potential supports that can be utilized to support change? Who or what are they, and how can they be involved in future plans?

Some case-management models have emphasized the existing strengths of the client. This is consistent with current practice models that have rejected the focus upon psychopathology or problems. They emphasize the client's own resources and potential as the foundation for change and see this as a more positive and constructive beginning point than the traditional negative focus of mainstream approaches. This strengths model "allows us to see possibilities rather than problems, options rather than constraints, wellness rather than sickness. And once seen, achievement can occur. As long as we stay in the muck and mire of deficits, we cannot achieve" (Rapp, 1998, p. 24).

In Stage 1, the client's niche and social environment are assessed. This includes their living arrangement, recreational outlets, work, and relationships. Their individual strengths—including aspirations, competencies, confidence, resources, and social support system—are all assessed in the strengths model, which ultimately seeks to empower the client by developing each of these.

Stage 2: Planning

This stage requires clear, honest, open discussion of the client's goals and aspirations, as well as discussion of impediments that may interfere with the achievement of those goals. Sessions typically include realistic appraisals of resources that vary from defining the quality and strength of the social relationship existent with family and friends to the level of debt and the credit rating of the client.

In this stage, the concept of *partnership* is essential. The individual client is *not* viewed as a victim, patient, or "sick" person or as powerless. He or she is seen and related to as a competent individual who brings a variety of strengths and resources that must be utilized to improve the quality of life and environment. If the social worker is too aggressive in "taking charge" or telling the individual what to do, the opportunity for genuine long-term empowerment is diminished. In this planning stage, the worker can offer suggestions, weigh options, evaluate different paths, and support the directions that appear to be the most efficient. However, it is essential that the individual client take the lead, not the worker.

For the case-management process to both achieve and maintain its goals in the future, the client must have confidence in his or her own competency. This necessitates supporting clients as they learn the process of taking care of themselves and developing their own plans. The worker can best help at this stage by engaging the individual in a dialogue that demonstrates respect for the client's ideas, thoughts, and hopes. Modeling certain behaviors, such as realistic appraisals of available resources, is helpful because it educates the client in learning to independently make similar appraisals.

The professional worker no doubt will have greater knowledge of formal resources available in the community as well as more experience with strategies for utilizing and developing personal resources in general. However, the client has more potential knowledge of his or her own strengths and resources; it is often up to the worker to help the client better understand how, when, and why those resources need to be used. The types of resources typically needed include social support systems, stress-reduction outlets, medical care, health information, and basic human resources such as enough money for food and housing. These are described in more detail later in this chapter.

Stage 3: Linking and Coordinating

Stage 3 is the action phase. It arrives only after the worker and client have clearly and concretely defined problems, strengths, resources, and impediments. They have formed a mutually respectful partnership and are now ready to try out their plan. Their plan essentially consists of connecting and coordinating resources, supports, and aid into an integrated, efficient, and constructive system that will allow the client to resolve his or her initial problem. Clients generally arrive with many problems, as well as strengths, so the plans that are developed are necessarily multifaceted. Some examples follow:

> MINDY: *Mindy's problem is that she is a 16-year-old single mother who wants to finish school, move out of the house of her abusive father, and*

become economically independent. Her strengths consist of a proven history of achieving well in school; a high degree of motivation and confidence; excellent social skills; and a supportive network of friends, teachers, and clergy. The plan that she developed with the social worker at Catholic Social Services involves enrolling at a special high school for young, single parents; moving out of her parents' home and into an apartment with her successful older sister who wants help with her own two children; and redeveloping a new network of supportive friends. She is now beginning that process by talking with her sister and arranging a clear schedule of mutually helpful child-care times, which she is coordinating with her new school. Her sister has also agreed to let Mindy have Friday nights free, as long as she watches the three children on Saturdays.

BILL: *Bill is a 30-year-old unemployed alcoholic whose wife left him after he hit her in a drunken rage. In spite of his recent behavior, Bill has many strengths such as a long history of sobriety, employment, and great love for his wife, whom he had never struck before the one incident. His plan is to continue to talk with Joan, the case manager at Family Social Services, to try to better understand and change his violence. He has also agreed to join AA, since he now recognizes that alcohol is a definite problem. He has set up weekly sessions with Joan, who is an experienced social worker with expertise in treating alcoholics. He has joined a support group that meets weekly to emotionally support unemployed men as well as allowing them to discuss, review, and share information about job openings in the community.*

ANN: *Ann is a 53-year-old depressed African American woman whose grown children no longer speak to her. She rarely leaves her cramped apartment due to a variety of physical problems and obesity. Her single pleasure is attending services at her church where she is a highly respected member of the choir. A social worker in her congregation, who works as a case manager at the local community mental health center, talked Ann into talking to one of her colleagues. They agreed that Ann needs to redevelop the relationships with her children, get a thorough physical exam, and talk with the center's psychiatrist about antidepressants, which had helped Ann years ago when she was similarly depressed. Ann has called her two children—with support from the social worker—and Ann's children are coordinating a series of exams with a local hospital that specializes in treating obesity in conjunction with a weekly meeting where women meet to support each other in a weight-loss program.*

Stage 4: Monitoring and Supporting

Even the best of plans require change, modification, and improvement. They also require that the worker and client maintain vigilance in assessing progress. Sometimes additional resources are required, and, invariably, certain supports such as professional or formal sector supports from the case manager are stopped.

The case manager may find that Mindy and her sister are not compatible or that the school is unable to accept her. Bill may find a job very quickly and find that the alcohol and violence were aberrant behaviors directly related to the unemployment. Ann may respond well to the medical care and group support but decide that only her daughter is supportive while her son is only a source of stress and therefore not one to be brought into her support system.

Without monitoring the progress in a reasoned and objective manner, there is no way to ascertain whether the case management is achieving its goal. The worker and client ideally will maintain an open, nonjudgmental attitude about progress that will allow them to recognize what is working and what is not working. Case-management interventions will invariably require fine-tuning and changes as goals are reached, discarded, or modified.

Supporting the client's growth, change, and progress are also essential. If Ginny stays in school in spite of some classmates spreading rumors about her, she will need the case manager to tell her what a great job she is doing. When Bill goes to his 20th job interview, gets rejected yet again, and calls his wife to talk about it instead of going to a bar, he needs to be told that he is doing the right thing. When Ann loses only two pounds and begins to feel depressed but calls friends from the support group instead of either eating or feeling sorry for herself, the case manager needs to say that Ann should be proud of herself for making progress, as slow and difficult as it may be. These accomplishments are the first steps in achieving their goals, and the first few steps are always the hardest.

Stage 5: Summarizing, Evaluating, Reinforcing, Crediting, and Closing

There are five tasks related to ending a case-management intervention: (a) summarize and review, (b) evaluate change, (c) reinforce specific improvements, (d) credit the client, and (e) close.

First, *summarize* the past history of change, beginning with a discussion and agreed-upon description of the initial problems and strengths. The series of gradual, sequential, incremental changes in behavior, attitudes, emotions, and social interactions should all be reviewed. This helps the client to clearly see where he or she has changed and made improvements. It further supports the fact that change is a process and struggle that takes time, effort, and a plan—but it is doable.

Second, objectively and realistically *evaluate* current strengths and concerns. Even at the closing, discussions that provide accurate feedback to the client are very useful. For instance, during the case-management process, certain lifelong patterns of behavior may have become apparent. These may include tendencies to be overly self-critical or to become repeatedly involved in destructive or abusive relationships. Open and honest feedback is useful regarding the fact that this pattern is likely to repeat itself unless the client remains vigilant. Open and objective evaluative review and discussion at the closing also serve to model the ongoing need of the client to be self-aware and conscious of how and why certain decisions or behaviors are maintained. The client needs to incorporate a capacity to self-evaluate honestly throughout life.

Third, *reinforce* specific changes that the client has learned. For instance, a young mother who had begun abusive behavior toward her infant will be encouraged to "stop and talk" rather than "hit and yell." Presumably, the new, more adaptive behaviors she learned during case management will have some degree of self-reinforcement by the fact that they have alleviated conditions that were initially presented as problems. Now she should know clearly and concretely what she needs to do if that same problem reoccurs in the future.

Fourth, *credit* the client for his or her own growth and change. A critical aspect of empowerment involves getting clients to see that *they* have the internal, independent ability to improve their lives and situations. While it is true that the social worker served as a guide through the process, the client needs to know that, now and in the future, he or she can utilize those new learned behaviors, attitudes, and insights without the social worker.

Fifth, *close* or *terminate* the case-management process. Bring closure by saying "good-bye." Leave the client with assurances that he or she is very capable of dealing with the issues initially presented. Many social workers "keep the door open" by telling clients that they can come back if necessary. This is not to encourage a return visit but, rather, to let the client know that you care and will be available even though the client should now feel reasonably confident of functioning well and independently without you.

RESOURCES REQUIRED FOR CASE MANAGEMENT

Case managers are often viewed as providers and coordinators of resources. Although the specific approaches and techniques vary considerably based upon the client's needs and the agency's approach, certain common needs consistently reappear whether the case manager is working in a child welfare setting, a family social service agency, a mental health clinic, or an independent clinical practice. There are three categories of needed resources that case managers are required to have access to: (a) *social resources,* including an ability to improve social support systems and reduce stressors in the client's system; (b) *informational resources,* particularly relative to medical care and health information; and (c) *physical resources,* including basic needs such as economic aid and housing.

Social Resources

Social resources and, particularly, an adequate *social support system* are the sine qua non of case management. Without the active involvement of family and friends, as well as a network of professionals who take a genuine interest in the client, case management is unlikely to be successful. Clients must be actively engaged and personally involved with others who know and care for them. The *informal support system* can be composed of a brother, a sister, a wife, a husband, a neighbor, a colleague at work, a fellow church member, or a team member in a bowling league. The *formal support system* of professionals may involve other social workers, nurses, doctors, clergy, lawyers, teachers, or any of many others.

The level and nature of this involvement can vary tremendously. Many clients do not have the prerequisite social skills or resources needed to independently develop support systems. Due to problematic development in their childhoods; trauma; low self-esteem; or a variety of social, psychological, or medical reasons, many of them have little or no history of independent relationships developed by themselves. As a result, social workers need to be precise in their initial assessments, taking particular care to clearly define the current level of support but also understanding the client's past history.

For instance, social workers often treat depressed or anxious adults who are currently dealing with problems of social adjustment such as job loss, divorce, health problems, or stress related to physical or psychological trauma. A standard approach by a social worker may be some discussion with them about others they spoke to or confided in as the problem developed. Most people actually talk to no one, even as significant issues of depression develop (Yamatani, Maguire, Rogers, & O'Kennedy, 1996). Those who even discuss their concerns do so with family or friends, not with social workers. This is typical and should be expected, but it also explains why the clients who come in to see social workers instead of seeking out family or friends are particularly at risk. These are the people who do not have a support system; often, have not had one in the past; and do not know how to develop one.

Support system development is an essential skill for case managers. There are five stages to developing such a system: ventilation, assessment, clarification, planning, and restructuring (Maguire, 1991, 1993). In Stage 1, the client is encouraged to release his or her feelings and emotions. Stage 2 involves assessing present and past support systems, with a particular sensitivity on the social worker's part toward being aware of historical patterns—isolation or, simply, difficulties in forming such needed ties and linkages to others. In other words, if the client is a self-described "loner," the level of intimacy of the potential system must integrate that level of comfort and not attempt to push a closeness or size that will in all likelihood be rejected by the client because it increases rather than decreases stress. Stage 3 is clarification, which involves helping the client to diagram or map his or her network (Maguire, 1983, 1993) or do an ecomap or genogram (Hartman, 1978). It may simply involve more detailed discussion of past and present friends, relatives, and social interactions. Planning—Stage 4—requires that the social worker and client team together to strategize and practically consider a course of action. Such planned actions may include either the social worker or the client calling or visiting past acquaintances or friends, with an idea of talking to them about themselves or their problem. Finally, restructuring the system, which is the process of making connections to others, will help to provide the personal, social resources needed to help overcome the problem (Maguire, 1991). Case 4.1 provides an example of support system development.

Case 4.1: Support System Development

Jim R. was a 32-year-old single librarian. He had lived with his mother up until two years ago. He initially appeared to be extremely rigid and guarded as he described his recent feelings of depression. His affect and avoidance of certain topics suggested that he was not disclosing certain information, so the social worker was particularly supportive in telling him that he could talk about anything. In fact, after she noticed his red hands and his cautious mention of germs, she mentioned how some people feel comfort by frequent washing, particularly when they feel under stress. This allowed him to ventilate, and he indicated that he was depressed because he had an extreme fear of germs, being touched, and being in most social situations. He then described a series of obsessions and compulsions that he knew to be "silly" and irrational but that he could not control. Furthermore, these behaviors precluded his having a "normal" life and had made him a depressed and anxious social isolate.

The social worker remained very accepting and supportive, even mentioning that ritualistic and compulsive behaviors such as washing three times—never more and never less—are frequently associated with his problem. Jim was very relieved that the worker understood his concerns and assessed them as neither "crazy" nor pathological. In fact, as they worked together to clarify when the symptoms appeared, it became apparent that Jim had, in fact, a tremendous sense of humor, great intellect, and even close friendships, as long as these friends did not physically touch him.

A behavioral plan emerged that gradually got Jim to the point of hugging certain people as long as he wore a particular coat that he already deemed "dirty but wearable." The plan also involved increasing attempts at dating, a goal that Jim felt to be important. Restructuring his system and linking him to others involved problem solving and social skill development as his initial premature attempts failed. For instance, without consulting the social worker, he asked a woman out on a date because she was friendly and frequently came to the library. When she politely but firmly rejected his date proposal, Jim became quite depressed and embarrassed and briefly decided to resume his self-isolation. However, the case manager got Jim to reassess his growing social support system and recognize that it provided him with immeasurable satisfaction and that closer, more intimate relationships may ultimately develop as he incrementally interacted with others, but they were not essential for him at the present time.

Stress reduction outlets, recreation, and plain old fun are all vastly underrated. In fact, clients themselves are often the first to question the practicality of going out and having fun when their marriage is deteriorating or their children are causing intolerable levels of stress. However, the validity of the research that connects stress reduction to diminishing symptoms is no longer questioned. The problem with the introduction of this particular resource by case managers tends to be that people consider recreation to be frivolous and unimportant relative to other needs of clients typically seen by social workers. On the surface, this is rather apparent. Also, clients tend to see themselves and their own needs as low priorities, often as a reflection of their own poor self-images.

Clients need to be helped to be objective and realistic concerning themselves. Human beings, like any other organism or even machine, must be "fueled," energized, or stimulated in order to grow. They need positive outlets. Depressed and overwhelmed clients are sometimes shocked when the social worker suggests exercise, taking a night out to dance, or even having a night out with old high-school buddies.

Timing and sensitivity are essential in the introduction of this resource, but social workers themselves are often reluctant to suggest such outlets. Treatment does not have to be painful and arduous. Timing the introduction of enjoyable outlets for times when the client will be more receptive increases the likelihood of success. For instance, an overwhelmed single parent who spends the initial session angrily venting about his or her acting-out adolescent does *not* want to be advised to go out and "have fun." However, after this necessary ventilation, an informative discussion of *stressors* and their documented negative effects on both the physical and psychological well-being of individuals may be helpful.

The analogy of a steam-release valve or whistling teakettle suggests to clients that when pressure from stress builds, it has to be released or it boils up and could even "explode." Individual social systems are damaged by long-term stress, so these stressors must be reduced or eliminated. They cannot remain within. The body is like a machine, and it must not be overloaded or it will malfunction. Dancing, singing, talking to friends about nothing, strolls on the beach, shopping, and, particularly, any activity involving laughter are potentially very therapeutic.

Recreation is a planned resource that offers an alternative mind-set to a client whose previous focus had been entirely negative. Strategically, the social worker is adding a new and alternative pathway for the client's attention. Cognitive therapists and researchers suggest that problems such as depression are at least maintained, if not originated, by the individual's proclivity toward perceiving virtually everything in black or white, good or bad terms (Burns, 1980). Thus, the depressed or overwhelmed client seen by most social workers comes in with a predisposed tendency to filter out positive, alternative perceptions of life and to exclusively focus upon negatives—such as his or her presenting problem. By reinforcing an approach that gradually and incrementally introduces alternatives to the client's pervasive negativity (i.e., recreation or fun), he or she can shift past patterns of negative cognitions. Breaking this cognitive pattern is essential; and, the more appealing, rewarding, and exciting the social worker can be in discussing appropriate recreational outlets, the better.

Another reason that clients themselves are not too receptive to recreation for stress reduction is that they do not see themselves as priorities. This may be related to issues of poor self-esteem, depression, guilt, or the pressures of caring for others to the detriment of their own needs. Whatever the cause, the result is clients who fail to inject themselves or their needs into the equations that define their own lives. Many clients will take care of the overwhelming needs of their demanding children rather than take an occasional night out to see a movie or even take a walk. The result is a self-inflicted resentment compounded by a self-imposed dilemma—they must take care of others, and they resent doing it.

Frequently, the practical and reasoned discussion of these conflicting behaviors helps to get clients to the point where they will consider alternatives to their actions. If they are helped to see that they must reprioritize their activities, putting their own basic health needs as a priority rather than something to be considered after everyone else is taken care of, then they might choose to relax. Often, the best argument a social worker can use to convince selfless but overwhelmed and increasingly resentful clients to care for themselves is that they cannot help others if they are too overwhelmed to function. If they really want to continue to help their children, spouse, or whomever, they must first protect and replenish their own social systems. Case 4.2 provides an example of recreation for stress reduction.

Case 4.2: Recreation for Stress Reduction

Molly was a recently divorced, White mother of three teenage children. She tearfully described herself as "a failure at everything." The social worker supported her in letting out her feelings and ventilating but also began asking whether these various "failures" were really Molly's "fault." As they discussed this, it became apparent that Molly's abusive and alcoholic former husband was, as Molly laughingly admitted, "no great loss." In fact, once Molly moved past her unrealistic self-blame, she quickly recognized her great strengths as evidenced by her care for her family.

Molly worked 50 hours per week while actively supporting her children's various sports and school activities. In fact, she came to the social worker because she had to work overtime one night and therefore missed the school play in which her 13-year-old daughter played a major role. The daughter would not forgive her mother for her "lack of caring," thus reinforcing Molly's worst fear, that is, that she was a failure. The social worker supportively but realistically challenged Molly about her definitions of failure and whether that definition was consistent with her rather heroic efforts to provide for her family.

Molly and the social worker developed a time sheet and examined where Molly was spending her time. It was apparent that she was overwhelmed with demands and had literally no time to relax, think, unwind, exercise, talk to others, or rejuvenate. In fact, she was physically and psychologically stressed and, thus, unable to efficiently function. It was agreed that Molly would "give herself permission" to go out with her closest high-school friends at least once a week and that she would realistically assert herself with her children. In short, she would go to certain events, especially if she enjoyed them, but she was not going to be able to volunteer to run or even attend some of their activities. Furthermore, she decided to hike every morning with her son, allowing them to talk and enjoy each other's company.

Information

Medical care information and *health information* are necessary resources for case managers. Holistic orientations, which recognize the linkages between mind and body, are essential, and proper medical treatment is a vital component of that care. Social work education has incorporated a *biopsychosocial* orientation, which has replaced the purely *psychosocial* theories of the past. We now know that severely debilitating disorders often have physical, not purely psychological, etiologies. Schizophrenia, bipolar disorders, and psychoses are primarily the result of genetic and biochemical imbalances. Common disorders, such as depression, are recognized as being significantly affected by biochemical changes in the system, and many even argue that major personality traits are genetically predetermined (Kramer, 1993; Gerhart, 1990).

Case managers need to have access to psychiatrists and other physicians to provide the full range of needed resources. If a case manager is working with an individual who is lethargic, feeling helpless, hopeless, suicidal, and isolated, then that individual is clinically depressed; and treatment today requires a psychiatric consult. Case management, combined with cognitive techniques and appropriate antidepressants, successfully treats such disorders at rates unimagined a few years ago and at a speed (typically two to five months) that could not have been achieved without psychopharmacological support (Bentley & Walsh, 1996).

Another need for medical care is related to the general but pervasive effects of subtle aches, pains, and disorders that so severely diminish the quality of life. Case management is a multifaceted and aggressive approach. As a result, all facets of life and sources of difficulty are carefully assessed and then aggressively pursued; so, when a client says that, in addition to the marital and family problems, he or she also has a backache and occasional migraine headaches, the case manager needs to make a quick referral. There may be significant neurological problems that are maintaining, if not essentially causing, the interpersonal problems.

Case managers are often well aware of the need for referral in cases in which there are obvious physical problems or where the behavior, insight, affect, or orientation in time or place is so disturbed that psychiatric or other medical attention is clearly needed. However, a more common but less obvious need for such a resource involves the symptoms of diabetes, epilepsy, post-surgery effects, and a wide variety of somatically related problems from high blood pressure to ulcers. Neurological disorders can manifest themselves in very subtle ways, as can the effects of strokes. From slurred speech to inexplicable loss of energy, the case manager needs to recognize that physical and social emotional problems interconnect in complex ways. It is far better to make a referral to a physician to have a client checked over than to wait for months as marital or family interventionist efforts fail due to a brain tumor that has been growing and, essentially, causing the problems at home.

Health information and education are essential resources in this holistic and broad endeavor of case management. Social workers routinely ask clients about their eating and sleeping habits and routine, as well as educating them about health concerns relevant to sexually transmitted disease, balanced nutritional needs, consistency in sleep patterns, and activities to increase or decrease to improve their health.

Teenagers and senior citizens are among the populations that are often at risk for general health concerns. Teenagers have tremendous growth spurts that necessitate healthy food for strong growth. Lethargic, inattentive, and sometimes irritable teens are not just displaying normal behaviors for their age. These symptoms are often manifestations of poor diet and inadequate sleep, compounded by growth and the belief among teens that they do not need to take care of their bodies. They are often unaware of their limitations or, at least, of the fact that they must nurture their bodies if they expect to function well. Social workers often see teens who try to survive on three or four hours of sleep per night while subsisting on high-fat, high-sodium fast food and no fruit or vegetables. Discussions of eating and sleeping patterns and the need for paying attention to those concerns are a part of the case manager's focus.

The aged are also at higher risk for health problems. Due to the increased likelihood of chronic health problems, as well as the normal physical changes in old age, elderly patients are often unaware of a need to shift eating or sleeping patterns (Gerhart, 1990). When these patients live alone, the social isolation and lack of social stimuli or even feedback regarding appearances can lead to health deterioration. Many elderly can do well with even less sleep than needed in their youth, but their nutritional needs frequently do not get met when they live alone and fail to "go through all the fuss" of making healthy, well-balanced meals for themselves on a regular basis. Case managers often can increase social systems and meet health and nutritional concerns by encouraging older clients to visit each other for meals, eat out together, or share favorite dishes or recipes in regular meals together. Case 4.3 gives an example of an elderly client.

Case 4.3: An Elderly Client

John was a 71-year-old White retiree whose wife of nearly 50 years had recently died. He had spent the last 20 years of his career as a car salesman and had a good relationship with his three grown children. However, he came in to see the medical social worker only after his eldest daughter and his cardiologist insisted on the referral. John reluctantly agreed to come in "just to talk" for three sessions.

John began the first session by angrily saying, "I don't know why I have to come here. Sure I'm depressed and angry. Why shouldn't I be? My wife died, my kids are never around, my heart doctor says I'm getting worse, and, frankly, I really don't see much reason to keep on living."

The social worker was supportive and empathic and even agreed that "It looks as if things are pretty rough right now." When John realized that the social worker seemed to be quite supportive, he admitted that he was very frightened that he was going to die soon. He had lost a considerable amount of weight, was irritable, easily upset, and could not eat or sleep comfortably without his wife. For John, this was an admission of weakness. The more he tried to be "strong" and "act like a man," the worse he became. He reluctantly admitted that he had even cried a few times and saw that as a sign of being "just a weak, dying old man."

The social worker surprised John by saying she was impressed with his resilience and ability to carry on as he had. However, she also discussed with him the fact that his "keeping this all inside" could be making his condition worse and that his children were very worried because they knew he was suffering in silence. They discussed how the body needs sleep and proper nutrition to function, particularly when a stressor, such as the loss of a loved one, happens.

John asked several questions and seemed initially reluctant but agreed to confide more in his kids, get out of the house more often, exercise, and let his kids prepare nutritious meals for him until he felt willing and able to do that for himself.

Physical Resources

Basic human needs include not only the provision of survival needs but also the capacity to independently achieve them. *Economic resources* for food and other essentials, as well as adequate *housing,* must be provided before virtually any other service. Clients with significant disabilities, particularly where reliance or dependence on others for assistance is needed, require a sense that they are capable and have inherent strengths and resources. The principles of the basic Maslow pyramid, which depicts the essentials of food, shelter, and survival on the bottom or foundation before achieving higher-level needs, is understood by most. In short, our clients have to first have the basics before other, higher-order needs can be addressed. Mental health interventions, or "psychotherapy," are luxuries for someone who has no food or shelter. Case managers need to provide the most basic resources first, and only after that can they go on to address the higher-order needs.

Social workers and, particularly, case managers are continuously redefining and reintegrating these basic, mundane, and less-exciting resources into their interventionist repertoire. Should social workers with bachelor-level or even master's-level degrees use their client time to go to the grocery store to show them how to shop? Should case managers help clients clean their homes, bathe their children, develop a budget, mend their clothes, or prepare a meal? For most case managers, the answer is "Yes." Status concerns are giving way to practical realities in the helping professions, and the direct-service professionals who are unwilling to provide simple but basic essential needs such as money, clothes, food, or housing are not helping their clients as effectively as they could.

This shift toward the provision of basic resources by highly trained social workers has resulted from the years of experience with long-term clients in health and mental health settings (Moseley & Deweaver, 1998; Gerhart, 1990). Deinstitutionalization failed as a movement in the 1960s, 1970s, and 1980s not only because linkages and coordination of services were poor but also because practitioners were not trained to provide for the essential basic needs of their clients. Patients released from psychiatric hospitals did not need therapy to stay out of the hospitals as much as they needed to learn how to prepare their own meals, clean their homes, take buses to jobs, and buy their own clothes. Not only were clinicians untrained in teaching those skills, but they frequently had a disregard for such simple tasks and felt it was an inappropriate use of their expertise. Such concerns still exist, and, indeed, professionally trained social workers should legitimately question whether they personally have to spend the time to perform some simple tasks; but case managers must see that these basic needs are met and that someone is clearly assigned to teaching the client how to live independently—doing their own shopping, cooking, cleaning, and developing ties to their community.

Economic resources and employment opportunities are needed for many of the clients of case managers. As discussed in the previous section, there are certain basic, essential needs; and money, as well as the opportunity for independent acquisition of money, is among them. Many of the clients of social workers are members of populations that have been disadvantaged politically, socially, and economically. African Americans, gays, women, the disabled, and a long list of others have not been allowed to achieve social or economic equity. The pay scales for women are still far below those of men, and minorities of color have clearly not been allowed full access to jobs, good schools, training, or the supports to even achieve such economic independence, such as adequate child care.

Case managers must provide those resources, as well as assisting clients in the continued task of developing economic resources independently. As the old saying goes, it is better to teach a person to fish than to simply provide the fish. Even in a society in which biases are strong and doors to economic opportunity are closed to some, the case manager still needs to work with the client to seek out opportunities and develop the skills required to achieve economic independence or at least connect the client to a resource that will provide the requisite aid. Advocacy is an increasingly important part of providing access to such resources. In tight economies, resources such as government aid, as well as jobs in industry, become scarce. Clients who are already at a disadvantage due to racism, sexism, bias against disability, or a lack of knowledge or experience in working in such systems need guidance as well as an advocate who knows these systems and is willing and able to exert pressure and demand justice.

Housing has enough complex issues of its own to merit special attention. Housing is far more than just a roof over one's head. It signifies that one has a base, a place where one belongs and can return to for security. It allows one to become part of a stable and essential community; and it is a concrete and important symbol of stability in the life of a client whose life is otherwise chaotic, depressing, and stressful. Perhaps that is why the homeless, in particular, are such a disadvantaged group; they lack the most basic essential of life, a permanent place they can call their own, where they can relax and escape from stress and the overwhelming and chaotic events affecting their lives.

Housing for the poor is difficult to find. Realtors have left this market, and government subsidies have declined. Considering the increasingly dangerous and torn social fabric of urban and even rural life, the need for a safe haven becomes obvious, even as it becomes less common. Not only does housing provide protection from the elements such as rain and snow but it also is needed to protect individuals and families from the dangers of crime, drugs, and violence. The homeless are left to the mercy of natural and human elements that simply cannot be accepted in a supposedly civilized society. In a society of rich and poor, the struggling, working poor are particularly at risk in keeping their homes and families together. Recessions and job losses force this precarious group out into the street, making the likelihood of some modicum of stability virtually impossible. It is both an inhumane and poor social policy to have such woefully inadequate housing stock in this large and bountiful country.

SUMMARY

Case management has evolved over the last decade from being perceived as a rather simple bureaucratic task performed by nonprofessionals to a complex and demanding intervention that requires a wide range of knowledge, skills, and resources. Although a variety of models exist, there is some agreement that most case managers need to be *resource coordinators, service providers, planners, monitors, supporters,* and *evaluators.*

The focus of case management is not therapy or even service provision. It is managing, coordinating, and guiding a client through a series of steps. These include an *initial assessment,* which defines both problems and strengths; *planning; linking and coordinating; monitoring and supporting* gradual change; and, finally, *summarizing and closing.*

The provision of and coordination of needed resources are essential to all case management. Those resources vary according to the specific issues presented by the client. However, case managers typically need access to *social resources* to develop social support systems and to reduce stressors in the environment; *information* about medical care and health; and, finally, *physical resources,* including economic aid and adequate housing.

GROUP INTERVENTIONS

Individuals belong to multiple groups. Archaeologists and anthropologists have provided evidence that humans have always congregated in groups. Evidence—and speculation—from prehistoric society indicates that people gathered in small groups to hunt and to provide mutual protection, just as most animal species do. Basic animal instincts actually may underlie this need to form groups and to fulfill needs other than merely procreation or maintenance of the species.

This apparent biological imperative to gather in groups is supported by research looking at the fascinating group dynamics seen in wolf packs, which are notoriously cohesive, as are packs of elephants, apes, and a wide variety of other animals. Animals develop a clear "pecking order" and pattern of interaction, dominance, affection, and a range of degrees of closeness of relationships within the group. Humans are also social animals who instinctively gravitate to one another in groups—particularly that type of group called the *family*—to share concerns, find direction in life, solve each other's problems (or sometimes add to those problems), and otherwise provide protection and support.

HISTORY

Unfortunately, the first relatively modern attempt to analyze group dynamics was Gerard Le Bon's (1895) description of the group dynamics evident during the French Revolution. Mobs ruled, and, seemingly, the most vicious group behaviors predominated. Le Bon focused on the single-mindedness of the rioting masses and concluded that such groups have the potential to make people lose their individual identities and engage in a frenzy of destruction and other behavior that they would never consider doing on their own. This initial foray into a modern understanding of group dynamics viewed groups as potentially dangerous entities that could collectively undermine the good in people.

It was not until the 1940s that other serious academic efforts were initiated to understand how group dynamics affect people. Kurt Lewin's (1951)

120

fascinating and groundbreaking work in *field theory* claimed that virtually all human behavior could be understood and predicted if social scientists could establish the patterns of interaction, influence, and control of the field, environment, or social system of individuals. Lewin saw behavior as being a function of the *field* present whenever behavior occurs. He used mathematical models to concretely present the whole *gestalt,* or structure, that affects behavior. By 1945, when Lewin accepted the position of director of the Massachusetts Institute of Technology's Research Center for Group Dynamics, he had developed many of the statistical approaches used today to objectively measure and define group and other social forces that can be used to predict and understand human behavior.

Another historical precursor to the modern understanding of groups was Harry Stack Sullivan's (1953, 1954) *interpersonal theory,* which, like field theory, led social scientists and, subsequently, clinicians away from the Freudian *intrapersonal* focus and toward an empirical *interpersonal* orientation. Not only did Sullivan recognize the significance of people's interactional effects on each other but he actually gave such factors primacy in the construction of theories of personality development and virtually all human behavior and motivation. His theory says that personality is a purely hypothetical construct that cannot be understood or even observed apart from interpersonal situations; so, personality only manifests itself in relation to other people and the appropriate unit of study is not the individual alone but in the context of interpersonal situations.

The conscious use of group dynamics as a therapeutic force did not develop until the end of World War II. As many thousands of veterans were returning from the trauma and horrors of battle experiences, the traditional one-to-one, long-term psychodynamic practitioners were simply overwhelmed and forced to treat many people together in groups. They found that such group therapy approaches were not only helpful but were, in fact, more successful than their much more expensive and time-consuming individual efforts. Schools of social work soon began developing social group techniques designed specifically to support and strengthen the obvious therapeutic factors seemingly inherent in groups (Reid, 1991).

By 1955, *social group work* was officially recognized by the National Association of Social Workers, and early group work pioneers were struggling with developing group methods, as well as defining their place in the social work profession. From the 1940s through the 1970s, the appropriate use of groups in the profession was hotly debated. This historical evolution and struggle within group work helped to define the profession of social work (Reid, 1991; Vinter, 1974a, 1974b).

Many different group work orientations developed, with some defining groups as tools to support democracy or citizen participation, others defining them as tools to teach people how to relax and use leisure time, and still others recognizing their potential for radically altering individual personality or working through significant interpersonal problems. Vinter (1974a, 1974b) was central in getting the profession to recognize the treatment function of group work. He referred to the worker as the *change agent* who focuses on individual change by using direct and indirect means of influence, marshaling these forces to meet their particular needs. His suggestion that the group is both the means and the context of treatment has been the basis for much discussion in the field.

This chapter examines the major classifications of groups, types of groups, the basics of getting started, group composition, stages of group development, group norms, the group worker's tasks, and the therapeutic factors. Case examples of groups at work are used liberally as a way to take this essential knowledge and apply it to the rather demanding group situations that clinical social workers typically encounter in the field.

CLASSIFICATIONS OF GROUPS

The *classifications* of groups can best be described in terms of dichotomies: open versus closed; homogeneous versus heterogeneous; and the basic classifications of primary versus secondary and psyche versus socio groups.

Open versus Closed

Open versus closed refers to whether the group remains open to new members or whether it is closed, maintaining the same membership throughout the existence of the group. Open groups have greater turnover, so members are less likely to develop the stronger bonds of mutual identification common to homogeneous ongoing closed groups. Open groups are frequently used in inpatient hospital or psychiatric settings in which new patients come and go quickly but need to relate to patients with similar physical or emotional problems to compare and understand their own experiences. The sessions are generally both cathartic and educational, and the pace may be relatively rapid.

Closed groups more consciously use the relationships that form. As members get to know each other better, they learn how to trust and, thus, to open up to fellow members with whom they interact on a regular basis. The composition of such groups is important since the members spend considerable time together, usually over the period of many months. The stages of development may unfold more slowly as people recognize they are committing a large amount of time, effort, and trust to those with whom they may discuss their innermost thoughts, fears, plans, and histories. In most instances, these are people with past difficulties or even traumas in their relationships with others, and so their hopes for improvement are tinged with doubts. Their need for closeness and intimacy is often counterbalanced by past experiences of hurt or rejection.

Ongoing closed groups are, therefore, particularly therapeutic in their potential to help members develop the capacity to share, learn, trust, communicate, and interact with others in ways that were previously impossible for them. Group cohesiveness, altruism, sharing advice and life experiences, and decreasing the sense of isolation as members learn about themselves in dynamic interaction with those whom they learn to care about and trust are all well-documented reasons for the formation of the in-depth dynamics of ongoing closed groups.

Homogeneous versus Heterogeneous

A *homogeneous* group is a group in which members share the same common problem or life circumstances, whereas *heterogeneous* groups are mixed in terms of presenting problems. Thus, homogeneous groups typically have a specific problem or diagnosis such as eating disorders, alcoholism, incest survival, obsessive-compulsive disorders, or recent divorce. Within heterogeneous groups, the members have a variety of problems and diagnoses although even they most often require a common level of functioning or ego strength. A heterogeneous group may have members who are depressed, overstressed at work or home, dealing with marital or family problems, or undergoing life crises.

Homogeneous groups tend to gel more quickly because of the natural bonding that comes from immediate mutual identification and the healing emotions that develop through finding and interacting with a group of "fellow sufferers." Immediate and strong bonding is typical of homogeneous groups wherein the affect is high and a past sense of isolation may have existed. Groups of Vietnam War combat veterans, recent widows, rape victims, or abused spouses tend to bond quickly. Heterogeneous groups take longer to develop and tend to be less cohesive initially. However, they may ultimately be preferable for more in-depth treatment because of their capacity to delve deeper into issues and confront problems from a variety of often conflicting styles and perspectives (Yalom, 1985, 1995).

Basic Classifications

The most basic classifications distinguish between *primary* and *secondary* or *psyche* and *socio groups*. A *primary group* is a small group that meets over time and in which relationships are formed; it has a defined purpose and identity. A *secondary group* is larger and, although it has an identity (e.g., all social workers or all Catholics or Croatians), its members do not typically know each other or even interact face-to-face. They may, however, have a strong emotional bond. For instance, all paraplegics or Vietnam veterans may feel a natural bond even though they do not know each other. A *psyche group* is a small inwardly oriented group that meets to share interpersonal problems for the purpose of growth, understanding, and change. A *socio group* is outwardly oriented and exists for the purpose of affecting change in society, a community, or a legislative or political structure.

TYPES OF GROUPS

Group *types* include therapy, counseling, encounter and sensitivity, self-help, and support groups. In current practice, most social workers interact with many types of groups in several capacities. They are therefore encouraged to refer to the more advanced textbooks that provide in-depth information about groups. Even the descriptions of the types of existing groups vary considerably. For instance, Zastrow (1999) lists the types of common groups as social conversation, recreation–skill building, education, problem solving and decision making, self-help, socialization, therapy, sensitivity, and encounter. However, others (Henry, 1992; Yalom, 1995) suggest that there are five most commonly encountered types. These are introduced and discussed in the following paragraphs.

Therapy Groups

A *therapy group* deals with significant interpersonal or emotional problems in depth. Its members may be inpatient or outpatient, and the presenting problems are often defined by diagnoses in the *DSM-IV-TR* (2000). The purpose of the therapy group is to use group dynamics in a psychotherapeutic manner to effect change in patients who need to explore and confront severe disorders or lifelong patterns of behavior. Therapy groups or group psychotherapy types can be further defined by their specific therapeutic approach. There are, for instance, *psychodynamic groups* (Grotjahn, 1977); *cognitive groups* (Beck, 1976); *behavioral groups* (Rose, 1990); and other therapy groups of a homogeneous nature that psychotherapeutically confront problems such as eating disorders, post-traumatic stress, victimization from rape or incest, and virtually all other diagnoses.

Counseling Groups

A *counseling group* helps members to deal with interpersonal problems from a here-and-now perspective by examining the process and interactions of the members. Group members are taught to adapt and utilize what they learn in that process to improve ongoing relationships and behaviors that have been problematic. Counseling groups do not delve quite as deeply as therapy groups and are usually shorter in duration.

Encounter and Sensitivity Groups

Encounter and sensitivity groups were widely used in the 1960s and 1970s as opportunities for healthy, well-functioning people to improve their interpersonal skills as well as develop new insights about themselves and their behavior. These groups shifted from a more academic or training orientation when Carl Rogers began to work with them, imbuing his here-and-now orientation with his focus on personal encounters between people motivated to be self-actualized. Corporations use these groups as a way of developing better supervisory and management skills for employees.

Self-Help Groups

Self-help groups consist of people who share a common problem or concern and who come together as peers to understand or solve that problem. Typically, they are directed by nonprofessional leaders who empower themselves or one of their members to facilitate the group. Some self-help groups are inner-focused and work to provide each other with mutual support around such issues as addiction (AA), obesity (Overeater's Anonymous), or problems with single parenting (Parents Without Partners). Others are more outwardly oriented or political, such as the National Organization of Women (NOW) or Families of Adult Mentally Ill (FAMI).

Support Groups

Support groups can be considered self-help when they are directed by their own members, but often the groups are led by social workers or other professionals. The common purpose of support groups is to share ideas, suggestions, and advice and to provide support. They often form on the basis of a common tragedy such as a divorce or because of societal biases such as homophobia. In such instances, there is a healthy emphasis on recognizing that members should not self-blame but, rather, should learn to live with or respond to the biases and prejudices of others in a constructive manner. For instance, survivors of incest, rape, or alcoholic parents find great help and solace in sharing their experiences with other survivors who help them to understand their feelings by reflecting and discussing common reactions. So, if one member begins to experience depression or "self-blame" for whatever happened to him or her, a fellow member often angrily and appropriately confronts that person with the fact that he or she was the injured party or was victimized and that it was the perpetrator who was wrong. This same observation might not have been previously possible for the individual to make regarding himself or herself. The group helps members to externalize and objectify the experience since they see it in relation to their fellow group members. Members quickly consciously recognize that the guilt and self-blame that are inaccurately displayed by fellow members are equally untrue in relation to their own experiences.

BASICS: GETTING STARTED

Setting

The *setting* or room where groups meet must meet certain essential requirements. For both practical and symbolic reasons, the place where people gather must be neat, clean, well-lit, ventilated, and comfortable. If the room is too large, such as in a gym or auditorium, members may feel unprotected and small or relatively insignificant. In fact, they almost invariably end up huddling in a corner under such circumstances. Likewise, it is not beneficial to crowd groups into a small space. This also leads to discomfort and a feeling of being restricted or even subtly pressured to relate, which would likely have the opposite effect. The setting must also be quiet, closed, and free of distractions.

Interruptions

Interruptions should not be tolerated. Group sessions must not be interrupted by telephone calls to members or to the social worker, by individual therapy, by family visits (for inpatient groups), by other activities or groups, or by even mild sickness. Some social work agencies and residential or inpatient treatment settings regularly, but inadvertently, undermine the tremendous therapeutic effects of groups by allowing interruptions. This is done by agencies that excuse members or that require members to miss a group session whenever the members' individual therapists schedule sessions to see them. Even social activities or arts and crafts sessions occasionally take precedence over scheduled group therapy. The clear but countertherapeutic message in these instances is that the group is not very important.

Inpatient psychiatric groups are notorious for interruptions, and some even meet out in the open common rooms where staff and others drop in and out or idly listen for entertaining stories from troubled members. This is very inappropriate. The clear message that must be reinforced over and over, verbally and behaviorally, is that the group is very important; the time allotted for those sessions cannot be usurped.

Confidentiality

Confidentiality is essential; if a social worker cannot protect it by having a closed, secure, consistent time and place to meet without distractions, then it is better not to have a group at all. The simple but unambiguous message that must be conveyed is that no one outside the exclusive membership of the group will ever know what is discussed within the group. Obvious exceptions, which need to be addressed, might involve the necessity of discussing clinical records with treatment staff, supervision, or the occurrence of certain emergencies such as suicidal behavior.

If clients are sincere in their desire to resolve or work through their problems in the context of their group, then they must always be on time and ready to talk and explore issues in an open and in-depth manner. Of course, this requires a high degree of trust, and some clients have difficulty in this area. The social worker therefore clearly conveys the message that whatever a member says in the group is important and will be treated sensitively and protected in utmost confidence.

Frequency and Duration

Practical issues—such as the nature and severity of the problem; the needs and motivations of members; and even the resources of the agency, hospital, or practice—will invariably dictate the *frequency and duration* of group sessions. However, as a general rule, standard outpatient treatment groups meet weekly for 90-minute sessions. Since groups do involve several people and their dynamics are more complex and sometimes even cumbersome than individual interventions, they typically take some time to develop before the group discusses substantive issues. The standard 50-minute or hour-long session used for individuals is insufficient to get into issues in depth, though any session over two hours at a time tends to lead to fatigue. Support groups and self-help or mutual aid groups tend to meet on a monthly basis with a time range of from one to two hours, while inpatient groups may even meet as often as twice a day to make the greatest possible impact during hospitalization.

Group work in social work has also utilized marathon sessions. These are extended group meetings that last from 4 straight hours to 24 or even 48 hours of continuous discussion, confrontation, support, and feedback. Marathon sessions are not often used in outpatient treatment since the typical course of improvement necessitates time (such as a week between sessions) to thoroughly integrate and comprehend what was discussed in the previous session. In fact, research indicates that, 12 weeks after these dramatic marathon encounters, there were no differences in the results between members of those groups and those in individual treatment who had not been in marathon group sessions (Lieberman, Yalom, & Miles, 1973).

Group Composition

The selection of members for a group requires a decision regarding individuals who will *not* be appropriate. Attempts at balancing group composition between assertive, talkative members and quiet members or similar attempts to prejudge a group's potential interactions have generally failed. Human behavior is simply too complex, and people react to each other in group settings in relatively unpredictable manners because of many factors. The individual who presents himself or herself at individual intake as calm, detached, and articulate may appear anxious and unable to speak at a first group session that includes an aggressive member; or, a very depressed, lethargic individual may become uncharacteristically talkative in the presence of a socially or physically attractive fellow group member. When one compounds all of these complex but often subtle interactional possibilities based upon the number of members in the group, the notion of "fine-tuning" or even balancing groups becomes understandably daunting, even absurd.

There are two generally agreed-upon rules for membership or group composition. First, the group members must be at similar levels of ego strength or functionality. Second, certain individuals should *not* be included, at least in mixed or heterogeneous groups (although homogeneous groups composed entirely of such people are often the treatment of choice).

The term *similar ego strengths* refers to individuals who have similar capacities to comprehend or process communication. A person who is literally too "abnormal" or who deviates too far from the norm of the group in terms of behavior, ability to communicate, or ability to understand the level of discussion or because of significant deviations from the other members intellectually or cognitively should not be included. For instance, an individual with severe dementia or organic brain damage will be excluded from discussion in a typical heterogeneous treatment group and will become the group deviant because he or she cannot "fit in" or interact at the same level. This result is countertherapeutic for both the individual and the group as a whole.

The second basis for choosing membership in heterogeneous treatment groups involves specific problem classifications or diagnoses of individuals who are less appropriate for heterogeneous groups. Social group workers find that these individuals perform poorly in mixed groups and instead require individual treatment. Occasionally, these individuals achieve a level in their individual work at which they can join a group. Alternatively, they may do well in homogeneous groups where the particular concern or disorder can be specifically addressed (Yalom, 1995).

Less Appropriate Candidates for Heterogeneous Groups   *Withdrawn, schizoid personalities* are extremely shy and emotionally deficient individuals. These individuals, who are sometimes diagnosed as schizoid personalities, include individuals who are incapable of displaying, communicating, or apparently even experiencing typical human reactions. They withdraw in virtually all types of emotional interactions. The *Social Work Dictionary* (Barker, 1995) defines *schizoid* behavior as being "characterized by an ingrained pattern of aloofness, social withdrawal, indifference to the feelings of others, and a restricted range of emotions. Often described as 'loners' " (p. 335).

Monopolists, a term used by Yalom (1995) in his list of particularly problematic patients in groups, refers to one who is unable to share time or attention with others and is compelled to talk incessantly. These individuals are not simply talkative people. In fact, reasonably talkative individuals are excellent for groups. Monopolists are individuals who become anxious whenever anyone else talks or becomes the focus of the group. It is important to also distinguish between monopolizers and simply anxious people who excessively verbalize initially as a way of dealing with transitional insecurity in early group sessions but who eventually "settle down." This latter type of person often helps the group to get started, whereas the monopolist interferes with that process by stopping anyone else from self-expression, thereby leading to disastrous consequences for the group.

Depressive personalities are individuals who are chronically predisposed to seeing the world negatively, excluding virtually all positive perceptions while focusing entirely upon negatives. These are not depressed individuals, who often respond well to groups, but, rather, are persons who will manage to find the cloud in even the bluest sky. Their core personality or worldview is tainted by a pervasive gloom or darkness that undermines their capacity to "improve" since treatment inherently implies positive or constructive change. Such individuals are unable or cognitively unwilling to accept positive change or growth and are, therefore, best treated by individual cognitive therapy with the possibility of moving into a group when positive changes occur.

Depressive personalities discount and, therefore, significantly undermine the therapeutic potential of a group and each of its members by persistently verbalizing their views. They believe that virtually all aspects of life are bad or hopeless; furthermore, any change, improvement, or instructive insight shared in the group by others is simply an aberration. The typical response of individuals with a depressive personality is negative. Therefore, if a client joyfully shares with the group a successful exchange with an abusive partner, he or she will be met by the depressive group member with scorn or the warning that "You shouldn't get too excited. You know you're just a weak doormat and next time you'll back off again like you always do." A group facilitator cannot risk the potential of the entire group by including individuals who are not yet capable of incorporating or accepting obvious signs of positive change and improvement.

The term *conversion disorders*—formerly known as hysterics, true hysterics, or hysterical reactions—refers to individuals who somaticize or convert psychological disorders into focalized physical problems. Freud treated many "hysterics." Even Hippocrates referred to this disorder many centuries ago. In this disorder, an individual takes a traumatic incident such as viewing the death of a parent by a gun and then develops "blindness" or, in essence, denies his or her own physical ability to witness such a painful event again. Many social workers, particularly Freudians, view this disorder in terms of its symbolic significance. An individual with a conversion disorder would not respond in a heterogeneous treatment group because the individual believes his or her problem to be physical, not psychological. The group would be similarly confused by the inclusion of this individual with an apparent physical problem. A homogeneous treatment group composed of conversion disorder members would be an excellent treatment choice since it can focus immediately, directly, and completely on the denial, conversions, and even symbolisms relevant to all members in common.

Manic, overly reactive, or extremely dramatic individuals are frequently poor candidates for groups because of their effects on others. Again, this is not a reference to moderately overreactive persons, who are, in fact, excellent candidates. This exclusion is for people who scream and run out of a room for fear of contagion when another group member sneezes or coughs. These individuals are so agitated or extreme in their reactive behavior that they make other group members withdraw out of disbelief, fear, or confusion.

Sometimes, such individuals behave this way to draw attention. In other instances, the manic or hyperactive individual exhibits extreme but directionless thoughts, verbalizations, or behaviors. Either way, these clients need individual treatment and are fairly destructive within mixed groups. Even homogeneous groups with this composition would be extremely difficult to facilitate or manage, although such groups are potentially therapeutic in well-controlled inpatient settings.

Antisocial personality disorders, psychopaths, and *sociopaths* refer to categories that vary in terms of social science perspective, presumed etiology, and even historical definition. Essentially, these are individuals who not only lack the capacity to empathize or even care about others but they also have the potential to be dangerously self-serving. Psychoanalysts describe psychopaths as lacking a superego and, therefore, unable to feel guilt or even develop a conscience. Biologically oriented professionals suggest that it is at least partially genetic and that such individuals are lacking a basic organic capability to feel a genuine concern for others.

Behaviorists, sociologists, and social systems–oriented clinicians prefer the term *sociopaths*, which suggests that the social environment in which such individuals were born and raised was so deviant and pervasive in its effects that the individual cannot relate to healthy, caring relationships. The best known of these individuals are the multiple killers Charles Manson and Jeffrey Dahmer. Traditional forms of group treatment that rely upon some capacity to understand and, therefore, relate to the problems and emotions of others have limited effect. Homogeneous groups of such individuals using strict controls and behavioral goals in settings such as prisons or forensic inpatient facilities can positively modify behavior.

It is important for social workers to balance the best interests of the individual as well as of the group. Individuals who need to be excluded from heterogeneous groups are better served in individual treatment or, occasionally, in homogeneous groups, where the specific, idiosyncratic needs of that type of presenting problem are addressed. The type of individual who epitomizes that need for homogeneous grouping is the *alcoholic or addicted individual.*

Drug and alcohol addictions are problems that should be treated in homogenous groups of fellow addicts and not mixed with other treatment problems. While the treatment of choice for alcohol and other addictions is group therapy, individuals are not well served when they are combined with a variety of dissimilar individuals. In such instances, their tendency to avoid, minimize, and deny their disorder may limit their opportunities to truly confront the addiction and focus on it above all other problems.

Occasionally, alcoholics and other chemically addicted individuals may be put into heterogeneous treatment groups. This can only be done if the social worker recognizes that the addiction itself will not be significantly affected. Only a homogeneous group of fellow addicts can result in a positive treatment outcome, but a heterogeneous group may help with other related problems. As long as an alcoholic is an active member of AA or, initially, of a homogeneous treatment group designed for alcoholics, he or she may additionally profit from another mixed group as well where problems such as their depression or family issues can be addressed.

Case 5.1 presents a staff discussion of developing guidelines for starting a group.

Case 5.1: Starting a Group

The senior social work staff have been asked to attend a meeting with several psychologists, psychiatrists, and psychiatric nurses to develop guidelines at their agency, the Family Service Counseling Center of Cincinnati. This agency has been asked to develop groups due to its long and successful history with them. However, the large insurance company that provides managed care to its many members first wants to know if the staff of the agency has the interest and capability to begin such an endeavor. The insurance company also wants the staff to give them some guidelines regarding appropriate referrals. The staff decided to use the five "getting started" issues (setting, interruptions, confidentiality, frequency and duration, and composition) as the basis for their discussion.

"I want to thank all of you for coming in with such brief notice, but National Health Company, which is the biggest insurer in this area, wants to contract with us to run all of its groups. Their thousands of members include the young and old, male and female, all racial and ethnic groups, and the whole range of both physical and social/psychological problems. Let's begin by discussing whether we can realistically get started. What do you think?" the senior social worker asked her staff.

"Well, we have four conference rooms that we've used for years for groups here at the main office," began one social worker.

"Make that three. The fourth one was Tom's old office, and if we try to get more than six people in that space, people get too crowded," said another.

"Okay. We need at least six people in the group in addition to the facilitator but not more than nine. We physically have the settings for three groups here, plus another four group rooms at the satellite office."

"Great. But how about facilities for the elderly or disabled? We don't even have adequate wheelchair access. And I believe that National Health Care owns the Forman Center, that nursing home on Fifth Street. They'll want us to run groups there as well."

"That's no problem. I've been there several times, and they have a conference room and a nice big day room where the residents meet and mingle."

"Well, the conference room is fine, but the open day room is out of the question. Whenever I've been there, the nurses and other staff are constantly coming and going with medications, telephone calls, and just people 'hanging around.' "

"What's wrong with hanging around? Frankly, I think that can be therapeutic in that setting."

"Sure, I agree, but you can't run a group there. Not only are the interruptions distracting but there is no assurance of confidentiality. We can't have people talk about serious issues and problems in a big, open room where anyone walking through can listen in."

"Okay. We've talked a little about getting started with kids and seniors. How about the majority of these people? Aren't they going to be adults with everything from chronic health problems to severe psychological problems?"

"Not necessarily," said the director. "National will still use St. Francis Hospital for psychiatric services for more severe cases, both inpatient and outpatient."

Several members laughed, and others started talking among themselves, so the director said, "It seems there is some concern here. Sue, you look worried."

"I am," replied Sue. "You know that St. Francis is only treating its own inpatient people, so we would still have to see some clinically depressed people as well as a wide variety of other problems from mild family disagreements to functional schizophrenics and people with bipolar disorders. And what about drugs and alcohol? We do not have the expertise in that area."

"Those are all good points, Sue. What are your thoughts on that?" asked the director of her staff.

"It's doable. Let's face it. We're like every other social service agency around here. We see that range all the time. As long as we do not have to see the most dysfunctional who would not benefit from our typically 'mixed' groups, we'll do fine. Most of our real treatment or therapeutic groups already have a variety of presenting problems or diagnoses. As long as the groups consist of people who can all relate at some meaningful level, and no one is too 'deviant,' those heterogeneous groups are great."

"I don't like that term 'deviant.' What do you mean?" asked the social work student who had been quietly taking notes up until now.

"I mean that you cannot have one person in the group who stands out so far from the rest that he or she will just never fit in. I know that sounds pretty subjective, but it tends to be the individual who cannot follow the discussion because of significant intellectual deficits or psychological disturbance."

"So what do you do with them?" asked the student, sensing that the agency was considering dropping groups for its most needy clients.

"You form homogeneous groups for them. That's by far the best approach. We can set up some homogeneous groups for different types of physical disabilities and other groups for some of those long-term psychologically dysfunctional people who need therapy but in a supportive or psychoeducational context rather than in an insight-oriented group."

"By the way, the same concept is true for any drug or alcohol groups we might run," interjected the student's field instructor, sensing that the student was still not convinced that client needs were really being met. "Right now, we don't have the specialized expertise required to lead groups of people addicted to drugs or alcohol. The fact of the matter is that we have to hire new staff who will run homogeneous groups composed entirely of alcoholics or addicts. They do not do very well with their addictions when mixed in with others. They tend to maintain their denial and often avoid their addictions unless grouped together and put into groups designed just for them where the right mix of confrontation and support is provided."

"I think we're really coming up with some practical and realistic answers and guidelines here, but can we actually schedule these groups?" asked the director as she enthusiastically took notes.

"Sure, as long as we all switch to the night shift," said an experienced but skeptical staff member as the entire staff laughed nervously.

"When you have groups like this, there is no way you can schedule during the daytime. If there are so many different groups, we'll have to schedule every hour from five o'clock on," he said despondently.

"Actually, it's worse than that. We'll need a minimum of an hour and a half per group, and, to really get these to work, we need to schedule them every week." Several staff groaned as the social worker continued. "These groups really are great if you do them right, and not all of them have to meet every week. For instance, for the support groups or the psychoeducational groups where the focus is less on therapeutic insight or complex problem solving, you could get by with bi-weekly or even monthly sessions. It's really only the more mainstream treatment groups where you need the weekly sessions and usually a more open-ended membership. The others might be workable as close-ended workshops. You know, where you say right at the beginning that you'll run 8 to 20 sessions, maintaining the same members throughout the sessions. And you focus on teaching members social skills or providing more of a supportive environment dealing with a single common problem that each member shares. They primarily need to learn how to cope or manage the issue."

"Those groups are also a little less problematic in relation to confidentiality." Several nodded in agreement. "People understandably worry when they come into some therapy groups. They're afraid someone in the group will talk about those innermost personal problems to others."

"That's a good point. In fact, it's so obvious that I sometimes forget to emphasize it since it's just a given part of my social work background, but our clients don't know this."

"Absolutely true. However, I think it has to be emphasized in some of the close-ended support or psychoeducational groups as much as in the open-ended therapeutic groups."

Several nodded in agreement. The director ended the staff meeting, saying, "Thank you all very much. You've done a great job in providing us with some guidelines on beginning a wide variety of groups."

STAGES OF GROUP DEVELOPMENT

The main reason to study and understand the way groups grow and develop is that practitioners must be able to anticipate and support that progress. For instance, knowing that groups typically develop some balance-of-power conflicts soon after the early polite phase can allow the social worker to plan for and resolve such conflict. Likewise, the ending phase of the group typically results in a discussion of issues and problems that the worker may have thought were resolved long ago but that need to be revisited as members prepare for life without the group. The role of the group facilitator is to be a supportive yet sometimes confrontive leader who guides the members through these stages. The more he or she knows what to expect, the better prepared he or she will be to plan and support the group's progress.

The stages of group development are essentially the same as stages observed in the process of the formation of any other relationship. The task of the group facilitator is to make the process more efficient and effective by getting individuals to open up and share thoughts, fears, past transgressions, and hopes for future improvement. The stages are predictable and comparable to a situation in which two people meet in a potential dating relationship.

- *Beginning* The two persons are a little reserved as each checks out the other person. The two only discuss safe topics, while often unconsciously comparing each other to others they have known with similar appearances, thoughts, opinions, emotions, and histories. There may be some nervous ambiguity based on desires to get to know each other but also fears of being hurt—or just wasting time. So some "approach-avoidance" feelings arise during this awkward phase.
- *Setting guidelines* Some differences develop as the two individuals decide whether to continue seeing each other. They will find that some interests vary and that they need to discuss their different preferences. One may want to go bowling or to a sporting event, while the other may prefer a movie or dinner at a good restaurant. If the couple can comfortably resolve those inevitable differences, the relationship will

grow. If the differences lead only to angry and unresolved conflict in which neither will compromise, then the relationship will stop or stay stuck until the couple can work out the differences. How the couple deals with this stormy or conflictual stage often "makes or breaks" the relationship. Many relationships either end or reach an impasse at this phase.

- *Agreeing* The third stage of a growing relationship involves setting norms and further clarifying likes and dislikes. The two persons may now see themselves as a couple after having spent some time and effort in working through various small differences and learning to adapt to each other's styles, needs, feelings, and behaviors. There may even be renewed efforts to consciously change to maintain or improve the relationship. Thus, one of the two will stop pushing efforts to go bowling since the other has no interest in it but will continue to occasionally suggest watching at least major football games on television. One might begin suggesting movies and restaurants that would not only be unobjectionable but also might actually be enjoyable for the other, thus bringing them closer together with common interests. If they talk openly about their relationship and how it makes them feel, then they grow as individuals and as a couple.

- *Working* The working stage for this hypothetical couple arrives when they have become committed to the relationship and are getting a great deal of enjoyment and growth as a result of being together. They have gotten past the superficial niceties and are no longer overly concerned if they see each other as they are—without makeup or pretense. If the couple can reach this stage, then they have found something worthwhile and profoundly significant. Ideally, they each finally have someone with whom they can really share life's problems in a manner that allows them to be themselves—or even better than the way they used to be. A relationship that nourishes their best instincts and gives them an improved sense of self based on concern, support, and honest communication from each other is, indeed, a cherished part of their lives.

- *Ending* Finally, there is an ending. While couples may do this by committing to each other (such as in marriage or in an agreement to be monogamous), they may also agree to stop seeing each other when the relationship no longer meets the needs of each person. They may part ways, amicably or otherwise, with each person ideally being able to learn and grow from the experience.

Groups follow these same stages if properly led. The task of the social worker is to support the healthy development of the group by being open, honest, nondefensive, and nonjudgmental and by doing everything possible to keep communicating. In the analogy of the couple, the process is described as normal and healthy; and, indeed, it is. But it is not necessarily the norm in society. Relationships often falter and die, or they move on at only a superficial level because people feel that they cannot really say what they feel. The task of the group worker is to guide the group members through the ideal stages of relationship formation.

There are other models of the stages of group development. Historically, the best-known and most widely used description of the stages of group development in the field of social work is that of Garland, Jones, and Kilodny (1965). They observed groups of normal children and adolescents age 9 through 16 in organized group settings and saw the development of five specific stages. The first stage, which they describe as *preaffiliation* or *approach/avoidance,* is one of polite distance and ambivalence. In the *power and control* stage, group members test the leader, establish rank or status among members, develop cliques, and may exclude some members or even drop out of the group. *Intimacy* develops in the third stage as the members grow in their acceptance of the group and even see it as similar to a family. The fourth stage, *differentiation,* further allows for individual differences, partially based on recognition of the group's acceptance; strong, supportive cohesiveness; and caring. Finally, at *separation,* members in this stage reflect upon and summarize what has happened.

The other most frequently cited model of group stages is the one by Tuckman and Jensen (1977) and Tuckman (1965). This model first describes *forming,* which is tentative, polite, ambiguous, and filled with silences. Next comes *storming* in which hostility develops, attendance is poor, ideas are criticized, and members interrupt each other. *Norming* involves efforts to agree on rules and develop consensus while becoming more supportive. *Performing* is the problem-solving stage in which people can make decisions together and work together cooperatively and with less emotionality. The last stage is *adjourning,* when members disintegrate the group, often indicating regret, and emotions once again increase as they separate from one another.

Sue Henry's insightful four-dimensional approach to social work groups focuses very clearly on the importance of the stages. Her *Group Skills in Social Work* (Henry, 1992) devotes separate chapters to each of the issues and dynamics of the six stages she defines: *initial, convening, formation, conflict/disequilibrium, maintenance,* and *termination.* She stresses that the stages are never perfectly linear and that groups revisit the stages periodically, moving forward and backward.

GROUP NORMS

Norms are standards of expected behavior. They are less precise than rules but more pervasive. While rules can be clearly described and infractions are, therefore, obvious (e.g., a member was late or interrupted another), following or not following norms is more difficult to monitor.

There are six norms, several of which originated with Garland, Jones, and Kilodny (1965), that are relevant to current groups. The social worker needs to model, facilitate, and explain these norms to the members:

1. *The group is a unit.* The facilitator reinforces the cohesiveness and therapeutic force of the group by asking for the *group's* reaction or ideas and often using the terms *us, we,* or *ours* rather than focusing on separateness. This norm suggests that the group is a *unit*—a unified, single system of support and caring for each member. It also deliberately deemphasizes the social worker as the leader or expert so that *group* dynamics can be stressed.

    This norm is particularly salient after the group gets comfortably started and has gone through its first two stages (i.e., the *beginning* stage and the *setting guidelines* stage) and progresses to the third stage, *agreeing.* There is often a desire or commitment at that time to bond and become a unit or come together in a conscious and deliberate way.

2. *The group is important.* This seemingly obvious norm is often undervalued. Groups are sometimes subtly devalued within treatment settings by the way they are scheduled, interrupted, composed, or facilitated by untrained leaders. Scheduling a convenient time and place tells clients whether the agency or facilitator genuinely wants the group. For instance, if a new group is scheduled during the middle of the day when potential members have family and work obligations, or meets in a dingy room in the basement, then the potential members are given a message that they are not seriously being encouraged to join; or, if they join the group, they are not well respected. Interruptions, as previously mentioned, have occasionally been allowed in agencies that would never consider interrupting individual treatment sessions.

    The manner in which some agencies compose groups is inefficient. For instance, some agencies "store" clients in groups to wait until individual (interpreted as the *real* treatment) can begin. An equally inappropriate standard exists in agencies in which the less-"interesting" or less-introspective or less-motivated clients are put into groups so that individual treatment can be reserved for those who can gain the most from it. The importance of a group can be appropriately reinforced when agencies use social workers who are well trained in group dynamics and who recognize groups as being an extremely therapeutic tool for change. Such staff members model their attitude toward the group by their enthusiasm and commitment, and they clearly convey their regard for the group, its members, and its therapeutic potential.

3. *Each member is important.* This is not a refutation of the first norm but suggests that each member has worth in helping other group members.

Group members typically focus on the social worker for direction, advice, and counsel. Initially, members may tend to minimize the possible therapeutic gain of listening to fellow members. In fact, they often feel that their fellow members are unlikely to be too helpful since they obviously have similar problems of their own. This attitude can change quickly as the facilitator encourages members to talk and share experiences with one another as a way of learning new insights or behaviors from each other. The group facilitator certainly is important but primarily as a model and facilitator. As such, he or she must give enthusiastic and genuine support to the opinions and verbalizations of every member. The facilitator may initially need to deflect the focus away from him or herself and toward the client members as a way of demonstrating regard for those members and also as a clear way of showing that each member has valuable ideas and thoughts. This emphasis on showing high regard and esteem for the persons who compose a group also has inherent therapeutic value by virtue of the support, care, and recognition demonstrating the worth of the person.

4. *Nonjudgmental and open attitude.* This norm encourages openness and a genuine acceptance of others, including their thoughts, attitudes, and past and ongoing behaviors. This acceptance is not the same as supporting or condoning any behavior. For instance, groups are the treatment of choice for victims of such socially deviant behavior as rape, child molestation, and sexual assault. The clearly modeled norm of nonjudgment allows group members to talk openly and freely, probably for the first time in their lives, about a particularly heinous act in which they have been victimized. Such victimization becomes more burdensome and intractable with time when left to fester without opportunities to talk and explore their hurt with others. The same nonjudgmentalism lets victims discuss their own doubts and inappropriate self-blame in ways they never could with family or well-meaning friends. Thus, the victims of incest, rape, or abuse have the freedom to explore their victimization without other group members naively or inappropriately judging them or their reactions.

By the same token, the aggressors must be provided the opportunity to reflect openly about their past behavior. Rapists, child molesters, and perpetrators of incest are understandably condemned by society. However, from a purely therapeutic standpoint, such condemnation is countertherapeutic. It disallows a thorough discussion or exploration of the causes or bases for the behavior. Then the causes of the behavior are suppressed even more, making it more difficult to treat. Homogeneous groups of aggressive perpetrators allow a forum for the aggressors to begin returning to some semblance of *normalcy* as opposed to *deviancy*.

This is the first, but perhaps the most important, step toward resolving or treating their problem.

5. *Groups require risks and trust.* Successful groups are invariably those in which members have to "take the plunge" and open up to others by divulging thoughts, feelings, and behaviors they have never entrusted to anyone else. The members of many groups facilitated by social workers are particularly unfamiliar with trusting others; consequently, they do not risk further hurt or pain by verbally putting themselves in a vulnerable position. This sensitivity to their vulnerability is precisely why groups have such tremendous potential for them. A supportive group that gives members an opportunity to trust others, for perhaps the first time in their lives, encourages them to express what has caused them lifetime suffering. Victims can finally say that their stepfathers molested them and they hate them. Aggressors can admit that they have beaten their own children when they have used drugs; or they can admit that they cannot control their addiction to alcohol, sex, or gambling.

The act of taking verbal risks within a group setting indicates to the individual and to fellow members that they believe others care and will help them, not hurt them. This act is therapeutic since it requires that the risk takers make a conscious decision to let their guards down and trust others to enter their private world of pain, suffering, and self-recrimination. Even the powerful therapeutic dynamics observed in effective groups will have difficulty ending these challenging and complex problems. However, if the group worker can move the members toward taking risks and trusting others, tremendous opportunities in the treatment process are likely to develop.

6. *Groups are flexible and spontaneous.* This norm refers to the need for the structure and topics of discussion to remain flexible. Groups should not be too structured or unstructured. In fact, there is a need for a balance or even a tension between the two extremes. Shorter-term groups that have an educational component (e.g., dealing with diabetes or being a caregiver for parents with Alzheimer's disease) will necessitate weekly topics and possibly some didactic presentations. Longer-term treatment groups are usually better left relatively unstructured to deal with here-and-now issues that relate to concerns of the group at the moment.

This is not to suggest that treatment groups meet from week to week without a clear direction. Quite the opposite is true. The social worker goes into each session with a list of concerns and issues that need to be addressed while remaining flexible. The facilitator may go into the session with the idea that there are three or four issues that should be addressed at some point soon. For instance, he or she may decide that the last session was particularly quiet, perhaps due to an argument over parenting between two members. Or the social worker may have decided that one or two specific members, or the group as a whole, should be more actively encouraged to take risks and that a structured exercise in trust building will be attempted at the following session.

Of course, spontaneity and flexibility should still be maintained. Thus, if a member comes to the group wanting to share a significant issue, and if it furthers the worker's goal of opening the group up more, then the worker would support the spontaneous discussion.

Finally, *rules* within the group should be discussed. Although the term *rules* may seem rigid, some *rules* are essential and cannot be broken without negative ramifications. How these rules are communicated will vary based upon the group. For instance, a highly motivated support group of single mothers might only be encouraged to attend regularly and be on time, while also being instructed to only allow one discussion to take place at a time during the sessions. On the other hand, acting out adolescents might actually need a clear (and possibly printed) list of rules. These rules cannot be overly rigid (e.g., *no swearing* may severely limit the vocabulary of some members), but rules help prepare the group and provide direction from their initial session.

No name-calling might be a rule suggested in an early session in the context of explaining that group members need to be clear in what they say to each other. In other words, the social worker prepares the group members by explaining that they must use *descriptions* of behaviors or feelings toward another member rather than vague or often intimidating names or insults. Other typical rules include a commitment to attend all sessions (unless there is a severe emergency); an agreement to be at the meetings on time; and even to be open, honest, and flexible.

TASKS OF THE GROUP WORKER

In the most basic terms, the job of the social group worker is to begin the group, help it grow and develop, encourage meaningful interaction, and bring the group to a close. More specifically, there are eleven tasks:

1. *Select members.* The social group worker needs to be aware of the issues of *group composition,* which addresses individuals for whom groups are not recommended. The group worker must also recruit members by talking to colleagues about the goals and purpose of the group and then calling and meeting with potential members. Occasionally, recruitment is very easy. Some individuals are highly motivated to participate and will strongly request that they be allowed to join. Many transitional support groups for recently divorced individuals or the recently unemployed may

quickly become filled with individuals who are highly motivated to talk. In other instances, the group worker may have to aggressively recruit and convince members such as the depressed who are without hope for themselves or alcoholics in denial. A related task involves ensuring that potential members can or will make a commitment and that their schedules, finances, and time constraints permit them to join and attend regularly.

2. *Physically set up the group.* This involves not only choosing a convenient setting (as previously described) but also ensuring that the room is always open when the group arrives, that chairs are arranged in a circle, and that coffee is available when appropriate. These mundane and seemingly minor details often either "make or break" a group. If the group meeting place is repeatedly relocated, or if the scheduled meeting time is occasionally changed, or if the room is not appropriately set up on time, a group can fail. Inconsistency in such seemingly minor details can easily discourage or confuse clients who usually have some degree of ambivalence about participating in a group setting. Some may conclude that the group worker is either poorly organized or disinterested, which could be sufficient reason for potential members to quit the group.

3. *Prepare the members.* Either before the first group session or more informally during the course of the first few meetings, the social group worker needs to prepare the members for their constructive and informed involvement in the group.

   First, the group worker must educate the group members in the way the group will work and how all members can help each other. He or she must explain how individuals are all products of their interactions with others. Further, it must be explained that the group will provide a structure in that each person can learn more as he or she interacts. Then those interactions will be analyzed and explored.

   Second, the group worker needs to anticipate problems related to the inherent slowness in "start-up time" or possible delay in addressing the problems of each individual. Ambivalence needs to be discussed early and openly with the worker, encouraging both questions and ventilation from the onset of the group interaction. A great deal of support and assurance is needed while preparing members for initial problems such as feeling that they are being ignored or given less attention than others. Realistically, the first few weeks of the group sessions will witness a great deal of insecurity among group members. This may result in a higher likelihood of premature termination or dropping out since group members are forced to wait to share the facilitator's time and attention. The social worker should prepare the members for this possible disappointment by discussing it and assuring people that the group will grow and develop from this slow and awkward stage into a highly supportive and therapeutic system *if* they are patient and make a personal commitment.

Third, the group worker prepares the members by asking for and discussing expectations. Have they had previous group experiences? What were they and were they valuable? What are their fears or concerns? The facilitator might even encourage discussion of negative stereotypes of groups such as the notoriously confrontive and invasive group techniques of the 1970s or even those used today by some cults. It may be helpful to address the preconceived notion that group interventions or therapy are similar to individual therapy but that members have to interact with each other as they develop a therapeutic system called the group.

4. *Set a tone and model it.* The group worker needs to be a model in relation to the *norms* of the group by discussing and showing members that the group is to be a supportive unit that is important in their lives. Each person in the group needs to know that he or she is important and will be respected. No behavior, thoughts, or verbalizations will be judged or demeaned. The tone of the successful group also requires openness, trust in others, and confidence that what one shares with the group will be seriously considered. Finally, by modeling spontaneity and an unrehearsed, genuine display of emotion and concern for the group and all of its members, the worker can make the members feel more comfortable, relaxed, and open to reexamining themselves and their lives.

Fundamentally, the practitioner needs to model behaviors and attitudes that include openness, a nonjudgmental style, appropriate confrontation, and support to every member. Members need to be encouraged to talk to each other, not just to the facilitator; to take risks (although this may not be well received initially); and to openly explore thoughts, histories, and perceptions of themselves and the other members. These behaviors and attitudes should be demonstrated and modeled by the facilitator, not merely given as verbal instructions. In most respects, the process of facilitating a group is one of modeling the natural, healthy, supportive tendencies inherent (or at least potential) in virtually all people. However, social workers facilitating groups frequently need to accelerate and enhance that process by conscientious demonstration.

By the same token, it is necessary for the facilitator to be wary of modeling countertherapeutic styles, such as defensiveness or intellectualization. Group workers can expect to receive some degree of anger from members in early sessions since the group worker often represents an authority figure. If a group worker's response to a member is defensive, such a reaction can stifle further exploration. Similarly, while intellectual or vague psychodynamic conjectures may be appropriate in discussions with a co-facilitator *after* the group session, these same vague, abstract interpretations are counterproductive if engaged in during the sessions.

5. *Establish flexible goals and objectives.* The social worker running the group must come to each session with clear goals and objectives. Progress notes describing the group's dynamics should be meticulously maintained and reviewed. Major issues and concerns—and whether they have been sufficiently addressed—should be monitored. The worker reviewing and writing these notes must also ask, "What is *not* happening that should be?" "Are members avoiding certain issues?" "Are there unresolved past conflicts that affect current group dynamics?" "Are some members becoming passive, avoidant, or hostile toward others?" As such questions and their responses develop, the social worker can set specific objectives for each session while keeping track of overall therapeutic goals for the entire group. The task of the social worker is to keep the group and its members on target toward the achievement of therapeutic goals. Before each session, the worker may develop or review a list of objectives such as the following:

> Have Don clarify the remark he made to Mandy last week concerning her difficulty in relationships with men.
>
> Encourage Cindy to be more open. She has been unusually quiet and looks depressed. Nothing happened in the group to cause this, so what is happening in her new marriage?
>
> Bill missed the previous session and had a very vague excuse. He has been hostile and sullen, particularly toward Alice, his former friend in the group. This is confusing the other group members since their relationship has been dramatically reversed. Did Bill and Alice meet outside the group against the rules? How should I discuss this in the next session?

Such questions become agenda items and objectives to be addressed and resolved from session to session. If other pressing issues develop and the group time can be better spent addressing the newer, more immediate problem, then the worker can deal with that first. But the predetermined list of objectives must also be dealt with and soon thereafter to maintain the flow of the group. A moderate balance between addressing immediate problems or changing concerns and keeping track of the group's central purpose and direction must be maintained.

6. *Ensure full and open interaction.* The social worker needs to ensure that members are talking to each other, that everyone is involved and no one

is excluded, that they feel comfortable in talking and dealing with their problems by sharing with their fellow members, and that any hindrances to communication are clearly addressed.

Such hindrances may include both the individual members' personal difficulties (which are also the reason or part of the reason for their being in the group) and problems in the interpersonal dynamics of the group. Members come into the group with problems that can be generally understood in terms of faulty interpersonal relationships (or misinterpretation of them), and they bring those flawed interactional styles into the group to be examined. As members interact with one another in their typical flawed patterns, the group worker can help members understand what they are doing, why they are doing it, and what effect it has on their fellow group members and their peers outside of the group.

7. *Focus on here and now.* A distinct advantage of groups over individual treatment for examining interpersonal behavior is that the group is like a laboratory or controlled setting. Group worker facilitators objectively examine the combinations and interactions of members as they interact. The facilitators can improve the communication process by providing ongoing, interactive, or "real-time" input.

Group worker needs to take full advantage of the active, ongoing behavior of the members by keeping a focus on what is happening between and among members as it happens. Thus the facilitator does not have to rely upon the client's faulty or biased perspective regarding his or her interactions (e.g., "My wife says I criticize her all of the time, but I don't"). As members interact, they become oriented toward exploring and understanding their interactions from an objective, clear, and analytical perspective. When the group member who denies his negative and critical behavior exhibits that tendency in the group, the facilitator can point it out at that time (e.g., "John, this is the third time in ten minutes that you have criticized Louise. Do you think that this is the kind of behavior your wife seems to dislike?").

When a group member angrily explodes at another for being controlling and abusive, the facilitator and fellow members are right there to help that person understand what they are doing, why they are doing it, and how it affects others. It is difficult, if not impossible, to deny or resist feedback on a problematic behavior when it is clearly exhibited in a group session and pointed out at the same time. If a significant unresolved issue from childhood or from a recent relationship has surfaced, the "explosive" member can be helped to understand that he or she has a right to discuss attendant feelings. However, the way these feelings are being manifested as a pervasive anger directed inappropriately at the wrong target is not helpful to anyone. In fact, it is harmful. By inappropriately displacing their legitimate anger onto a particular population (e.g., all older men or women or people in authority), an individual impedes his or her potential to develop meaningful relationships or to work through his or her anger.

The here-and-now focus of groups allows members to point out to each other dysfunctional patterns, habits, or styles. As these past behaviors and patterns are displayed in the group sessions, the facilitator and the members can supportively provide feedback. Discussions should develop within the group concerning each member's perceptions of other members; and, since honesty and openness are encouraged, members are given, perhaps for the first time, clear feedback on their behavior and attitudes and how these behaviors affect others.

8. *Confront.* Some social workers have difficulty with the task of confronting group members. It is helpful for a group facilitator to remember that *confrontation,* or providing clear, often critical information to a person who needs it, is extremely therapeutic. Groups that focus on the here and now with honesty and openness lend themselves rather easily to supportive confrontation.

Typically, such behaviors as avoidance, displacement, anger, hostility, and the whole plethora of feelings and attitudes that develop into negative interactional patterns need to be addressed in groups. For example, the individual who has a long history of avoiding intimacy because of past unresolved issues of abandonment or abuse will also avoid intimacy and openness within the group. With the facilitator's direction, the group will ultimately need to confront the member with this avoidance.

Similarly, a group member who begins to look at and understand past problematic interactions based on unresolved feelings becomes very anxious. Historically, he or she has dealt with anxiety-producing relationships and concerns by avoiding relationships, thus avoiding pain in the short term but ultimately suffering from loneliness and self-induced social isolation. The facilitator and the group must confront the member and point out how he or she has displayed avoidance within the group. For instance, this individual will probably miss the session after his or her avoidance issue is first discussed. Painful as it may be, the member needs help in seeing the connection between old unresolved abuse or abandonment issues and current patterns of avoiding intimate relationships. When he or she misses group sessions that are anxiety producing, this affords an opportunity to supportively confront the individual with a clear example of his or her problematic behavior within the group.

9. *Provide feedback and analysis.* The group facilitator needs to clearly understand the interactions of the group and then provide feedback to members in ways members will hear and understand. Modeling this clear and supportive feedback process then becomes a norm for other members. Group members quickly learn that the purpose of the group is to help each other by providing care, support, and understanding and then sharing that understanding with each other.

If the facilitator shows concern through constructive observations and feedback on the behaviors, feelings, and interactions of all members, then members respond similarly. The group session becomes an exciting therapeutic event in which members come to take part in the process of learning about themselves and others. Group members gradually develop a style similar to that of the facilitator whereby they are sensitive to the way they and their fellow members affect each other by their words and actions. They learn to verbalize their feelings and observations to each other as well as come to expect and even welcome constructive feedback on their interactions within the group.

As members learn to incorporate this self-analytic and objective feedback, their self-understanding develops. They may recognize that their displaced anger is not "crazy" or bad but is counterproductive. This insight, provided through the group's feedback, can allow members to work through to the *real* sources of their anger. Their long histories of angry interactions with others can now be replaced by more open relationships, unencumbered by the misplaced anger that inappropriately distanced people in the past.

10. *Begin and end the sessions.* Group facilitators need to start each session with ideas, topics, or concerns. Often, this translates into getting individuals to communicate and focus on concerns in an organized manner. For example, the facilitator might begin the session this way: "Well, we looked a lot last week at Ginny's concern that the group was avoiding Bill and that Bill felt he had no real problem with his fistfights or drug use. I believe that Sue was starting to give us her reactions when we had to end last week. . . " If the group does not pick up on this, then the facilitator must make note of the continued avoidance and resistance and maintain efforts to explore this issue sometime later or confront the issue here and now.

Beginning and ending sessions are not only transitional times. They also tend to be the most awkward and crucial times. The beginning of a session lays the foundation for subsequent discussions; without clear and informed direction from the facilitator, the session may falter or wander aimlessly. So, too, ending a session is crucial because it is a time when structure needs to be reasserted or the group will lose direction. The facilitator must lead the group toward closure, which requires a summary of whatever has been discussed along with some observations and suggestions for subsequent discussion in the following session. Transitional times may be difficult for some members. These time periods may not flow as comfortably as discussions in the middle phases of group sessions. The facilitator can best use the beginning and ending times to reinforce insights and relevant observations that occurred in the session and to predispose the group toward dealing with issues that need to be addressed later.

11. *Encourage therapeutic factors.* This last group worker's task serves to introduce a basic and often quoted study. Initially defined by Irvin Yalom (1985, 1995), a psychiatrist and eminent group therapist, the "curative" or "therapeutic factors of groups" are, in his viewpoint, "natural lines of cleavage that divide the therapeutic experience into eleven primary factors" (p. 3). Those therapeutic factors of groups are essential to any successful group, so supporting them is an important task.

Therapeutic Factors

Experienced social work practitioners eventually recognize that their interventions are not based upon a narrow list of techniques or a "bag of tricks." Successful interactions are based upon a set of underlying dynamics that direct and define the appropriate course of action. New students in the field of social work invariably find comfort in having specific "things to do" under various circumstances or at different stages of interventions. Unfortunately, such narrow techniques are too often inappropriate for some populations at certain times. A balance must be struck between having a well-organized structure for each session and allowing for maximum openness and availability for spontaneous in-depth discussion of those feelings and concerns that are most pertinent to members at the moment. Rather than placing too much focus on either the process or the program, experienced group facilitators find that encouraging the development of the therapeutic factors inherent in well-led groups tends to be an excellent guideline.

Several group researchers have focused on trying to define the specific therapeutic or curative factors that seem to typically develop in successful groups. Those that social workers find the most useful in their own practices include (a) instillation of hope, (b) self-understanding, (c) imitation, (d) learning from interaction, (e) universalization of experience, (f) reality testing, (g) acceptance, (h) self-disclosure, (i) altruism, and (j) guidance (Reid, 1991).

In a classic work by Corsini and Rosenberg (1955), the following nine therapeutic factors were presented:

1. *Acceptance*—a sense of belonging and being emotionally supported and accepted by the group

2. *Altruism*—a sense of being important in the lives of other group members by being helpful to them
3. *Universalization*—a realization that the client is not unique and that other people share similar problems
4. *Intellectualization*—the process of learning or acquiring knowledge
5. *Reality testing*—the evaluation of issues such as personal values, family values, hostility, frustration, and personal defenses as events within the group unfold
6. *Transference*—strong attachments to the therapist and/or other group members
7. *Interaction*—the opportunity to relate to other people within the group
8. *Spectator therapy*—gains made by observing other group members and, in part, by imitating their behavior
9. *Ventilation*—the release of feelings and the expression of ideas previously repressed

Some types of groups, such as self-help groups, find that only certain therapeutic factors become evident. Five factors that are seen as particularly therapeutic in self-help groups follow:

1. *Cognitive restructuring* gives members an opportunity to develop new perspectives on their concerns.
2. *Hope* develops as members witness other members improving and overcoming problems similar to their own.
3. *Altruism* allows members to feel better about themselves by being in a position of helping others.
4. *Acceptance* involves the realization by members that the group will support and accept them, in spite of their problem.
5. *Universality* involves the realization that members are not as isolated, different or alone as they had thought (Borman, 1979).

For advanced social workers in diverse practice settings, certain therapeutic factors seem particularly relevant. The reader is referred to Yalom (1985, 1995) for an in-depth description, but many social group workers have also addressed these factors. The following discussion reflects the best and most current thinking and research in the use of therapeutic factors of social group work.

Hope and Belief   These terms refer to the inherently therapeutic gain evident among members who believe the group will help. Group members who believe that treatment is purposeful and effective and will eventuate in improvement are biased or predisposed toward a positive outcome. By the same token, individuals who begin treatment with the firm belief that it will not work and is, in all likelihood, a waste of their time, will probably prove themselves to be correct. Yalom (1995) cites a variety of clinical studies from both individual and group studies that support these related phenomena. *Hope* is the foundation for change; without it, there is no motivation to try to change or improve. With it, the individual can move forward in expectation that one's pain and suffering can be alleviated and life can be fulfilling.

Groups are by their nature vehicles in which members observe and subsequently affect each other. As members observe the positive effects of the group on each other, they are witnessing unassailable evidence that this group is helping other members to deal with life's problems; they possibly find joy and satisfaction. An example would be the dramatic effect that attendance at *Alcoholics Anonymous* (AA) meetings frequently produces. As person after person gives testimonials, describing a sad and hopeless addiction and the countless difficulties this addiction caused them, fellow members can recognize themselves in the same situation. They also see that fellow alcoholics who follow the *Twelve Steps* and commit themselves to adherence to the AA program actually do improve. This dynamic has no such counterpart in individual therapy. In fact, most practitioners have witnessed the disbelieving reaction of new clients when social workers assure clients that their lives should improve. Initially, clients may not *believe* this, and social workers may lose credibility by well-intended assurances to new clients who lack hope.

Belief as a therapeutic factor has been viewed negatively by some. It is cited as evidence that treatment interventions are comparable to naive or childish beliefs. Like Peter Pan, if one truly believes, one can fly (Gross, 1978). The comparison may have some validity; but, if belief in getting better increases the likelihood of successful treatment outcome, then it should be used. Belief and hope are important and legitimate factors in successful treatment since *lack* of hope is a major counterforce in any treatment. The direct observation of improvement on the part of fellow members of a group who share common problems and who improve as a result of the group probably is the most unequivocal and dramatic evidence a person can receive to instill a belief that life can indeed improve.

Martin Gross (1978) mistakenly compared this therapeutic component to the charlatans, faith healers, and quacks who use people's gullibility and insecurity to "cure." However, even if this positive outcome *is* based on an empirically unresearchable basis such as a belief in religious relics, mysticism, or the powers of another person such as a social worker to "cure," then such beliefs must be used effectively. Having lived and worked for three years on the Sioux reservation in Pine Ridge, South Dakota, this writer personally witnessed significant therapeutic gain based on an individual's deep and unalterable belief in shamans and Sioux spiritual leaders and their teachings. Positive treatment outcomes are derived by exorcisms or driving out evil spirits. If people improve as a result of this belief, then it is therapeutic and the beliefs must be understood and utilized therapeutically for the benefit of clients.

Universality   The therapeutic factor whereby group members recognize that they are not alone and therefore do not perceive themselves as odd, deviant, or unacceptable is termed *universality*. As group members come to share common problems, thoughts, histories, hopes, and fears, they see themselves in each other. If they had been self-isolating and distancing from family and friends before joining the group, their participation reverses that process.

The sense of isolation or self-loathing that afflicts many clients when they first enter treatment is often underrated. A person feels somehow so different, abnormal, damaged, or "sick" that they believe that others would despise or shun them. It is difficult to even contemplate beginning the long and potentially painful process toward acceptance. It is a particularly sad irony that those who often feel the most alienated are, in fact, victims, not the perpetrators. It is often the *victims* of abuse, incest, rape, or pervasive and long-term insult and degradation who are the most vulnerable to this developing sense of "differentness." Their own sense of embarrassment and misplaced guilt has often been reinforced and encouraged by their perpetrators.

Universality is an extremely strong and essential factor in undermining counterproductive thoughts and emotions related to the client's feelings of being "abnormal" or "deviant." Homogeneous groups of victims of abuse, incest, or rape or even children traumatized through divorce and the loss of a parent (Kalter, Schaefer, Lesowitz, Alpern, & Kickar, 1988) achieve dramatic therapeutic results through the use of universality. Individuals who have previously seen themselves as "damaged" and who frequently isolated themselves for protection from the fear of embarrassment or pity are particularly helped. This self-inflicted isolation leads to withdrawal and an even deeper feeling of deviancy, embarrassment, and worthlessness. However, by joining a group of fellow victims who have also engaged in self-blaming, these victimized individuals can find a new acceptance—from others and from themselves. They can be supported by other group members who have been through the same horrors and subsequent self-doubts and misplaced blame. They can personally see that some of their thoughts and behaviors were counterproductive but very understandable and that others in the group thought and acted in the same way.

Through this kind of sharing and acceptance, a member's once secret recriminations can now be more easily discussed and worked through. Universality allows group members to interact with others in the group who know of their problem and share it—yet who accept and understand them. They see that their negative self-perceptions of being so very different and unworthy of love or even understanding and acceptance were misplaced. Now they can finally put their traumatic histories into perspective and more freely explore their current thoughts and feelings with peers who truly accept and understand them.

Imitation   Imitative behavior within groups commonly manifests itself soon after one member has taken some decisive and constructive action. For instance, if a single member of a group stands up to an abusive or insulting partner or employer, often another member will imitate that behavior. It is the facilitator's task to focus upon and support such behavior. Time may be spent in the group sessions talking about the successful confrontations individual members have while the whole group supports and reinforces such successful behavioral change.

This dynamic is not usually based on significant insight or even conscious reflection. Typically, it involves *unfreezing,* which refers to the breaking of a habitual pattern of behavior for a new and more therapeutic behavioral response. After discussing the group member who had for many years accepted the demeaning or even insulting treatment by parents or lovers, other group members will decide to copy, model, or imitate that individual. Instead of passively accepting the insults, a wife may finally defend herself from an abusive husband and even confront him with his inappropriate behavior. When this highly successful response is shared, the other group members will join in the joy and success of having helped this person change. They will also consider responding in the same manner, having seen it work for another group member with whom they identify. Since members identify with each other, one member's success is shared or even multiplied by the rest of the group, which is a very satisfying therapeutic experience. Other group members may wonder if they can have the same degree of success if they imitate the same behavior. A flurry of therapeutic activity is sometimes clustered into several successive and highly successful sessions at which several members enthusiastically describe how they "did what Jenny did."

This particular imitative factor is sometimes cited as a concern in relation to copying negative behaviors. Social workers who have not experienced groups suggest that members are also capable of imitating dangerous or countertherapeutic behavior. There is, however, no evidence to support this concern. Since the specified purpose of therapeutic groups is the amelioration of a problem through open and honest interaction with others, no ethical group social worker will sanction deviant or countertherapeutic behavior. Deviant behavior is discussed, of course, but the group dynamic is extremely powerful in demanding conformity to certain constructive norms of behavior. Behavior deemed unacceptable by the group will inherently be discouraged, not promoted.

For instance, social work students might fear that a group composed of rapists might be as likely to imitate the deviant behavior of other group members as they would the positive behaviors. While there is always a danger of someone misusing the group to learn new deviant behaviors, this happens *in spite of* the group, not because of it. In short, there is no guarantee in this field that people will always be honest, sincere, and genuinely motivated to change for the better. However, the likelihood of persons in therapeutic groups imitating deviant behavior is an anathema to treatment groups. Such an outcome could only occur in the context of secretive or dishonest use of the group; when such misuse is discovered, the offending member is immediately confronted and often removed from the group. In instances in which group members were court-ordered to the group, which occurs occasionally for groups of rapists, pedophiles, and others, the appropriate referral is back to the court.

Cohesiveness   The sense of support, caring, belonging, and unconditional acceptance a successful group develops is referred to as *cohesiveness*. This factor is more active than universality as members demonstrate their care by being supportive, by sharing experiences, and by offering feedback and insights to each other. Cohesiveness refers to the bonding that invariably takes place in successful groups.

For many group members, this kind of bonding and acceptance may be a new experience that allows them to receive and give affection as they enter into a new set of positive relationships for the first time. Cohesiveness does not mean comfort or even that members always enjoy each other's company. Cohesive groups are those groups capable of dealing with *conflict* and those groups in which members develop relationships to the point where they express their feelings openly and honestly. When members are angry or hurt or in disagreement, they express these feelings rather than holding them in and allowing them to fester. Dealing successfully with conflict within the group represents a significant developmental stage for these members. Group members cannot grow or develop unless they can confront and deal with conflict successfully, and this requires some degree of group cohesiveness.

Sharing Information   This factor involves two types of sharing: (a) the social group worker provides information to the members, and (b) the members share information with each other. The social worker prepares the group members by explaining the group's purpose and providing guidelines and ideas about group dynamics or the particular focus of the group, such as family conflict, schizophrenia, post-traumatic stress, or the effects of divorce. This factual, didactic information may vary considerably depending upon the type of group. Treatment groups rely more on interpersonal dynamics; thus, objective facts are less relevant in treatment groups than in theme groups or psychoeducational and shorter-term groups whose partial purpose is to inform members about a problem.

The second aspect of sharing, in which group members share information with one another, is extremely useful for several reasons. Sharing or giving by one caring member to another is significant. Members get to know each other and develop relationships just by the initial sharing of basic factual information. This is normal and healthy and is the basis for further trust. As described in the stages of group development, most groups and relationships begin with this sort of polite discussion with a focus on less-emotion-laden concerns.

Another reason such information sharing among fellow members is so important is that it increases members' sense of ownership of the group. After all, it is their group, not the leader's. As members give helpful aid or facts to each other, not only is their individual importance enhanced but so too is their investment in the group.

In addition, their information may be more relevant than that of the social worker and less encumbered by agency politics or relationships. For instance, in health-related groups, members may have more information than the social worker about better and less-costly orthopedic devices or supplies; or, members may more openly discuss their observations about hospital or agency staff. The social worker may have ethical and professional concerns preventing unguarded statements about a surgeon, nurse, or fellow social worker whose skills may be less than those of other staff members. Group members do not have such constraints and may be in a better position than the social worker to make certain assessments.

Altruism   A therapeutic phenomenon unique to groups is *altruism,* which can be defined as a regard for the welfare of others without concern for personal reward. Some individuals who join groups have both a poor sense of self-worth and diminished confidence. Individual interventions may actually reinforce that diminished status since, in effect, clients present themselves to the "more capable" professional who takes care of them because they cannot help themselves.

On the other hand, within groups, members are empowered. Members have the capacity to be helpers, not passive recipients of services. As members are encouraged to share their thoughts, suggestions, advice, and stories of past successful encounters, fellow members regard them differently. When one member offers another member advice, that act is as therapeutic for the receiver as it is for the giver. Members who have previously felt worthless find they are given opportunities to prove they have much to offer to other members who listen to them and respect the help. There is therapeutic value to the respect one receives from peers who show regard for what one member says to another.

Altruism, as practiced within groups, is not so much an act of self-sacrifice as it is a demonstration of one's own merit and competence. In a group, no therapist needs to say, "You are getting better. . . . Good work!" The evidence is there for members to see in the regard the other members have for them. The therapeutic feedback so common to individual work is neither as necessary nor as therapeutic as the positive regard experienced by group members who act altruistically.

Alcoholics Anonymous (AA) provides an excellent venue for altruism. Sponsors and fellow members eagerly run to the aid of another member who is fighting temptation to drink or who has been hospitalized. As marvelous and generous as the AA members are in going to extremes to help each other, so it is equally clear that such altruism is a profoundly therapeutic statement to themselves. The message is that they are such functional, good, caring, and resourceful individuals that they can even extend their wellness and strength to others who are in need of it.

Altruism also helps individual group members become less self-absorbed. Many who come into treatment are so focused on their own problems and difficulties that they think of little else. This is not helpful; and, without interaction and subsequent concern for others, their self-absorption exacerbates the problem. In a group, members are required to think of others, to become less engulfed in their own misery, and to consider the problems of others. This behavior breaks a self-pitying pattern because members are encouraged to think of others and help them.

Reworking the Family of Origin   There is an inevitable recapitulation of family dynamics observed within groups. People first learn how to interact with others by interacting at home with their own families. In some instances, the learned behavior is dysfunctional. In families in which secrets are kept, aggression is reinforced, abusiveness is accepted, or intimidation is the norm, these same behaviors typically are maintained in outside relationships, fostering a reoccurring pattern of dysfunctional interactions.

One does not need to be a Freudian to recognize *transference* within groups. Members interact with one another as they would in their families of origin with sibling rivalry and competitiveness for the parental figure of the social group worker. The use of co-facilitators, one male and one female, is a helpful device for observing and even fostering this phenomenon. The social worker then has the option of deciding to what extent these early developmental issues should be explored. Psychodynamically oriented psychotherapists explore, uncover, and otherwise work through these early experiences by interpreting and delving into clients' childhoods and issues with parents. Likewise, most social group workers address such issues in the group, if only in the context of how these issues affect current relationships or even group behavior.

Current social work practice, particularly in managed care settings, in HMOs, and with chronic or long-term care clients, is using social group work extensively. However, the field is also generally moving away from the *psychodynamic* orientations. Groups have no more of a historical basis in psychodynamics than individual or family interventions because of its focus on the here and now. However, ignorance of this dynamic or of the effects of early childhood on the formation of relationships could jeopardize effective group work. Group workers will observe each member misinterpret statements or make highly inaccurate observations about other members' intentions or even observed behavior based on individual early family experiences. While it is unnecessary to regress the group to therapeutically resolve each member's repressed or unresolved childhood traumas, it *is* often necessary to help members put the effects of childhood into perspective.

The effects of childhood or family-of-origin dynamics invariably affect current relationships, patterns of interactions, and interpersonal relations. The social group worker's task often involves pointing out and supportively confronting members as they inappropriately respond to behaviors or motives of others when there is no apparent basis for their response within the group. Group workers frequently observe members angrily accusing other members of being hateful, critical, or controlling or even plotting against them even when there is no evidence of such behavior. If a reaction or behavior happens in the group, then it typically happens in other settings as well. Such unresolved historical responses may be a major factor in the inability of clients to form trusting relationships, or in their pattern of getting involved in arguments, or in their tendency to suddenly and prematurely end relationships or jobs as soon as an authority figure expresses disapproval.

Running from an abusive parent may have served a purpose during childhood; however, if it is carried over into relationships with actual or potential partners, employers, or teachers and manifests itself in the group, this issue must be addressed. Groups provide excellent opportunities to put such reactions into their proper perspective. Open, frank discussions of how that behavior manifests itself within the group, followed by the member's insight and memories relevant to how and why such behavior started, may be sufficient to bring about significant change. This type of clear demonstration of interpersonal behavior, coupled with the support and feedback of fellow group members who have observed it, may be more effective than years of psychoanalysis. Undoubtedly, it is more efficient.

Life and Developmental Crisis Issues   Treatment or support groups can be very useful in helping clients confront the major issues of life and how to resolve them. Both directly and indirectly, group members can discuss, argue, and explore questions like "Why did this tragedy happen to me?" "What is wrong with me that I cannot sustain a marriage?" "Why am I dying of a terminal disease while others live?" or "Why did God allow me to be born with this deformity (or schizophrenia or learning disorder or bipolar disorder, etc.)?" Of course, there are no clear answers to any of these questions and even the questions may need to be reworked. However, groups are perhaps the best available means for exploring, and at least partially resolving, major issues such as these, which most self-observing people need to address at some point in their lives.

Interpersonal Learning   This involves a wide variety of experiences. It is based in the notion that people are a product of their interactions with others in their present environment as well as in their past. For social workers, interpersonal learning is a familiar concept, since the field of social work focuses so often on how people continuously affect and are, in turn, affected by their environment. Groups are powerful vehicles to foster a conscious understanding of this potential growth process. Groups encourage members to learn more about themselves, their thoughts, and their feelings by developing an ability to assess their individual interactions objectively.

An effective, supportive, and therapeutic group involves a constant and exciting exchange of insights, observations, and advice. Members are continuously reminded by their social group worker to learn, grow, and reflect on their observations in the sessions. Each group meeting is another opportunity to build upon the last session and for members to help each other by interacting openly, honestly, and with a constant orientation toward self-growth.

SUMMARY

There are a wide variety of groups used in contemporary practice. There are different classes of groups, such as open or closed and homogeneous or heterogeneous. There are also different types of groups: therapy, counseling, encounter and sensitivity, self-help, and support groups. Basic factors to consider when starting a new group include the appropriateness of the setting, avoiding interruptions, assuring confidentiality, the frequency and duration of sessions, and the composition of the group. Some individuals are not appropriate for heterogeneous groups and instead should utilize either individual treatment or homogeneous groups. These candidates include extremely shy, withdrawn, or schizoid individuals; monopolists; depressive personalities; those with conversion disorders; manic or overly reactive individuals; antisocial personalities; and those addicted to drugs or alcohol.

Groups develop typically in five stages that are similar to the development of most normal relationships. There is a beginning, then a time to resolve differences and set guidelines, then an agreement or "norming" stage, then a productive working time, and then an ending. Several models of group stage development were examined. Norms that are developed in most successful groups include the following: the group is a single unit; it is important; each member is important; the group is nonjudgmental and open; it requires risks and trust; and it is flexible and spontaneous. The major tasks required of social group workers include selecting members, setting up the group, preparing members, setting and modeling a tone, establishing flexible goals and objectives, ensuring full interaction, maintaining focus on here and now, confronting, providing feedback and analysis, beginning and ending sessions, and encouraging the development of the therapeutic factors. The therapeutic factors that are most helpful to groups are belief and hope, universality, imitation, cohesiveness, sharing information, altruism, reworking the family of origin, dealing with life crises or developmental issues, and interpersonal learning.

FAMILY SYSTEMS INTERVENTIONS

THE FAMILY AS A SOCIAL SYSTEM

The family is a social system. The family forms the basis of identity for all individuals and provides the psychological and developmental foundation for subsequent growth. If the family is stable, loving, supportive and sensitive to its task of teaching and nurturing all members, then it is a tremendously positive force in the fulfillment of one's potential. If it is erratic, hostile, uncaring, neglectful, or abusive, it can be the source of irreparable damage to the developing children and great emotional pain for the adults.

In today's complex and often stressful society, the family system invariably becomes the primary source of either help or hindrance. When social workers intervene with this system, they draw on a vast array of skills that include their knowledge of the development of individuals, family systems, group systems, cultures, the community, and society as a whole and how each of these impacts specifically on the family that comes to them for help.

The essence of a system is that its various components interact and affect each other whenever any single part is affected. The family is the perfect example; every significant event that happens to any family member reverberates throughout the family system. Examples include the following:

- A 3-year-old daughter who catches a cold. The child's illness affects her mother and her siblings as they change their schedules to respond to the need for new emergency child care arrangements. This situation could possibly bring the mother and child closer together while alienating the teenage daughter who has to cancel her date with a boyfriend to watch her sister.
- A teenage son who is failing algebra. Consequently, his older sister tutors him, the father scolds him, and the mother meets with the teachers to try to see how to help. This further angers the father who insists, "The lazy kid should deal with the teachers on his own."

- A mother who leaves her abusive boyfriend. The teenage son has been beaten defending his mother and sister, which tightens their family bond as they distance themselves from the now isolated, violent boyfriend.
- A hyperactive 10-year-old boy who begins therapy and confronts his alcoholic parents. The parents then stop scapegoating him and begin to target the next youngest child rather than confront their own problems.
- A 9-year-old daughter who begins throwing temper tantrums every time her parents begin to argue. Her behavior diverts attention away from the couple's problem.

From the family systems perspective, it is difficult to imagine *any* significant act or behavior that does not have systemic ramifications. For better or worse, the family is a system, and, in many instances, its individual members cannot be understood or treated in any effective way other than through intervening with the entire system. In each of the examples provided, any social worker trying to intervene on an individual basis without working with the family system would probably fail. See Box 6.1.

FAMILY THERAPY MODELS

Fortunately, the days exemplified by Box 6.1 are gone. Any social worker treating a young child without focusing upon the family would be questioned today. In fact, the 1970s and early 1980s witnessed an explosive growth in the use of family therapy with a focus that suggests most treatment approaches, even for adults, were inappropriate in limiting treatment to the individual. Many social workers shifted their focus away from individual treatment and toward family therapy models and variations, which became a dominant approach in all of the helping professions.

There is yet another shift in social work's orientation to the family. Managed care and the emphasis upon brief, broad-based systems interventions generally allow for the significant inclusion of the family as a unit of intervention. However, the family *therapy* approach, as opposed to a family *systems* approach, is often questioned by social workers who see the former as more narrow in its psychotherapeutic focus (Aronson, 1996; Franklin & Jordan, 1999).

Before explaining the theory, stages, and techniques used in current family interventions, it is useful to first briefly list and describe the many different models found among family therapists (see Box 6.2).

6.1   *Historical Example*

I lived and worked in an institution for severely disturbed children for two years. This was a highly regarded institution that served as a placement setting for social work, psychology, and psychiatry students. It was psychodynamic in orientation, and occasional attempts by staff to make the institution more behavioral, systemic, or eclectic were generally met with the response that this center would never compromise its high standards. Further, these autistic and other severely disturbed children were being provided with the very best type of care, that is, long-term, insight-oriented psychotherapy.

This center was eventually forced to completely revise its program and start a new behavioral and short-term unit. Many local professionals decried the loss of a great setting, but my personal reaction was one of relief, knowing that the lack of a family systems–oriented approach to the treatment of this vulnerable population was very problematic. For years, the senior analysts had successfully "protected" these children from the continuation of the "damage" their parents had inflicted upon them. The psychoanalyst who directed the institution held the view that the family, particularly the mothers, had caused these symptoms through their lack of bonding, through double binding, through contradictory communication, or through any number of other often subtle rejections or insults to the developing child's fragile ego.

Prior to the revision of this program, the families were virtually ignored and the children spent years in this facility. The few occasional family visits were invariably traumatic, further supporting the staff's views that the families of origin were, indeed, the sources of the problems. The antagonism between the staff and the families was palpable. Some families became convinced that they had done something irreparable to their children, though they often had difficulty understanding *what* they had done to their children that was so harmful. Some parents even avoided or missed their scheduled, rare appointments completely. Later they would often admit that their guilt was overwhelming.

6.2   *Family Therapy Models*

The distinctions among the many models of family therapy are often somewhat forced in the crowded literature of family therapy. There are many variations of family therapy:

- Structural family therapists include Salvadore Minuchin, Ronald Liebman, Harry Aponte, Braulio Montalvo, and M. Duncan Stanton.
- Strategic family therapists include Jay Haley, Richard Rabkin, Paul Watzlawick, Richard Fisch, John Weakland, Mara Selvini Palazzoli, Cloe Madanes, Peggy Papp, Lynn Hoffman, and Bradford Keeney.
- Behavioral family therapists are Gerald Patterson, Neil Jacobson, Robert Weiss, Robert Stuart, and Gayla Margolin; and some might include the cognitive work of Aaron Beck.
- Experiential family therapists are represented by Virginia Satir, Carl Whitaker, Shirley Luthman, David Keith, Augustus Napier, and Walter Kempler.
- Psychodynamic family therapists include Nathan Ackerman, Helm Stierlin, Ivan Boszormenyi-Nagy, James Framo, A. C. R. Skynner, D. Scharff, and J. S. Scharff.
- Bowenian therapists include Murray Bowen, Tom Fogarty, Monica McGoldrick, Edwin Friedman, Michael Kerr, Thomas Pepero, and Harriet Goldhor Lerner.
- Network interventionists include Carolyn Attneave, Ross Speck, Uri Rueveni, and H. P. Laqueur.
- Psychoeducational family therapists are Carol Anderson, William McFarland, and I. R. H. Faloon.
- Solution-focused therapists include William Hudson-O'Hanlon, Insoo Kim Berg, Moshe Talmon, Michael White, Tapani Ahola, and Michael Weiner Davis.
- Feminists are Elizabeth Carter, Peggy Papp, Olga Silverstein, Maryann Walters, Virginia Goldner, Rachel Hare-Mustin, Lynn Hoffman, Morris Taggart, and Dorothy Wheeler.
- Pioneers in family therapy include Gregory Bateson, Don Jackson, Milton Erickson, Theodore Lidz, Margaret Singer, Lyman Wynne, and John Bell.

Although there may be disagreement with both the names and labels applied to some of these family therapy models, as well as with the accuracy of who is included in each area, this listing is an indication that family therapy covers a wide range of methods and individuals.

REASONS TO SEE FAMILIES TOGETHER

The reasons to see families together are many and varied. Several of the primary reasons are addressed in subsequent paragraphs.

Observe and Understand Interactions

Observing family members together in an office or home allows the worker an opportunity to directly see the family dynamics and interactions as opposed to relying on the necessarily biased perspective of an individual family member. The social worker can observe, for example, how the father undermines the mother's authority or how the adolescent girl manipulates the father against the mother to achieve her goals. If the father comes in alone for individual treatment, he may well portray himself as the parent who reluctantly has to do all of the limit setting or disciplining because the mother is unwilling or unable to do so. By the same token, if the adolescent girl is seen alone, she may portray the mother as being unfairly hostile toward her and the father as being her sole source of support.

Such biases are to be expected and are normal. Few experienced workers would accept a client's initial viewpoints as being anything other than subjective. In fact, individual treatment can be a process of helping the client to view such experiences as they are in reality. However, the direct observation of the family by an objective family systems–oriented worker is an efficient way to assess the interactions, hierarchies, rivalries, jealousies, and influences in a manner that seeing the client individually would not allow.

Provide Balance

Seeing the family together minimizes the likelihood of the worker being biased or "taking sides." In family sessions, the worker can see and hear everyone's perspective. In individual sessions, the worker may hear repeated descriptions of how one partner in a relationship feels that he or she contributes to the relationship and supports the other partner and receives only criticism and abuse in response. The worker may well conclude that this relationship is extremely detrimental to that client and, therefore, encourage the client to leave the negatively portrayed partner.

Encouragement to take such action may be warranted, but the likelihood also exists that the partner is, in fact, extremely supportive and caring and that the client's depressed symptoms are negatively skewing his or her perspective. By including the partner in family sessions, the worker may be in a better position to see the beneficial and therapeutic aspects of the relationship and work toward reinforcing those aspects rather than being negatively biased toward a major source of support for the client.

Provide Rational Structure

Having the family together as a unit in an office establishes a degree of social sanction, structure, or even pressure to behave or interact in a socially accept-able manner. Family members may be less inclined to treat each other too harshly in front of a stranger, particularly a professional social worker whom each member may want to impress in a positive way. While the worker can anticipate a rather natural and genuine dialogue among family members in the office or even at a home in the worker's presence, the early sessions may also be slightly inhibited because they are being observed.

This *halo effect*, in which the family is initially more reasonable and polite, may be somewhat artificial. However, from a clinical perspective, it is thera-peutic since it provides a subtle social pressure to at least appear to be appro-priate. Family members may, therefore, express their differences but will do so in a relatively socially acceptable way to avoid being perceived by the worker as being the unreasonable or irrational family member.

Begin Open Communication

Family systems interventions are based upon communicating, not just talking. Communication implies interaction, hearing, listening, responding, under-standing, and reacting to feedback. From the very first session, families are put into milieu in which clear, honest, open communication is the norm. This norm can be overtly and verbally stated by the worker who may say: "We are all here to try to understand each other and come closer as a family. The best way to do that is by really listening to every family member; trying to understand their issues and concerns; and then having everyone else respond, discuss, and agree or disagree in some reasonable, open, honest, and clear manner."

FAMILY TREATMENT TECHNIQUES

It is difficult to define the techniques of family therapy because the field is so complex. Both family and group interventions cover the social work and psychotherapy continuum from long-term, insight-oriented to short-term behavioral approaches. As such, the techniques vary tremendously and may even be diametrically opposed. For instance, a psychodynamically oriented family therapist such as Nathan Ackerman would allow the family to strug-gle with their history as a family while Jay Haley would begin immediately with defining clear goals and performing homework tasks that would be evaluated and monitored weekly. Needless to say, their approaches are completely different.

However, certain common techniques have emerged in recent times. The common factor among all of these techniques is a systems orientation with an emphasis upon brief, validated, effective methods. Furthermore, social work values and ethics are placed into the family context. Among the values that define social work are the priorities put upon diversity and sensitivity to different cultures. This value has the effect of requiring that social workers pay attention to such culturally defined mannerisms as eye contact, physical closeness when speaking, and deference given to elders. The most widely accepted techniques today are (a) reframing, (b) questioning, (c) examining interactional sequences, (d) providing directives, and (e) respecting physical cues.

Reframing or Relabeling

(Minuchin & Fishman, (1981) describe *reframing* or *relabeling* as helping the family to redefine or interpret a problem. For instance, if a single mother loses her job and becomes more easily depressed or stressed, her teenage son may interpret her behavior as simply "mean." A family therapist would likely help the son understand his mother's new behavior as being "preoccupied" or "worried." The focus of blaming the mother shifts to a more accurate understanding that his mother is concerned and dealing with a real threat to the family.

Another example would be a father whose discipline of his son has become a dangerous power play and therefore likely to escalate and fail. The son's label of "abuse" may not be accurate or helpful if it only leads to defensiveness by the father. However, by reframing the behavior as one of "parenting" or helping the son realize the effects of his behavior, then new, alternative ways of bringing order to the family might be addressed (see Case 6.1).

> **Case 6.1: Reframing**
> The Simons are an African American family who referred their 14-year-old son because of a recent arrest for theft, poor school performance, and an increasingly angry and defiant reaction to his stepfather. Their relationship had been very good up until the last year when Kamal began associating with some youngsters who the parents suspect are gang members. The stepfather, John, is a supervisor at the post office and readily admits that he has often spanked Kamal. Kamal says he now hates his "abusive stepfather" and recently reported John to the police and to children's protective services after an incident in which John punched Kamal and Kamal hit him back before running away overnight.
>
> In this third family session, Marie, the mother, angrily but tearfully explains, "I won't have my boy show disrespect to his father. John has been good to us, and we have two little ones now. Kamal's a good boy, but I won't let him join some gang and get killed or hooked on drugs. I'm always in the middle, and things are just getting worse."

Kamal interrupted, "Well how come he won't show me some respect? You think I'm gonna let him beat me up? You don't do nothing to help me! That sucker gave me a bloody nose last time. If I can't take him myself, then me and my boys will bring him down."

"I'm the man in this family. You're just some stupid punk who thinks he's tough," said John as he glared at Kamal.

The social worker stopped John by positively reframing his intentions that were "to redevelop some appropriate parental rules and help Kamal to do better at home and school while avoiding involvement with gang members."

John readily agreed that those were his goals. Marie and Kamal were asked to give John ideas concerning how to achieve those goals without labeling John as "abusive," while agreeing that there must be mutual respect. Once the anger was defused slightly, the three of them worked with the social worker in subsequent sessions to establish agreed-upon goals that required mutual respect without any physical forms of punishment.

The purpose of reframing and relabeling, as demonstrated in Case 6.1, is to help the family find new, constructive ways of interacting. A husband or wife may feel "rejected" by a spouse who is increasingly distant because of medical or financial reasons. The problem is not one of rejection, but the partner needs help in cognitively viewing the issue. In this instance, reframing leads to a shift in attitude and behavior from one of distancing, anger, and hurt to one of support and a recommitment to the relationship.

Another aspect of reframing is the development of *positive connotations* (Hanna & Brown, 1995) or "ascribing noble intentions" to the problem as a way of getting family cooperation. While negative labels such as *hateful, crazy, mean,* or *bad* all tend to distance family members and rarely suggest ways to work constructively, positive terms tend to do just the opposite. *Hate* therefore becomes reframed as *worried; crazy* is seen as *concerned; mean* is replaced by *upset;* and *bad* becomes *frustrated.* Whether the social worker uses *positive connotations,* which are always positive from the client's perspective, or *reframing,* which is not always positive but redefines a problem, both are designed to lessen some of the strong emotions related to certain labels and to "depathologize" a problem so that a family can communicate openly and relate the problem to normal events addressed by any family.

Reframing a problem requires sensitivity to the family's understanding of terms, not the social worker's. Too quickly relabeling a *spanking* as *abuse,* or *loud arguments* as *intimidation,* may lead to significant family members leaving therapy. The choice of words is important, and the way people understand and interpret them must be sensitively addressed. Ultimately, the word or term chosen as the descriptor of the problem should be one that is accurate without negatively stigmatizing or labeling any one family member. However, accuracy takes precedence over subtlety. If a problem is clearly one of abuse as opposed to strict discipline (which varies widely in different cultures), then it must be defined and framed as such.

Questioning

Questioning, including the manner in which it is done, is an important technique in most treatments but particularly in family work. The goal of questioning is not so much to get answers but, rather, to get the family to think and examine their dynamics realistically. The Milan team of family therapists uses *circular questions* (Boscolo, Cecchin, Hoffman, & Penn, 1987) to better understand how certain problems evolved and how they currently affect family interactions and problems. The four types of circular questions are those that (a) help define a problem, (b) establish the sequence of interactions, (c) compare or classify questions, or (d) help to develop an intervention (Hanna & Brown, 1995).

Michael White (1986), a solution-focused family therapist, is known to use questions for two major purposes: to look for exceptions to the stated systematic behavior or to get more specific instances of how the family interacts (Hanna & Brown, 1995). He might ask questions such as "Have there been times when the two of you did *not* fight? Can you tell me about those instances?" Efforts are made to help a family focus on the circumstances surrounding their rare enjoyable times together rather than continuing to rehash and blame one another in a perpetual cycle of blame. Families are asked to examine the specific times, places, and circumstances surrounding those events as a way of counteracting a negative and seemingly hopeless communicative pattern (see Case 6.2).

> **Case 6.2: Questioning**
> Bonnie (age 36) is a single parent with two teenage boys named Bill (15) and Jim (12). Her plans to have her boyfriend of two years move in with them were stopped when Bill "disappeared" for a night, saying he would leave home if Glen (38) moved in. Jim has an excellent relationship with Glen and thinks his big brother is being a "jerk" for all of the trouble he is causing, and Bonnie is increasingly angry at her older son for potentially ruining the best relationship she has ever had. She also separately confided to the social worker that Glen has begun distancing from her because of Bill's antagonism and her hopes to develop a permanent relationship are diminishing.
>
> The last two sessions deteriorated into accusations against Bill by Bonnie and Jim, and Bill is now sulking angrily but silently in his chair, refusing to talk even to defend himself. The social worker realizes that he has let this go too far and is now trying to reverse the focus and feelings of all members: "Okay, so I get a pretty clear idea that the two of you feel that Glen is a good guy, but I don't think Bill really agrees. What does he do that's so good? How does he help you? Jim, you claim that Glen really likes your big brother, but what makes you say that? Bill has a right to feel the way he does."
>
> The social worker was attempting to support Bill and get him to reengage in the discussion but in a positive and constructive way. He soon drew Bill into the discussion, having sensed that it was not so much a matter of Bill disliking Glen as it was fearing that Glen would replace him in his mother's affection and in his role as "the man in the family." Those issues were addressed very openly, and,

once Bill was assured that his mother was definitely not "replacing" him, he was enthusiastic in positively responding to the questions regarding Glen.

Examining Interactional Sequences

Family therapists frequently help families to look at *how* they interact. Who talks to whom? Do some members talk for others? Who listens? Who leads, and who follows? Do some members interrupt others? Who does this? When? Why? How? What are the alliances?

Structural family therapists focus their questions more on trying to clarify the functions and structures of various subsystems such as marital, sibling, or parental. Strategic family therapists are more symptom oriented and help the family explore how, why, and when the family problem is supported. In both models, the social worker tries to get families to objectively look at patterns of interaction and influence and how those interactions contribute to family dysfunction (Hanna & Brown, 1995).

Interactional sequences and patterns develop within families with very little conscious awareness. Parents are often unaware that they consistently undermine each other or are far more affectionate with one child over another. They may not be aware of ingrained alliances; or, if they are aware, they may be unable to change those alliances that are problematic. The family therapist focuses upon specific behaviors and their sequences, not attitudes or feelings. This allows the family to objectively look at itself without a focus on right or wrong, blame or pathology. Gradually, the social worker helps the family to become aware of interactional sequences. Examples follow (also see Case 6.3):

1. Whenever the father tells the daughter to help with chores, the grandmother criticizes him.
2. When the teenage son uses drugs, the mother defends him, or the other son becomes depressed, or the father goes on an alcoholic binge.
3. Whenever the single mother goes out on a date, the son develops a stomachache or some other physical problem and the daughter cries for her to stay home.
4. Whenever the high-achieving daughter receives another academic award, her brother finds a way to draw attention to himself.
5. Whenever the father begins dating a new woman, his 12-year-old daughter criticizes the woman's hair, makeup, and personality and compares the new woman unfavorably to the former wife, her mother.

Case 6.3: Examining Interactional Sequences
Jenny divorced her alcoholic husband 6 years ago and reluctantly returned to her parents' home with her 3-year-old daughter Mandy. The grandmother has taken over child care for Mandy who is becoming "spoiled" and antagonistic to her mother who works all day and some evenings as a waitress. Jenny is now feeling

depressed and increasingly marginalized at home where she is beginning to feel that neither her mother nor her daughter really love her or even care that she works exhausting hours to support them. She has also begun to abuse alcohol, justifying it by claiming that alcohol is the only way she has to relax and escape the pressures of home and work.

The social worker quickly decided to have Jenny come in with her mother and daughter after the first session. In the family session, the social worker noted that Mandy, who was beautifully dressed in a cute outfit, sat close to her grandmother while Jenny, looking fairly disheveled after a recent binge, sat several feet away. The grandmother began the session, staring at her intimidated daughter as she said, "You know, that one is just like her father. He was a drunk, too. I don't know what would happen to this precious baby of hers if I didn't take care of her."

Little Mandy's affect quickly changed from that of a smiling three-year-old to a quietly crying toddler as she stared at her mother, who was also now in tears. After several moments of silence, Jenny looked over at the social worker and said, "See that? Didn't I tell you? Hell, I might as well be a drunk. Dad was a drunk 'cause Mom treated him like dirt and all he got was criticism and a lot of mean, nasty comments."

At this point, Mandy started crying and the grandmother motioned for her to come and sit on her lap. When that happened, Jenny started to get up to leave saying, "Forget it! This isn't going to work. Where's the nearest bar?"

The social worker responded, "Let's just settle down a bit and kind of look at this. Jenny, please have a seat. I know this is hard for you, but I really got the feeling last week that you want things to change and get better. Let's at least try to figure out what's going on here, and maybe we can improve things for everyone."

For the remainder of the session, the social worker essentially led a discussion that tried to examine what had just happened in that brief period. In a nonaccusatory, factual manner, each of the family members agreed that sometimes Grandma gets angry toward Jenny, and, when she does, Jenny either drinks or leaves the house for work or to see friends. This upsets Mandy because Mandy thinks her mother doesn't like her, so she cries to Grandma, who says, "Mommy is being bad again, but I love you even if mommy is gone."

In subsequent sessions, the social worker helped the three of them talk about their anger and fears as well as their hopes and aspirations for the future. They also discussed how their interactions followed a fairly predictable sequence that needed to be altered. Jenny realized that it was neither accurate nor helpful to suggest that her mother "made her drink." Obviously Jenny had other, healthier choices, and she agreed to go to Alcoholics Anonymous to better understand alcoholism.

The grandmother recognized that Jenny was trying her best. Jenny loved her daughter and appreciated her mother's help but was feeling left out and feared that the grandmother was turning Mandy away from her own mother. In later sessions, the grandmother was also helped to realize that some of the anger and disappointment she felt over Jenny was actually unresolved issues toward her deceased alcoholic husband. Jenny had always been a great deal closer to her father than to her, and the grandmother resented it. She was determined to have the granddaughter's love even if she had to alienate her own daughter.

The social worker tried to help each person see how she played a role in this interactional sequence of events. The worker also helped each to see that, by openly talking about their fears and genuine concern for each other, they could also agree to alter the events. Jenny did not have to drink or leave whenever her mother criticized her. The grandmother did not have to criticize her daughter's efforts, whether out of anger or fear of losing her granddaughter. And even Mandy was helped to see that she could go to her mother and talk when she was feeling frightened, and her grandmother would not be angry when this happened. This pattern of behaviors could change and be replaced by more constructive responses once it was understood.

These interactional sequences cannot be altered unless they are consciously known; and, in families dealing with stress, they cannot be known until someone helps the family objectively look at itself. The social worker, therefore, asks questions that help the family to see how their behavior maintains problems and symptoms. This often leads to a recognition that the behavior must change.

Providing Directives

Some family therapists "restructure" family interactions, even assigning homework to various members. The father who "picks on" one child will be told to spend time daily with that child and give him or her specific, genuine verbal support. The grandmother who undermines her son-in-law will be told to support the son-in-law's appropriate efforts in getting the son to clean his room. The mother who consistently and inappropriately criticizes the teenage daughter's appearance will be directed to avoid such negative comments and verbalize her pride in the girl's academic accomplishments instead.

The structural family therapists use "restructuring" to change the balance of power within a family. For instance, a controlling father might be directed to be more flexible with an adolescent and allow him or her to use the family car without rigid restrictions. Or a family will be told that future sessions will focus on the alcoholic behavior of a parent rather than the poor school performance of a child who is inappropriately trying to direct the focus toward him.

Experiential family therapists may even give families "new rules for effective communication." These "rules" would require each member to speak in the first person and say what he or she is thinking or feeling. Family members cannot speak for another family member or even presume to know what another family member feels without letting that person express his or her thoughts or feelings. In addition, family members must take responsibility for their own feelings. Family members cannot blame others for "making them" feel bad or guilty; nor can they blame other family members for their own alcoholism or drug abuse. Third, affective communication requires family members to be direct with each other and say what they want the other to do. They may be directed to say to a mother or brother that their alcoholism or verbal abuse must stop or that they do not believe the other is trustworthy with money (Hanna & Brown, 1995).

Directing a family to change requires trust and good, open communication among the family members and the family therapist or social worker. Change involves a shift in the balance and structure of the family that means that someone is giving up something to another member. The parent may give more control to an adolescent; or one partner may relinquish control to another; or one family member may be required to completely refrain from a particular behavior such as shouting, hitting, or drinking. Directives only work when the family is invested in improving their patterns of influence and communication. As long as the family therapist maintains a focus on the family as a single system, then the members can openly discuss the fact that change requires loss and gain, give and take, and sacrifice for the sake of the family.

Respecting Physical Cues

This technique covers a range of seven different physical actions, including (a) eye contact, (b) breathing, (c) sitting, (d) positioning, (e) diversions, (f) voice modulation, and (g) greetings. *Eye contact* standards vary from culture to culture, and certain Native American and Asian cultures consider it offensive to look into another's eyes. Social workers need to be aware of and sensitive to this cultural difference. Many other clients resist or are reluctant to make eye contact for reasons associated with their presenting problem. In those instances, it may be diagnostically informative to note a client who has low self-esteem who gradually accepts or even initiates eye contact. A goal to work toward may be increasing eye contact as long as it is not culturally contraindicated.

Breathing has a subtle rhythm that varies among people and often within the same session. In family sessions, it is useful to match the breathing of the family member whom you want to join. This is an effective way of identifying with a certain family member by literally getting into the same rhythm as the client. It also allows for the potential of getting other family members to relax and think. A highly reactive, overly emotional family member might be encouraged to communicate better and regain self-control by breathing deeply and slowly, just as the social worker does. Care has to be given that the suggestion is accepted as one of support, not criticism.

A similar technique involves *sitting* in the same manner as a family member. If a client crosses his or her legs a certain way or leans forward or backward at various times, the social worker can follow with similar actions. However, caution must be exercised not to insult a client if this technique appears to mimic a client. Furthermore, sitting in a manner similar to the client's must also be moderated when the stance is clearly defensive, proactive, or reactionary. An example would be when a client folds his or her hands across the chest and moves away from the others.

Positioning refers to the physical location or place where members choose to sit. A mother sitting close to her three children across from the father who is sitting alone is an obvious example of his isolation. The one who is separate is often the family's identified target or "problem" member. It may be the pregnant teenage daughter or the drug-abusing son or the alcoholic mother or father. Alliances are apparent in many families simply by observing positions.

Structural family therapists might suggest changing positions as a way of physically restructuring family dynamics, whereas strategic family therapists would more likely point out the patterns and relate them to previous discussions concerning the interaction among members. Either way, members are allowed an opportunity to objectively observe patterns and comment on them or even change them. Parents might be encouraged to sit together rather than be separated by their children. A mother might be told to sit with or even hold the hand of her daughter as the girl confronts an abusive uncle.

Diversions are behaviors in family sessions that draw the focus away from the *real* problem. The diversion is usually acted out by the family's designated problem member. The 3-year-old who has severely regressed will suddenly throw a tantrum, or the 14-year-old will forcefully change the topic from the father's drug use to her own sexual experimentations. In many families, the children divert attention away from major, ongoing problems such as alcoholism or marital discord by drawing attention to themselves. Rather than suffering through another episode of seeing a drunk parent or two parents fighting, the child "acts up" in a family session.

Diversions prolong problems; they do not help alleviate them. This self-sacrificing behavior on the part of one child also frequently begins an unfortunate pattern for the child. The same three-year-old who throws a tantrum in a family session rather than listen to her parents yell at each other will be similarly inclined in later life. She may be developing a pattern in which she will yell and scream concerning her boss in later life whenever anyone confronts her with her own alcoholism. Or, the 12-year-old becomes a 40-year-old who may still be blaming herself for her infidelity, this time to her third alcoholic partner.

Voice modulation involves the modeling of a calm, clear, and quiet tone and volume of speaking in sessions. Communication is the essential factor in families; and people do not listen when others shout, threaten, or verbally over react. The social worker may find it necessary to interrupt a family member who is shouting accusations and to suggest calmly that, while his or her anger may be well justified, the most effective way to be heard is to speak clearly and slowly.

The social worker usually does not have to give any verbal directives regarding voice modulation, since it is sufficient to model the behavior. Families learn from the social worker, and much of what they learn is through modeling or imitation. The initial accusatory and chaotic family sessions can be transformed into reasonable discourses on ways of helping each other by simply lowering the volume and pace of the discussion, thus allowing people to respond to the content of the communication rather than reacting to its affect.

Greetings set the tone of sessions. It is important that social workers greet and address each family member in a welcoming and appropriate manner. The social worker may need to examine whether he or she ignores or is less attentive to children or the elderly so as not to diminish that member's status in family interactions.

Recognizing cultural differences is important. A social worker who inadvertently ignores the grandmother in a family of Asian descent may have alienated and insulted the entire family before the session begins. Similarly, the husband or father in some cultures expects or demands greater attention or even subservience from other family members. Many social workers understandably find such sexist patterns offensive. However, a balance that is sensitive to cultural differences yet instructive for families must be developed. For instance, people in some cultures might expect the social worker to greet the father with more respect than the wife or children. Rather than alienating this central figure, it may be best for the social worker to greet all members very warmly while being careful not to insult the father or his status. This respectful greeting is particularly important if this same "head of the family" is disadvantaged in the labor market and, therefore, being supported by his wife.

STAGES

The stages of family intervention vary due to the differing underlying theories, goals, and methods. However, the following model of six stages of family intervention uses the major methods and incorporates the leading models used in contemporary clinical social work.

Stage 1: Beginning

Family system interventionists focus a great deal of time and attention on the beginning sessions. In some instances, they write about the importance of *joining* or making the initial connection and relationship with the family Haley's (1976) social stage emphasized the need to begin right away with homework assignments and establishing clear goals, but only after putting members at ease with casual discussion about the weather or parking. This initial joining helps to set a tone for the rest of the intervention.

The tone or style can vary considerably, as one might expect from the previous list of different family therapy approaches. Minuchin and Fishman (1981) define three distinct categories or styles used in family work to join initially with the family: (a) the close, (b) the median, and (c) the disengaged position. In the close approach, the social worker starts by working and allying with one family member, then another, and so on until each member is successfully joined in a therapeutic alliance. Another approach is the median position in which the social worker is an active listener who remains objective and neutral but encourages each member to talk. The third style for a family worker involves using that of the "disengaged therapist." This therapist remains distant and separate from the various family conflicts so that he or she can serve as a director or neutral expert who encourages and supports the position of some members while discouraging others on the basis of facts and objectivity.

The beginning phase of family intervention usually involves gathering information about the problems and strengths of the family. This entails collecting data as well as making observations about the norms and roles of family members. The social worker observes whether the norm of the family is open or closed communication and whether they defer to certain members or have a hierarchy or pattern for decision making.

Norms can be assessed by watching responses to open-ended questions related to family values and social interactions. For instance, if the social worker asks if the family is involved in the community, the responses are likely to vary; but the important response to observe is related to the degree of openness, tolerance, social interaction, or defensiveness exhibited. To whom does everybody look when such questions are asked? Do the others agree or disagree? What are the divisions or subsystems within the family as various members begin to take sides in response to questions? Do some members seem angry, frightened, depressed, or anxious as they respond? Do they look to others before expressing their opinions? Does their affect change as they look at different family members?

When asked about the division of tasks and responsibilities, family members will probably differ in perceptions. Members may indicate that they do a great deal of the housecleaning, shopping, baby-sitting, or other tasks; while other members disagree. Where are the agreements and alliances? Where are members in agreement? For instance, all members may agree that Dad is the disciplinarian, or Mom is the breadwinner, or Brother Bob is the bully.

Either a genogram or a social network diagram is recommended as a graphic tool to subsequently understand behavior and family dynamics. Some clinicians may want to have each family draw separate networks and then compare and contrast them among themselves, assessing the various points or people who are commonly included on the individual diagrams. This is a useful approach to efficiently yet objectively begin discussion of relationships among family members and others in the social environment (see Case 6.4).

Case 6.4: Stage 1: The Clements Family
Jim and Amy Clements, both age 34, came in to Family Social Services with their two children, Betsy (age 16) and Jim Jr. (age 12). Jim is unemployed, and Amy's income from working at a grocery store is inadequate and without health benefits. When Amy took Betsy to a doctor recently, they found that Betsy was not pregnant, as they had feared, but she did have a sexually transmitted disease

(STD), which required treatment. When Jim found the medication and learned from his tearful daughter that it was for an STD, he hit her. No one spoke about any of this for three weeks, and all were tense and avoidant of each other. After a recent incident in which Jim again struck Betsy as she snuck into the house at 3 A.M., the police were called. A policewoman with experience in domestic violence told them she would not arrest Jim as long as the family went to see a social worker at the local Family Social Service Agency.

After greeting everyone and some general discussion of the parking situation, the social worker gathered general information and then asked each family member to describe the current family situation. She noted that everyone looked to Jim after Amy spoke, and she sensed some fear or hesitation. Jim rather defensively stated that "This family had no problems until Betsy started hanging with some bad kids."

Betsy avoided eye contact with her father and looked furtively at her mother as if asking her to say something. Amy looked back and forth between her husband and her daughter and finally said, "I think we've had problems for a long time."

In spite of the social worker's support, Amy said, "I don't want to talk about it right now."

The social worker recognized that there were some secrets and a long history of avoidance, so she decided to simply commend each of them for coming in and beginning this process. She also drew a family genogram with input from all family members and encouraged a relaxed discussion of tasks, roles, and the social life of the family and each of its members.

Stage 2: Setting the Tone

Family members invariably copy and emulate the social worker's behavior in the sessions. The behaviors that the social worker wants to support and model for family sessions include (a) respect for all members, (b) openness, (c) honesty, (d) objectivity, and (e) moderation in response.

Respect for all members entails polite and supportive inclusion of everyone with a genuine desire to give everyone an opportunity to express themselves. The 80-year-old grandmother, the 8-year-old daughter, and the alcoholic father all have an equal right to be heard, even if the family norm has been to ignore or denigrate individual opinions. By setting this tone of respect for all and by including everyone, the worker is already shifting the family structure toward a more balanced pattern. At times, this modeling involves diminishing the role of some family members. For instance, a controlling, domineering, or even abusive father may be in the habit of dictating the behavior of other family members. As the social worker supports the free expression of family members who were previously quiet but who need to be heard, resistance can be expected.

Openness and honesty are essential to communication yet often elude families with problems. In fact, a common theme addressed by family systems therapists involves *secrets*. Family secrets typically relate to abuse, incest, or addictions. In some instances, family members may even be coached to keep the truth about those issues from the social worker. These are difficult and sometimes highly defended family traits, so the worker must gain the trust and support of the affected members before proceeding too far. If the worker is seeing the family specifically because the abuse has been reported and that is the focus of intervention, then the process is significantly helped. The worker can address the issue from the beginning and model an open and nonjudgmental attitude from the onset of treatment.

This *open,* nonjudgmental approach is essential, particularly in the early phases, because the worker needs to keep the secret in the open to improve the family situation. Secrets related to abuse, incest, or alcohol or drug addiction invariably cause guilt and embarrassment. To successfully work through such issues, they need to be openly and honestly discussed, giving each family member an opportunity to discuss the issue and explain his or her behavior, feelings, and responses.

Objectivity is another trait that is modeled in setting the tone. Postmodernists suggest that facts and objectivity are relative and subject to individual interpretation. The 16-year-old girl who stayed out all night and her father who hit her will see the situation very differently, with the daughter claiming abuse and the father claiming he felt the daughter needed to be severely disciplined. In such instances, both family members may need to change behaviors; so the worker needs to first model objective appraisals of the family dynamics before more appropriate, constructive discussions of changes in behavior can begin.

Objectivity is particularly important in family interventions, because, in the highly charged atmosphere of some sessions, each member is very sensitive to alliances and often hopes to get the social worker to ally or agree with him or her. Objectivity and even neutrality therefore are particularly important (and sometimes difficult to maintain), because even the appearance of "siding" with one family member implies that the worker is therefore "against" someone else.

Moderation in response refers to modeling a tone that encourages objective communication, listening, respect, and openness. The families seen by social workers frequently exhibit behavioral extremes; that is, they scream, accuse, get indignantly defensive, and generally fail to see the middle ground or the valid opinion of fellow family members. Through the modeling of a quiet, supportive, calm tone of voice and a genuine respect for all, the communication will improve as the extremes of behavior diminish. It allows for the balanced "middle ground" to assert itself. When families stop shouting and accusing, they can begin to genuinely listen and hear each other (see Case 6.5).

Case 6.5: Stage 2: The Clements Family

After gathering the facts and observing some initial dynamics, Ms. Johnson continued to set the tone for the sessions. While being objective and moderate in her interactions, she also modeled a degree of openness that was initially difficult for this family. She questioned them about family violence, alcohol and drug abuse, and sexuality. Ms. Johnson showed respect for Betsy's developing need for more independence and even intimacy but also supported the fact that her parents had understandable and legitimate concerns for her safety.

Jim objected to his daughter being out until 3 A.M. Furthermore, he said Jim Jr. should not be there at these sessions and should not know of his subsequently hitting Betsy or the police intervention. However, Jim Jr. quickly responded that he knew all about it and thought his sister was absolutely right in staying away.

"She probably knew Dad was going to hit her again, just like he always does when he's drunk," said Jim Jr. as his father glared menacingly at him.

Jim Jr. now looked tearfully at the social worker and said, "And how come that jerk Betsy's seeing hit her? He's meaner than dad!"

The family secrets around both physical abuse and alcoholism were now clearly in the open. It was now in the open that Betsy's boyfriend was also violent. Ms. Johnson wanted to maintain this openness and objectivity without completely alienating and marginalizing the father. She turned quickly to Jim Sr. and said, "Jim, this must be very hard for you to hear, but do you remember how hurt you were when you heard that your wife and daughter kept secrets from you? Maybe the whole family would be better off if we looked at some of these issues and got them out in the open so we can move forward."

Stage 3: Clarifying Interactions

In this stage, the social worker begins discussing observations about how people act within the family. The tone should be moderate and questioning rather than too authoritative since the worker wants to model an objective and accurate environment. Family members will legitimately disagree on a wide variety of issues from who washes the baby to who takes responsibility for paying the bills. Although part of the goal in this stage is to develop an accurate picture of both behavior and the division of tasks, the other goal is to begin genuine communication. Clarifying interactions involves getting all family members to openly and honestly dialogue around family patterns and alliances.

The social worker will make frequent observations such as "It seems to me that Lisa and Marge (mother and daughter) agree when it comes to entertainment or what to watch on TV. But when it comes to Marge's boyfriend, then Mom, Dad, and even your grandmother feel that Marge is wrong." The mother, Lisa, may then modify this, adding, "Well, I don't really mind him like her dad and grandma do. I just think she needs to slow down. You know, date other boys and not stay out so late."

The father might say, "Well that's no different from what I'm saying. I just don't think a 14-year-old girl should be out so late during the school week."

The social worker will use this dialogue to point out that there are clear agreements and disagreements at times but that these can be resolved through open discussion and a better understanding of how, when, and why issues get resolved. The worker uses a combination of stating observations about interactions and alliances and asking all family members for their assessments. This models a pattern for family members to become more consciously aware of their responses to others and subsequently supports an increased capacity to reconsider those patterns. For instance, the daughter may have historically agreed with her mother on nearly all issues but has recently been placed into the middle of a marital dispute in which her dating is identified with her parents' problematic marriage. As the family discusses and clarifies their current interactions, the fact of this displacement of facts and feelings will be brought out into the open (see Case 6.6).

Case 6.6: Stage 3: The Clements Family

Ms. Johnson knew that this third stage was critical for the Clements family. In fact, she was unsure if Jim would return since his son had revealed the family's secret about his violence and alcoholism. She knew that Jim was reluctantly willing to come only as long as his daughter Betsy was seen as "the problem." Now the focus might be on him and his lifelong pattern of secretiveness, binge drinking, violence, and overall insecurity based partially on his recent job loss. Jim did not want to talk about any of this, even his strong suspicion that his daughter had been abused by the boyfriend, just as by him. Only his wife's prodding and the policewoman's insistence had forced him to these sessions.

Amy Clements called and canceled their next session, leaving a message that stated that she would call if they decided to come back. The social worker had expected this cancellation and called Amy immediately. Amy vaguely hinted that Jim did not want to return and felt that he was being focused upon when he believed Betsy was the problem. The social worker was already well aware of this family dynamic in which Amy enabled Jim to maintain his avoidance and denial but then became deeply resentful of him. Amy had been turning more to the daughter, Betsy, as a friend and even reinforcing much of her daughter's relationship in spite of her discomfort with the violent, older boyfriend.

The social worker convinced Amy to come in again with the family. She then engaged the family in a discussion over Amy's initial pleasure in seeing her young daughter being so well treated by a somewhat older boyfriend but also her subsequent anger. Amy added, "I liked the boy at first. I even kind of envied Betsy until she came home all beat up. Then I just wanted to kill him. I don't know why I got so mad. Maybe 'cause he reminded me of Jim who can be so nice and sweet, and then he drinks and gets mean. I can take it. Hell, I'm used to it. But no daughter of mine is going to tolerate what I did!"

In spite of Jim's obvious discomfort, the social worker supported Amy's cathartic discussion of her fear of Jim, whom she still loved, and Amy's vicarious enjoyment of her daughter's relationship. The family structure was shifting as Amy, Betsy, and Jim Jr. all became more empowered as they recounted instances of Jim Sr.'s violent, drunken outbursts. The social worker encouraged Jim Sr. to respond; although, by this time, he knew he was not allowed to be intimidating or threatening. When his responses were clearly inaccurate, defensive, or self-serving, the social worker firmly but nonjudgmentally challenged or questioned his statements.

Stage 4: Restructuring

At this stage, the worker becomes more directive, engaging the family in the process of using the insight and information they have developed from previous sessions. They now know of their patterns of interaction and behavior, and they are ready to change dysfunctional patterns. There will not be complete agreement, but certain obvious and agreed-upon maladaptive behaviors can be restructured. Behaviors that are clear, specific, and relatively easy to modify may be the first to change. For instance, if the previous sessions have been open and nonjudgmental, then the objective descriptions of drug or alcohol abuse, as well as physical, sexual, or emotional abuse, can be restructured. The social worker's task at this stage is to take the family to the next level. They have rationally discussed issues of displacement, enabling, family alliances, and inappropriate interactions. Changing all of those involves a family discussion and agreement (see also Case 6.7).

- The father will be told to refrain from all comments about the teenage daughter's attire.
- The 10-year-old son will agree to have a neighbor watch him if his single mother goes out on a date. If he feels sick, the neighbor will take him to a doctor or otherwise help him, but the mother's date will not be canceled.
- The grandmother will stop making critical comments about her son-in-law to her daughter or grandson. If she has concerns, she can discuss them objectively at the next family session.
- The parents will stop criticizing the teenage son's friends. All have agreed that these are not really "bad kids." The son will agree to be back at home before 9 P.M. during the week.
- The 12- and 14-year-old children will agree to clean their rooms and perform other reasonable and agreed-upon tasks at home to help their single mother. Friday night will be reserved by all to be "family night."
- Dad will attend two AA meetings per week and attend the weekly support group for anger control. Other family members will refrain from making any derogatory comments about his past behavior but will immediately call the police and go to a safe place if he comes home with any alcohol on his breath.
- Mom will make at least two positive statements about the teenage son to him per evening. He will agree to complete homework assignments, as reported by the school guidance counselor.

Case 6.7: Stage 4: The Clements Family
Jim Sr. reluctantly and defensively returned to the next few sessions. He initially denied his alcohol abuse and violence but gradually admitted to it when his wife, daughter, and son all described incidents in which he had either directly or inadvertently hurt each of them. Jim indicated that neither of these behaviors had been in existence for long and that they began soon after he lost his job. The others said that he had always abused alcohol and threatened them, although they agreed that he had become much worse since he lost his job.

Jim Sr. began their eighth session in an uncharacteristically emotional manner. On the verge of tears, he admitted that he drank too much but that he did not remember ever hitting anyone in the family. He knows he did it, and that frightens him because he grew up in a family in which his father was a violent alcoholic and Jim Sr.'s greatest fear was that he would become like his father, whom he hated. Amy, who had become increasingly assertive and less depressed in the last few sessions, indicated some ambivalence: "Jim, I know you love us all, and, up until the last year or so, you've been a good husband and father. But now, I don't trust you, and I'm afraid of you. You need help, and I'm tired of making excuses for you while you just get meaner and blame me and the kids for your problems."

For the next few sessions, the social worker supported family discussions that looked realistically at the problematic patterns and behaviors but also asked for specific ways to change these behaviors. The social worker had each family member discuss and then write down exactly what he or she would do under future circumstances.

Jim agreed to attend two AA meetings per week plus go to two job interviews per week and join a support group for men. He also agreed to stop all drinking and refrain from all physical violence. The social worker and the three family members supported this but encouraged him to focus on one day at a time. They also developed contingency plans in case he did not succeed.

The daughter, Betsy, somewhat surprisingly announced that she had broken up with her boyfriend. The family actually laughed together when she said, "He had all of Dad's bad qualities, and none of his good ones." She also volunteered to stay home during school nights and help her brother with his homework. She and Jim Jr. agreed to raise their overall grades by one grade by the end of next term. Both of their grades had deteriorated in the last year, and this was seen as a very realistic and achievable goal.

Jim Jr. had been a model of openness in the sessions; and, other than some deterioration in grades in the last year, he had nothing else to change. He did, however, agree to let his sister "babysit" one night per week so that their parents could go out together.

Amy enjoyed her new empowered feeling. A great deal of resentment and fear had developed toward Jim Sr. Although the marriage had deteriorated severely in the last year, she indicated that, even before that, her husband had been very intimidating and that his drinking binges had existed for years. She decided that she would no longer make excuses for Jim or enable any of his behavior. She also agreed to go out with him once a week without the two children and see if they could change their marriage into an honest and open one with clear communication. She decided to stop criticizing Jim for his lack of a job but would instead support his job-finding efforts. Amy also announced that she was returning to school and had signed up for courses at the local community college, an activity that Jim had previously discouraged.

Stage 5: Monitoring and Evaluating

Change and restructuring are ongoing processes that require constant effort. When dealing with long-term, ingrained patterns of family interaction, such change is difficult. Family members need to be supported as they attempt new behaviors. If the family and the social worker have defined clear and observable behavioral changes, then the monitoring of those changes becomes relatively easy. For instance, if the father agreed to make no negative comments about his daughter's attire, then the sessions can include discussion of whether this did or did not happen. If, instead, the agreed-upon structural change had been something less behaviorally precise, such as "improve his attitude" toward his daughter, then it would be difficult if not impossible to monitor.

Gradual and incremental behavioral changes are also preferred since they are more likely to lead to success. The mother of a 10-year-old boy with attention-deficit/hyperactivity disorder might agree to give her son his medication twice a day, as well as calling the boy's counselor at school every Friday and accurately reporting the feedback to her son at their agreed-upon Friday night dinners. Each of these behaviors is clear enough that the social worker can monitor these behavioral changes at the weekly family meeting. If they did happen, then the mother is supported and reinforced and they may discuss slightly changing the behaviors. If they did not happen—for instance, the mother missed giving him the medications on three occasions—then the reasons for this are discussed objectively.

The ten-year-old boy will agree to stop calling his mother names, finish all homework assignments on time, meet twice weekly with the guidance counselor and keep him or her informed of his homework and academic performance, take his medication twice a day, meet with his mother every Friday after she has spoken with the guidance counselor to monitor his school work, and attend the weekly family sessions. By keeping these behavioral changes clear and achievable, the monitoring process is fairly straightforward (see Case 6.8).

Case 6.8: Stage 5: The Clements Family

The social worker maintained her supportive and open manner with the family but also made a point of thoroughly monitoring and evaluating each of the changes agreed upon by family members. Jim Sr. reported that he did attend two AA meetings, went to two job interviews, stopped drinking, and had no instances of violence. He had been unable to find a support group, so it was agreed that that change would be deleted.

Betsy helped her brother Jim Jr. on only two nights. Both of them decided they could get more accomplished separately, and, after some discussion and assurances that this was accurate, it was agreed to change the goal to only twice a week that Betsy would help. Betsy reported receiving a "B" on a recent term paper, which was considerably better than before. She also stayed home on Friday and actually enjoyed watching Jim Jr. while their parents went out together.

Jim Jr. did his homework and studied twice with his sister's help. He had not had any tests, but his guidance counselor called Amy to tell her that Jim seemed to be doing very well.

Amy had no reason to make excuses for Jim Sr., and all agreed that it was quite an accomplishment to *not* have to make that change. She stopped criticizing her husband for his lack of a job and was extremely supportive when he reported his two job interviews. Their evening out alone was described by both Amy and Jim as very strained, so it was agreed that they will go to movies, followed by a cup of coffee, rather than just "try to talk." Amy was also enthusiastic about the two courses that she would begin the next week.

The social worker discussed and reinforced each of these successes. However, she noted that Jim Sr. had been vague and elusive when asked about the location of the AA meetings as well as the names of the two companies where he interviewed. He became defensive when asked for more information and said, "What's the matter? Don't you believe me?"

The social worker received a recorded call at work one morning from Amy. She was extremely upset. She said that Jim Sr. had returned to the home drunk, and, when she confronted him, he angrily blamed the social worker for causing the problems in their family. Amy uncharacteristically and angrily disagreed. Jim took a swing at Amy and missed, but she got the two children to leave the house with her. She called the police and had him arrested. At the emergency family session the next morning, the social worker met with Amy, Betsy, and Jim Jr. Amy had learned that her husband had not attended any AA meetings, had gone on only one job interview, and had continued drinking during the time when he claimed to be abstinent.

The social worker reminded them of how well they had done at changing behaviors that were not related to Jim Sr. It was agreed that Jim would not be allowed back into the house until he was able to reach his previously agreed-upon changes. They also discussed the fact that there would be a need for an outside, objective monitor for Jim. They all agreed to three more visits to support their own positive changes and to reintegrate as a family without Jim Sr.

The social worker later met separately with Jim Sr. She was firm but not judgmental as she gave him the feedback that he was not helping himself by his dishonesty, continued violence, and alcoholism. She also confronted him with his continued pattern of avoidance and blaming others for his behavior. She reviewed a long list of behavioral changes he would have to make before Amy would even consider letting him return. She tried to leave Jim with a clear action plan and some hope for the future but also made it clear that his future with his family was dependent upon his taking responsibility for making some significant changes.

Stage 6: Closing

The final stage of family intervention is a *review* of the process, *support* for positive changes, and a *summary* of whatever needs to be done in the future. For brief family intervention, in which there have been only 8 to 12 sessions, then the last 2 sessions are needed for closing. For longer-term interventions, an additional session or two is used.

The review of the process involves discussing the various changes and insights that developed. It is helpful to have individual family members comment on their own as well as their relatives' changes. This review also serves to clarify and therefore reinforce specific behaviors. It reminds family members of what they need to do. For instance, simple but effective behaviors such as increasing compliments and stopping negative criticisms may have had dramatic and quick results when first tried by a family. The family may have had years of experience with negatively critical communication. Even though the family intervention taught them to change that pattern, the behavior could easily revert to the old pattern. The social worker should review this new communication style and why and when it can be used.

The closing stage is also used to support specific changes. If a family member has learned to become more assertive or has returned to school or has improved grades, then each of those positive behaviors can be discussed and encouraged. A discussion of possible future impediments also helps, with a review of what did or did not work in the past to accomplish certain changes. For instance, individual family members may have learned to accept responsibility for their own behaviors rather than blaming others or circumstances for their own actions; or, a family member may have been *too* willing to accept blame or responsibility for the behavior of others. It is useful at closing to support the maintenance of new learned behaviors by clarifying when, where, how, and why these changes should be continued.

The closing stage is also used to clearly define and list or summarize each change for future reference. Family intervention is an intense and complex process, and the number of changes, as well as the new insights gained, may be many more than either the social worker or the family members had realized. If the worker has maintained a clear behavioral focus or has relied upon a behavioral or cognitive case record (see the behavioral and cognitive chapters for examples), then this summary is a rather easy "re-listing" of previously agreed-upon tasks or goals. Even where the case record does not allow for such lists, the summary involves an exhaustive and precise description that will serve as a guide (see Case 6.9).

Case 6.9: Stage 6: The Clements Family

The social worker recognized that the Clements case was not exactly a "typical" family intervention example since, ultimately, Jim Sr. separated from the others who then at least temporarily restructured as a family. However, in reviewing the dynamics with Amy, Betsy, and Jim Jr., there was some agreement that the three of them had considerable strength that they supported in each other. Jim Sr. tended to undermine open communication, denigrate and intimidate each of them, and avoid or deny rather obvious behaviors.

The social worker believed that it was *not* her role to further criticize the now absent father. In fact, it had been only through her consistent objectivity and moderation that the family opened up and saw and communicated their previously denied fear and dislike of him and his behavior. She knew from experience with families that she could eventually get the family to consciously accept and then communicate their concerns only by modeling openness and objectivity. If she had been too critical of Jim Sr. in early sessions, he would have successfully stopped the sessions or the others may have even defended him.

In reviewing the process, she commented regarding the degree to which they had all grown in insight, confidence, and behaviors. Amy, who was initially depressed and noncommunicative yet extremely angry and resentful, was now quite different. Amy was a relaxed and confident woman who had gained new strength by standing up to her abusive, alcoholic husband. She also had developed a new, open pattern of communication with Betsy and Jim Jr. that was devoid of the secretive denial patterns fostered by her husband.

Betsy's self-esteem and confidence had grown immeasurably, and they all discussed the fact that she now knew that relationships with men were not all based in abuse or intimidation. In fact, Betsy spoke of her realization that relationships were improved and strengthened when there was openness, honesty, mutual respect, and equality. She and her mother cried together and held hands as they discussed their agreement.

Jim Jr. commented that "Everyone seems a lot better off now," but he hesitantly added, "I miss Dad sometimes. I know he did some bad things, but I don't think he's all bad."

The social worker agreed and commended him for his insight: "Maybe your dad will change. In his own way, I'm sure he does love you. It's up to him now to make some changes. In the meantime, you'll still see him, and there's a good chance that the two of you will be even closer than you were before."

In the last three agreed-upon sessions, the social worker supported each of the previously agreed-upon behaviors that did not relate specifically to Jim Sr. Together, they listed behaviors that would be useful in the future. The three of them had restructured the family into a rather supportive system now that Jim Sr. was gone. The possibility for his returning was left open, but it was agreed that he would not be allowed back until he had been sober and tested for sobriety for six months and had made other major behavioral changes.

SUMMARY

Families epitomize social systems in that virtually all of the important actions that affect individual family members impact on the rest of the system and cause change. There are dozens of different models and approaches to family intervention, and they vary somewhat in technique. However, there is some agreement that seeing families as opposed to seeing individuals alone often has certain advantages. By seeing people within their family systems, the social worker can observe the interactions and understand the family members' behaviors. Seeing families also provides balance so that the worker is less likely to be biased by separate individual statements. Furthermore, by seeing everyone together, the worker can provide a rational structure or setting in which family members may be more inclined to begin the process of genuine, open communication.

The many varied techniques used in family intervention include reframing or relabeling, questioning, examining interactional sequences, providing directives, and respecting physical cues (which include eye contact, breathing, sitting, positioning, diversions, voice modulation, and greetings).

There are six stages to family interventions: beginning; setting the tone, which includes modeling respect for all members, openness, honesty, objectivity, and moderation; clarifying interactions; restructuring; monitoring and evaluating; and closing, which includes reviewing, supporting, and summarizing the changes made.

PART three

ADVANCED TECHNIQUES
WITH INDIVIDUALS

PSYCHODYNAMIC INTERVENTIONS

HISTORY

In the last two decades, psychoanalytic theory and psychodynamic interventions have undergone several major changes. Contemporary methods based in ego psychology, object relations, and self psychology have been particularly adaptive to the demands of social work in today's climate (Strean, 1996; St. Clair, 1996).

Psychodynamically based interventions and the relevance of childhood development and experiences were the subject of endless and often heated debate throughout the 20th century. This approach was the basis of social work practice through the 1950s and later, even as it became the subject of a great deal of criticism from researchers and practitioners. It is unclear precisely how certain aspects of this approach are to be used. However, it is still universally accepted that early childhood experiences, along with other social, environmental, and genetic factors, interact to shape a person; and the psychodynamic perspective adds an invaluable perspective to that understanding.

So how are social workers to recognize the tremendous impact of childhood, parenting, early family dynamics, and their undeniable effects on individuals without returning to a reliance upon long-term psychoanalytic methods? Can some of the helpful and essential perspectives of the psychodynamic approach be utilized without resorting to prolonged insight-oriented therapy? The answer is an emphatic "Yes." In fact, most of the major texts on brief social work interventions indicate that the psychodynamic model is still one of the three bases for current brief interventions with either cognitive-behavioral and strategic-structural family work (Wells, 1993) or with problem-solving and mixed-eclectic types (Epstein, 1992).

Many social workers today have some ambivalence concerning psychodynamic interventions that rely on psychoanalytic theory and utilize psychoanalytic psychotherapy as a basis. Most recognize that the advent of psychoanalytic theory and its applications virtually gave birth to the field of modern psychotherapy. However, there are many social workers who believe that some of the values of the psychodynamic interventions are inaccurate, sexist, or culturally biased. These values reflect the Victorian, upper-middle-class culture of the times.

Sigmund Freud wrote and worked at a time soon after the Victorian era. The people of that era were highly repressed, at least among the middle and upper classes that generally formed Freud's clientele. His patients grew up in an era in which normal sexual instincts were viewed as wrong and bad and in which these instincts had to be consciously denied or repressed. This repression of normal, healthy urges led to anxiety, conflict, and occasional outbursts of inappropriate rage or depression, frequently directed at people who were not the appropriate targets of such expressions. Yet, the era during which psychoanalytic therapy began was a time when women were maintained in clearly subservient positions with limited economic or political power. The overly sexualized focus of Freud's theories was frequently inaccurate and even led to his parting of ways with Carl Jung. Many females of that era were undeniably frustrated; and the sexualized theories were appropriate metaphors reflecting the pervasive sexism of those times.

Freud was the first who recognized this dynamic of the psyche. He pioneered a reasonably clear, consistent theory for understanding how and why the mind acts as it does. His groundbreaking work in personality theory and childhood development is still considered one of the major breakthroughs of modern science. Whatever one's view of either the personality or theories of Sigmund Freud, most would argue that his impact on 20th-century psychology and beyond was widespread and revolutionary.

Social work mainstream has been shifting away from classical psychoanalytic interventions and toward object relations or self-psychology applications. However, even those social workers engaging strictly in short-term or managed care owe much to psychoanalytic theory. For instance, the concept of unconscious thoughts and events as the basis for motivating seemingly irrational behavior is a well-accepted fact of human behavior. Other psychoanalytic concepts such as transference, regression, repression, meaning and purpose in some dreams, and, at least, the clarity and internal consistency of the psychoanalytic theory of personality and stages of development have been accepted in varying degrees by the social work community. Social work practice owes a great deal to psychoanalysis even though the theory is not used in practice today as frequently as it was in the past.

In the past, the terms *clinical social worker, psychiatric social worker,* or, simply, *therapist* have all been used to denote people in the social work profession who practiced psychotherapy. *Psychotherapist* itself is an equally ambiguous term that is used in a narrow sense to describe only psychodynamic or insight-oriented therapists, or, in a broader context, to include behaviorally or cognitively trained practitioners. In either application, the role of psychotherapy in social work is being redefined.

From the 1940s through the 1970s, many social workers in mental health or children- and family-oriented social service agencies utilized approaches that were based on psychoanalytically oriented theory. These theories were typically Freudian or Jungian and focused on intrapsychic phenomenon and early childhood experiences as the bases for intervention. Social workers typically practiced psychotherapy by combining their social work orientation, which focused on environmental and social forces, with a psychodynamic orientation, which focused on reworking childhood or unconscious or repressed issues.

During the 1960s, when community organization reached its prominence in social work, the *psychotherapists* in the profession went from being viewed as the high status advanced practitioners to "part of the problem," a particularly damning description in those activist, politically charged times. Insight-oriented psychotherapeutic social workers were increasingly on the defensive.

The development of effective generalist and broad-based ecological and systems approaches in response to managed care concerns and economic pressures has further put into question the need for long-term approaches. However, a knowledge of the effects of childhood, family history, traumas such as abuse or neglect, bonding, and long forgotten or repressed memories from developmental years is even now undeniably central to the understanding of a client's current behavior and functioning. So, the debate continues concerning the proper place of therapy or psychotherapy in the social work profession.

However, virtually all definitions of the social work perspective toward practice refer to the field as being reliant on a *bio*psycho*social* perspective. This *psychological* component of the perspective is one that recognizes that childhood experiences and, particularly, the dynamics of one's family of origin, are central factors in defining one's personality, attitudes, behavior, and even adaptability to later functioning in roles such as student, worker, mother, father, police officer, or drug dealer. The importance of these early experiences and their effects is questioned not so much as the practicality or even helpfulness of recovering or reworking such phenomenon but as a necessity or prerequisite for helping the clients of social workers.

For some clients, such as adults who were abused as children and who subsequently distance themselves from any intimacy, the need for insight-oriented psychotherapy seems essential. In many other instances in which clients are oriented toward insight or viewing the origin of their marital or family problems as stemming from their unresolved anger toward a parent or a trauma that they initially only vaguely remember, psychotherapy also seems warranted. Precisely how this psychotherapeutic intervention is applied depends upon the needs of the client, the knowledge and ability of the social worker, and the agency's resources or receptivity to psychotherapy.

The advocates of psychoanalytic psychotherapy maintain that the quick and easy treatments that rely upon mere symptomatic changes are relatively ineffective. They charge that *symptom substitution* is likely to occur, wherein problems and symptoms based upon underlying unconscious factors will simply surface in other behaviors or symptoms unless the underlying cause is confronted.

Thus, the young man who is unable to form positive relationships with women because of an unresolved anger toward his mother can be behaviorally trained to interact positively with one or more particular women; but he will continue to display that anger toward others. Psychoanalytically oriented practitioners claim that his still-existent underlying anger will continue to be displaced onto other women who serve as substitutes for the hated mother figure. If the cause of his behavior (i.e., the unconscious anger) is not worked through and brought to the conscious and resolved through psychoanalytic techniques, the psychoanalysts claim that no amount of simple symptomatic behavioral change will be appropriate since the underlying cause still exists. As a consequence, his anger will exhibit itself in some other way.

Current psychoanalytically oriented social work practice is very different from Freudian analysis. Freud's theories were and are extremely significant (see Box 7.1), but his many followers recognized that he erred in certain ways. Also, his techniques, which provided breakthroughs for many of his clients, were too long and time-consuming and at times either ineffective or, at least, inefficient compared to many more recent psychoanalytically based approaches that focus upon the ego, object relations, or the self. Over the years, social workers have modified basic psychoanalytic practice and, generally, made it more reality based and ego oriented. Its many applications are also more efficient, more cost-effective, and briefer, thus assuring its use within even the most cost-oriented managed care settings.

Variations of Psychoanalytically Oriented Practice

There are at least four major variations of psychoanalytic theory and practice that follow a continuum: (a) purely *Freudian psychoanalysis,* (b) *psychoanalytic psychotherapy,* (c) *ego-psychological intervention,* and (d) *psychosocial treatment.* Furthermore, there are two additional separate psychoanalytic variations that do not quite follow this Freudian continuum: *object relations* theory and *self psychology* (often associated with Heinz Kohut), which are

The Life of Sigmund Freud

Sigmund Freud was born in Freiberg in Moravia in 1856 in an area of Austria that is now part of the Czech Republic. He was the eldest of seven children born to Jakob and Amalie [Amalie was Jakob's second wife and 20 years his junior]. When Sigmund was 4 years old, the family moved to Vienna where Jakob was a wool merchant. Freud recalled a good, although somewhat distant, relationship with his father, whom he saw as an authority figure. His mother was the more affectionate parent, and he was close to her until her death at age 95 (Sharf, 1996).

Freud received his medical degree in 1881 from the University of Vienna and spent his early professional years studying anatomy and neurology while engaged in general medical practice. However, his interests became increasingly oriented toward understanding the thoughts, emotions, and behavior of individuals and, particularly, the causes of such behavior. Freud began working with Joseph Breuer, with whom he collaborated, and together they wrote about the case of Anna (Breuer & Freud, 1895/1955), which used both catharsis and hypnosis to treat a hysterical conversion reaction. Although they later parted ways, Freud continued his studies of what he referred to as *unconscious motivations of behavior.* He also further developed his motives of repressed sexual drives and instincts as the bases for some behaviors. These trends in his theoretical development were an anathema to the physicians of his day who viewed etiology as wholly related to the brain. By 1900, Freud was widely rejected by the medical establishment of his day for his highly unorthodox viewpoint; and his book *The Interpretation of Dreams* (1938b) completed his isolation.

Freud used but later lost interest in hypnosis, which had been developed by Mesmer and Charcot. Freud believed that the effects of hypnosis were too limited. In spite of having met and viewed Charcot's highly dramatic hypnotic sessions with typically hysterical patients, Freud was disappointed in the fact that such change was not maintained for patients after the hypnotic trance.

Instead, he developed his own theory of personality based on the unconscious. While some view his capacity to accept the ostracism of his peers and manage to vigorously work in isolation as the example of a devoted and tireless idealist, others view his isolation more negatively. They see Freud as one who was unable and unwilling to accept any view other than his own. These detractors cite the example of the famous Vienna Psychoanalytic Society, which met in his home beginning in 1902, as an example of Freud's preference for followers rather than peers who could help develop his theories.

viewed by some as the most relevant for social workers in contemporary practice (Strean, 1996; St. Clair, 1996).

Freudian Psychoanalysis

A variety of terms are currently used to denote psychodynamic practice. The terms *psychoanalysis* and *Freudian analysis* usually refer to the purest of the psychoanalytic approaches or those that most closely follow classical Freudian techniques. In Freudian psychoanalysis, the client is frequently requested to lie on a special analyst's couch, become very relaxed, and free associate. *Free association*, which is described in more depth later in this chapter, involves verbalizing whatever comes into one's mind, regardless of whether it makes sense or is immoral, unusual, or irrational. The psychoanalyst views the patient as an individual who represses many thoughts and painful memories. This repression leads to a variety of unresolved conflicts and anxiety. The patient must be relaxed, unguarded, and open to resolve most conflicts that have been focused within the unconscious.

The purpose of this technique is to get the patient to bring to the fore and discuss those unconscious and repressed problems so that they can be resolved through greater understanding or insight. The analyst's primary technique is the interpretation of thoughts, behaviors, symbols, and dreams as a means of reaching back into the unconscious. Childhood memories and intrapsychic turmoil are explored in-depth since those are the factors that motivate current thoughts and beliefs. Here-and-now issues are not dealt with except as manifestations of underlying, unresolved issues. As a result, the analysis typically takes at least three years and sometimes twice as long, with two to five sessions per week. The goal is a reworking of the personality structure.

Psychoanalytic Psychotherapy

Freud himself was not a "pure Freudian" or classical analyst. Although he used and developed the classical techniques of free association, dream interpretation, uncovering the repressed, symbolic interpretation, and blank screen, his interpretations were, at times, more here-and-now oriented. Psychoanalytic psychotherapists are more oriented to present, functional problems than the "pure" analysts. The patient's time in treatment is therefore shorter, usually one to two years, and the patient and therapist typically talk face-to-face rather than relying on an analyst's couch. The interpretations used are still vehicles for uncovering unconscious phenomenon, but the interpretations are more likely to have present, reality-based implications than to be used solely for the purpose of uncovering. The psychoanalytically oriented psychotherapist is more sensitive to the needs of reality, the ego, and conscious day-to-day problems. This type of psychoanalyst may show more personality affect, provide some degree of support, and engage on a more personal level than the pure analyst, who avoids such personal interactions because such behaviors may undermine the needed development of transference toward the analyst.

Ego Psychology

Ego-oriented psychoanalysts (or analysts) are, as the name implies, more focused upon the ego and the conscious needs and concerns of the patient. The analyst sees herself or himself as more of a psychotherapist with an emphasis on helping the patient to cope more effectively with reality by resolving only those issues that lead to current dysfunction, anxiety, depression, or other difficulties. Whereas the pure analyst works toward a more thorough resolution of the psyche and the psychoanalytically oriented psychotherapist focuses on a more narrow resolution, the ego-oriented psychotherapist focuses primarily on the conscious and current problems and uses psychoanalytic techniques on a more efficient basis. Ego psychologists may, in fact, avoid the use of overly regressive psychoanalytic approaches that uncover deeply repressed or very early trauma. Among the more prominent ego psychologists is Anna Freud, Sigmund's daughter, whose work added to a better understanding of the defense mechanisms and who added immeasurably to the field, particularly in the treatment of children (Freud, 1936).

Erik Erikson is another ego psychologist who developed a theory of eight stages of development that must be successfully negotiated for an individual to grow and mature into adulthood. His developmental theory is perhaps more relevant to social work than the Freudian stages because it relates more to social and practical or ego-related issues. At each stage in the Eriksonian model, there is a crisis or developmental task that must be mastered. If that task is not successfully negotiated, then the next stage cannot be fully developed. Subsequent problems related to that particular stage will manifest themselves throughout life. Those eight stages are described later in this chapter's section on developmental stages.

Psychosocial Treatment

The term *psychosocial* has two generally accepted definitions. The first refers to the general, nonspecific concept of the term as a descriptor for any theory or approach that broadly encompasses a recognition of human behavior being the result of both psychological and social forces. The second use of the term is to describe a social work approach developed by Florence Hollis (1964) and used extensively in social work practice. It is described in several places throughout this book and is considered the primary brief variation of psychodynamically oriented social work methods (see Chapter 10).

Psychological forces include early childhood and family developmental histories, intrapsychic and repressed issues, and symbolic interpretations of behavior or dreams on the basis of their relevance to behavior, attitudes, and self-concepts. *Social forces* include environmental and current systems that affect behavior, attitudes, and self-concept—such as unemployment, divorce, health problems, or stress related to caring for children and parents—and employment and economic concerns. The ongoing effects of racism, sexism, or ageism are also social forces typically considered.

Object Relations

Object relations theorists focus upon early childhood experiences and the formation of psychological structures such as inner images of the self and the other, or *object*. The *object* in object relations theory refers to someone (or something) toward whom desire or action is directed. Individuals relate to a variety of objects. Furthermore, emotions and feelings have objects. An individual can love his spouse or fear his boss.

Representation is central to object relations theory. It refers to the way in which an individual psychically represents or possesses an object. An individual's frames of reference are either *internal*, which refers to subjective mental images, or *external*, which refers to objective, observable reality (St. Clair, 1996).

Object relations–oriented social workers suggest that, as they develop from infancy to adulthood, individuals develop a mental expression of the self that gradually becomes differentiated from the mother and then from the rest of the world. *Self-representation* is the internal or subjective expression of the self as it is experienced in relation to significant *objects* in a child's environment. One's self-representation establishes the way the individual relates to the world. If an individual's self-representation is that of a victimized, abused, and subjectively powerless or pitiful individual, then that individual subsequently relates to others on the basis of this representation, regardless of objective successes and accomplishments.

Self Psychology

The concept of the *self* differs from the concept of the *ego* since the ego is an abstraction that cannot be observed; whereas the *self*, or the *self object*, as Heinz Kohut (Sharf, 1996) suggests, is "not a person (a whole love object) but patterns or themes of unconscious thoughts, images, or representations of another" (p. 43). Kohut, the founder of *self psychology*, often focused upon narcissism, which he saw as being its own form of pathology that needed specialized treatment. Kohut disagreed with Freud's belief that narcissistic individuals could not be successfully treated because they could not form healthy relationships. Kohut believed that narcissistic individuals could form relationships or object relationships but that these relationships were narcissistic; that is, these were relationships with the self (St. Clair, 1996).

In treatment, self-psychology–oriented social workers are very empathic to these clients with damaged notions of self and they help the client to form a cohesive self. This process is called *transmuting internalizations,* whereby the clinician helps the client to develop normal adult psychic functions for the self such as reality testing and realistically regulating self-esteem.

PERSONALITY THEORY

Freud hypothesized that the personality is made up of three entities identified as the *id,* the *ego,* and the *superego.* The *id* is the most primitive, basic, and instinctually based component of the personality. The id exists from birth (or before) and seeks only its own gratification. Eventually, the ego and, later, the superego develop from the id. The id is governed by the pleasure principle, and some of its biologically based instincts are immoral and asocial. The id desires the expression of these instincts regardless of consequence or costs.

Eventually, the *ego* develops from the id and serves as a more realistic coordinator or executor of the personality. It thrives to help the individual meet his or her needs and basic, primitive instinctual desires; but, the ego also recognizes reality and the need to achieve desires, goals, and demands by interacting with real-life forces. The ego operates on the reality principle and works with the id to help it achieve goals by waiting for more appropriate targets for the discharge of energy or by interacting with the environment to more successfully negotiate the fulfillment of those needs. The ego is the administrator of the personality; it forces the more primitive and potentially dangerous instincts to be stopped or at least held in check until a more realistic or appropriate way of discharging the needs can be found or developed.

The *superego* is comprised of the *conscience* and the *ego ideal.* The superego begins developing between the ages of three and five and grows and adapts, with its major development being in the earlier years. It consists of the traditional values and norms of society as interpreted for the child by the parents. It decides right from wrong and sends signals such as guilt and anxiety to the ego as a way of further supporting and directing the ego in the attempts to meet id-driven needs, instincts, and realistic pursuits of the ego. However, this is achieved in a fashion that considers the needs of others, society, and an idealized self.

The id, the ego, and the superego are simply theoretical constructs that form an enormously useful basis for understanding human behavior. These constructs cannot, however, be empirically validated in any direct or measurable sense; but they can be used to form a clear, consistent, and logical basis for understanding, interpreting, and treating feelings, emotions, and behavior.

Even clinicians who do not use psychoanalytic techniques must be versed in this personality theory, as well as in the developmental stages described by psychoanalytic therapists.

BEHAVIORAL ISSUES IN THE STAGES OF DEVELOPMENT

Clinicians who use psychoanalytic approaches also are required to be well versed in understanding how individuals grow and develop. This approach generally follows Freudian theories of developmental stages in which the individual progresses through an oral, anal, phallic, latency, and then genital phase. Within these stages, certain body parts are focused upon or, as psychoanalysts would describe it, this libidinal energy becomes cathected onto these parts. The theory states that at any stage of development the maturing individual may become "stuck" or fixated at that stage as a result of psychological trauma, extreme stress, or anxiety. Furthermore, individuals may regress to that stage later in life when feeling particularly threatened or insecure.

The *oral stage* (birth to 18 months) is the earliest and, therefore, the most primitive stage. The infant's energy is focused around eating, sucking, and the mouth. Fixation at this stage would manifest itself in the most primitive of behaviors such as schizophrenia or psychotic depression.

The *anal phase* (18 months to 3 years) is one in which the activities are based on toilet training and the developing discipline to retain or pass feces. This is a symbolically important stage since it represents the time when children are becoming consciously aware of their power to retain or give. Toilet training itself can be conflictual for some; and, if there is sufficient anxiety around this developmental stage, the individual can become fixated here or regress to personality characteristics that are "anal" in character, such as stubbornness; withholding; controlling; or extremely neat, fastidious, or rigidly punctual characteristics. Reaction formation that may be related to this stage includes messiness or rebelliousness.

The *phallic stage* (3 years to 5 years) is focused around the genitals; typically, the developing child is oriented around stimulating or showing his or her genitals or looking at his or her own body or that of others out of curiosity or pride. A child in this stage is still extremely self-centered; but the need for love, admiration, and caring is increased at this stage as the child begins to form more mature bonds. For instance, the Oedipus and the Electra complexes develop at this stage. The Oedipus complex refers to the Greek tale of King Oedipus who unknowingly fell in love with his mother and killed his father. The Electra complex in females similarly involves the instinctual love of the young girl for her father, with the added component of jealousy of the same-sex parent. This stage is typically resolved during this age for most normal, healthy children; although those who do not successfully resolve it may be fated to maintain frequent patterns of immature and often unrequited loves for opposite-sex parent figures.

The *latency stage* (usually 5 years to 7 years) begins after the phallic stage. Although there is some debate in the field regarding the degree of sexual interest at this age, it is a transitional stage preceding adult sexuality.

The *genital stage* describes adulthood and its mature integration of sexual and emotional development.

Erikson's Eight Psychosocial Stages

Erik H. Erikson (1963) was a psychoanalyst whose interest was in other cultures and how children and adults developed in varying cultures. He was among the first to examine adult development and to recognize that individuals change, grow, and adapt throughout their lifetimes. Furthermore, he directly studied the ongoing question of the causes of human behavior: "In every field there are a few very simple questions which are highly embarrassing because the debate which forever arises around them leads only to perpetual failure and seems consistently to make fools of the most expert. In psychopathology such questions have always concerned the location and cause of a neurotic disturbance. Does it have a visible onset? Does it reside in the body or in the mind, in the individual or in his society? . . . In recent years we have come to the conclusion that a neurosis is psycho- *and* somatic, psycho- *and* social, and *inter*personal" (p. 23).

Erikson's insightful stages resulted from his direct observation of children in different cultures and relied upon objective anthropological methods with normal populations—as contrasted to Freud's observations, which were partially derived from Freud's work with his patients. Erikson's eight psychosocial stages are presented and discussed in the following sections.

Trust versus Mistrust (Infancy)

The newborn must learn to trust that the caring mother will be there to feed, nurture, and provide essential care. If such basic needs are not met, the infant will grow to be mistrustful and incapable of relying on others or trusting them, thus significantly reducing the likelihood of forming close attachments later in life.

Autonomy versus Shame and Doubt (Early Childhood)

Toilet training, which is the first activity requiring some active mastery on the part of the developing infant, is crucial in subsequent activities involving confidence. If the small child is warmly supported, encouraged, and praised in this process, he or she grows into a more comfortable and potentially confident and independent person. If excessive criticism and multiple failures are focused upon by critical or demanding parents, shame and diminished capacity for autonomy ensue.

Initiative versus Guilt (Preschool Age)

Erikson, as well as Sigmund Freud, theorized that young children must resolve their anger toward their same-sex parent and stop engaging in fantasies toward their opposite-sex parent. They must successfully resolve their rivalry and use their energy to engage in successful activities and play with others as a way of taking initiative and developing competence. Without such a resolution, guilt over such frustrated fantasies develops, leading to a diminished capacity to actively develop relationships.

Industry versus Inferiority (School Age)

Cognitive as well as social skills necessary in school are central in this stage, and one's sex role identity is a focal issue. The child who develops these required skills enhances his or her sense of adequacy or industry, whereas insufficient growth in this stage culminates in a sense of inadequacy and inferiority.

Identity versus Role Confusion (Adolescence)

Erikson saw this stage as extremely important in establishing a foundation for adulthood. Adolescents are required to develop some assurance that others see them as they see themselves. At this stage, adolescents confront the meaning or purpose of life and begin to independently establish future goals. They begin to recognize that they need to independently accept responsibility for who they are and what they are doing with their lives. Without this developing sense of self-identity, it is difficult to establish a purpose for being; and decisions regarding many upcoming adult responsibilities are likely to be difficult to define.

Intimacy versus Isolation (Young Adulthood)

At this stage, the young adult is learning to work with others and to form closer attachments. Some intimate relationships may develop, and the young adult may initiate close relationships. Isolation can develop if the young adult cannot master cooperative, close interactions.

Generativity versus Stagnation (Middle Age)

The stage beyond taking responsibility for oneself is that in which a person becomes responsible for helping others. By helping others develop and grow, one continues his or her own maturation. Those who do not develop this sense of responsibility will stagnate and miss the energizing adult feeling associated with contributing to the growth of others.

Integrity versus Despair (Later Life)

A sense of personal worth and accomplishment accompanies older adults in or near their sixties. There is a sense that they have generally done well and have experienced most of whatever any person could ask of life. Those who reach this age feeling they have not accomplished their life goals, even in a very ill defined way, experience a despair, regret, or sense of a lack of value or purpose to their lives. They feel that they have not contributed anything of value and fear that they cannot contribute to others or find meaning to their lives in their remaining years.

DEFENSE MECHANISMS

Perhaps the greatest disservice that history has perpetrated on Freud has been the fact that Freud himself, his ideas, and his original writings have been obscured and, ironically, misinterpreted and misanalyzed. Freud was a scholar and highly literate individual who wrote poetry and history and brought the lives of saints into fascinating discussions with his patients. Yet, if he were a practitioner today, probably no major professional journal would publish his narrative case examples. His work was replete with connections to literature and the arts, and he displayed a marvelous understanding of a wide variety of problems. For instance, Freud used Leonardo da Vinci and his painting of the Madonna as an example of sublimation and a way for da Vinci to deal with the loss of his mother at a young age. Repression was explained in the case of a woman's lost love but only after Freud helped her make a connection via a poem by Keats that deals with the god Apollo (Freud, 1938a and b).

In today's empirical and quantitatively oriented environment, Freud's case studies with their highly subjective interpretations would be considered very unscientific. However, the repudiation of certain psychoanalytic concepts due to their inherent inability to be quantified may ultimately limit today's social workers. Psychoanalysis is central to debates and controversies over current practice because it is historically dominant; yet, the teaching of psychoanalytic concepts is being deleted at schools of social work, which rely upon quantitative clinical outcome methodology to discredit the traditional, long-term psychoanalytic approach. It may be useful for social workers to make a clear distinction between psychoanalytically oriented clinical techniques that are often long-term in nature and certain psychoanalytic concepts that seem to be self-evident and essential to understanding practice.

For instance, the concept of defense mechanisms is well accepted in everyday living as well as in practice. The degree to which they need to be addressed, or even whether they should be ignored, may be debated, but their existence and descriptions are marvels of psychological understanding and awareness. Cognitive and behavioral therapists frequently choose to ignore defense mechanisms, but most of them accept the fact that defense mechanisms do exist. The question for many in current practice is the degree to which their existence should affect interventions. Psychosocial therapists, existentialists, Rogerians, humanists, and ego psychologists believe the defense mechanisms are overly emphasized by traditional psychoanalysts, particularly those analysts who use symbolic interpretation extensively for seemingly unconnected behaviors. But very few social workers in practice today, a hundred years after defense mechanisms were first described, can deny the tremendous significance of defense mechanisms as factors in the history, evolution, or treatment of mental health problems. Social workers have to know how, when, and whether to incorporate the knowledge of their existence into practice.

Although psychoanalysts originally viewed defense mechanisms as somewhat pathological since they distort reality, they later viewed them as understandable and even healthy responses for defending the ego from real or perceived assault. The general concept behind defense mechanisms is that individuals must adapt to unacceptable thoughts, so they distort them to meet their needs, which usually involves diminishing anxiety. Past recollections, thoughts, or id impulses are changed (distorted) into something that is not realistic.

The listing of defense mechanisms varies by different authors. Anna Freud defined the principal defense mechanisms as repression, projection, reaction formation, fixation, and regression. Sigmund Freud initially saw displacement (along with identification) as primarily an aspect of personality development rather than a defense mechanism. Current lists vary, but typically include repression, denial, rationalization, intellectualization, isolation, projection, displacement, and reaction formation.

Central to all psychoanalytically based psychotherapy is the notion that the defense mechanisms must be dealt with in a way that will help the patient to gradually understand and work through the unconscious thought or impulse that is being defended. Defense mechanisms falsify and distort reality and subsequently one's behavior as individuals act on these distortions. The task of the psychoanalytically oriented social worker is to change or eliminate the defenses and free up the psychic energy so that the patient can more effectively and directly deal with reality. Through the careful process of well-timed interpretations and explorations of the unconscious, patients are helped to understand that there are better, healthier, or more adaptive means of dealing with the feared unconscious phenomenon.

Timing and *sensitivity* are essential factors in the psychoanalytic process of working through the defense mechanisms. These mechanisms were developed to defend the ego, so it must be recognized that they do serve a purpose. The social worker or analyst must be careful to avoid premature interpretations. For instance, the football player who represses his homosexual urges through sublimation in his sport or even though overreaction with extreme bias toward homosexuals will not be helped by premature suggestions that he is homosexual. Quite the contrary, if such an interpretation is even hinted at too early in therapy, the understandable response of the patient will be extreme anger, denial, and even the loss of credibility for the analyst who would even suggest such a consciously unacceptable and absurd notion.

The primary reason that psychoanalytic psychotherapy is such a slow, arduous, and often painful process is that a great deal of psychic energy goes into defending the ego from these thoughts and unconscious impulses. The more threatening and anxiety provoking the impulse, the greater the energy the patient must exert to repress the impulse or to defend against it coming to the conscious. At some level, the social worker and the patient are, at least initially, working at cross-purposes. The patient is often "driven" into psychotherapy because the defense mechanism itself has caused the person great pain or difficulty; yet, the individual cannot give up the defense for fear of the even greater pain of that which hides in the unconscious. It is clear why psychodynamic intervention must involve a long, sensitively timed process that works toward letting the defenses diminish while slowly working back to the origin of the problem. The origin of the problem must first be explored through a long process of interpreting symbolic thoughts, dreams, and actions and through free association and the therapeutic use of transference. Only then can the patient let down the defense mechanisms since they are no longer needed. If the dreaded unconscious basis for the defense mechanisms is found to be manageable, then the patient can finally understand and better accept his or her underlying problem through the help of the psychodynamic intervention.

In the following sections, each of the most commonly accepted and observed defense mechanisms are defined and explained with case examples and descriptions of clinical interventions.

Reaction Formation

This defense mechanism involves replacing the unconscious anxiety-producing thought or feeling by its opposite thought or feeling. Love is typically replaced by hate. The assessment of this defense mechanism is typically developed by the observation of a certain exaggeration or overly dramatic presentation in the behavior or by a seeming compulsion to behave in this way. For example, the patient feels he or she has to do this but does not understand the reason; or a patient is simply so anxious in the extreme and inappropriate feelings or actions displayed that observers cannot help but question whether it is not a cover-up of the patient's real feelings.

The patient protects himself or herself from the unwanted unconscious impulses by anxiously, compulsively, and enthusiastically replacing that thought with the opposite, thus assuring himself or herself and anyone else that the unconscious thought could not possibly exist since the patient acts in such a completely opposite manner. In many instances, the reaction formation is diagnostically supported by the fact that the patient simply protests too much.

Psychoanalytically oriented psychotherapists need to be careful in their judgment of this defense mechanism. At times, very strong and seemingly exaggerated emotions are real and genuine. So the patient who engages in "gay bashing" may in fact be a genuine bigot who hates homosexuals and needs help dealing with that very real but counterproductive feeling. Similarly, the overly rigid, organized, compulsively neat person may not be reacting to an unconscious fear of losing control, as some psychoanalysts would suggest, but, rather, may be obsessive-compulsive.

Case 7.1: Reaction Formation

Jane was a 26-year-old single mother of a severely handicapped 3-year-old daughter. The father of the child stopped all contact when it became apparent at the birth of their daughter, Melanie, that she had Down's syndrome and that it was quite severe in its effects.

When Jane initially came into treatment, she indicated that it was for depression and anxiety that were probably related to her stress and lack of social support. However, she quickly indicated that Melanie was not at all the cause of it. In fact, Jane's only "joy in life" was caring for Melanie, who required constant attention but was "the greatest kid in the world and the best thing that ever happened to me."

Jane's attention to Melanie was almost constant. This was not only because her daughter was unable to feed, clothe, or bathe herself but also because Jane felt that no one else was sensitive enough to Melanie's unique needs. Jane's mother was no longer allowed to care for her granddaughter after she suggested that Jane was spoiling Melanie and once even suggested that Melanie could be helped by more professional care, possibly even in a residential setting. For 3 months after that suggestion, Jane never let her mother even see Melanie.

The psychoanalytically oriented social worker asked Jane to bring her daughter into a session and was struck by the fact that Melanie was impeccably dressed and clean while her mother Jane was disheveled and dressed in shabby old clothes. Jane rapidly and almost angrily told the social worker how cute and well behaved her daughter was in a constant stream of verbiage that prevented the social worker from saying a word throughout the session.

In Case 7.1, for example, Jane is defending against a repressed and unconscious disappointment and anger concerning her daughter Melanie. The birth of a severely handicapped child often involves a narcissistic trauma to oneself, as the child is viewed as an extension of the self. This disappointment and the subsequent anger are, at a conscious level, totally unacceptable and irreconcilable with the fact that the child is a product of oneself and the responsibility of the patient. Jane's anger at Melanie was further exacerbated by the rejecting father who abandoned them both upon being told that his daughter was "defective." Jane felt an overwhelming need to repress this unacceptable anger and disappointment, so any conscious thought on her part that was motivated by this disappointment had to be immediately squelched or else it would overwhelm her with anxiety. The analyst's task became one of very slowly and gradually interpreting some of Jane's overly reactive and defensive statements for what they were—cover-ups for her real feelings.

Timing and the formation of a trusting bond between the social worker and patient are essential. If the social worker interprets Jane's defensive statements too early in the process, she will reject the interpretation and, in all likelihood, the analyst as well. But the analyst can very slowly and gradually break through the defense to the point at which Jane can recognize that her feelings are understandable and acceptable and not necessarily incompatible with being a good and caring mother for a child who needs special attention. In fact, Jane needs to see that her reaction formation, which distorts both her feelings and her ability to understand the reactions of others or even her daughter Melanie, is counterproductive. As Jane is gradually helped to recognize the reality of the limitations of her daughter in certain ways and Melanie's need to be helped to deal with the realistic demands of life in a way that challenges Melanie to meet her best potential, Jane and Melanie will both be helped.

Repression

Repression occurs when a thought or impulse is forced out of the conscious because it arouses undue alarm. It was one of Freud's earliest concepts and originally was developed in his work on the development of the personality. Freud divided the personality into the id, the ego, and the superego; and he divided the mind into the conscious, the preconscious, and the unconscious. Freud felt that unconscious material was relatively inaccessible to the conscious mind because it was repressed or hidden there. Repressed thoughts are essentially thoughts that are so upsetting that they are put into the unconscious so that they do not consciously arouse anxiety. However, the repressed thoughts sometimes enter into the preconscious where these thoughts are more accessible and also occasionally more anxiety producing.

Repression takes the form of *displacement* in many instances. Typically, this displacement is manifested in some symbolic way; so, a young man who resents his authoritarian father, but whose anger toward his father is consciously unacceptable, displaces the anger onto other authority figures. For instance, the young man views his teachers as mean, demanding, and hateful when they may not have any of those qualities. Repression can also take on physical symptoms. A man could become impotent or a woman frigid as a displaced repression of sexual desires that they find consciously unacceptable.

Psychoanalytically oriented social workers suggest that there is nothing accidental about slips of the tongue, forgetting certain names, or mistakes in reading or writing. To these therapists, these verbal errors have deeper meanings and these mechanisms are all repressed parts of the preconscious or foreconscious. In his *Psychopathology of Everyday Life*, Freud (1938a) explained that the process of forgetting names usually involves a predisposition to forget the name, a process of suppressing it that took place before, and some association with an outer issue that is used in place of the "forgotten" one.

Freud's case examples are fascinating in their process. In one, he gradually helps a brilliant young woman patient understand how and why she selectively changed Keat's poem "Ode to Apollo." Freud had previously been talking with this woman about Victor Hugo and Hugo's belief that love can turn grocery clerks into gods. The woman said that this is so and that love is a wonderful experience with frequently terrible disappointments. She recounted her love for a young man whom she idolized. He was an actor, and all of her friends warned her against this young man. Her "Apollo" eventually disappointed her severely when he left to marry a wealthy woman. The patient and Freud later discussed the Keats poem, which she recited but managed to change in several significant ways to deal with her disagreeable experience in which her own god had turned out to have been far worse than most mortals. Her recalling of the lines of the poem reflected her current mental state.

Case 7.2: Repression

Sister Jean was a 30-year-old Catholic nun from an Irish background. She lived in a community of other nuns who were all members of the Dominican Order. Although she found them to be a good, supportive support system, she had become increasingly anxious, depressed, and unable to sleep. She was unable to talk with her fellow nuns because they were all much older and because "some of what I dream about is too disgusting to talk about."

Sister Jean had entered the convent after high school and was proud of her vocation and her teaching assignment with fourth-grade children. When she began talking to the psychoanalytically oriented social worker, Sister Jean was encouraged to free associate while reclining on the couch. Initially, she protested that this seemed "silly" and unnecessary and she was unable to say anything. The analyst asked about her dreams, which she said were upsetting but which she felt had nothing to do with her current depression or anxiety.

For the initial 4 months, Sister Jean said very little even though her anxiety seemed to be actually increasing and her ability to sleep was lessened—typically with her suddenly being aroused at 2 or 3 in the morning because of "upsetting dreams" that she could not recall. As she began to accept the quiet but seemingly accepting and totally nonjudgmental analyst, she got past her resistance and was able to talk about some aspects of her dreams. They were all of a sexual nature and typically included thoughts of intercourse and other sexual behavior with

unknown older men or with the father of one of her students. As she came to realize that she could talk and think about such issues and that her analyst did not
condemn her for her "sinful thoughts," she gradually opened up more.

Sister Jean's free associations began to focus on her childhood and her father,
whom she said she loved dearly. She described him as an idealist and a romantic
who loved her deeply but cautioned her often about the "sins of the flesh." She
never dated during high school because she did not trust the intentions of the
young boys and none of them quite measured up to her father. Her father had died
over a year ago, but she immediately insisted that his death had nothing to do with
her depression or anxiety and certainly nothing to do with her "dirty" dreams.

After nearly a year of sessions, Sister Jean very hesitantly mentioned that the
analyst had been in her dreams. Furthermore, the analyst noted that Sister Jean
had developed some speech and behavioral mannerisms that were childlike in
their quality and her dress had become both more youth oriented and seductive.
Several months later, she elaborated on the sexual nature of her dreams about the
analyst and, when she did, she told him that it was hard for her to talk about it
with him since she knows that he disapproves of her sexual thoughts and he will
see her for what she is—"a bad person who cannot control my dirty thoughts and
dreams." The analyst encouraged her to talk about her assessment of him and her
thoughts about the dreams, what they meant, and why she saw him as condem-
natory of sex.

These discussions were extremely difficult and painful for Sister Jean. Her
ultimate admission that she had sexual urges was difficult for her, and her realization that she had deep love and even sexual feelings toward her recently
deceased father was even more painful. However, after nearly three years of slow
and painful exploration of deeply repressed material through free association,
dream analysis, interpretation of symbolic and actual behavior and feelings, and
particularly through gaining self-acceptance and insight into the nature of sexuality as a normal part of everyone's life, Sister Jean improved. The symptoms
stopped; but, more importantly, the patient's insight and understanding developed into greater self-acceptance.

Case 7.2 involves several major classical psychoanalytic issues in addition
to repression. These include resistance, an unresolved Oedipus complex,
interpretation of dreams, working through the transference, and repression.
These are dealt with in depth in the next section, which discusses psychoanalytic techniques, and are briefly considered here as well.

The Oedipus complex (or *Electra complex,* which some prefer as the term
for females) became evident in Sister Jean's attitude toward her father. Her
love for him and her unresolved and repressed sexual feelings toward him not
only precluded her subsequent relationships with men but also became significant issues in the analytical process. The patient needed to understand
these repressed feelings toward her father that were causing her difficulty in
the present. Her current anxiety and sleep disorder were, no doubt, initiated
by the recent death of her father. This death forced the repressed sexual urges
into the preconsciousness, which often manifests itself in the form of dreams.

Dreams are generally either wish fulfillment or ways of working through
repressed material from the unconscious. Since such material is not acceptable

to conscious thought processes, dreams are frequently used as vehicles for at least partially resolving and dealing with thoughts that force themselves into the less guarded and undefended sleep states. They frequently become activated when some trauma such as a death activates the need to consider repressed or otherwise unconscious material. Essentially, it is a way of bringing such issues closer to conscious awareness as they slip past the guard of the defense mechanisms and force open repressed thoughts. Since even in dream states patients are unable to see the repressed material, they usually manifest themselves symbolically. So fires, volcanoes, tunnels, and cigars all become symbolic representations of passion, orgasms, or female and male genitalia. Such symbolism has become commonplace in modern culture and is often central to classical movies by Federico Fellini and Ingmar Bergman, as is the more humorous use of symbols by Woody Allen.

Sublimation

Sublimation is not a classic Freudian defense mechanism. In fact, sublimation is described by Freud as a type of displacement in which socially unacceptable urges are modified or converted into socially acceptable behaviors or thoughts. Sublimation is also atypical in that many current psychoanalytically oriented social workers as well as nonpsychoanalytic psychotherapists actually encourage it as a healthy response to stress or even anxiety. Sublimation is the process of acting out unacceptable thoughts and impulses in a positive and constructive way. Traditionalists still view it as unhealthy in that it does not resolve the underlying problem. However, most current psychotherapists and, particularly, holistic practitioners who are more concerned with behavior than underlying causes are often content with working through problems by sublimating the anxiety rather than going through the long and arduous task of psychoanalysis.

Sublimation frequently is seen in sports and recreational outlets. Active games of tennis or basketball that may exhaust but subsequently relax previously anxious or depressed individuals are good examples of sublimation. Rather than violently assault one's father, boss, or spouse, individuals who sublimate their anger will go out and smash a tennis ball, drive a golf ball, or play an aggressive game of basketball. Slightly less pent-up emotions can be resolved through gardening, particularly planting seeds that need to be nourished and developed. Some may take care of pets or volunteer to help other individuals as a way of fulfilling inner needs.

In nonpsychoanalytic circles, some of the therapeutic effects of sublimation are viewed positively from both a psychological and a biological perspective. The healthy effects of sports have become commonly accepted, and even terms such as *getting the adrenaline flowing* or *getting one's second wind* (as the result of increased lung capacity and more efficient flow of oxygen) or the hormonal changes in athletes are now well documented. These effects are nearly universally encouraged as ways of working through frustration and anxiety and as healthy outlets that allow the body to respond against the negative effects of the stress of modern everyday life. Psychoanalytic psychotherapists currently view sublimation as a healthy but less than ideal way of dealing with unconscious or repressed material that ultimately still needs to be resolved. Holistic therapists view sublimation as an appropriate and acceptable means of actually working through the symptoms or effects of problems and typically see no need to resolve the underlying cause. See Case 7.3.

Case 7.3: Sublimation

John was a 35-year-old carpenter who was devoted to sports. He was completely immersed in a life of watching, playing, and talking about sports. He would go from the baseball to the basketball to the football season, fanatically supporting his home teams and retreating into depressed moods when they performed poorly. He also was an avid player and member of local basketball, baseball and volleyball teams.

John's life consisted of his work and sports, and even his work was in some ways used as a vehicle to help his training. John's work was such that he could have avoided hard, strenuous lifting, or exercise; but, instead, he sought out jobs that involved heavy lifting as a means of keeping in shape. When he was not working or involved in a sport, he was training either by running or weight training. Although John was not an exceptional athlete by nature, he and his teammates agreed that his "hustle" and hard work more than made up for his fairly average natural athletic skills.

John came into a social worker's office only at the insistence of his friends after he physically assaulted one of his teammates for not trying hard enough in a game and for lacking team spirit. This particular outbreak was more of a projection on his part. At age 35, John was no longer able to keep up in his basketball league with his younger teammates and projected this "laziness" onto another.

John was socially isolated in spite of what was ostensibly an extremely active social life. However, his social life consisted of playing sports, not genuinely interacting with any of his colleagues at even the most superficial level. While his teammates invariably went out for a few beers after most games, John refused to go and even criticized the others for breaking training. Their attempts to "fix him up" on dates always failed because he said that a woman would only get in the way of his excelling in sports. After multiple attempts, his teammates stopped asking him out socially or trying to find him dates. In fact, they began to distance themselves from John as he became increasingly fanatical concerning sports and the activities that the friends viewed as merely fun and a means of relaxation.

John reluctantly came to see a psychoanalyst only after his basketball coach, who was a social worker by profession, insisted that John see this analyst after he punched a teammate who was not running quickly enough down court to help with defense. The coach suspended him from the team until he received help. The coach remarked that John was getting much worse lately and questioned whether it was time for John to quit the team since he could not realistically keep up with some of his younger teammates.

John reluctantly admitted to his female psychoanalytically oriented social worker that he had become upset with himself lately since he was doing so poorly in sports. He explained that he had tried to exercise more and work out harder and that his whole life was devoted to sports, but he was simply unable to do as well as his younger teammates.

After a few sessions, John also confided to his coach that while the analyst "seemed like a real nice lady," she probably "couldn't understand what sports mean to a guy like me." The coach insisted that John must return to the analyst and tell the analyst about his misgivings. Somewhat to John's surprise, the social worker seemed to accept this concern about her and merely encouraged John to talk more about his concerns and to say whatever he wanted to—even if it did not seem relevant. John accepted this as a game of sorts even though he was initially very frustrated with this analyst. She told him nothing of herself, not even if she liked sports. However, John eventually came to enjoy just talking (free association), and he surprised himself in the many sessions when he began by talking about sports but eventually found himself frequently talking about his childhood and his relationship with his father. His father had been a minor league baseball player who died at age 50 of cirrhosis of the liver after years of alcoholism. John remembers his father as being cold and abusive, but his father's negative behavior often changed when the two of them engaged in sports together. Even though John's father frequently criticized him for not trying hard enough or being good enough in sports, at least it was a way of interacting.

This way of achieving love through athletic endeavors also became the way John channeled his excessive anxiety and energy. John had been a poor student and probably had an attention deficit disorder with hyperactivity as a child, yet he was able to finish high school and even achieve some degree of popularity by lettering in three sports and becoming captain of the baseball team.

Eventually, John ended his sessions in tears. He became aware of the fact that his total immersion in sports was his way of trying to get acceptance or love, and he avoided all other "normal" interactions because of extreme anxiety in relation to his social skills—just like his socially inept, alcoholic father. John developed insight into the fact that he strongly identified with his father.

The analyst had also been somewhat surprised by John's progress. She had an average interest and knowledge of sports but felt that there may be a real problem in the transference phenomenon when it became apparent that the major parental figure for John was his father. However, by strictly adhering to a very neutral response pattern (called a "blank screen" technique), John gradually began transferring his feelings about his father onto her, accusing her of only caring about him if he did well in sports and otherwise being distant or erratic toward him. John's anger also came out as he came to grips with his poor social skills and low self-esteem, which had been exacerbated recently as his misplaced devotion to playing sports became increasingly difficult to maintain.

Projection

The mechanism by which one's own anxiety-producing thought or impulse is converted into a different, objective-feared source is called *projection*. Essentially, instead of admitting consciously to the real (but unacceptable) thought that "I hate her," the patient instead deals indirectly with the thought by turning it around and saying "she hates me." Highly competitive but insecure individuals who superficially maintain self-esteem by comparing and competing

constantly with others may do so by explaining that it is the unfortunate competitiveness of others that keeps them on guard and always having to respond
to the challenges of others by competing with them. Siblings will complain
about their brother or sister as always feeling the need to impress their parent
even though it is they who are forced to seek these parental indications of
acceptance. Such conscious explanations are also referred to as *rationaliza-
tions,* which generally include any reactive and often unrealistic explanations
of defensive behavior rather than actually being defensive behaviors themselves. Projections provide relief by attributing the source of the anxiety to
some external source rather than to an individual's own unacceptable and
primitive urges. By externalizing the source of the anxiety, it becomes at least
indirectly accessible. However, projections are distortions of reality and therefore become counterproductive in one's interaction with others.

A projection is also very confusing in that one essentially blames another
for his or her own feelings. This defense mechanism puts onto another that
which belongs to the self and is often particularly infuriating to the individual
who is the object of the projection. Some projections are the result of transference that may further infuriate as well as confuse others. For instance, a
man at a work setting views a coworker as being very similar to his brother.
This brother has historically been the object of a projection of being jealous
and competitive. If the man begins acting out the projection against the fellow
worker (e.g., competing with this coworker for the approval of the boss), the
coworker's initial confusion will eventually turn to anger at this individual who
rather inexplicably competes with him and displays unwarranted anger. This
innocent coworker is blamed for "starting it all by his jealousy and competitiveness," even though the reality is that the coworker is simply a reminder of
the brother. See Case 7.4.

Case 7.4: Projection

Bill is a graduate student at a large midwestern university. Although he has been
doing reasonably well, he came to see an analyst because he had recently become
mildly depressed and lethargic and his informal academic support group was no
longer as helpful as it had been. In fact, one of the women in this group of friends
and fellow graduate students was becoming an obsession and source of concern
and frustration to him because he saw her as being in competition with him.

Bill is the second child of a family of three children. His sister, who is three
years older, has already successfully finished a Ph.D. from a top university. Bill
says he loves his sister and has always been very impressed with her knowledge
and ability. He indicates he is very proud of her accomplishments and talked at
length about her brilliance and his pride in her. By contrast, he views himself as
a very easygoing, relatively passive individual with a fair amount of ability but certainly not in the same league with his sister. Bill's one complaint about his sister
is that "she had an unfortunate need to put me down or belittle me," particularly
in front of their parents. Bill said she did not need to do this since he accepted
her intellectual superiority and that his parents seemed to prefer her.

These details about his sister were presented at his sessions only months after he came in for therapy and then only in response to the analyst's questions about his early childhood memories and his family. Bill had initially talked about one of the young women in the group and admitted to having become almost obsessed with her. He claimed that she would not stop belittling him. He said it came to a climax a month before he started therapy. They had invited a young professor from their department to join them at a local bar for their weekly discussions and support sessions. Bill was enjoying himself immensely explaining his viewpoint to the professor when Emily, his nemesis and fellow grad student, rudely interrupted Bill with a cutting remark. Bill was so devastated that he became silent, then excused himself and left the group. Bill was further enraged because virtually all of the other members of the group told him individually that he had acted very inappropriately or that he had made a fool of himself by over-reacting to Emily. Bill felt that Emily had deliberately turned the group against him as well as having insulted him. He was now depressed and suicidal since the group and its support had been so essential to him during this stressful time, and it was entirely Emily's fault.

During the first couple of months, Bill's therapy sessions focused upon his anger toward Emily and her "petty put-downs" and competitiveness. The analyst never disputed these claims but only occasionally asked for clarification or else she simply encouraged Bill to say whatever he wanted. When the focus shifted more to Bill's family of origin, his affect became more animated and anxious, which he described as probably reflecting his love of family. When the discussion narrowed down to his older sister, Bill was exuberant in his praise for her and his relative inferiority. The analyst naturally began interpreting some of Bill's perceived put-downs from Emily as being similar to what he had wanted to say to *her* "deep down inside." Bill laughed at the suggestion and said that Emily and his sister were not at all similar. In fact, he had never understood how Emily had even been accepted into graduate school whereas his sister, by contrast, was brighter than nearly every one of the faculty.

Bill missed the next two sessions because of "illness"; then he arrived 20 minutes late for the following session. The analyst suggested that perhaps she had said something or made an interpretation at the last session that was problematic to him. He assured her that was not the case, although in his own mind he had begun to wonder whether this analyst was really as qualified as he had initially thought. After all, her interpretations seem to suggest that the rather stupid, insulting Emily, who had deliberately turned his best friends against him, was somewhat similar to his beloved and brilliant older sister. Bill was also feeling some confusion in his own mind regarding the analyst. He had to admit that she reminded him of Emily when she made her more naive and rather insulting interpretations but also seemed a bit like his big sister who knew the answer to nearly everything.

After 8 months of therapy, Bill was frustrated with the process. Although he and his analyst had discussed his childhood, his parents, his sister, and his current dilemma with graduate school, as well as Emily and his loss of his friends and support group because of her insults and plotting against him, he felt that he was still no better. In fact, he was very angry with his analyst and her lack of direction, casual insults, and naive interpretations that often were, as far as he felt, completely wrong and inappropriate. He considered stopping the sessions.

Before doing so, he happened to run into one of the members of his support group. Bill had carefully avoided all of them for many months, particularly this member who was the dominant leader. Bill even changed his telephone number. He felt that they had betrayed him when they sided with Emily against him. When Bill saw his former friend and group leader on the street, Bill tried to simply say hello and continue on his way. However, the friend insisted that Bill talk to him that evening. In a long, heated, and emotional discussion, this group leader confronted Bill with the fact that he and all of the other members, including Emily, were very hurt and surprised that Bill had abandoned them. He said that Bill had overreacted to Emily when she briefly interrupted his discussion with the professor. This group leader adamantly disagreed that Emily had insulted Bill then or at any other time. Bill stormed out of that discussion with his former friend but was overwhelmed with the realization that there may have been some truth to it all, especially since his analyst had seemingly suggested some of the same dynamics.

Bill's subsequent therapy session was emotional, cathartic, and very tearful. Bill's usual composure and restraint were replaced by a torrent of tears, fears, and accusations. He accused the analyst of being like Emily and his sister and admitted to having felt a real rage toward the analyst who seemed to look down on him from her superior position and intellect. He also admitted to a great deal of confusion and a beginning realization that perhaps Emily had not really meant to insult him and that, in fact, he had rather consistently verbally attacked her or at least felt as if he wanted to do so. His friend and former group leader said that neither he nor Emily could understand or accept his obvious disdain for Emily and that Bill's subtle insults seemed petty. Bill had been unaware of this. However, he realized it had merit when he was confronted by this former friend, his analyst, and by his own growing suspicion in therapy that it was he who was easily threatened and competitive and openly hostile toward people who (like his sister) seemed smarter, better liked, and more respected than he.

This cathartic session was a turning point in therapy. It helped Bill recognize that he projected his feelings of competitiveness onto Emily who, in turn, was only a transference image of his successful and deeply resented older sister. The analyst who was a reminder of his sister had also become the object of considerable anger.

Bill's case involves the dynamics of catharsis, transference, resistance, avoidance, and re-creation of family dynamics, in addition to the obvious projections. Catharsis is the emotional working through of a problem. It is an essential factor in psychoanalysis. Freud recognized that simply talking about issues in an intellectual and detached manner is not sufficient. Cognitive therapists and behaviorists who are often accused of being overly detached and who rely on mechanical responses to a problem to the exclusion of feelings also recognize the importance of catharsis. If the psychoanalytically oriented social worker is too intellectual and abstract and distant from the strong emotions and feelings of the patient, then true change is unlikely to happen. Bill was prone to being avoidant, passive, and emotionally repressed. He had probably been growing in his insight in the early months of psychoanalysis but was too emotionally guarded and reserved to really be in touch with his feelings. He needed to be emotionally challenged at the time when his analysis was forcing him to ask questions about himself. This challenge was presented to Bill by his friend and group leader.

Re-creation of family dynamics is frequently observed secondary to transference but is particularly evident within groups. Bill's informal support group had been very significant for him emotionally. Bill had re-created his family dynamics, with Emily representing his sister and the group leader representing his father. The confrontation by the powerful father figure/group leader, whose authority was difficult for Bill to challenge, lead to a crisis and a cathartic experience. Through interpretation, the analyst suggested that Bill was projecting his hostility and insulting behavior onto Emily who was, in fact, innocent of everything with the exception that she reminded Bill of his sister. The unconscious hostility and competitiveness toward his "sister" Emily, which he had converted into a safer observation—that she was the one who was hostile and threatened—was unavoidable. The respected father figure/group leader had supported the analyst, and analysis had already helped him reach a point of considerable anxiety and growing suspicion that he was inaccurate in his feelings.

Avoidance is evident in Bill's staying away from the group as a primitive but very common way of simply not dealing with anxiety-producing or threatening situations. Avoidance was also clearly evident when he missed two therapy sessions and part of a third as a way of not dealing with the analyst's increasing insistence about connections between Bill's feelings about Emily and unresolved issues about his sister.

Avoidant personalities who deny reality and avoid the negative circumstances of their actions ultimately become trapped. As one "successfully" avoids reality and the potentially constructive options that are offered, the behavior ultimately leads to fewer options and finally to none at all. It is a sad and rather vicious path for many who find avoidance in their youth to be a short-term means of helping them get away from negative circumstances. However, these earlier successes, which only encourage the process, ultimately lead to a dead end or a series of psychological dead ends. Bill (Case 7.4) avoided or denied unpleasant realities and even his support group when they failed to take his side against Emily.

PSYCHOANALYTIC TECHNIQUES

The psychoanalytic approach has an extremely rich theoretical base. However, it is not as clear and precise in defining its techniques and practical applications as the cognitive and behavioral methods. Most undergraduate psychology, child development, and social work majors are well aware of the personality theory, developmental stages, and even the defense mechanisms but are completely unaware of what a psychoanalytically oriented psychotherapist actually does.

There are, in fact, a number of techniques that are used by psychoanalysts and psychoanalytically oriented social workers that clearly reflect the theory described in this chapter. Primary techniques include use of transference/countertransference, blank screen, interpretation, dream analysis, uncovering repressed, free association, and regression.

Use of Transference/Countertransference

The concept of *transference* is central to psychoanalytic psychotherapy. It refers to the fact that people relate to others partially on the basis of their previous relationships with others, particularly significant others from childhood such as parents. This phenomenon is well accepted by nonpsychoanalysts, although its significance and active use in therapy are debated.

In psychoanalytic interventions, the therapist invariably sees the patient begin to relate to the analyst in the same way the patient related to a significant figure in his or her development, typically a mother figure or father figure. The analyst is in a position of authority, much like a parent, and it is quite natural for the patient to transfer his or her feelings and attitudes toward a parent or other significant authority figure onto the analyst. The analyst allows and encourages this process since psychoanalytic theory posits that most problems initiate in early childhood years as a result of faulty parental relationships.

The problems of the patient are viewed as resulting from unresolved, traumatic, or otherwise dysfunctional patterns of relating that were developed in childhood. It is believed that current problems of the patient such as poor self-esteem, a history of defying authority figures, marital conflict, or generalized and displaced anger toward others are the result of the patient's unresolved feelings toward the parental figure. For instance, patients with poor self-esteem based upon overly critical parents will misinterpret a positive remark or feedback as negative or sarcastic because, in growing up, that is what they expected from their mother or father. Patients who had very controlling, intimidating fathers will overreact with great fear or anger to relatively mild suggestions from others concerning their behavior because they are accustomed to the highly emotional and controlling suggestions from their father. Within their own marriages, patients will relate to husbands as they did to their fathers or to a wife as they did to their mothers or, finally, to a psychoanalytically oriented social worker as they did to either parent.

Countertransference refers to the feelings and attitudes that the social worker develops toward the patient as the result of the patient's past. One of the primary reasons that psychoanalytically oriented social workers are encouraged to undergo analysis themselves is to help them understand some of the feelings that result from their own past and how those feelings may affect their interaction with their patients. A homophobic social worker must confront and work through personal feelings before working with homosexual patients, just as a male analyst who has deep-seated resentment toward assertive females (like his mother) must work through or resolve those issues before being able to successfully work with assertive females (see Case 7.5).

Case 7.5: Transference

Ginny was a 14-year-old girl who was asked to leave the eighth grade of her parochial school 3 months before graduation. She had rarely attended classes for the past school year; and, when she did attend, she was highly disruptive, physically and verbally assaultive toward teachers and classmates, and rumored to be both using and selling drugs.

She had previously but unsuccessfully attempted therapy earlier in the year, and her mother took her to the social worker primarily to ask him for help in getting Ginny hospitalized or institutionalized where she could receive help. Soon after Ginny and her mother came into the social worker's office, they became embroiled in an angry confrontation that ended when the mother stormed out of the office, telling the social worker to "just get this lousy little slut out of my house. I'm tired of her screwing up my life and I don't want her affecting her little sister." Ginny remained seated in her chair, angrily glaring at the social worker and barely concealing her rage and hurt. Finally, the analyst said, "Well, this seems like a pretty rough situation with your mother."

"Who cares?" asked Ginny angrily. "She's a bitch and I hate her. . . . I don't know why she wastes my time bringing me into stupid shrinks like you."

"I'm not really sure either. What do you think?" asked the social worker in a relatively neutral tone.

Ginny stared for a moment at the analyst, clearly attempting to "size him up." This analyst was unlike her previous therapist, who seemed phony in his attempt to be supportive and take her side no matter how blatantly "bad" she had been. He also did not come across as coldly as the behaviorist she had seen who wanted her to begin counting her "outbursts" at home and at school. In fact, the social worker reminded Ginny of her father who had divorced Ginny's mother but who had always been very affectionate and supportive of Ginny. Ginny immediately liked the social worker even though he said very little.

Since she was unable to establish what this social worker wanted her to do, Ginny just began to talk about herself, her feelings, and her past, essentially ignoring him. The "blank screen" approach displayed by the worker allowed Ginny to treat the worker as if he were her beloved, missing father. After nearly an hour of just "griping" and letting it all come out, she was amazed at how quickly the time had passed. She was also surprised that she actually liked this social worker even though he had said very little and simply nodded and supportively encouraged her to say whatever she wanted.

Blank Screen

The *blank screen* technique involves the use of very nonreactive, emotionless responses to the patient. The social worker accepts the fact of being an object of transference and uses the blank screen as a way of increasing the transference and resolving issues that may significantly and negatively affect current relationships. By reacting quite neutrally during analysis, the social worker creates a personality vacuum that allows the patient to create for him or herself the personality of the significant authority figure and put it in the person of the social worker. In the mind of the patient, the social worker becomes the intimidating father or the critical mother.

This is therapeutically desirable because this transference phenomenon allows the analyst to help the patient successfully experience and rework the relationship in a healthier context. By actively encouraging transference to develop, it brings to the conscious those earlier repressed and unresolved feelings and issues toward the mother or father figure and gives patients the opportunity to recognize that they had treated all males as intimidating authority figures or all females as negative and critical. By fostering transference, the patient gradually intellectually and emotionally comes to the awareness that a pattern had developed that was counterproductive, unnecessary, or pathological in their relationships with others. Over time, as the analyst helps the patient achieve greater insight into how these feelings are transferred unfairly or inappropriately at times onto others, the patient gradually resolves those earlier issues of anger, intimidation, or poor self-esteem. The patient sees that the social worker onto whom they transferred those unresolved feelings is, in fact, a different person who is helpful and supportive.

Interpretation

Psychoanalytic theory suggests that unconscious thoughts and repressed memories drive certain behaviors. Past repressed memories form the basis for behavior that may not be consciously intended. An individual may, for instance, repeatedly undermine possibilities for affectionate relationships in spite of a conscious desire to form one. Social workers frequently work with individuals who say that they desperately want to marry or develop a close, intimate relationship. However, those individuals repeatedly undermine the possibility of such relationships by subtly distancing from the potential partner or by acting in a manner that is counter to their verbally stated conscious desire. An analytically oriented social worker would help these patients to gradually and consciously recognize that behaviors such as "accidentally forgetting" to meet potential partners for an important engagement or arriving "just a little bit drunk" on a first date with a recovering alcoholic potential partner is not just "accidental."

Experienced analytically trained social workers help clients to consciously make the connection between unconscious memories and current behaviors. Timing and trust are essential in making appropriate interpretations because the patient is defending himself or herself against the conscious awareness of these painful memories (see Case 7.6).

Dream Analysis

Dream analysis is rarely used by social workers. Dreams are believed to be preconscious thoughts that become known to individuals during the unguarded, undefended dream states. Repressed memories that are normally unknown to the patient consciously become more accessible during sleep. Those memories that are beginning to reach consciousness, usually because of current issues, are difficult to repress. These unconscious memories frequently manifest themselves symbolically in dreams. A patient who fears his abusive father may be unable to consciously accept his or her rage, so he or she will dream that he or she kills a frightening demon in a dream. The patient may remember the dream and describe it to an analyst without consciously recognizing the demon as representing the "evil," dreaded father.

A patient may recall a reoccuring dream in which he is drowning and is terrified. This same patient may describe the mother as abusively controlling and domineering. The social worker will help the patient to make the conscious connection between the frightening control from the mother and the feeling of drowning (see Case 7.6).

Uncovering Repressed

Thoughts and memories that are too frightening to accept consciously become repressed. At times, these repressed memories may be related to specific traumatic events such as rape or incidents of physical abuse. Individuals "forget" these incidents, but they cannot be erased. These subconscious, repressed memories often have a profound effect on behavior and attitudes even though the individual is not consciously aware that the incident ever happened.

When such traumatic repressed memories negatively affect clients, psychoanalytically oriented practitioners argue that the memory must be made conscious, that is, the repressed memory must be recovered. In fact, analysts believe that simple behavioral treatment that only changes the client's responses or behavior is insufficient. Analysts suggest that a behavioral therapist may train a traumatized woman to positively interact with men. However, if the behaviorist does not resolve or uncover the repressed memories of early childhood abuse, then the woman's likelihood of ever developing a trusting relationship with any male is minimal (see Case 7.6).

> **Case 7.6: Uncovering Repressed, Interpretation, and Dreams**
> Jason was a quiet, withdrawn, depressed, and sullen 15-year-old who was referred to Joan Bach, MSW, a psychoanalytically oriented social worker, because Jason was failing several courses at school. He and his mother had recently moved back to the Pittsburgh area from Connecticut, where Jason's father was an architect and occasional contractor who had a history of bipolar disorder and cocaine addiction. Jason's mother Claire also reported a history of her husband physically abusing her. Claire's attempts to minimize the physical abuse and even defend her husband were reasons for concern by Joan. Claire was 40 years old and managed the children and house full-time. She was depressed, anxious, and insecure, having left her husband and three other children to escape from his abuse and because he had openly maintained an affair with another woman.

Jason came to Pittsburgh with his mother because he had bronchitis and recurring bouts of pneumonia. However, using upper physical problems as a reason to move to Pittsburgh from Connecticut was only later recognized as an excuse for escape. Sickness of some sort was, in fact, the only escape within that family, in which a history gradually unfolded of a father and husband who brutally verbally and physically assaulted his wife and four children. Whenever the father became manic or paranoid, he took out his own anxiety and insecurity on his family by berating and belittling each of them for their inadequacies, failures, and insensitivity—all as rather obvious projections of his own fear. The more out of control the father's life became, the more rigidly and harshly he would demand conformity and perfection from his wife and children. Since his mood swings varied tremendously as a result of his bipolar disorder and drug and alcohol abuse, the family became nearly immobilized by fear. The father took complete control over the family.

Jason subconsciously recognized that his father would not abuse him if Jason was sick in bed. Consequently, Jason and his mother indicated to Joan Bach that the two of them left Connecticut to stay with family in Pittsburgh because of Jason's health even though both were evasive and vague about his medical history and current treatment regimen. This evasiveness was not conscious. In fact, both consciously believed that the real reason they left Jason's father was because of Jason's health and, secondarily, because Claire felt that she and her husband needed some time away from each other. After further sessions with Claire and in response to a series of very specific questions, it was revealed that her three children, ages 8, 10, and 12, who had stayed behind with her husband, were often left alone overnight. In fact, the father's new 28-year-old friend had virtually moved in with them. Claire was referred to the agency for individual therapy when her defensive denial system rapidly deteriorated and as she began to recall frightening dreams. The more depressed and frightened she became, the more she depended upon and clung to her erratic, controlling, and abusive husband.

Jason was the eldest child and had become a quiet loner having few friends or interests. His affect was neutral; and, while he was cooperative and seemingly interested in treatment, he would not indicate any motivation, nor would he talk much beyond simple responses.

The social worker surmised that Jason did, in fact, want to understand himself and his family better. However, his history of abuse from adult authority figures was one in which the adult yelled, accused, and assaulted him. His only defense was to withdraw and not respond in any way or he would risk further retribution for no reason whatsoever. Any past defense, verbal or physical, led invariably to increased assault. Therefore, the social worker proceeded cautiously with Jason, never pushing or demanding but always working with Jason to help him understand his feelings and how those feelings were related to his father.

When Jason was just beginning to open up, the dialogue in the sixth weekly session went something like this:

SOCIAL WORKER: *So it seems that at the time maybe your father was having some problems with his work and would come home in a bad mood?*
JASON: *Yeah. I don't think he hated us or anything. I guess he didn't know how to . . . uh, change. . . . He couldn't help it. . . .*
SOCIAL WORKER: *So, your father was having a rough time because of the bipolar problem or his cocaine use and he would come home and might not*

be quite in control of his own feelings and get angry at you and your mother and maybe some sort of fight would develop? (See Clinical Note #1.)
JASON: *Yeah. Sometimes it would get pretty bad. . . .*
SOCIAL WORKER: *Bad? In what way?*
JASON: *Well, you know . . . sometimes he would just yell at us or call us names like "stupid idiots" or say things like "you're all lazy—you'll never amount to anything."*
SOCIAL WORKER: *Uh, huh.*
JASON: *Yeah. Sometimes I think it affected me in some ways.*
SOCIAL WORKER: *Oh, really? You feel that some of these problems or rough family times may have affected you?*
JASON: *Well, I guess when somebody yells at me or tells me I'm stupid and stuff like that, I just want to shut down—or get back at them.*
SOCIAL WORKER: *So you kind of wanted to get back?*
JASON: *Well, you know . . . to feel like you're not there—to disappear— or to have my father disappear. Sometimes I even think I'd like to say something back or do something to him.*
SOCIAL WORKER: *So at times you feel like saying or doing something to respond?*
JASON: *Sure, especially when he's mean to Mom or even hits her or something like that. Maybe she kind of deserves it at times. (See Clinical Note #2.) But . . . I don't know. . . .*
SOCIAL WORKER: *It seems you aren't too sure about whether she deserves that?*
JASON: *(somewhat angrily) How could she deserve that? It's not her fault! (See Clinical Note #3.)*
SOCIAL WORKER: *Yes, I guess you are . . .*
JASON: *(he interrupts angrily) Do you think she likes the way he treats her?*
SOCIAL WORKER: *It sounds like it's pretty rough for all of you.*

Clinical Note #1: The social worker is being extremely careful here not to be critical of the father at this early point in therapy. This is necessary in spite of the father's obvious brutal behavior, because at this time Jason is very defensive about his father. Even though Jason is intellectually aware of the fact that his father is bipolar, addicted, and abusive, he will still defend him and is very sensitive to any hints of criticism. The social worker cannot be critical of the father yet because Jason views his father emotionally as an omnipotent figure whom he cannot afford to alienate.

Jason's insecurity, depression, and frightened emotional dependence on his father would make any criticism of the father tantamount to a criticism of Jason and would quickly lead to rejection of the social worker in favor of the father. However, the social worker does need to allow for Jason's free expression of negative feelings. Thus, the social worker will remain fairly neutral in tone and affect—a technique called "blank screen." This technique is used to encourage free expression of feelings concerning the father. Because of this transference, Jason will relate to and start treating the social worker in the same way he relates to his father. This allows for a re-working of the pathological dependence into a healthier therapeutic relationship with this social worker/father figure.

Clinical Note #2: At one level, Jason's perception is that his mother, who feels and acts "inferior" to his powerful father, must deserve the treatment she receives. It would be too threatening for Jason to believe the obvious fact that his father's abusiveness and pathological need to control the family is a response to his father's insecurity, his feelings of inferiority, and his loss of control. Jason needs to be helped to gradually reach that conclusion by delving beneath his defensive denial system.

Clinical Note #3: This sudden anger was directed at the social worker since Jason perceived the worker as being critical of him. Jason's conflict and ambivalence about defending his mother are being revealed even though his mother is a clear victim in an abusive relationship and his father is the perpetrator. The transference phenomenon is also apparent now in that Jason is directly expressing anger about his mother's mistreatment. The social worker has encouraged the transference to allow the appropriate expression of anger, fear, love, and hate to be initially directed at the social worker as a surrogate for the father.

Session #20: Children and adolescents who are in powerless relationships with abusive or controlling parents typically displace their object of anger onto another, less threatening choice such as a teacher as a way of venting at least some of their anger. Also, they typically develop passive-aggressive response patterns to threatening authority figures because they fear direct confrontation with adult authority figures who are seen as very powerful. In this session, Jason and his social worker are beginning to deal with his history of passive-aggressive behavior in which he fails in school as an angry but inappropriate way to "get back" at his controlling father. His father tried to pressure Jason to excel in school. Instead, Jason frequently missed school due to various vague illnesses and indicated open disdain and dislike for the teachers whom he viewed as "mean, controlling, and abusive."

> JASON: *Well, I called the school like you said I should.*
> SOCIAL WORKER: *Oh, so you did get in touch with them?*
> JASON: *They said I already failed two courses and might not even pass the other three. That's so unfair. It wasn't my fault I was sick for all of those tests and classes.*
> SOCIAL WORKER: *(nods) Um huh . . .*
> JASON: *They're real jerks. You'd think they could give a guy a break. . . . They just don't care whether you fail or not. Jerks.*
> SOCIAL WORKER: *They didn't show any concern one way or the other, huh? Seemed like real jerks. You really do seem to be angry.*
> Jason: *Well . . .*

Clinical Note #1: The analyst had not directed Jason to call the school but had interpreted to Jason that his failing courses and multiple absences were a passive-aggressive way to get back at his feared father's controlling behavior. Jason felt powerless throughout his childhood in relation to his domineering father and had adopted an angry, sullen, passive-aggressive response by which he would fail at anything in which his father wanted him to achieve. Jason was not only unaware of the basis for his behavior; he vigorously denied it when the social worker initially hinted at it. The social worker had helped Jason to understand his dynamic, as well as helped him come to the realization that such behavior was hurting Jason far more than his father. Jason's behavior was counterproductive and a misdirected displacement of his anger. By interpreting the school failures as passive-aggressive means of retaliating for his father's feared abusiveness, the social worker helped Jason to consciously rework his feelings.

Free Association

The technique whereby practitioners support and facilitate the client's unguarded, open, unstructured verbalizations that may tap into the subconscious is *free association*. Typically, analysts instruct clients to relax. The analyst uses phrases such as: "Say whatever you want. . . . Do not worry whether it makes sense or not. . . . Relax and say whatever comes into your mind." In classical psychoanalysis, which is rarely practiced by social workers, the practitioner directs the client to lie on the analyst's couch and talk, facing away from the practitioner. The client may be asked to say whatever comes into his or her mind related to the father or mother or early childhood experiences.

Word association is an additional method of delving into subconscious or repressed memories. In word association, a client is asked to say the first word that comes into mind in response to a cue word. The practitioner may say "White," and the client will respond with the word "Black." If the practitioner says "Father" and the client responds "Fear" or "Hurt," then the practitioner realizes that the client has a fearful association with the father, and that association needs to be explored or uncovered. Word association is a relatively efficient and fairly commonly utilized method for social workers as a diagnostic approach and as a means to begin delving into subconscious memories.

Regression

Regression is common and frequently encouraged in traditional psychoanalysis or psychotherapy. Social workers rarely regress patients during the course of psychodynamic intervention, although patients do tend to regress without the deliberate use of the technique. For Sister Jean (see Case 7.2) to truly resolve deeply repressed Oedipal feelings, she needed to be allowed and even encouraged to become a youngster once again—to dress, act, look, and subsequently think more like the youngster she was when her feelings toward her father were more consciously available but before they were repressed. She reverted to an earlier age and unconsciously even became more seductive. This regression is viewed as therapeutically necessary as a way of getting into touch with those feelings by returning to the time when they were less repressed. The analyst must be careful to accept this regressed behavior with the understanding that it is a transitional stage. Once the repressed Oedipal urges are worked through and resolved, the patient can securely return to his or her appropriate age. The dreams that this patient started remembering and that frequently became distressful coincide with such repression. Both are related to the lessening of the control of the repression and are related to preconsciousness more than to heavily guarded unconscious material.

Timing is important for all of the psychodynamic techniques. Premature and threatening interpretations that are too close to the repressed memories will be denied by the patient and will probably increase the guard and defenses. On the other hand, well-timed interpretations of dreams, behavior, and symbols—that is, timed for when the patient is beginning to have insight and awareness into the real meaning—are crucial to progress.

SUMMARY

The psychodynamic approaches are no longer the dominant mode of practice in social work, but knowledge of the personality theory, developmental processes, defense mechanisms, and major techniques are all essential. There are dozens of psychodynamic variations. Current approaches utilized by social workers and others include Freudian analysis, psychoanalytic psychotherapy, ego psychology, and the psychosocial approach. Self psychology and object relations theory are additional psychodynamic methods that are currently used. Psychoanalytic theory describes the personality as being composed of the id, the ego, and the superego. Psychoanalytic stages of development include the oral, the anal, the phallic, the latency, and the genital stages, although Erikson's eight psychosocial stages may have more relevance for social workers.

Defense mechanisms falsify and distort reality and are seen in normal as well as in clinical situations. The defense mechanisms include reaction formation, repression, sublimation, and projection. Techniques used by psychoanalysts and psychodynamically oriented social workers include the use of transference, blank screen, interpretation, dream analysis, uncovering repressed, free association, and regression.

BEHAVIORAL INTERVENTIONS

GENERAL DESCRIPTION

There is a certain beauty in the logic and consistency of behaviorism that is not found in any other model. Behavioral models say that behavior can be predicted and controlled as long as one observes and controls the antecedent conditions, the behavior itself, and the reinforcers. These models say that behavior is learned or conditioned and that unobservable theories or constructs about subconscious or repressed material are simply irrelevant to the appropriate treatment goal of changing behavior or alleviating symptoms. Behavior is typically seen as a response to a stimulus that may be either internal or external. The social worker's intervention, therefore, involves assessing the stimulus-response (S-R) pattern or connection and then modifying that connection where the response is inappropriate or maladaptive. Behaviorism is also a relatively scientific and research-based approach that highly values the measurement of clear, observable behaviors. It stands in stark contrast to the orientation of psychoanalytic theory.

HISTORY

Ivan Pavlov's classical research in which he conditioned dogs to salivate when a light was turned on laid a foundation for treatment applications. B. F. Skinner later brought this notion of modifying behavior into the mainstream of practice. Skinner was dedicated to a scientific study of behavior and focused on observable and measurable behaviors rather than the presumed subconscious emotions and constructs upon which virtually all other clinical theorists based their therapeutic interventions. Skinner stressed that behavioral scientists needed to focus upon research that would help in the understanding of the logic and order of individual behavior so that therapists could anticipate, predict, determine, and modify that behavior (Skinner, 1953, 1971).

Skinner did not argue against the possibility of the existence of unconscious forces but argued that the science of human behavior and therapy must be based upon observable phenomena. He suggested that further research was needed to understand how and why people behave as they do. His theory of *operant behavior* recognized that certain behaviors could be increased by reinforcing them and that other behaviors (such as negative or harmful responses) could be diminished or extinguished by negative reinforcement. He worked to measure and refine the effects of punishment or withholding reinforcement to gauge the effects. Skinner's focus was therefore largely on the environmental events that preceded the studied behavior and how these events led to consequent responses. Therapy involved altering this sequence so that the responses of the individual were always positive and productive rather than destructive.

Skinner also stressed that a baseline of behavior had to be established and that the past history of responses needed to be measured. This notion of measuring and counting behaviors was a radical departure from the field of social work at that time. The field was dominated by psychodynamic psychotherapists whose focus was on abstract concepts such as ego strengths, libido, subconscious motivation, and the Oedipus complex—none of which could be observed, let alone measured.

Another pioneering behaviorist in therapeutic circles was Hans J. Eysenck (1960), who also argued for quantification and clarity of interventions. Eysenck's reputation was initially founded on his early publications, which were highly critical of the poor therapeutic outcome of the psychodynamic therapists of his day. Eysenck led the way for the many dramatic new changes of the 1950s, which included Carl Rogers' client-centered approach as well as the advent of the behaviorists. Eysenck and researchers in social work (Fischer, 1973) claimed that approximately two-thirds of the clients who came into psychotherapy eventually improved whether they were in treatment or not. They essentially claimed that psychotherapy, as currently practiced among psychodynamic therapists and social workers, was a waste of time and did no better than just leaving clients alone (Eysenck, 1952; Fischer, 1976,1978).

A fourth major historical figure in the development of behavioral psychotherapy was Joseph Wolpe (1966), who pioneered the technique known as *systematic desensitization* that is described later in this chapter. He was also one of the earliest psychiatrists who was highly critical of the research methods of psychoanalysts of his day. In the 1960s, the five clinical research standards that were generally accepted were (a) symptomatic improvement, (b) increased productiveness, (c) improved adjustments and pleasure in sex, (d) improved interpersonal relationships, and (e) the ability to handle ordinary psychological conflicts and reasonable reality stresses. Such general criteria obviously did not meet the more clearly delineated preferences for behaviorists. Wolpe argued that only one of them—symptomatic improvement—is always relevant. He went on to indicate that the psychoanalytic cases that were cited as successes in psychoanalytic research were indeed failures even by the accepted standards of the time.

Wolpe's development of systematic desensitization was a breakthrough for the treatment of phobias and other anxiety-related situations. This technique was also a stark contrast to the relatively long, tedious, and relatively unsuccessful psychodynamic interventions used with the same disorders. Systematic desensitization is based upon certain basic behavioral tenets such as building slowly and incrementally upon successes that are self-reinforcing. Wolpe also suggested that relaxation and positive associations need to be developed to replace fearful associations for treatment to be successful (Wolpe, 1958; Wolpe & Lazarus, 1967).

There is a major group of scholars in the field of social work who successfully integrated behaviorism into practice. Arthur Schwartz, who started the first behavioral track at the University of Chicago, wrote *The Behavioral Therapies* (1982), which along with Edwin Thomas's *Behavior Modification Procedure* (1974) and Richard Stuart's *Behavioral Self-Management: Strategies, Techniques and Outcomes,* (1977), put the entire profession onto a behavioral direction. Sheldon Rose (1977) did the same for social group workers. These contemporary pioneers not only integrated the social and environmental perspective into the previously rather sterile approach but also oriented the approach to social workers. In varying degrees, they also recognized the need for eclecticism at a time when social work practitioners were still torn between feeling a need to pick either a psychodynamic or behavioral approach. Perhaps most importantly, these research-based social workers freed the social work profession from its reliance on clinical psychology for direction in methodologically rigorous clinical research. Although these four scholars are mentioned here for their historical significance, they have all continued to publish and exert a tremendous influence to the present day.

The strength and appeal of behavior modification is in its logic and consistency. Most applications are based upon learning theory or conditioning. *Learning theory* says that people learn responses to situations, often as children; but those responses may be inappropriate or counterproductive in other situations later in life. So the child who was rewarded whenever he or she whined or threw temper tantrums would use the same behavior to reach other goals in later life. However, as an adult, this behavior is no longer acceptable or productive. Since a potential mate or employer is less receptive to such behavior in social and work situations, the individual, upon reaching adulthood, is often confused by a series of rejections or job losses when he or she demonstrates inappropriate behavior that was reinforced by parents during childhood.

The concepts of cause and effect or stimulus and response are basic components of understanding behavioral approaches. Many behaviorists instruct their clients in this basic concept. If they behave in a certain way, they can logically expect a certain response. Thus, if they throw a temper tantrum or even a more adult variation of it such as hitting someone or screaming at them or having some overly reactive emotional outburst, they will be told to expect a response of distancing, rejection, return anger, loss of job, or loss of affection. This response, which is different from that of their parent, must be learned and understood as a direct effect of their behavior. They are instructed to understand that their behavior causes an effect in others and that they need to learn new behaviors to minimize or extinguish such responses in others.

One of the reasons for having clients maintain written baseline records is to reinforce the awareness of this causal relationship. So clients are told, for instance, to record every time they have an outburst or overreaction. Clients are instructed to document the antecedent conditions as part of this record. Clients record whatever preceded the outburst (such as a rejection or frustration), the maintaining conditions (e.g., people in the vicinity paid attention to them), and the result (e.g., they did or did not get what they wanted as a result of the outburst).

Over the years, behavior modification has evolved and developed into many different adaptations and schools. Some practitioners apply it in a *general* way in which they talk with clients to help them to understand the causal nature of behavior and the need to learn new ways of behaving to attain goals. This behavioral orientation has much in common with cognitive approaches. Other practitioners are very *structured* and specific and use a variety of charts, contracts, and clearly delineated steps to incrementally modify a client's behavior. The next section of this chapter briefly describes the major common foci or characteristics of behavioral social work.

BEHAVIORAL FOCI

Although there are tremendous variations in what practitioners view as behavioral beliefs, the following eight are the major foci:

1. *A focus on clear, observable, and measurable behaviors over vague feelings or emotions.* Behavioral social workers rely upon graphs, charts, and counting of specific behaviors as targets of intervention and as tools for describing the environment, antecedents, or consequences of behavior. Vague descriptions of feelings are deemed too imprecise to be workable. Clients are helped from the initial intake and throughout the process of the intervention to be succinct and precise in their descriptions of discrete observable phenomena.

Graphs and charts recording clear, preferably observable, behaviors are developed and maintained throughout the intervention to measure behavioral change. Common examples include charting the number of cigarettes smoked, the amount of food eaten, the weight gained or lost, the frequency of crying behavior, tics, anxiety attacks, phobic responses, aggressive behaviors, or abusive actions. Accurate counts of such behaviors are maintained; and progress is routinely monitored as the number of the client's behaviors or critical incidents moves in the desired direction, usually with a decrease in the frequency of the problematic target behavior (see Case 8.1).

Case 8.1: Clear, Observable Behavior

Sue was a single mother of two who lived in a household with her 50-year-old mother who supported her and her children. Her mother referred her 23-year-old daughter because she had recently broken up with the father of her two children. Sue smoked heavily, would not talk, find a job, or even adequately care for her children. The mother said that Sue had always been very quiet, passive, and dependent on her for everything.

Sue walked into the social worker's office with a slow shuffle, staring at her feet as she moved forward. She dropped into a chair and sat silently, playing with the tissue in her lap. When the social worker asked how she might help and what brought her in, Sue replied, "My mother made me see you. I don't have any problems, and this is a waste of time."

The social worker patiently and supportively encouraged Sue to talk but was only able to get Sue to indicate, "Life stinks. I don't even know why I smoke all the time. . . . I can't even get up out of bed to take care of my kids. . . . I just don't know what's wrong with me, let alone have any idea of what to do."

The first two sessions were spent on clarifying, specifically, what behaviors were so upsetting. At first, Sue seemed to be incapable of being precise, at one point angrily saying, "You're supposed to be the expert. Why do I have to do all the work?" Eventually, she at least described her typical day; arising at noon, watching TV, smoking, and occasionally calling friends. The social worker repeatedly encouraged Sue to specify what she did until finally a pattern became clear. Sue did very little yet bitterly blamed her mother, past boyfriend, and society in general for her lack of a job, education, or opportunities for her children. Although she was not clinically depressed, Sue was overwhelmed but very invested in issues of blame and guilt. The social worker consistently supported the connection between behaviors and responses and generally did not respond to her occasional more vague complaints, asking her to specify behaviorally whatever she thought was a concern.

Although social workers do not typically deal with smoking-cessation programs, the social worker chose to use this as a focus for three reasons: First, it was a learning opportunity in which the worker could instruct Sue in a clear example of behaviorism. This was deemed to be important since Sue was historically a very disorganized, passive-aggressive person who lacked a history of seeing her behavior have any effect in her environment. Second, smoking is a significant health hazard that was reinforcing Sue's perception that she could not control her environment. Third, smoking depressed her; and if this narrow and specific behavior could be stopped through a behavioral approach, then other broader problems such as parenting issues, jobs, or even self-esteem could be addressed later.

Sue and the social worker developed a form to keep track of the number of cigarettes Sue smoked. She was also to check off on the form whether she was at home or not and the time of day. Sue immediately tried to lessen her smoking behavior but was clearly instructed by the social worker not to do so. She was to continue to smoke as much as before to establish a clear baseline of behavior. Sue became somewhat enthusiastic about the procedure, although she was impatient to begin diminishing her smoking behavior. After a week, the clear pattern of frequencies and circumstances of smoking developed and Sue and the worker developed an alternate reward for Sue as they slowly but gradually cut back on the number of cigarettes smoked.

Sue was also assisted in developing a list of actions she could take to deal with her children's "lack of opportunities," as she initially described it. It eventually became clear that this term referred to the fact that both of her children had been suspended from school because Sue had not been getting them ready for school in the morning. It was very difficult for Sue to admit this; but, as soon as she realized that the social worker was neither blaming nor judging her, she opened up to the process of keeping meticulous records of when she arose, the time she took the children to the bus stop, the amount of time she spent with them on their homework, and even the rewards she gave them for their incremental improvement in grades.

2. *A focus on immediate, causal events and series such as the setting, antecedent events, and consequences of behavior.* Behaviorists frequently conceptualize behavior in terms of cause and effect or, more often, stimulus and response. Understanding the environmental setting in which target behaviors are most likely to appear is critical. Clients are required to keep records describing the settings of their problematic behaviors when they occur. As accurate records describing the settings emerge, clear patterns are also likely to become evident.

For instance, some sexual abusers will begin to note that they engage in their behaviors only when they are alone with vulnerable victims in isolated places. Cigarette smokers may see that they only smoke at home, at work, at bars, or when they are anxious. Depressed clients may begin to note that the symptoms of crying or lethargic behaviors only manifest themselves when they are alone at home in the evenings. Schizophrenics have been helped by charting their occasional hallucinations or delusional thinking, thus establishing that these disturbing symptoms only manifest themselves when they are alone with nothing to do.

Immediate antecedent events typically involve behaviors such as, in the case of an adult, taking a drink before engaging in abuse or, in the case of a child, being bored and anxious before striking a classmate. These antecedent events differ from the settings in that they are more precise and immediate and typically describe actions rather than settings or environments. Behaviorists often attempt to help clients recognize that by engaging in certain seemingly benign behaviors (e.g., having a few beers with friends or simply having nothing to do during long, anxious weekends), the clients predispose or set up a condition in which subsequent, problematic behaviors are more likely to occur. Clients are often instructed to chart their behaviors, tracking whatever they are doing beforehand, as a way to help in understanding the sequence of events so that they can learn to stop engaging in the events or to avoid the settings that antecede the target problem behavior. For instance, a child molester will be told to avoid going to schools or playgrounds, since his or her history may have revealed a pattern in which he or she goes to these settings before all past molestations.

There are also certain events that maintain, reinforce, or support the problem behavior. These events might include parents engaging in the same pattern of overeating as their obese child or dependent spouses or partners accepting, condoning, or even protecting the client from negative consequences. The spouse who makes excuses for the alcoholic partner, the acting-out child, or the abuser helps to maintain the problem for the client.

Consequent events follow the problematic behavior and are usually focused upon as reinforcers of the problematic target behavior. These consequences are also clearly and precisely charted as documentation of the series of events typical of problem behavior. Clients soon recognize a pattern in which they have been rewarded by positive consequences rather than negative consequences for behavior that they wish to extinguish, control, or at least diminish. A common consequence of tantrums for children who act out in public is the immediate reward of parents' giving in to demands. This reinforces the child's tantruming behavior and increases the likelihood that more tantrums will follow in the future. The unfortunate immediate consequence of excessive drinking for alcoholics is that the painful symptoms of withdrawal subside if they maintain themselves in a stupor. Each instance of excessive drinking is followed by another drink as a consequence of the attempt to stop the withdrawal. This reinforces the alcoholic's drinking as physical dependence increases and his or her social life becomes increasingly unrewarding (see Case 8.2).

Case 8.2: Immediate, Causal Events

Jenny was a single, 35-year-old fourth-grade teacher in an inner-city school. This was Jenny's eighth year at the school, and she felt that the job was becoming increasingly difficult and even frightening. Her colleagues and her principal were also concerned about her increased fearfulness and anxiety and encouraged Jenny to talk to the school social worker who had a reputation as a highly experienced behaviorist and group/classroom consultant.

Jenny initially indicated that she felt that the children at the school were somehow less disciplined than in the past, and she did not believe she was doing anything different than she had ever done. The social worker encouraged Jenny to describe precisely when the children misbehave and clearly and behaviorally describe what they do. Jenny and the social worker developed a chart that had columns to indicate the time of day of the problematic behavior, a brief description of the behavior, the individuals involved, the activity the class was engaged in when the behavior happened, Jenny's response, and, finally, the class response to her.

The result of her charting was a shock to Jenny. Within two days, it became clear that the disruptive pattern emerged at 9:20 every morning, just as the class shifted from English to math. Jenny frankly admitted that she loved teaching English literature almost as much as she hated teaching math. The school district had required her to teach a new approach to math that she neither understood nor respected. She said that she gets almost physically ill every day at that time but insisted that the students could not notice her change in attitude. The charting further indicated that Jenny tried rather consistently to regain control of the class for 15 to 20 minutes, typically losing virtually all of the math class time to attend to the discipline of several of the more disruptive students.

The social worker reviewed the charts with Jenny, objectively pointing out that the disruptive behavior was exhibited in the context of the math class. This is when Jenny was personally uncomfortable. By dealing with the disruptions instead of the dreaded math content, she did not have to teach the material that made her so very uncomfortable.

Jenny was helped to see the flow or order of event. She clearly saw that her discomfort with the math class preceded the deterioration of behavior. Jenny's erratic, halfhearted attempts at regaining class control typically did not "work" until after that period was over and she began teaching social science. The social worker helped Jenny to develop better skills and greater confidence in teaching the math class. Jenny was also encouraged to talk to the head math teacher to discuss her concerns regarding the way the material was taught. Jenny was soon able to modify the way the class was taught and found that she enjoyed the class once she understood the material and deleted the confusing content. This resulted in a comfortable transition at 9:20. She no longer had a need to angrily berate her students during the math period.

3. *A focus on defining behavior empirically, logically, and objectively rather than philosophically.* The status differential between psychoanalytical and behavioral approaches may be explained in part by the observation that analysts are the philosophers of the field while behaviorists are the mechanics. B. F. Skinner shocked much of the world, including most social workers of the time, with his books *Science and Human Behavior* (1953) and especially *Beyond Freedom and Dignity* (1971). These writings completely rejected mainstream perceptions of human behavior. His insistence that all behavior was logical, consistent, observable, measurable, and even controllable was counter to the accepted psychodynamic theory, which stated that behaviors are the result of unconscious thoughts, feelings, motivations, and instincts.

The notion that humans are subject to clear, definable manipulation and modification was and still is a profound concept. This was a very deterministic and mechanistic viewpoint. Skinner revolutionized the way individuals were to think of themselves, much as Freud had done a half a century before him. Critics lambasted Skinner in both the media and, even more viciously at times, in the professional journals. While the extreme overreactions and seeming misinterpretations of much of what he said have subsequently subsided, it is still a humbling theory to suggest that, at least behaviorally, humans are mere products of certain stimuli in the environment that essentially "cause" them to act in certain predictable and modifiable ways. The more simplistic behavioral models that viewed behavior in a straight linear causal fashion have been updated with much more complex and even interactive models, but the overall concept remains.

Of course, the other result of this clear bias toward objectivity is that it significantly increased the applicability of the scientific method to the previously murky field of human behavior and abnormal behavior. Behaviorism introduced a whole new realm of research possibilities that was not particularly adaptable to the philosophy that accepted such imprecise tenets as the Oedipus complex; penis envy; oral, anal, phallic, latency, and genital phases of development; and the interpretation of dreams through symbolism.

The empiricism espoused by the behaviorists has also been challenged by some *postmodern* social workers who suggest that empiricism is not the true objective perspective that it claims to be. Such supposedly objective observations are, in fact, filtered through the viewpoint or at least the language of the predominant culture. Thus, empiricism is actually a biased perspective that may not accurately present the objective reality of groups or subcultures whose language and perspective are quite different (Hartman, 1991) (see Case 8.3).

Case 8.3: Logic and Objectivity

John was a 41-year-old recently divorced father of two teenage children. He had left college 20 years earlier, indicating that he knew more than the professors. He was intellectually oriented and often tried to engage the social worker in discussions of the meaning and purpose of life. This was evident whenever the session examined his underlying hurt and insecurity over his wife leaving him for another man, claiming that John was "hopelessly lacking in emotions." This had hurt John far more than he could admit, even to himself, so he preferred to discuss human feelings in the abstract rather than to discuss his own painful feelings. When the social worker confronted John with his pattern of switching to abstract, intellectualized, and sterile discussion whenever the subject of his divorce arose, John denied it. However, after the social worker clearly described three instances of the behavior in the last 20 minutes of their session, he did admit that he felt uncomfortable with the topic and it made him anxious.

John said, "So what can you do about stuff like that anyway? I don't know if I had some mid-life crisis or if I just can't love anyone. I really did love my wife, and I miss seeing my kids every day. I never told you this before, but I think about killing myself. What's the point of living if everyone you care about leaves you, and you don't have the slightest idea of why they did it? What can I do to put any meaning or purpose into life?"

This breakthrough allowed the social worker to help John recognize that he needed to understand and confront his feelings. The pain of divorce would gradually subside only if he worked to more clearly understand what happened and what part he and his ex-wife played. It was explained to John that his great love of logic could be put to good use in understanding the causes and effects of the divorce. While this objective appraisal could be painful at times, it was infinitely less painful than his long and protracted avoidance of the real problem.

John soon began to describe the circumstances of the marriage and divorce, quickly recognizing that, as his wife withdrew from him, he became increasingly avoidant and critical of her. John was helped to see that the divorce was not caused by a vague "mid-life crisis"; nor was it caused by his ex-wife's "low self-esteem," which some "jerk" whom she eventually married had the unethical audacity to try to address. Instead, John was encouraged to describe the multiple incidents of coldness, verbal abuse, and insensitivity that he displayed.

The purpose of that rather painful but objective description of behavior was to get John to concretely relate to the consequences of specific behaviors. He was discouraged from pitying himself or even engaging in self-recrimination. He was helped to see that his behavior toward his ex-wife had consequences and that he suffered a great deal himself by not being more aware of his behavior and recognizing his emotions more clearly. The social worker and John spent two sessions writing a three-column exercise describing his inappropriate behavior, his ex-wife's response, and then the preferred behavior that he was to consider in the future.

4. *A focus on reinforcements in which behavior is viewed as modifiable through the contingent management of positive and negative reinforcement.* Central to behaviorism is the belief that behavior can be modified through the appropriate use of positive responses such as rewards for behavior that is desired or sought, while negative reinforcement can be used to diminish or extinguish behavior that is undesirable.

At the simplest level, this may involve giving money to a youngster as a positive reinforcer for each high grade on a report card. Such simplistic responses may seem naive to some professionals, but many social workers have been humbled in the past by grandmothers and others who simply "bribe" children to do better in school.

I had such a humbling experience myself. After spending three months with an underachieving adolescent who was reluctantly forced to see me by his parents, the boy suddenly started to study; stayed at home instead of seeing his young drug-abusing friends; and showed all the signs of being less depressed, angry, and rebellious. In reality, this 13-year-old boy wanted a "face-saving" way of returning to school but was unable to do so while caught in a power struggle with his parents. As his social worker, I was seen as simply another adult who was trying to force him to conform. The grandmother's reward of money allowed him to say to his predelinquent peer group that he was motivated to change his behavior, or at least his study habits, for his own sake. As so often happens, the improved study habits led to improved grades that diminished the tension at home with his parents. It also allowed the boy to disengage gradually from the potentially dangerous peer group whose behaviors had admittedly frightened the youngster.

Reinforcements are events that follow a behavior. They are used to alter the frequency of a behavior. Operant theory suggests that behavior operates to produce a reinforcement and there is a contingent relationship between a behavior and its reinforcing event. Positive reinforcers are used by social workers to follow behaviors they wish to increase. Negative reinforcers are events that will increase the frequency of behaviors if the reinforcers are removed following the behavior. For instance, a parent will yell at a child until he or she stops teasing a pet. As soon as the child stops, the yelling is withdrawn.

Reinforcement techniques are also central components of *classical conditioning*. Pavlov demonstrated years ago how he could *condition* a dog to salivate when it heard the sound of a bell by reinforcing the association between the sound of the bell and being fed. By ringing a bell consistently immediately before feeding, the dog was conditioned to associate the stimulus of a bell with food. The pairing of the conditioned stimulus (the bell) and the unconditioned stimulus (the food) was reinforced, and the salivating response was strengthened by the reward of food. Eventually these learned responses to previously unconditioned stimuli will weaken or cease completely when the response (food) is no longer paired with the conditioned stimulus (the bell).

A related technique is *extinction*. *Extinction* is the elimination or weakening of a conditioned response by discontinuing reinforcement after the response occurs. For instance, the mother of a young toddler may have inadvertently reinforced her child's tantrum behavior at the grocery store by giving the child candy as soon as the child became restless, cried, or began a temper tantrum. The social worker would instruct the parent to stop her previous response and instead ignore the child's behavior by not responding, which would lead to extinction of the tantrums.

Two other concepts related to reinforcement are *discrimination* and *generalization*. *Discrimination* refers to the capacity of an individual to only narrowly respond to a specific stimulus and no other, even a similar one. Just as a pigeon can be conditioned to respond to two pellets of food and not one or three, a person can be conditioned to respond to constructive but not to destructive feedback. *Generalization* refers to broadening the response to similar situations, not just the single, narrow stimuli that had been reinforced as the basis for response. For instance, a desensitization technique may be used to treat a person for a phobia of dogs. In in vivo desensitization, a dog (as opposed to simply the mental picture or *imagery* of a dog) will eventually be used to practice a learned response of relaxation as opposed to fear or anxiety when the stimulus of a dog is presented. However, the social worker must continue the desensitization procedure to ensure that the client generalizes the learned, relaxed response to *all* dogs, not simply the one used during the treatment conditions.

Reinforcers are sometimes listed in order, thus displaying a *hierarchy of reinforcers.* A client may be asked to talk and then compile a list of possible rewards for certain behaviors. A 10-year-old schoolchild may indicate that her favorite things in life are frozen Snickers bars, playing with her friend Sally, going to movies with her father, and visiting her grandmother in California. The issue of *availability of reinforcers* must first be considered here; in this instance, the cost of traveling to visit her grandmother may necessitate deleting it as a reinforcer. Alternatively, particularly if that reward is a top item in her hierarchy list, it could be used as an ultimate reinforcer when her grades are significantly improved. So, her list becomes: (a) playing with Sally, (b) going to a movie with her father, and (c) having a frozen Snickers bar.

The highest reinforcer, visiting her grandmother, would be a reinforcer worth saving. Since this is a strong but expensive and not easily available reinforcer, a behaviorally oriented social worker would not use it initially. Instead, the social worker and the child would work on slow, incremental, easily achievable short-term goals (e.g., the child would get a Snickers every time she completed her homework and would go to a movie with her father if she had a whole week of completing all homework. However, only after some period of success with these tasks would the social worker again introduce the possibility of the trip to her grandmother's. Since this choice is such a strong and expensive reinforcer, it would be saved for the bigger but later goal of improving all grades by one letter grade if that was a realistic and achievable goal based upon the girl's history of progress (see Case 8.4).

Case 8.4: Reinforcements

Sandy and Ray came in for marital help. The first session was loud, acrimonious, and hostile. At the second session, the social worker asked each of them to list on a sheet of paper three positive actions or behaviors that his or her spouse had demonstrated toward the other that made him or her feel good and closer to the other. This exercise failed. The exercise quickly degenerated into a power struggle as they accused each other of "never" doing anything decent for the other.

The social worker then suggested a separate session for each of them. This worked very well in that, alone, both partners said that they had once loved the other and still felt hope for the marriage; but each perceived the other to be increasingly cold, distant, and hostile. Even in the separate session, each partner agreed that in recent months the other had not done one single kind act toward his or her partner. Each felt unappreciated, overwhelmed with stress, and frustrated in what each genuinely perceived as past attempts to reconcile.

With each partner's permission, the social worker began the next joint session summarizing an amazingly similar list of shared concerns of both partners and also stressed that each appears to be committed to the marriage and willing work to make it better. However, they both feel frustrated in their attempts.

Without any further discussion between the husband and the wife, the social worker again asked each of them to make a list of positive, appreciated actions on the part of the other spouse. This time, the exercise worked better. Sandy listed three actions that Ray had done in the past that she appreciated: (a) Ray took out the garbage last week without being asked, a job that had become a major point of contention for them. (b) He came home from work last week, smiled, and kissed her. For months prior to their coming in, Sandy said Ray either ignored her or seemed to stare angrily at her. (c) Ray took Sandy out to dinner and complimented her on how nice she looked.

Ray listed the three behaviors from Sandy that he appreciated: (a) They made love one night for the first time in 5 months. (b) Sandy called Ray's mother just to have a friendly chat. This had been a problem in the past, since Sandy resented her mother-in-law for interfering; but Ray had insisted that his mother liked Sandy and felt hurt by Sandy's seeming rejection. (c) Sandy surprised him with actually encouraging him to go out one night with a small group of neighborhood friends who play cards and drink beer together once a week. Previously, Sandy strongly objected, even though Ray accurately described the group as a good opportunity for him to just relax with a nice group of old high-school friends.

These lists of reinforcers served as the basis for the next two sessions in which Sandy and Ray mutually reinforced each other's behavior.

5. *A focus on incremental steps that use short-term, easily achievable tasks that are gradually broadened to achieve behavioral goals.* Reinforcement patterns frequently become quite involved to achieve more complex behavioral goals. Behavioral research consistently shows that success breeds success and, likewise, failure often leads to more failures in behavior. Therefore, behavioral social workers try to assure success by beginning with easily achievable tasks. For instance, the compulsive eater who wants to lose 50 pounds and gain control over his or her inability to control gorging behavior when feeling anxious will initially be encouraged to stop focusing on that ultimate 50-pound-loss goal. Instead, after the initial collection of baseline behavior (which is described later), the client and social worker may agree merely to set aside a small period of time during the day when the client will agree to not eat. This may even be a time when the client does not normally eat, such as between 2:00 and 7:00 in the morning.

A depressed and lethargic client may agree to simply set the alarm clock for 9:00 in the morning, sit up in bed, and then go back to sleep. After this task is performed free of anxiety, the next incremental step may be to briefly get up out of bed. These seemingly easy tasks must be designed carefully with the client to allow him or her to finally feel some degree of success and potential mastery over the previously uncontrollable behavior (see Case 8.5).

One of the major accomplishments by behaviorists is the highly successful method and technique called *systematic desensitization* (Wolpe, 1969; Granvold, 1994). For phobias, this appears to be the most widely accepted treatment available. However, this technique has also been used with a wide variety of other problem areas from stuttering and tics to the treatment of behavior in individuals with schizophrenia and other psychotic disorders.

Systematic desensitization is based on the notion that certain stimuli arouse anxiety that, in the extreme, become debilitating, such as phobias. Since a person cannot be both relaxed and anxious at the same time, the social worker uses this approach to countercondition the client so that he or she will gradually and incrementally associate the anxiety-provoking stimuli, such as a phobic object, with a relaxed response. The process involves three stages: (a) deep muscle relaxation, (b) the development of a hierarchy of anxiety-provoking situations, and (c) counterpoising the anxiety-provoking situation with the learned relaxed response. This process and other desensitization techniques are explained in detail later.

Another incremental aspect of behaviorism is known as *shaping*. Shaping is a behavioral technique in which various incremental steps are used to gradually develop an ultimately desired complex behavior. The classic experiment in this area is with pigeons or other animals. Each small, incremental turn in the desired direction of making a complete turnaround is positively reinforced. Ultimately, the pigeon is shaped into doing a complete turn before being rewarded with a pellet of food.

Case 8.5: Incremental Steps

Jill had been suspended for fighting in her ninth-grade class at a conservative parochial school. Both the referring teacher and Jill's mother agreed that Jill had changed in the last year from a fairly outgoing, confident youngster to a rather angry, depressed, and increasingly withdrawn and combative adolescent. They also both suspected drug abuse.

When Jill came into the social worker's office, she angrily glared at the worker as she held back her tears. The social worker addressed Jill's apparent sadness and the fact that something must have happened to her that she has changed so much in the last year. The worker also told Jill that she was there to help and that what-ever Jill shared with the social worker would be confidential (although any suicidal concerns would require discussion with her mother). After some testing, anger, and missed sessions, Jill finally tearfully said that a tenth-grade boy she liked had become sexually involved with her and then told everyone at school. Since Jill wanted and agreed to have sex to keep the boy, she felt doubly hurt and humiliated.

At this point, Jill had no interest in the boy; but she felt that her life was ruined because all of her good old friends from this conservative religious school must think she was a "slut" while the boy actually seemed to be proud of his behavior. She said that the worst part of this was the rejection by her girlfriends at school, most of whom she had known all of her life. After considerable discussion of sexism and her accurate perception that she had been unfairly victimized, Jill and the social worker discussed ways of re-developing the ties with her former friends.

The social worker asked Jill to talk about one of the former girlfriends who had been nice or who seemed less hostile than the others. As the two of them talked objectively about Jill's social system, Jill said that, actually, several of her old friends seemed to continue to be nice, but she had avoided them. It was agreed that Jill would call her one best former friend and possibly invite her over after school. This worked extremely well. This friend assured Jill that most of her old friends knew the boy was a jerk, and he had been shunned by all of the girls at school. Jill was still concerned that "everyone knows" and blames her, but Jill's friend suggested having two more of the girls join them the next day at McDonald's, their usual meeting place. The four of them met, and Jill, who by this time was quite comfortable in talking about the incident and her feelings of rejection, was met with an outpouring of support. Her friends said they could not understand what had happened since Jill had been so cold toward them. Jill was invited to an overnight party at the home of one of the friends, and her entire former network joined them.

If the social worker had not been so very slow and incremental, this approach would not have succeeded. Jill's initial belief that "everyone" rejected her was factually inaccurate but overwhelming nonetheless. Jill had to begin with achieving her objective with one safe friend. Success is essential in this behavioral incrementalism. It is essential that the social worker always begin with small, easy, and clearly achievable tasks that then slowly build toward achievement of the larger objective. That ultimate objective was reinvolvement with the close network of former girlfriends. However, during the initial phases of treatment, that ultimate longer-term goal is generally ignored. After each of the small incremental successes is gradually achieved, then that ultimate goal becomes easily achievable as simply one more task on the continuum.

6. *A focus on the initial assessment.* While all approaches give significance to the importance of the initial assessment, behaviorists are distinctive in three ways. First, they intervene on the basis of the client's statement of the problem, not the social worker's view of the "real" problem. Behaviorists accept the client's perception. This is unlike some psychodynamically oriented social workers who see the early descriptions of the problems as stated by the client as somewhat ill informed because of repression, defenses, and other largely unconscious forces. Behaviorists highly regard the client's capacity to define his or her own problem, which must then be made specific, concrete, and workable from a behavioral perspective.

A second unique aspect of the behavioral assessment is the fact that behavioral social workers require that the client *not* change his or her behavior until sufficient data is gathered to establish a consistent baseline of behavior. This is an important and sometimes difficult goal to achieve. For instance, as smokers start to count the number of cigarettes or as obsessive-compulsive individuals count their obsessive thoughts or acts, they almost invariably want to try to immediately change. After all, that is why they came to see the social worker. However, clients are told to make no attempts to alter their behavior during this initial baseline assessment period.

This occasionally develops into ethical dilemmas when treating child or spouse abusers or sexual offenders, and some practical remedies often need to be developed. However, behavioral interventions are highly dependent upon realistic, accurate data relevant to the presenting problem. Behavioral alterations during this assessment period not only would provide insufficient data but also would be inaccurate. This issue is particularly relevant when significant others such as friends, teachers, or relatives are involved. For instance, the teacher who may have made the referral may quickly note that the child who was referred becomes disruptive only when the teacher is poorly prepared or the assignments are boring. The understandable tendency is for the teacher to try to immediately modify his or her own behavior, which is clearly an antecedent condition. Similarly, the parent who is gathering the initial data on his or her son who is physically abusive to another sibling may quickly observe that the boy hits his sister soon after the parent hits the boy. This antecedent behavior on the part of the parent, which is often denied or not initially mentioned, must be carefully examined while protecting the child.

The third unique aspect of behavioral assessments is that they typically define only from two to four precise behaviorally specific problems. The initial phase is one in which the social worker works closely with clients to help them clearly specify these limited numbers of target problem behaviors. For this reason, many behaviorists are also considered brief therapists. Once the three or so target problem behaviors have been successfully treated, treatment ends. Behaviorists, like most brief therapists, are deliberately narrow in their focus. If significant childhood trauma is discovered while behaviorally treating a child abuser, the behaviorist is generally disallowed from exploring that tangential but important issue. On the positive side, they can focus all of their intervention time and resources rather than prolong or even dilute the process by pursuing many other varied problems (see Case 8.6).

Case 8.6: Initial Assessment

Bill was a 17-year-old honor roll high school student whose behavior, grades, and social life had all recently deteriorated. He was extremely polite to the social worker and indicated a willingness to improve his situation but seemed inordinately evasive and anxious in spite of his verbal assurances of motivation. After two sessions, the social worker and Bill decided that Bill's two specific problems were (a) poor grades and (b) increasing social isolation.

Bill and the social worker developed a 2-week plan to do all homework assignments and have his teachers sign his homework to show to the worker. They also developed a short-term goal of calling two of his friends on the track team and one young woman he had dated and still liked. Progress on the homework went well. The tasks were gradually increased to getting at least a C in the three subjects in which he had received Ds last semester after three years of making nearly all As.

The social isolation goals were only partially achieved. He called one of his old track team friends, as Bill and the social worker had agreed, but he stalled in calling his former girlfriend, even after 3 weeks of discussion of this seemingly simple task. The social worker supportively confronted Bill with this and, after a missed session, Bill came in and said that his "real problem" was that he thought he was gay. He had briefly experimented sexually with another boy and was now simply unsure of his sexual orientation but knew he had no interest in calling his old girlfriend. He was also extremely frightened about his father's potential reaction as well as the reaction of his straight classmates.

After some discussion about sexual orientation and the fact that it is perfectly normal and healthy to question, it was decided that Bill should talk to another social worker within the agency who specialized in issues of sexual orientation and adolescence. In the meantime, Bill and the initial social worker continued work much more successfully on the same two initial problems while Bill separately and thoroughly dealt with his sexual orientation issue with another social worker.

7. *A focus on contracts, mutual agreements, and goals.* A behavioral characteristic that is increasingly shared even by nonbehaviorists is the development of a contract or written agreement. The contract is part of the initial assessment and typically specifies four conditions or areas of agreement involving (a) the behaviors of the client, (b) the behaviors of the social worker, (c) the agreed-upon behavioral goals, and (d) some description of the tasks required to reach those goals.

The behaviors of the client typically refers to the development of a written, agreed-upon statement to the effect that the client will attend all sessions on time and will be completely honest in providing data regarding his or her behavior. In addition, the client agrees to perform the tasks required of him or her to successfully change behavior and reach the agreed-upon behavioral goal or outcome.

The behaviors of the social worker similarly refers to a written agreement that the social worker be there for the client at all sessions and be honest, accurate, and clear in his or her feedback. The social worker will also agree to perform specified tasks in fulfillment of the goal of helping the client to stop, start, or otherwise change the agreed-upon behavior.

The agreed-upon behavioral goals refers to a concise, behaviorally specific statement of the desired outcome. Examples may include:

Stop hitting my wife.
Stop smoking.
Stop eating other than at mealtime.
Fly in a plane.
Stop washing my hands more than two times per day.
Get up each morning by 8 A.M., get dressed, and read the paper.
Stop making negative comments about myself or my children.
Ride my bike, swim, or weight lift three times per week.

Contracts also lend themselves to the use of *problem-oriented records* or *goal-oriented records.* These are types of case records or clinical records commonly used and require clear documentation of problems and/or goals on all clients served by social work agencies. Such records are a contrast to some medical records that rely on diagnoses (such as from the *DSM-IV-TR,* 2000) and that are usually less behaviorally specific. Social workers who use problem- or goal-oriented records frequently contract with the clients regarding tasks, anticipated goals, or behavioral outcomes to be achieved (see Case 8.7).

Case 8.7: Contracts, Mutual Agreements, and Goals

Helen was a 74-year-old widow whose husband had died the previous year. His death was a surprise and shock. Helen was not only depressed but also extremely anxious since her husband had managed the finances and she was still uncertain of how much money she had or how to manage it well.

When Helen came in to see the social worker, she was tearful and so anxious that she was unable to focus or clearly define workable problems or goals. The social worker let her ventilate and supported her need to "get it all out." However, he also guided her toward looking objectively at her current situation, which Helen perceived as overwhelming and impossible. They discussed finances, and Helen indicated that her younger sister was already reorganizing her finances and had even assured her that she was actually quite comfortable financially, especially with the life insurance policy money.

It became apparent that Helen had resented her rather controlling husband and was now beginning to resent her sister even though she was only doing what Helen had requested. Strong feelings of anger, hurt, rejection, and insecurity flooded Helen; but a consistent theme of *wanting* to take control of her life emerged. Unfortunately, Helen had not been able to resolve the marital problems with her domineering husband before he died.

The social worker recognized that there was a great deal of unresolved anger, as well as feelings of abandonment. However, there was also a need to help Helen to become more confident in the process of regaining some control over her fate. While helping Helen to ventilate and accept her anger as normal, the worker also developed a contract with her. Helen took the lead in writing up an agreement that stipulated that she would do the following:

> Call the life insurance company after thoroughly reviewing the policy and get them to agree to a date and amount to be sent.
>
> Talk to my sister about taking care of my own finances. Have three separate meetings to review my ongoing bills and checking account, review my own and my husband's pension, and begin developing a budget.
>
> Call my friend Kate, whose husband also died last year, and thank her for her sympathy and past support and ask that we meet for lunch weekly, perhaps with some other mutual friends.
>
> Go to my husband's grave site and "talk to him." Many issues were left unresolved, both positive and negative, and I will express those feelings to him.

The last stipulation of the contract was Helen's idea since she felt that the sessions with the social worker tended to be very helpful in getting her to clarify and accept her feelings. Additionally, she felt a need to actively maintain connections with her deceased husband. The sessions following this contract all dealt with monitoring the progress toward each component.

8. *A focus on the inclusion of significant others such as spouses, parents, teachers, neighbors, and friends in treatment.* Behaviorism evolved from research labs and social or experimental psychology, not from medical and clinical settings. As such, it tends to be more egalitarian and inclusive of nonclinicians than more traditional approaches that value professional status and expertise. Behaviorists have even been criticized as mere technicians in comparison to psychotherapists. However, many behaviorists accept this criticism as valid and counter that technical skills, which can be taught to virtually anyone, can yield more positive treatment outcomes than those of highly trained psychotherapists.

Tharp and Wetzel's (1969) *Behavior Modification in the Natural Environment* was a milestone in behaviorism and treatment in general. This book encouraged clinicians to view teachers, parents, and significant nonprofessionals as the *mediators* in working with clients, particularly children. The clinician's role was seen as that of a trainer, not a therapist. In this model, social workers or other professionals trained in behavioral techniques worked with the teachers or parents of children who presented problems.

These significant others were actually seen as preferable to professionals in providing the direct services. One reason for this preference for using significant others as the mediators was that the mediators already spent a great deal of time with the child, much more than the typical one hour or less prescribed by most professionals. These mediators were, therefore, in a better position to affect the target behavior since they intimately understood the problem already, they were personally motivated to change it, they already had strong relationships with the child, and they may even have been in a better position to dispense social reinforcers. Hugs or praise are more valued when coming from a teacher or parent than from a therapist with no preexisting relationship. This mediator or significant other was able to stay in the social environment of the child for a long period of time, which was extremely beneficial in itself since so much research indicates that positive results of any type of therapy are diminished after extended periods of time. In fact, the positive effects of behavioral intervention are often extinguished if the social environment of the client is countertherapeutic or even neutral.

Furthermore, many behaviorists believe that they can multiply their own effects by training teachers, child care workers, and, particularly, parents and spouses who may in turn apply what they have learned to other children, family, or friends (see Case 8.8).

Case 8.8: Significant Others
Curtis was a 12-year-old boy who was referred by his sixth-grade school teacher for disruptive behavior and fighting. He was put on medication after being diagnosed as having attention-deficit/hyperactivity disorder. He was seen by a social worker who developed a hierarchy of reinforcers that included individual time and tutoring with the teacher. At first, the sixth-grade teacher declined the request to be involved, but the social worker met with her and explained that, in spite of Curtis's behavior, he was actually very fond of the teacher and had previously been incapable of focusing or working effectively. Curtis had told the social worker, "My teacher is the only one who cares. I know I was real bad in school, but she was always nice, even when she yelled at me. She also made me come here, and that's been good too."

After that discussion, the teacher spoke with the principal who agreed to release her for two periods per week to work independently with Curtis. Although the medication was credited with helping, it was also evident that Curtis needed the individual attention, affection, and academic help that only his teacher was able to provide. Since the teacher was also willing and able to provide the social reinforcers of herself and her time, her involvement as the mediator was a particularly powerful and effective reinforcer.

COMPARING BEHAVIORAL TO PSYCHODYNAMIC APPROACHES

It is an unfortunate historical artifact of social work practice that the field developed into different "camps." Social workers were either behaviorist or psychodynamic in orientation. There were, of course, many other smaller "camps" particularly related to brief or crisis interventions and such social work models as the problem-solving method or the task-centered approach, which are only two of dozens; but most models of social work intervention were variations of either psychodynamic, insight-oriented "talking cures" or behavioral approaches. Social workers in the 1970s and early 1980s felt that they had to choose between the two major approaches and the generalist applications, which were seen as less rigorous or effective.

Social workers throughout much of the 1970s who described themselves as being research-based, eclectic, brief treatment–oriented social workers with an emphasis on social systems and support, were in the minority of clinicians. There were still many in the field who felt that it was far better to be very knowledgeable in one area, either psychodynamic or behavioral (although there was strong disagreement as to which it should be). Generalists or eclectics were viewed as ineffective.

General behavioral applications are used by practitioners who choose to instruct clients in behavioral terms for certain situations. Cognitive therapists also use this approach, although the cognitive therapist may approach the client from a cognitive theory rather than from a learning theory foundation. In practice, the general behaviorist will guide clients in discovering that there is nothing psychopathological or even illogical about their seemingly destructive and incomprehensible behavior; but, rather, they were taught and encouraged to behave that way in previous situations that no longer exist.

Thus, a 25-year-old depressed and isolated female with a history of having been sexually and physically abused by her stepfather may present herself to a social worker because she is hostile toward or afraid of men. However, she desperately wants a good, supportive relationship with a man and hopes to develop a family of her own. Her fear and anger toward men may at times mystify and confuse her as she seemingly self-defeats her own efforts to develop a relationship with potential mates. In this highly simplified example, even a psychodynamic therapist is likely to use a general behavioral discussion of the unfortunate but understandable logic and consistency of her behavior. Her abusive stepfather conditioned her to fear and hate all men. She learned to defend herself as an adult by keeping men away for fear that they would hurt or abuse her. There is nothing psychopathological or even illogical about her behavior given her history except for the fact that she consciously wants to have a relationship and, subsequently, a family. Although behaviorists do not subscribe to the notion of unconscious motivations, they do see the same phenomenon as a learned response to negative stimuli. All men have become viewed in the same light as her stepfather even though all men are not behaviorally alike. A behavioral generalist would reinforce the fact that her generalization of abusive behavior to all men is inaccurate and that, by responding to men in a rejecting, hostile, and defensive manner, she is maintaining the response to her stepfather, which is no longer appropriate. In fact, it is inappropriate and counterproductive for her goal of developing a relationship.

The task of the advanced social work practitioner often involves making choices among various approaches. As previously discussed, there are several guidelines for making choices. Certain problems, diagnoses, or personality types lend themselves very clearly to one approach or another (Thyer & Wodarski, 1998); but it is also useful to back away from the specifics and use a broader view to compare psychodynamic approaches to behavioral interventions. There are several aspects of treatment that differ when comparing behavioral to insight-oriented treatment (Zastrow, 1999). They concern how each describes their understanding of (a) the causes of problems and the underlying theory, (b) problems versus diagnoses, (c) symptoms versus underlying motivators, (d) purpose of the intervention, and (e) goals.

Underlying Theory

Psychodynamic and insight-oriented psychotherapy or interventions are based on the theory that problems are caused by unconscious and unresolved or repressed issues. These consciously unknown issues must be understood, and it is through resolving the repressed and gaining insight into the unconscious source of the problem that help is achieved. Psychodynamically oriented social workers believe that early childhood dynamics are particularly significant in determining feelings, emotions, and subsequent behavior. Transference, wherein patients relate to others partially on the basis of unconscious similarities to their parents or other significant (or traumatic) people in their histories, plays a significant role in treatment. Clinicians work under the assumption that underlying repressed or denied factors are the cause of later problems.

On the other hand, behaviorists see the source of the problem as being learned responses to situations. They posit that the client is essentially still responding to conditions that no longer exist and that these responses are, therefore, maladaptive or inappropriate in subsequent situations. Behaviorists do not see concepts such as the unconscious or repression as being relevant to treatment; and while some behaviorists may agree that psychodynamic theory has some validity (e.g., individuals are all clearly products of early family dynamics and apparently repress or "forget" some past traumas), they maintain that there is no need to deal with these underlying dynamics in interventions.

Problem Statements

Psychodynamic and insight-oriented social workers accept a medical model, which views problems in diagnostic categories, usually using the *DSM-IV-TR* (2000). Each diagnosis or problem needs to be understood by insight-oriented social workers in terms of the underlying dynamics and history. They believe that the problem is typically not consciously known or understood by the *patient* (the term used in the medical model for the *client*), since he or she has repressed it or the problem is otherwise unavailable for conscious or objective analysis. For psychodynamic and insight-oriented clinicians, the presenting problem as initially described by the patient is not really the focus of intervention. The "real" problem has to be discovered through uncovering repressed or unconscious material, typically from childhood.

For behaviorists, the problem is simply the problem. The behavioral social worker does not elaborate on the problem or try to understand it or analyze it in the context of the client's past. The early assessment phase for the behaviorist is very clear and unambiguous, although sometimes quite long and detailed. The therapist accepts the client's statement concerning whatever is bothering him or her. Insight-oriented psychotherapists such as psychoanalysts rarely accept the patient's statement of the problem at face value. For them, such statements are only beginning points from which they must embark to help the client work through defense mechanisms, repressed and forgotten past events and traumas, and other unconscious conflicts and anxieties that are, in fact, the real focus of attention.

Symptoms

Psychodynamically oriented social workers see symptoms as the overt and observable but decidedly secondary manifestation of the underlying problems. Crying, insomnia, lethargy, or suicide attempts are all symptoms of depression. These symptoms help the social worker as well as the client to better understand the real underlying cause of the problem; and this cause may frequently be understood in symbolic ways. For instance, patients who feel guilty about past sexual behavior frequently develop symptoms of compulsively washing their hands or taking baths as if to cleanse themselves of dirt. Similarly, conversion disorders or somatic symptoms such as paralysis or hysterical blindness are generally interpreted as symptoms of patients who were too frightened previously to act or move. Patients who were unable to rescue a child hit by a car are subsequently unable to walk or unable to see again.

On the other hand, behaviorists frequently see the symptom as the focus of intervention or the *problem* that needs to be changed. A behaviorist would directly attempt to stop the crying behavior of a severely depressed client or use systematic desensitization to stop an obsessive-compulsive client from excessive hand washing. Insight-oriented social workers and psychoanalysts would never consider directly stopping those symptoms but would, instead, work on resolving the underlying causes of the depression or obsessive-compulsive disorder.

Insight-oriented therapists sometimes suggest that it is inappropriate to simply try to stop the symptoms. If the underlying cause is still there, then the symptom will manifest itself in some other manner. This theory of *symptom substitution* has a great deal of logical validity; however, very little empirical evidence supports its existence. In fact, behaviorists generally suggest that insight-oriented therapists are so relatively inefficient and ineffective because they fail to recognize that the task of the therapist is simply to modify the symptom or the behavior, not to "waste time" with symbolic interpretations of unverifiable concepts or causes. At best, behaviorists indicate that, even if the underlying cause is related to some unconscious factor, developing insight into that cause seems to have little effect on behavioral outcomes. They point to the many cases in which patients work for years to finally develop insight into their traumatic childhood or anxiety-laden insecurity, yet they *still* cry excessively or wash their hands dozens of times each day.

Defining the symptom is far from being a heuristic exercise. Social workers are increasingly required to focus on overt, clear, and relatively treatable symptoms. However, if a woman presents herself with a set of standard symptoms of depression such as crying, poor hygiene, sleep disturbances, and eating problems but who has a history of childhood abuse, rape, or incest, then the underlying causes need to be addressed psychodynamically.

Goals

The goal of the insight-oriented or psychodynamic social worker is the resolution of the underlying unconscious cause of the feelings, emotions, and behaviors that cause difficulties for the patient. The goal of the behaviorist is to change the responses, behaviors, overt attitudes, and symptoms of the client. These two very diverse goals partially explain the reason for the relative differences in clinical outcome research. Using their more limited, observable and measurable goals, behaviorists are generally more successful in their outcomes than insight-oriented psychotherapists.

The goals of the insight-oriented psychotherapist frequently involve changing the personality of the patient. By reworking past unresolved problems that are the basis for much of the patient's underlying behavior, insight-oriented psychotherapists have significantly more ambitious goals than the behaviorists. It may take years of intensive analysis to help patients slowly regress or, at least, remember early childhood traumas, feelings, or significant interactions that still affect them in their adult lives. Few social workers have the training or inclination to conduct such long-term analysis, but it is important for social workers to know some psychodynamic theory and to be able to apply it whenever needed.

Insight into early childhood issues is believed to be essential before attitudes and behaviors can change. A 30-year-old heterosexual male client who verbalizes an interest but frustration in developing an intimate, trusting relationship with women may need help in exploring childhood relationships with his controlling, critical and "castrating" mother. The adult woman, expressing the same frustration, may need years of analysis to recall repressed incidents of sexual abuse by an uncle before being able to resolve her apparent fear and loathing of sexual intimacy with men.

Goals and subsequent methods of the behaviorists are radically different. In the case of the heterosexual man and women, the goal may be a series of social interactions with members of the opposite sex. Note that more complex and nebulous goals (e.g., forming a relationship, love, etc.) are to be avoided and that only clear, discrete, preferably measurable goals are developed. Thus, in both cases, the behaviorally oriented therapist might slowly and incrementally reward the man in his achievement of the necessary stages that culminate in a successful relationship. The behaviorist and the client would work together in developing a clear, multistaged process. *Stage 1* would be defining characteristics of the chosen partner, or describing attributes for a likely partner such as physical appearance, age, religion, or interests. *Stage 2* would be researching likely groups, organizations, or settings where such people might be found and/or at which social interactions might be fostered (e.g., a co-ed volleyball league, a church singles group, or an adult education class). *Stage 3* would be defining how, when, and where to interact. Some behaviorists might role-play what to say or how to act. Along each successive stage, the client or behavioral therapist will have established a reward system for successful achievement of each stage or even discrete tasks involved within the stages. A log would be kept, and the role of the social worker becomes one of monitoring the task achievement and the reward system, as well as altering the stages or tasks whenever needed.

The goals, techniques, and underlying assumptions are radically different for the psychodynamically oriented therapist and the behaviorist. The insight-oriented social worker focuses upon underlying causes; thus, the techniques are designed to uncover repressed traumas by developing insight into them. Therefore, the young man needs to work through his denial and repressed feelings about his mother to recognize that not all women are similar to her and that his relationship with her has had a significant effect on his present feelings about all women. Similarly, the woman must work through and uncover repressed memories of the trauma of her past abuse and deal with the pain it has caused her before being able to trust men.

To the behaviorist, these past traumas are not relevant in the treatment plan. The focus of the treatment is the pattern of avoidance or lack of action in making connections. This man and woman have to be reinforced to engage in behaviors that are designed to incrementally reach the goal of multiple successful interactions, that is, a dating relationship. In a rather simplistic generalization, one can say that insight-oriented social workers focus upon the causes while behaviorists focus upon the behaviors themselves with relatively little regard for the causes (see Case 8.9).

Case 8.9: Conditioning

Mrs. Green is a 63-year-old mother of three grown children, and her husband recently retired. She is ostensibly a very confident, warm, outgoing woman with a charming sense of humor. However, she came in to see the social worker at the

Memphis Family and Children's Social Service Agency because she is mildly ago-raphobic, claustrophobic, and anxious in social situations whenever she has to leave her home. She has an active family life as long as family members visit her. She even has a few friends who come to her home regularly. Mrs. Green manages to go shopping and occasionally, reluctantly, goes out with her husband for important social events. However, considerable tension was developing for her and her hus-band because she was unable to enter elevators or fly in airplanes. These behav-iors considerably limit her hopes for traveling extensively during retirement years.

Once it was established that she genuinely wanted to travel, particularly to see her children, the process of eliminating the barriers began. Since Mrs. Green became noticeably anxious when she discussed her phobias, the clinical social worker decided to begin treatment by getting Mrs. Green to relax by walking around the elevators in the office building. This was done because it conditioned Mrs. Green to be relaxed rather than anxious as they walked past the elevators. The social worker totally ignored the elevators in spite of Mrs. Green's anxious glances in their direction. Instead, the social worker maintained the interesting and relaxing discussions around family and friends that Mrs. Green enjoyed. They always returned for the last few minutes to the social worker's private office, where the worker said, "Well, that was fun. I noticed you looked at the elevators a lot, but there's really no rush to use them. If you'd like, maybe we could just con-tinue our chats outside of the elevator."

The social worker's agency was located in a large office/apartment complex that housed a variety of social service programs; doctors' and counselors' offices; and a great many residents, many of whom were quite elderly. Eventually, some of the residents joined in on their conversations. The point of conversing in a relaxed manner while in proximity to the elevators was to get Mrs. Green to asso-ciate relaxation rather than anxiety with the elevator.

By incrementally replacing an anxious response with a relaxed response when in the presence of elevators, small rooms, and, eventually, airplanes, the social worker helped Mrs. Green overcome her phobias. For her mild agorapho-bia and social anxiety, she was given similar assignments, that is, she engaged in relaxed discussion with family, friends, or the social worker until she was relaxed and all traces of anxiety were extinguished. Then she could move up to the next level of anxiety-related situations, replace the anxiety with a relaxed response, and move forward.

In addition to the process of conditioning Mrs. Green to be relaxed in the presence of previously anxiety-provoking stimuli, a second factor in the success of this intervention was the choice of a powerful reinforcer. The social worker quickly discerned that Mrs. Green was very sociable and close to her family, in spite of her condition. The social worker therefore engaged Mrs. Green's family and friends by integrating them into the process as social reinforcers. Close friends and family members met with Mrs. Green at the airport, near elevators, and at stores or restaurants. They were instructed in relaxation techniques, as well as being instructed in the necessity of a slow, incremental process. The social worker believed that this involvement of Mrs. Green's social support system intensified the process, diminished the time needed in treatment, and increased the likelihood of long-term success in the future.

Case 8.10: Systematic Desensitization

Joey is an 11-year-old boy with autism who lives in a residential treatment center. His evenings are spent with a small group of six severely disturbed boys who are approximately his age. However, the other boys correctly perceive of themselves as being more functional or "normal looking" than Joey. Furthermore, typical of youngsters this age, they are very sensitive to being different from other children. They began to resent Joey because he often talked to himself, threw occasional temper tantrums, did a great deal of self-stimulation, and occasionally hit himself. Joey also had a great many fears and phobias. Whenever Joey saw a dog while on any trip outside of the center, he became terrified and encopretic. This necessitated immediate returns to the center for a change of pants. It was also an extreme embarrassment to Joey and his other group members. Field trips were invariably cut short, and Joey was blamed for ruining their fun.

With Joey's blessings, it was decided to try to help him to overcome his fear of dogs. The process was begun by having Joey's favorite dorm counselor regularly read to him and show Joey children's books about small puppies. Typically, these books for small children depicted drawings of cute puppies that performed great or heroic feats or that were somehow imperiled. After a week of one-hour sessions developing comfort with these stories, Joey started to say that he liked puppies but did not like big dogs.

The next step in incrementally helping Joey involved looking at drawings of and reading stories that had larger, full-grown dogs. The context was always positive. A week of daily sessions was spent looking at these drawings and discussing the stories of how these dogs helped people. Successive weeks involved a series of very slow, gradual, incremental, and easily achievable steps that moved toward a field trip during which they would probably encounter someone walking a dog.

This systematic behavioral process was augmented when the live-in maintenance man, who was well aware of the desensitization process with Joey, offered to get a puppy to live at the center. After some discussions with other staff administrators and calls to the health department, it was agreed to ask Joey about this idea. The plan was to suggest that the maintenance man initially keep the puppy far from Joey. Joey agreed to this, and his affect and verbalizations clearly indicated that he genuinely wanted to see this puppy as long as it was kept far from him.

The day the puppy arrived was a joyfully anticipated event for all of the children, including Joey. However, the social worker suggested that Joey and his dorm counselor observe the puppy from the third-floor staff residential area where they could watch the puppy play with the other children at the far end of the courtyard. Joey himself almost immediately wanted to play with the puppy; but, knowing that Joey's feelings could change from desire to dread very quickly, the social worker insisted on maintaining observations from a long distance, which would be gradually shortened. Thus, Joey and the dorm counselor watched the puppy from the third floor for several days, then from the second floor, then from the first floor, and then from a much closer distance. Within one month of the puppy's arrival, Joey was petting and picking up the puppy. He and most of the staff and children referred to the pet as "Joey's dog." Joey loved the puppy and asked to take the puppy for walks on a leash in front of the center by himself.

The desired outcome with systematic desensitization and behavioral interventions is to gradually change behavioral responses (see Case 8.10). An emphasis upon the final, desired outcome itself can often induce tremendous anxiety; and some clients cannot be desensitized because they obsess about their phobic object, such as dogs. It is important throughout the behavioral process to deemphasize the final outcome and focus instead on achieving the very small, gradual, incremental stages as they occur one at a time.

Another common desensitization example, in which there is a need to focus on the small incremental stages, is in sexual therapy with men who have performance anxiety–related impotence. These men frequently obsess about their inability to have successful intercourse and, therefore, avoid having even minimal intimacy. The focus of this treatment approach must be on the relatively easy and comfortable achievement of the current or next step with virtually no attention paid to the final outcome or goal.

SUMMARY

Behavioral interventions historically presented a radical departure from the psychodynamic orientation that predominated in mental health and social work until the middle of the 20th century. Although behavioral interventions encompass a wide variety of variations and combinations with other approaches (particularly with cognitive methods), there are eight foci that are common to most behavioral models:

1. Clear, observable, and measurable behaviors
2. Causal and antecedent events and consequences of behavior
3. Defining behavior empirically, logically, and objectively
4. Reinforcements that modify behavior through their contingent management
5. Incremental, achievable steps
6. The initial assessment
7. Contracts, mutual agreements, and goals
8. Inclusion of significant others in treatment

Behaviorists differ from insight-oriented psychodynamic social workers in a number of significant ways. They differ in their understandings of the causes of problems and the theories that underlie those causes. They differ in respect to their views of *problems* as opposed to diagnostic categories; symptoms as opposed to underlying motivators; and the purposes and goals of intervention.

COGNITIVE INTERVENTIONS

Cogito ergo sum. . . . I think, therefore I am. This phrase is perhaps the most meaningful phrase ever uttered. One's thoughts define who one is and what he or she believes. The fact that a person thinks validates his or her existence, and the way that person thinks gives meaning and purpose to that existence.

The *cognitive approach* is the newest major treatment approach used in social work, and it is rapidly becoming the predominant approach. Some even suggest that the change from behavioral therapy to cognitive therapy is revolutionary (Baars, 1986). However, as in most revolutions, there is an evolutionary component as well. For instance, the constructivist approach that originated in cognitive therapy is now seen by many within the social work profession as being the dominant model (Franklin & Nurius, 1996). There are a variety of cognitive models that borrow both theory and practice techniques from a wide and diverse basis and that have evolved into an eclectic mix of behaviorism, psychoanalysis, cognitive psychology, and social-constructionist theories.

In this chapter, the three basic models of cognitively based interventions are examined: cognitive therapy, cognitive-behavioral interventions, and constructivism, as well as three related models. The commonalities of the approaches are described, followed by a section on the cognitive techniques. The chapter concludes with an examination of the cognitive treatment of the two categories of disorders most frequently associated with this approach: anxiety disorders and depression. Finally, a list of common cognitive distortions is included.

MAJOR MODELS

The cognitive approach is a relatively new model that has gained tremendous support among social workers because of its clarity, brevity, effectiveness, and logic. However, after three decades of change and evolution within cognitive treatment, it has become increasingly difficult to differentiate purely cognitive approaches from the many behavioral and other blended models.

There are many variations of cognitive treatment (Granvold, 1994; 1996; Mahoney, 1991), but even a brief list of the major models would minimally include rational-emotive therapy (Ellis, 1977); cognitive therapy (Beck, 1976, 1996; Beck, Rush, Shaw, & Emery, 1979); self-instructional training (Meichenbaum, 1977); and constructivist therapy (Granvold, 1996; Guidano & Liotti, 1983). Furthermore, social work textbooks in this area suggest that virtually every social worker needs to know the various problem-focused models (Granvold, 1994).

Six different cognitive models are described briefly in this section. The first three models are the major approaches that form the basis for most of the others: Beck's cognitive therapy, cognitive-behavioral treatment (CBT), and constructivism. The next three models are all applied interventions and include problem-solving or problem-focused interventions, Meichenbaum's self-instruction training (SIT), and Ellis's rational-emotive therapy (RET) model. Techniques are described later in this chapter. Readers are urged to refer to other texts (Beck, 1996; Granvold, 1994, 1996) and the original sources for more detailed descriptions of this highly varied, eclectic, and rapidly evolving approach.

Beck's Cognitive Therapy

In 1976, Aaron Beck published *Cognitive Therapy and the Emotional Disorders,* which described a new approach to treatment. Beck is a psychoanalyst who based this new approach on the work of Kelly (1955), Piaget (1950), and other widely divergent theorists to suggest that one's *thoughts* or *cognitions* form the basis for the activation of idiosyncratic cognitive *schemata,* which, in turn, lead to predictable patterns of cognitive, affective, and behavioral symptoms or responses by individuals. In other words, the main causes of emotions, motives, and, subsequently, behavior, are the conscious thoughts one has.

Therapeutic interventions aim directly at the dysfunctional thoughts, emotions, expressed motives, behavior, interpretations, and predictions, as well as at dysfunctional schema and underlying beliefs of the client. To accomplish change, cognitive therapists have developed techniques to understand and learn a client's patterns and habits of thought or cognition and then to work to change them. Dysfunctional thoughts are changed, which leads to changes in subsequent behavior. The social worker modifies the client's conscious perceptions and ideas until they are realistic. So the worker challenges, confronts, suggests alternatives, and questions the client's distorted thinking as a way of helping the client reassess the perceptions and beliefs that form the basis for his or her dysfunctional behavior and emotions (Beck, 1996).

The cognitive model says that there are cognitive structures that organize information from the five senses into cognitive propositions. A *schema* or *schemata* result that are the product of all of these structures and propositions.

Cognitive therapy targets these inaccurate or dysfunctional schemata. By helping the client change his or her schemata, the therapist teaches the client to think and, therefore, behave in a more constructive, consistent, or behaviorally appropriate manner.

The schemata, which are formed in early childhood, are the foundation for the subsequent beliefs, rules governing behavior, and overall philosophy or view of life. Though it is not easy to precisely define these schemata, they form the basis for evaluating, screening, coding, and categorizing all input or stimuli. These schemata are the filters through which one views oneself and the world (Beck, 1996; Granvold, 1994).

Cognitive therapists target the underlying schemata for change and often use certain "guideposts" to "zero in" with the client on counterproductive schemata. These distorted schemata are referred to as either *cognitive distortions, dysfunctional thoughts,* or *irrational beliefs,* depending upon the particular model chosen. A description of the most common of these distortions is included at the end of this chapter.

Cognitive restructuring is the primary method of Beck's cognitive model and is more psychoanalytic than behavioral in some respects. In fact, both psychoanalysts and cognitive therapists suggest that behavior is influenced by beliefs. The difference is that psychoanalysts emphasize unconscious beliefs, whereas cognitive therapists emphasize conscious beliefs (Sharf, 1996). Cognitive restructuring systematically focuses attention on the client's cognitive errors and recommends that the therapist and client collaborate in correcting them. Cognitive restructuring works particularly well with affective disorders such as depression and anxiety (Beck, 1996; Beck, Rush, Shaw, & Emery, 1979; Dulmus & Wodarski, 1998).

Cognitive restructuring focuses upon the three areas of cognitions, mood, and behavior. There is an interaction among these three areas, and the point of intervention can be directed at any one of them or at all of them together. For instance, internal stimuli, such as the client's own beliefs and assumptions (i.e., cognitions) can trigger *automatic thoughts*. These lead to emotional responses (i.e., moods), which in turn lead to biased behaviors that ultimately reinforce internal beliefs and assumptions.

However, external events can also set up *automatic thoughts* that lead to behavior and, eventually, responses by others, finally returning to affect external events. Cognitive interventions aim directly at the basis of the problem which is viewed as the distorted schemata or thinking. Therefore, the worker questions and challenges the client's thoughts, emotions, motives, and behavior, as well as the bases for each. The goal of treatment is to modify the conscious perceptions and views of reality to ultimately help the client's moods and views, thus affecting the client's behavior in a constructive and appropriate manner. The worker talks to the client, guiding him or her to reconsider faulty assumptions and inaccurate perceptions that have led to inappropriate responses.

The three basic problematic processes that are defined and used as points of intervention for clients are thoughts, emotions, and behavior. First, *distortions in thought processing occur* whereby the client's logic and sequencing of thoughts and actions are unrealistic or distorted. For instance, Jim thinks that Sally is angry with him because she walked past him without smiling or acknowledging him.

Second, *maladaptive emotional responses develop* wherein the client is hurt, angry, or upset needlessly. The emotional reactions are not only extreme, but they are based in faulty perceptions of reality. Using the previous example, Jim might return to his desk and think about how "rude" Sally is. He becomes increasingly upset with her and feels very angry.

Third, *faulty, exaggerated, or unrealistic expectations of others, self, and the social environment or conditions develop that lead to inappropriate behavior* and an exacerbation of the problem. Staying with the example, Jim might decide that he will no longer tolerate Sally's unfair behavior, so he angrily storms into his boss's office and loudly complains that he will quit if the boss does not fire Sally.

Cognitive therapists can intervene at any point along the continuum. First, the social worker would suggest alternative and more realistic observations by challenging the original thoughts. Or the social worker may help Jim by suggesting the possibility that Sally was preoccupied, did not see him, or was in a bad mood. The social worker suggests alternative beliefs or perceptions indicating that Sally's behavior may be unrelated to Jim.

Second, the worker could confront Jim with his counterproductive and irrationally angry and painful response. Jim would be helped to see that the unpleasant responses of anger, resentment, and hurt were self-induced and, therefore, are within his power to change.

Third, the worker could choose to focus on Jim's inappropriate behavioral response. Instead of going to his boss directly, he might be helped to develop different behaviors such as asking Sally for the reason she did not greet him or giving himself a 24-hour "time-out" period to calmly reconsider his many alternative, positive responses.

Cognitive-Behavioral Treatment

Cognitive-behavioral treatment (CBT) developed from what is now often referred to as *radical behaviorism.* The early behaviorists are best represented by B. F. Skinner and others in the 1960s and 1970s who developed a rather extreme *deterministic* view that stated that individuals are simply programmed organisms that respond to stimuli in somewhat invariable patterns that are both predictable and modifiable. This viewpoint significantly altered the way social workers and others in the helping professions treated clients. Although the clear linear logic of this model appealed to many researchers and academics, it also raised many existential questions concerning human nature, free will, and self-determination.

The cognitive approach provided the missing link for behaviorists. Researchers, theorists, and practitioners who were uncomfortable with or who had actually rejected the simplistic notion of pure, predetermined responses to stimuli were now offered a reasonable alternative theory by adding the notion of a mediating or processing component of the human organism. Thus, the classical stimulus-response (S-R) model was altered to become stimulus-organism-response (S-O-R). The reader is referred to the previous chapter for more details on behavioral theory and practice.

It is difficult to separate cognitive therapy from behaviorism since both use "in vivo exposure, positive reinforcement, modeling, relaxation techniques, homework, and graded activities. Cognitive therapy shares with behavior therapy the emphasis on a collaborative relationship with the client and the use of experimentation in trying behavioral and cognitive homework. Additionally, cognitive therapists attend to the feelings and moods of the client, incorporating empathic aspects of person-centered therapy" (Sharf, 1996, p. 406).

The next major models also provide some transition from radical behaviorism to the cognitive approach by recognizing the tremendous importance of the way individuals differentially construct or mediate reality.

Constructivism

Constructivism and its theoretically related "mediational model" (Granvold, 1994; Mahoney, 1991) say that the way that an individual or organism *perceives* the stimulus has a significant effect on how he or she responds to it. The perceptual process involves screening, evaluating, weighing, and understanding what one observes through one's own history and idiosyncratic perspective.

Social constructivism is a theory that states that what one knows or thinks is socially, culturally, and historically situated. Constructivism states that one cannot know reality apart from one's construction of it. These views stand in contrast to empirical positivists and objectivists who claim that reality is an objective fact, undifferentiated among individuals. Social work and the social sciences are currently vigorously debating these opposing viewpoints. The differences have profound implications for both research and applied practice (Thyer & Wodarski, 1998).

Objectivists and positivists are typically viewed as coming from the traditional empirical school of research that states there is an objective reality apart from the "knowers and the known." One's subjective response or even perceptions of that immutable reality is irrelevant for research purposes and, ultimately, for clinical practice research. The constructivists say that there are multiple truths or realities. Each reality is developed, by necessity, upon the viewer's construction of that reality.

The culture and the society in which each individual is raised shape the personality in ways that require each person to attribute different meanings and, subsequently, different behavioral responses to the same events. Each of the resultant perceptions of reality is equally valid; and, in fact, an individual cannot know reality in any way other than through his or her idiosyncratic viewpoint.

Constructivism has been embraced by social work for several reasons, but the two primary reasons are *cultural diversity* and *qualitative flexibility.* Constructivists are ideally well versed in the specific cultures of their clients so that they are aware of culture-specific concepts and knowledge (called the *emic approach*). However, they are also open to universalistic, intercultural perspectives that are sensitive to the tremendous variations of individuals within the same culture as a result of aculturation as well as individual personality differences unrelated to culture (called the *etic approach*) (Lee, 1996). A constructivist would combine the best of both by first trying to understand the client's perceptions as developed within that person's cultural framework while recognizing, as well, the unique reality of that individual whose viewpoint may be quite different from that of others who share that same culture.

The other reason that social work has been so receptive to constructivism is that many in social work have rejected the more rigid, hierarchical, quantitative, and, some say, paternalistic approach of objectivist empiricism. This older, traditional viewpoint, previously addressed in this book in relation to the debate between qualitative versus quantitative methods (Chapter 2), is central to constructivism. To constructivists, there is no single measurable objective "truth." In fact, quantitative empiricists who lay claim to single, immutable truth, as defined and often quantified by them, are viewed as insensitive to constructivism.

For instance, a common concern among many *feminist practice* social workers is that empirical objectivists, who are typically male, put themselves into the position of defining reality in their own authoritative way. Furthermore, these male-oriented researchers exclude the very different construction of the reality of females who experience, perceive, develop, and subsequently respond to their reality in ways that are quite different from males. Constructivists ideologically side with feminist practitioners and those who espouse developing techniques within a strong cultural, but individualistic, framework that is highly sensitive to *client self-determination.*

Constructivism is a philosophical position that states that we cannot know reality other than our interpretation of it and that our values and interests cannot be separated from our observations. In contrast, the objectivists and quantitative empiricists view reality as being neutral, stable, and ultimately quantifiable. Constructivists can trace their roots back to the Greek skeptics who asked, "How is it that anyone can claim to know anything?" Skepticism refutes absolutist and positivist claims and further argues that to even allow such absolutist claims to knowledge and truth, society turns over tremendous power and authority to those who "know truth" or can define it with their methodology.

The concept of "objectivism" suggests that there are absolute, "correct" ways of knowing and that, ultimately, truth and reality are the same for everyone. Such absolutist thinking has understandable historical roots in the industrial era and then the "age of science," particularly in the early 20th century, when the highly vulnerable and suspect "social sciences" were attempting to gain credibility among their highly quantitative colleagues in the "hard sciences." However, in a *postmodernist* era, which recognizes diversity and change as norms, a more individualistic orientation to client needs is necessary.

The treatment goal for constructivists "explores client's personal meanings and facilitates the transformations of those meanings in the direction of more viable representations of experience" (Granvold, 1996, p. 348). Constructivists focus on the promotion of meaning making and personal development as opposed to traditional treatment that treats or reduces a problem or symptom. Treatment is more creative than corrective, and "problems" are essentially opportunities to explore new meanings and meet developmental challenges (Granvold, 1996).

Dean (1993) describes five basic aspects of the constructivist approach and how they differ from mainstream treatment: (a) *assessment* is collaborative, nonhierarchical, and geared to individualistic formulations of the problem; (b) *use of theory:* constructivists accept multiple theories as alternative explanations with no single personal or theoretical perspective viewed as the "truth"; (c) *treatment* emphasizes client narratives with a focus on the evolution of meaning; (d) the *therapeutic relationship* is reciprocal and mutual although the client's perceptions are given greater value and attention than the worker's; and (e) *values* are central and focused upon and explored as a basic element of therapy.

Given this highly individualistic philosophical approach to treatment, it is not surprising that constructivists eschew specific, standardized techniques. "Skilled therapy (like all other complex skills) defies explicit mechanical operationalization. Techniques as tools of practice are not to be given greater credit than they deserve relative to other aspects of practice. . . . The development of a quality therapeutic relationship with such characteristics as acceptance, understanding, trust, and caring is a prime objective of constructivists. . . . [which] calls for more creative than corrective interventions" (Granvold, 1996, p. 350).

There are, however, certain practice techniques used by constructivists that are philosophically consistent with their perspective. These include (a) *exploration through questioning and challenging,* (b) *restructuring,* (c) *journaling or daily logs,* (d) *imagery,* and (e) *guided discovery.* Cognitive *restructuring,* which is the primary method of Beck's (1996) cognitive approach, has already been described. The other techniques are described later in this chapter.

Cognitive theorists and, particularly, constructivists say that emotions are experienced "as a result of the way in which events are interpreted or appraised. It is the meaning of events that triggers emotions rather than the events themselves. The particular appraisal made will depend on the context in which an event occurs, the mood the person is in at the time it occurs, and the person's past experiences. . . . [T]he same event can evoke a different emotion in different people, or even different emotions in the same person on different occasions" (Salkovskis, 1996, p. 48).

Case 9.1, Case 9.2, and Case 9.3, respectively, demonstrate how the factors of *context, mood,* and *past experiences* cognitively affect one's *construction* of an event.

Case 9.1: Context

Sue is a successful office manager who is being treated for anorexia and depression. She recently finished work on a new account, and the president of the company sent a memo to most of Sue's colleagues praising her. However, Sue admitted to her social worker that she was very confused by her own reaction to the seemingly identical feedback she received from three different people at work. When her good friend and confidant, Jenny, said, "Great job," Sue was proud and smiled and hugged her friend. When Bill, her main competitor for a promotion, said the same, she politely thanked him and walked away quickly to avoid him.

When her immediate supervisor also complimented her, Sue was terrified. This supervisor's incompetence had forced Sue to go over this person's head to do the work. In this context, Sue interpreted the feedback as a threat as if her boss had said, "I know what you did to me, and I'm going to repay you." Sue responded by going to the president of the company. Sue thanked the president, solidifying that relationship as a way of protecting herself from her boss's presumed recriminations.

Case 9.2: Mood

John is being successfully treated for a bipolar disorder by his social worker, who treats him in a biweekly psychoeducational support group. John is also taking Depakote, having switched recently from lithium since it depressed his mood. He meets on an "as-needed" basis with his social worker and recently came in with a concern that he responds erratically to the same situation: "My wife tries so hard to be supportive, but I treat her badly. Nearly every morning, she tells me how nice I look before I go to work. Some days, I love it and I thank her. Other days, I don't even hear her; I'm just a little out of it. Then yesterday, I almost hit her. I woke up scared as hell. . . . I think I had a nightmare. Anyway, she should have known to leave me alone, but she bothers me some mornings just by opening her damn mouth."

Case 9.3: Past Experiences

Sally is an experienced social worker at Family and Children's Social Services. She specializes in working with adolescents and their families. One day, she saw three youngsters who were each given a "C" grade for a subject in school. John, who has a history of poor school performance, was elated and decided to work harder at school now that he knew he could achieve passing grades. Billy, an average student, had very little response since most of his grades were the same. Mindy, a perfectionistic honor roll student, was suicidal and spoke of quitting school since she now saw herself as a failure.

Each of these adolescents interpreted the same event differently based upon his or her past experiences. Furthermore, each behaved in a different way as a result of that event, with one responding with a renewed dedication to school-work, one remaining behaviorally the same as in the past, and the third contemplating suicide.

Problem-Solving/Problem-Focused Treatment

The most behavioral of these major interventionist models of cognitive therapy and usually based on learning theory, *problem-solving/problem-focused treatment (PST)* pays less attention to thought distortions and schemata than the other three models. PST focuses on stress management, social skills, and assertiveness training. PST uses brainstorming to help clients develop an arsenal of alternative solutions to their problems. The client is taught to become his or her own "therapist," learning to apply behavioral techniques to problems such as eating disorders and improved social functioning (D'Zurilla & Goldfried, 1971; Spivack & Shure, 1974).

In PST, clients are trained by social workers to follow sequences that allow them to overcome a variety of problems. First, they are taught to clearly and objectively define the problem behaviorally. Next, they develop lists of alternative responses or ways of coping, followed by comparing, then selecting a strategy. Then clients evaluate the success of their responses, reconsidering alternatives. It is a useful teaching approach that focuses upon empowerment and the development of long-term adaptive skills. More detailed descriptions of the techniques mentioned here are included in a later section of this chapter.

Self-Instruction Training

A common cognitive-behavioral model of intervention that is particularly effective with generalized problems such as anxiety or depression, *self-instruction training (SIT)* focuses on *coping skills* and uses such behavioral techniques as systematic desensitization, stress-inoculation training, and other behavioral interventions. Donald Meichenbaum (1977, 1984) is the leading proponent, and his approach relies on positive self-talk (Bourne, 1990) and behavioral techniques to deal with panic and anxiety disorders. Meichenbaum uses a process called "guided discovery" to help the client assess cognitions and understand his or her "maladaptive thoughts." The social worker then helps the client reconceptualize problems in a healthier pattern and perspective. Finally, the worker trains the client to develop coping statements and strategies based upon these new ways of thinking about the problem.

Rational-Emotive Therapy

A third cognitive-interventionist model—*rational-emotive therapy (RET)*—is associated primarily with Albert Ellis (1973; Ellis & Dryden, 1987). Both Ellis and Beck (1976) developed their methods in the context of clinical practice and share several central theoretical notions. However, rational-emotive therapy tends to be more didactic than Socratic, and its methods can be very directive and confrontive. RET directs clients to accept the activating event–belief–consequences (ABC) model of distress. Social workers actively debate with clients about the client's "irrational beliefs," forcing the client to discriminate between wants and needs or between desires and demands.

While Beck relies on having clients monitor their own dysfunctional cognitions and *automatic thoughts* as a means of helping them develop their own conclusions, Ellis would vehemently point out the irrationality of the client's thoughts and argue the rationality of those thoughts with the client.

COMMONALITIES

Although there are many types of cognitive intervention, all models have at least six commonalities: (a) brevity, (b) a problem focus, (c) problem definition by the client, (d) partnership or team orientation, (e) activism for both the client and the social worker, and (f) homework assignments.

Brevity

Most cognitive interventions are *brief* and, therefore, relatively cost-effective and efficient. In fact, the tenth chapter of this book deals with brief interventions and includes several cognitive approaches that are specifically defined as short-term. Cognitive treatment is invariably short-term because it directly limits the number of sessions as determined at the beginning of treatment, sometimes using a written contract specifying anywhere from 4 to 20 sessions. Cognitive treatment does not become too prolonged by requiring the involved histories or intake information used with longer-term treatment, although some history is often needed to understand the schemata or patterns of thought. In addition, cognitive interventions do not require the development of a close therapeutic relationship with its transference and dependency issues, although trust is considered essential.

Problem Focus

Cognitive interventions tend to be *problem focused* with a clear behavioral orientation. Many cognitive therapists work in the initial session to get the client to define a limited number of clear, observable problems. The social worker's task is often one of questioning, challenging, and constructively confronting the client to think about or define these problems concretely. The worker helps the client clearly and concretely describe his or her thoughts, moods, or behaviors for two reasons. First, this focus upon problem clarity facilitates treatment by making behavioral goals more precise and, therefore, more likely to be achieved efficiently. Second, by forcing clients to struggle with defining clear problem statements, clients often develop some sense of control or mastery over the problem by minimizing the vague and abstract fears that typically form the basis for anxiety. Anxiety is essentially a fear of the unknown. By "knowing" that fear—that is, clearly defining it, along with its causes and effects—the client begins the process of regaining control of his or her thoughts, fears, and behaviors.

Problem Definition by Client

The client defines the problem, and the social worker assumes the task of clarifying, educating, and collaborating with the client but always refers back to the client's own interpretation of the problem. By consciously and deliberately deferring to the client and requiring that individual to struggle with a clear, workable problem statement, the sessions begin with a recognition that the client, not just the social worker, has chosen to address these specific issues. By being required to take "ownership" of the problem, the client typically recognizes that the responsibility for change must come from within.

Partnership

Through this *partnership,* the client and the social worker view themselves as a team working together to solve a problem. This avoids the difficulty of "one-upmanship" wherein the social worker is the "expert" and the client is the relatively powerless individual seeking help. By beginning the interventionist process on an equal basis, cognitive therapists *empower* their clients and behaviorally demonstrate that the client and the social worker together must take responsibility for the ultimate success of the intervention. There is an explicit understanding that the social worker and the client are a team or mutual support system that will help each other until the problems are successfully treated.

Activism

There is also an *activist* orientation to all of the cognitive-intervention models. Both the cognitive social worker and the client are expected to *do something,* not just talk. All cognitive-intervention models require ongoing monitoring and discussions of change in attitude, thoughts, and behaviors. When a client slips into old, counterproductive depressive schemata such as feeling that he or she is "no good" and might as well stay home from work feeling hopeless, the worker challenges all of those assumptions. Self-pitying patterns are not to be accepted by the client or the worker, and both are expected to consciously confront such beliefs as well as the behavior that results from it. Clients quickly learn that reverting to habitual patterns of thought and behavior will result in a confrontation by the cognitive therapist. Furthermore, the client is expected to personally challenge and confront himself or herself. Clients gradually become more *empowered,* refusing to remain passive or defeated by their own thoughts.

Homework Assignments

All of the cognitive models have *homework assignments* that take a wide variety of forms. Some social workers have clients keep *daily logs of dysfunctional thoughts,* particularly their old, automatic, negative ones. Clients may be assigned the task of developing alternative thoughts and then positive responses to their old schemata. This can be organized into a format called the *three-column technique,* which the client brings in to sessions to discuss with the worker. These and other techniques are described later in this chapter in the "Treatment Techniques" section.

The client may be given a reading assignment or asked to do one of the exercises from a cognitive self-help book (Bourne, 1990; Burns, 1980). Other assignments typically include learning and practicing relaxation techniques (Benson, 1975, 1985) or other behavioral techniques that also foster reexaminations of habitual patterns of thought and their behavioral outcomes. The cognitive approaches require a conscious, planned, and thoughtful examination of the underlying beliefs that form the basis for behavior.

TREATMENT TECHNIQUES

Cognitive techniques are a masterful blend of the best of psychodynamic and behavioral approaches. For instance, of the 7 cognitive techniques described, *questioning* and *challenging* have their origins in classical analysis, while *relaxation* and other methods of *stress reduction* are mainstream behavioral techniques. *Guided thinking* (or *visualization*), *thought stopping,* and the *three-column technique and log* are purely "cognitive" by the fact that they focus directly on the client's conscious cognitions. Other techniques have been addressed in the "Commonalities" section and indirectly in the previous section describing the various cognitive models.

Questioning

Questioning is a major technique among cognitive practitioners. The types of questions range from very practical and concrete to rather abstract and philosophical. Direct and practical questions are often used to help the client better clarify vague or contradictory thoughts, emotions, or behaviors.

Jenny, you just said that you thought your job was overwhelming and stressful, but now you are suggesting that you are bored and do not have enough responsibility. Which is it?

Or,

Bill, when you describe your feelings toward your wife, you mention a lot of anger and really hostile feelings; but you also seem to care very much about her recent depression. Much of what you have said suggests that you deeply respect and trust her. Can you kind of clarify these feelings? Do they all exist in some way?

Or,

Sue, you just started dating a man whom you describe as an alcoholic, and some of what you have said indicates that he really puts you down and is pretty insulting to you. When we began these sessions, you said repeatedly that you wanted to stop the pattern of dating or marrying abusive alcoholics like your father. Can you explain or help me to understand why you have begun a relationship with someone who sounds so much like the last three guys who were also abusive alcoholics?

In addition to the practical and concrete questions that frequently focus on inconsistent or contradictory thoughts, emotions, or behaviors, the *Socratic method* of questioning is also used. Typically, the worker asks the client questions as a way of helping the client grope with his or her true, inner beliefs or as a way to develop direction.

John, you've said that you tried to kill yourself because life has no purpose or meaning for you and you feel aimless, like you're just going through the motions, looking forward to dying. But I kind of wonder if we all don't deal with that in some way or another. It's just that some decide what has meaning or purpose for them and then pursue it, and some don't. So what's important for you? Did you ever wonder if maybe it's up to you to figure out some purpose for yourself and then pursue it?

Or,

Ann, you seem to have some pretty clear ideas about what you don't like. For instance, you don't like your job, husband, school, and a few other things; but we're having trouble developing a list of things you do like. Do you think we could kind of brainstorm and you could list for me the things that give you pleasure or satisfaction or real joy?

Challenging

Challenging is the second type of common cognitive technique. Challenging a client to examine contradictions, inconsistencies, or vague and abstract assertions is actually a very supportive and caring method. Some social workers may fear that it will alienate clients if they use this technique, but, actually, the opposite is true if the challenge or confrontation is done in an appropriately caring manner.

For instance, social workers often see clients who say that they must be "crazy" because they stay in relationships with people they sometimes love yet literally want to kill on other occasions. This is particularly true in abusive relationships in which the client's *self-esteem* is so low that he or she feels that better treatment is undeserved. These individuals gradually come to believe that they are fortunate to be in even an obviously abusive relationship because they are so useless and unlovable themselves, whereas their partners are seen as superior or at least as people with power.

Stating the obvious—that the client should leave that relationship—does not always work since family and friends have perhaps already made that suggestion, and the client's subsequent lack of action only makes the client feel more depressed and hopeless. Instead, the social worker needs to confront the client in an empathic manner that provokes genuine thought and self-reflection. See Case 9.4.

Case 9.4: Challenging

"Jill, you've told me that Carl has put you into the hospital three times with broken bones and that he has a long history of violence toward you and your daughter. Your previous two social workers found shelters for you and your daughter, but you went back to Carl and got beaten up again, as did your daughter. At this point, you've never reported this to the police or even gotten a restraining order. Are you suggesting now that you will go back to him, thinking he will change?"

Jill responded, "Yes, 'cause he said he might come in sometime and talk to you, and he's really sorry this time. You should have seen him cry and apologize. He said he just did it 'cause he was drunk and I kept bothering him about the bills. If I just stop bothering him so much, and he quits drinking, like he said he would, then I think we'll be okay this time."

"Jill, from what you've said and from your case record, this situation actually seems to be identical to the last few times," began the social worker.

"Wait. That isn't fair. This time Carl is going to go to AA and come in here to see you."

"Well, the records indicate that he agreed to do that on both previous occasions and he only came here once and quit AA after two meetings. He said that those drunks were worse than he and just made him want to drink even more," responded the worker in a factual but caring tone.

Jill quickly came to Carl's defense and blamed everyone but Carl for the long, recurring pattern. The social worker allowed and even encouraged this process. Then he challenged Jill on all of her "facts" and defenses of Carl, finally summarizing the history and stating the obvious prognosis. "Jill, in spite of your feelings, everything you have said and all of the facts and history that you yourself have described to me clearly indicate that you will be beaten up again and so will your daughter. Legally I am obliged to report the abuse of your daughter to the police and Protective Services, so she may be removed for her safety."

Jill began crying and said, "You can't do that."

"Well, actually I have to since I'm legally required to protect your daughter, so the only question left is whether you want to return to a boyfriend who will continue to beat you up or whether you really want this pattern to stop," said the worker, now holding Jill's hand.

In Case 9.4, previous attempts had failed and future similar interventions would have likely failed because Jill's past behavior was not appropriately considered. Jill needed to be *empowered* by making a genuine decision for herself. Previous helpers had told her what to do and probably did so appropriately under the circumstances. However, this more experienced cognitive worker perceived that Jill had a history of ultimately refusing to do what her past social workers suggested. It was deemed essential that Jill take action on her own behalf if the plan was to succeed. The worker had Jill make the arrangements to go to the shelter, and then the social worker helped Jill develop clear behavioral expectations for Carl, including multiple sessions with the worker and nightly AA. When Carl failed (as expected) to meet these reasonable expectations, Jill was able to leave, having successfully and consciously dealt with her conflicting and contradictory thoughts, emotions, and behaviors.

Relaxation

The third technique, *relaxation*, is associated with the *holistic* approach and behaviorism, as well as with cognitive interventions. Relaxation methods recognize the importance of the interaction of physical and psychological factors by helping the client to relax his or her body by consciously *focusing* on its functioning. *Deep relaxation* is a state in which one's body reacts in exactly the opposite way of how the body reacts under stress or extreme anxiety. Relaxation techniques are, therefore, particularly applicable for clients who suffer from anxiety and panic, which are conditions that have strong physical and physiological components. Relaxation techniques are also used for many individuals who are depressed, and these techniques may have positive effects for some phobias (Bourne, 1990; Benson, 1985).

The relaxation response involves a series of physiological changes that include decreases in heart rate, respiration, blood pressure, skeletal muscle tension, metabolic rate, oxygen consumption, and analytical thinking and increases in skin resistance and alpha wave activity in the brain (Benson, 1975, 1985). Evidence suggests that there is a generalization effect whereby clients who learn deep relaxation techniques reduce the severity of panic attacks and anxiety while increasing their energy levels and capacity to concentrate. Common deep relaxation methods include meditation, biofeedback, breathing exercises, and visualization of relaxing stimuli (Bourne, 1990).

Guided Imagery and Visualization

Guided imagery and visualization, or "guided discovery," are cognitive methods based on behaviorism that are particularly useful with anxiety, panic, depression, and some phobias. These methods are useful for self-instruction training and for relaxation. When used as a treatment technique or as a tool for improving performance, the client *imagines* or *visualizes* a desired goal and then repeatedly thinks of the process of achieving that goal. For instance, marathon runners imagine running their course and winning or pitchers in baseball visualize the perfect fast-ball pitch and see themselves doing it repeatedly.

There are two basic areas in which visualization techniques are used. For those suffering from a generalized chronic anxiety, visualization is often used in conjunction with deep muscle relaxation and meditation. For phobias and panic disorders, the technique is applied more specifically to the situation to desensitize and reprogram the client. Social workers can combine many varying methods (such as meditation, deep breathing, exercise, and relaxation techniques) with visualization to develop well-rounded and thorough interventions tailored to the idiosyncratic needs and problems of individual clients.

Visualization for anxiety uses guided imagery to relax an individual by having that individual imagine or visualize scenes that are calming. These visualizations are recorded on tape in either the client's own voice or that of the therapist. Some social workers prefer instructing clients to purchase prerecorded tapes, which are available at most large bookstores. The client routinely listens to these relaxing tapes either at bedtime, when the client gets up each day, or at work or school. A quiet, stress-free environment is essential. There are four stages to this guided imagery process: recording or purchasing the tape, preparatory relaxation, visualization, and return.

Stage 1: Recording or Purchasing the Tape   The tape-recorded scene itself must be thorough, clear, detailed, relaxing, and specific to the client's own needs. *Stress reduction* tapes are available in many bookstores. Alternatively, one can tape a relaxing scene such as those developed by Bourne (1990), which visualize passive muscle relaxation, sunlight meditation, a beach, a forest, or a globe of light. The tape recording should describe in vivid detail a distinct picture. Not only sights but also sounds, smells, and colors are to be included to add detail to the visualization. Whether the tape is self-recorded or a professionally developed tape purchased at a store, the script should be read and recorded in a slow, relaxing tone of voice with pauses of several seconds between sentences.

Stage 2: Preparatory Relaxation   The individual should be as relaxed and as free of stressful thoughts as possible before listening to the tape. To prepare for the guided imagery or visualization, the client needs to first go to a safe, comfortable, relaxing environment where he or she will not be distracted or disturbed. He or she may meditate, do a muscle-relaxing exercise, or simply clear the mind of all thoughts. Most clients prefer sitting in a comfortable chair with palms down and eyes closed. Breathing and respiration should be slow and steady. This preparation may take 5 to 10 minutes, but it is essential to get maximum results from the guided imagery or visualization process and the scene described on the tape.

Stage 3: Visualization   Visualization takes practice. Often the types of clients who are most resistant to this type of method are the very same clients who need guided imagery and visualization the most. The high-pressured, aggressive saleswoman or the frantic, untenured teacher who becomes anxious at the thought of "wasting time" with such nonproductive efforts is exactly the type of person who needs to relax and visualize. With practice, individuals improve in their ability to see the sights and colors, smell the aromas, and feel their bodies and muscles relax during visualization. Box 9–1 presents an example of the visualization process.

Stage 4: Return   The last stage involves a discussion of the process and its effects. Individuals are also encouraged to practice guided imagery and to monitor its success in future sessions.

The scripts for these visualizations can come from one of the self-help books or through a client-worker collaboration, but individualizing them is often helpful. For instance, many of these scripts involve the "penetrating warmth of the sun." For pale-skinned individuals, that particular image is actually very anxiety producing. Both the tone and the content of the script are important.

Systematic desensitization, as described in the previous chapter on behavioral interventions, is a classic example of the structured use of imagery for desensitizing clients with phobias or for helping clients become relaxed in situations that had previously terrified them. The first stage of this technique typically involves instructing a client to sit, relax, close his or her eyes, and visualize or develop a nonthreatening image relevant to the phobic object. A client who fears dogs will be helped to relax while visualizing a small puppy.

Thought Stopping

Thought stopping is a basic cognitive technique that essentially says that, since people act inappropriately because of the way they "think," then they must be taught to "stop" those thoughts. On the surface, the technique of "thought stopping" is naively simplistic; yet, it is effective because it cognitively directs the client to take control of his or her anxiety-producing inner thoughts.

Potentially inappropriate, destructive, or disturbed behavior often originates with the thoughts of vulnerable clients; thus, the clients themselves have

9.1   *Visualizing a Sunset*

You are sitting in a chair surrounded by beautiful flowers. You feel the gentle breeze washing over you as the aroma of the flowers drifts by. You are looking across a vast, empty beach, listening to the peaceful waves of the sea as they lap at the sand. The sky above you is slowly turning to vivid shades of red and orange and blue as the sun slowly recedes on the horizon.

You feel the warmth of the tropical breeze relaxing your whole body. Your right hand feels the warmth of the setting sun. Focus on it. Feel your right hand relax. The feeling of relaxation moves up your arm. You can feel every muscle, every fiber, relax. It feels like sand is slowly draining and leaving your arm. Your arm is becoming light like air. Every muscle in your arm is relaxed. Now your left hand and its fingertips feel the breeze as the warmth caresses them. Your whole left forearm feels light now as the muscles relax completely. . . . You are more and more at peace. Your shoulders gently drop as you let go. Your left hand and arm are now completely relaxed like your right hand, and you are feeling secure, relaxed, and free as the warmth of the breeze touches the tips of your toes. . . . All of the muscles, tendons, and nerves in your calves feel the warmth and caresses of the gentle breeze. . . . The warmth moves up; your thighs are penetrated by the gentle warmth of the breeze as the sun settles on the vivid horizon. Feel the breeze as it gently warms you, relaxing you . . . bathing you completely in a warm caress. Feel it soothe your stomach as all tension flows away. Your stomach muscles relax as you drift slowly into a deeper, quiet and peaceful feeling. Now feel the gentle breeze caress your chest. You feel more and more relaxed, and your breathing becomes slow, steady, and easy.

Now the breeze touches your face. . . . Your face and jaws relax as the breeze penetrates and softly touches your cheeks. Feel the warmth on your face as the breeze gently relaxes you and releases every tight muscle and tendon down your neck. . . . then your spine . . . healing and soothing you down through your back as your whole body softens into a deep, deep state of relaxation. . . . You feel secure, safe, at peace. . . . You drift more into peace as the warmth of the breeze heals you, relaxes every nerve, every cell. You enter a deeper peace, relaxed, at peace.

the power and potential to stop the precipitating thoughts before they progress to harmful behavior. The technique can be as simple as getting children to yell "stop" as soon as certain frightening thoughts first enter the conscious mind, or social workers can use thought stopping in conjunction with methods that directly address the physical responses. Often, a *series* of responses is needed that begins with teaching "thought stopping" combined with deep breathing and the replacement of anxiety-producing thoughts with equally powerful calming thoughts.

For instance, the client will practice first yelling or thinking "stop" while taking long, slow, deep breaths and thinking, "This will not last," or "I am strong and can stop this." Beginning a new activity as an alternative to the past, dysfunctional patterns helps by engaging the mind in a different direction. Visualization and guided imagery are often used with thought stopping as methods of replacing the conscious, anxiety-producing thoughts with their opposite, relaxing types of thoughts.

Three-Column Technique, Journaling, and Logs

The three-column, or triple-column, technique (Burns, 1980) and the similar method called a "daily record of dysfunctional thoughts" (Bourne, 1990, p. 180) are very useful, clear, graphic cognitive tools for helping clients recognize their patterns of counterproductive automatic thoughts. The first column is used by clients to keep a record of their negative automatic thoughts. The second column describes the type of "cognitive distortion" in which they are engaging. The third column is used by the client to describe the more appropriate "rational response." See Table 9.1.

The daily record of dysfunctional thoughts can vary in format, and some variations have five or six columns. In the five-column format, the first column typically briefly describes a problematic situation, followed by a second column that is used by the client to assign a value (from 1 to 100) to the strength of the related "emotions." A third column contains a statement of

TABLE 9.1 **EXAMPLE OF THE THREE-COLUMN TECHNIQUE**

Automatic Thought	Cognitive Distortion	Rational Response
I'm an idiot because I got a *D*.	Labeling and all-or-nothing.	I did not study. I can do well if I try.
John hates me. I have no friends.	Jumping to conclusions (mind reading); all-or-nothing.	John might be mad but is still my friend.

the "automatic thought" involved. The fourth column is for the rational response, and a fifth column is reserved for the "outcome." This outcome column is filled in after *rethinking* or even redoing the original situation more positively (Burns, 1980).

Another cognitive technique involves social workers instructing clients to maintain a *log* or keeping a *journal*. This technique is commonly recommended by constructivists as a way of helping clients to understand their own perspectives and thoughts more clearly. Logs and journals involve making notes to oneself as a way of encouraging self-discovery or stimulating emotions and self-awareness. Clients are encouraged to write about current events, past events, memories, dreams, fantasies, or life reviews. For some, the act of concretely placing these "thoughts" onto paper allows them just enough distance and objectivity to better clarify the meaning of their thoughts. Journaling requires some degree of organizing one's thoughts and emotions, which is essential in the process of examining where one's habitual, patterned thoughts and behaviors may need to be reexamined and changed.

COGNITIVE TREATMENT OF ANXIETY DISORDERS

The *DSM-IV* (American Psychiatric Association, 1994) lists the following anxiety disorders: (a) panic disorder with or without agoraphobia, (b) agoraphobia without history of panic disorder, (c) specific phobia, (d) social phobia, (e) acute stress disorder, (f) generalized anxiety disorder, (g) obsessive-compulsive disorder, and (e) post-traumatic stress disorder.

Panic is characterized by a feeling of extreme, irrational fear or terror, often associated with a feeling of doom. The attacks typically have a sudden, acute, and intense onset. Panic attacks usually last for only a few minutes, although milder "aftershocks" of apprehension may incapacitate the individual for much longer periods. Symptoms include shortness of breath, palpitations, chest pain or discomfort, choking or smothering sensations, and fears of "going crazy" or losing control. *Agoraphobia* is a fear of open spaces, although the predominant symptom is a fear of a panic attack while in a situation from which one cannot escape or where no one is available to help. A *specific phobia* involves significant anxiety provoked by clear exposure to a specific, feared object or situation, often leading to avoidance of it. *Social phobia* is extreme anxiety related to a fear of being embarrassed or critically scrutinized by others, leading to the avoidance of social or public situations (Plaud & Vavrovsky, 1998). *Generalized anxiety disorder* is a vague but pervasive fear unrelated to any specific stimulus or avoidance (in which case it is a phobia) or situation. This disorder is less intense than panic disorders that involve strong and debilitating physical responses, but it lasts for at least 6 months (McLellarn & Rosenzweig, 1998).

Obsessive-compulsive disorders (OCD) involve reoccuring thoughts, images, fears, or senseless impulses that uncontrollably intrude themselves into the client's thoughts (obsessions) and/or equally uncontrollable and irrational behaviors or rituals that the client feels unable to stop. Excessive hand washing and checking to see if a stove is off or a door is closed even though it has already been checked multiple times are common examples. Clients feel compelled to perform these acts as a way to ward off their feelings of anxiety but end up feeling embarrassed, shamed, and in despair because they lack control over this behavior, which they know to be irrational. Treatment for OCD involves a specialized mix of medications combined with specific behavioral techniques (Cohen & Steketee, 1998).

Post-traumatic stress disorder (PTSD) develops as the result of a severely traumatic event such as in a battle, at a car accident scene, an earthquake, or as the result of an assault such as a rape or violent attack. Symptoms of nightmares, flashbacks, avoidance, numbness, and depression occur. These symptoms develop soon after the traumatic event or sometimes after a delay of months or even years. Treatment for PTSD often involves psychotherapy and the client developing insight into the feelings and causes of the symptoms. Behavioral intervention is utilized to help develop responses that are more constructive (Vonk & Yegidis, 1998).

Anxiety disorders, panic attacks, and *phobias* have significant biological components. The nervous system is subdivided into a *sympathetic* and a *parasympathetic system* as parts of the *involuntary nervous system* or those responses that are automatic such as the heartbeat, digestion, and respiration. In a panic attack, the sympathetic system mobilizes a set of strong physical reactions that cause the adrenal glands to release adrenaline. This sudden and excessive amount of adrenaline can cause sudden profuse sweating; a quickened heart beat; rapid and shallow respiration; trembling; shaking; and a cold, clammy feeling in the hands and feet. In some instances, muscles tighten or freeze, stomach acid increases, and the pupils may dilate. Psychologically, the result is one of feeling completely overwhelmed, terrified, and out of control (Himle & Fischer, 1998).

The works of Bruce Thyer are particularly well regarded in describing behavioral and cognitive-behavioral methods of treating anxiety disorders (Thyer & Birsinger, 1994; Thyer, 1983, 1984, 1987). He uses a cognitive-behavioral technique called *exposure therapy*, which is based upon Joseph Wolpe's *systematic desensitization.* Before using the technique, the social worker must first establish that the client has an anxiety disorder and that there are clear and specific stimuli that evoke the anxiety. The stimuli must be recreatable in some manner (e.g., using pictures, tapes, audio, or verbal or physical representations). Furthermore, the client must be committed to working on change with the social worker as a partner. There must also be agreement that the technique will entail gradual exposure to the anxiety-evoking stimuli (AES) and that the stimuli are not a significant source of physical or realistic danger.

The process itself begins the same as any helpful intervention with the development of a good therapeutic alliance and rapport based on empathy, genuineness, acceptance, or positive regard. Treatment can be helped by suggesting reading assignments to the client that describe the process (i.e., Steketee & White, 1990; Barbior & Goldman, 1990; or Bourne, 1990). Such bibliotherapy helps the client see that he or she is not alone or "abnormal" in his or her problem and that the problem can be alleviated if the client simply stays in treatment and agrees to follow the program.

In the next phase, the crucial task of *stimulus mapping* begins. Since each person with a phobia or other anxiety disorder differs markedly in the way he or she responds, thinks, and acts, it is essential that a clear and detailed description of the AES be developed. For instance, even the seemingly clear phobia of dogs would need to be described in detail. Clients need to discuss and describe specifically whether they fear large or small dogs or any certain breeds more or less than others. Is it the fear of being bitten or of being chased that frightens them? Do small puppies also frighten them or dogs chained or on leashes? How close can they get and under what conditions (e.g., with friends or the social worker) before mild anxiety begins? Could they tolerate a dog better by being outside or behind a locked door?

A hierarchy of anxiety-evoking stimuli needs to be developed by the worker and client. The hierarchy begins with the least provoking and most tolerable situation (e.g., looking at a picture of a puppy playing with a ball) and then progresses to the most fearful stimuli (e.g., being bitten on the right leg by a large German shepherd while running from the dog in an open field with no protection). It is important to progress through this hierarchy in slow, multiple stages, although clients themselves are often quite willing to push forward to the next level, sometimes prematurely. Although Wolpe's (Wolpe and Lazarus, 1967) method of systematic desensitization stresses the replacement of anxiety with stress-reduction methods at each stage, the exposure-therapy method allows for somewhat higher levels of acceptable anxiety, at least with very motivated clients. Caution should be used since, behaviorally, a fairly traumatic "failure" at some level, such as a sudden panic attack when seeing a dog in the distance, could slow or even derail the treatment. Clients need a great deal of reassurance throughout the treatment process, particularly in reminding them that they are, in fact, in control of the whole process from beginning to end. If they find that they are becoming too anxious and want to slow down or even go back to get more comfortable with an earlier stage, then they can do so. It is up to them, and at no time will the worker push them to proceed at a quicker pace. The client may want to proceed more quickly than the social worker recommends. Occasionally, the social worker may need to slow the client down since the client may be overly ambitious in trying to reach the goal, only to find that they set back their progress because of an unexpected sudden panic or increase in anxiety levels.

COGNITIVE TREATMENT OF DEPRESSION

Basic Principles

Some of the most impressive results in cognitive treatment have been in treating depression (Beck, 1996; Dulmus & Wodarski, 1998). In fact, the approach was very suddenly but widely popularized in 1980 with the publication of David Burns's *Feeling Good: The New Mood Therapy*. This very readable self-help book was addressed directly to the millions of depressed individuals who wanted to overcome the devastating effects of their disorder. It even included a copy of Beck's Depression Inventory, which is now widely utilized in social work practice at the beginning of treatment for depression (Dulmus & Wodarski, 1998).

Burns (1980) delineated three basic principles that form the basis for cognitive interventions with depressed clients:

1. *One's moods are created by his or her own thoughts or cognitions.* It is the way that one thinks that essentially creates the basis for subsequent moods and behaviors. If one *thinks* that a situation is hopeless, then he or she will take no action to change the situation. If one *thinks* that the world is hostile, then he or she naturally protects himself or herself by relating defensively or offensively to others.

   Cognitions refer to perceptions or the way one looks at things. These cognitions define how one interprets, screens, or evaluates circumstances. "You feel the way you do right now because of the *thoughts you are thinking at this moment*" (Burns, 1980, p. 12). Burns's cognitive approach involves a great deal of logic, education, and instruction in helping the client to accept this premise. Once this is understood and accepted, the client is helped to rethink or more rationally examine his or her thoughts with the goal of affecting feelings and behavior.

2. *When a person is feeling depressed, his or her thoughts are dominated by a pervasive negativity.* Virtually everything a depressed person sees is perceived or thought of as negative, dark, or gloomy. Depressed people do not confine their negativity to just themselves but attribute it to all aspects of their lives and circumstances. Not only is there no hope with

their jobs but their husbands or wives also are seen negatively along with their world view of politics, the economy, crime, and essentially every other issue of importance to them. The future holds no hope and seems to auger only more pain and frustration in an unrelenting series of upcoming failures.

The world is a painful place for depressed people, and the belief that there is no sanctuary or even future hope is unbearable. The suffering impacts upon everything they say and do, often leading to the actual creation of the clients' worst fears. For instance, the depressed client who believes that his or her family, friends, and coworkers all dislike him or her will logically start to display either anger or sullen withdrawal from each of those elements of potential support. As such behavior becomes apparent to those persons around the client, the natural reaction from them will be anger or avoidance, thus eventually creating the environment most feared by the client. See Case 9.5.

Case 9.5: Negativity

John was a school cafeteria worker who was referred to the social worker at the school's Employee Assistance Program (EAP). John was variously described as being paranoid, angry, depressed, and hostile. Colleagues had also indicated that he was increasingly isolated and often misinterpreted their actions in a hostile manner.

The social worker met with John, who was outraged that his boss "made" him talk to this social worker. At first, John sullenly said that everything was fine and he had no problem. The social worker supportively suggested that some of his friends were concerned about him and she had come to try to help. John angrily told her to leave him alone and that he knew that she was just like everyone else at work who hated him and wanted him fired. The social worker calmly suggested that John seemed very angry; and if everyone hated him and plotted against him as he said, then it certainly was an intolerable situation for him. She asked him to tell her more and, using John's term that "every one of these backstabbing bastards hates my guts," asked for examples and evidence.

John had many examples to support his perception, but the social worker eventually challenged him on each in a caring but factual manner. By the end of the first session, John agreed with the social worker that "maybe not every single one of those bastards" hated him but that several of them clearly did dislike him. The social worker agreed that may be accurate, but they needed to begin by getting rid of the terms "all" or "every." Instead, they should look at specific instances and individuals with a realization that there is apparently a range of attitudes toward him at work, and some people may actually have at least partially positive feelings toward him. John reluctantly admitted this could actually be true.

3. *Research indicates that these negative thoughts are not valid and are, in fact, distorted.* This last principle has tremendous treatment implications since much of the cognitive approach involves ways of convincing depressed clients that, in spite of their vehement denial, their perceptions are invalid. While the world is imperfect and life sometimes difficult, it is not as horrible as they see it and they do have some control

over it. If this last message can be effectively conveyed and accepted by the client, then much of the therapy is accomplished.

This pervasive mindset is seen daily in social work practice. Individuals make complaints about their insensitive spouses, hostile neighbors, demanding bosses, and the overall feeling that the world around them is threatening and miserable. This perception is generalized to nearly all familial, social, personal, and professional aspects of the lives of depressed clients. Premature suggestions by the social worker that these situations are, in reality, much more positive are usually responded to by mixtures of anger, disbelief, and a general response that the social worker is naive and incompetent. It is important that the social worker is not seen as trying to "cheer up" the client with an inappropriately rosy, inaccurate picture of the real world.

Premature debates in which the social worker jumps too quickly into a logical argument concerning the nature of life or even general attitudes can also yield counterproductive responses. Arguments quickly alienate clients. Cognitive workers try to sensitively join with the client to minimize the likelihood that treatment would deteriorate into two opposing arguments, ultimately ending in the client leaving in angry disbelief. The worker often needs to wait for the appropriate time to help the client recognize that the world is not divided into two distinct camps of good or bad, black or white. There are many gray areas of life, and these can best be examined by reconsidering any extreme viewpoints, especially those that are negative and pervasive.

Case 9.6: Invalid Perceptions

Wendy is a depressed, 23-year-old, unemployed mother of two. She is suicidal and had been admitted to the psychiatric unit the previous day. At intake, she indicated that she had no friends and that her mother and neighbors all hated her. The social worker challenged her on these points, but Wendy insisted that these potential supports all intensely disliked her, and she was sure that none of them would be willing to help her in any way. With Wendy's permission, the social worker called Wendy's mother who tearfully related many past instances when Wendy rejected her help. The mother also said that Wendy's two sisters were equally concerned and that well-intentioned neighbors had called her several times with concerns that Wendy was increasingly isolated and hostile.

The social worker presented this feedback to Wendy in a clear "matter-of-fact" manner and subsequently scheduled sessions for the mother, sisters, and two neighbors to visit her in the hospital. In a supportive and empathic manner, the social worker consistently challenged Wendy to reexamine her social support system with more objectivity. Initially, Wendy accused the social worker of being unrealistically optimistic and of simply naively trying to "cheer her up." The social worker remained nondefensive but insisted that her goal was not to "cheer her up" but rather to help Wendy become more accurate and realistic in her perceptions so that she could move forward and develop a realistic approach to connecting with family and friends.

Distorted Thoughts

Depressed individuals tend to cognitively distort their thinking, thus negatively affecting both their moods and subsequent behaviors. These distortions have been widely described (Burns, 1980; Beck, 1996; Baucom & Epstein, 1990; Munson, 1994). They include:

1. *Dichotomous thinking* or "all-or-nothing" thinking. All aspects of life are perceived as good or bad, black or white, failures or successes. There is no in-between. This type of thinking is highly distorted and extremely destructive since eventually nearly every perception ends up in the negative or "bad" column of life. If a client's spouse fails to be affectionate, then that spouse must hate the client. If the client does not win a contract or make a sale, then the client is a hopeless failure. If a friend is critical of one thing, then the friend can "go to hell" for his or her lack of acceptance.

2. *Magnification* or catastrophizing is a way of thinking that vastly overemphasizes the import of some event or viewpoint. If the client has to wear an old or worn dress to work, "Everyone will think I look ridiculous. I'll be the laughingstock of the office." Every minor incident becomes blown out of proportion. A bounced check becomes the basis for "everyone thinking I'm bankrupt." Tripping in front of classmates automatically translates into the client believing that he or she is hopelessly clumsy and certainly despised by classmates. A slip of the tongue at work in which the client calls a customer by the wrong name becomes "an unbelievably insulting" predicament that is sure to lead to being fired from the job.

3. *Minimization,* which is the opposite of maximization for depressed clients, naturally applies only to the accomplishments or positive attributes of the client. Every practitioner has encountered clients who discount and describe their own successes as silly, unimportant, or just random luck. So the spelling contest they won at school, the raise they received at work, the three accomplished children they raised, or the promotion to a manager position are all described as inconsequential or irrelevant by the client. The client will say, "Anyone can do that" or "They had to make me manager; no one else wanted the job" or "The kids turned out all right in spite of me, not because of me. I had no effect on them."

4. *Emotional reasoning* refers to inferring that one's emotions are the same as facts and that one's negative emotions reflect the way things really exist. Thus, if the client feels disliked at work, the reality must be that everyone genuinely dislikes him or her. The client may believe that a person he or she likes recently turned against him or her when that

person failed to greet the client at work. The client then presumes that his or her anger is a valid basis for subsequent behavior and gives that person an angry glare when the client sees that person the next time.

5. *Should and must statements* are used by virtually everyone and only become problematic when clients use them extensively as a counterproductive means of self-motivation. For instance, "I *should* be a better mother or father or student" or "I *must* start spending more time with my son or schoolbooks." The problem with this type of cognitive distortion rests in its punitive and guilt-ridden nature. When carried to an extreme, these *shoulds* and *musts* simply become unachievable goals and, therefore, are constant sources of discouraging guilt.

6. *Labeling* is a form of overgeneralization with the additional problem of being vague and imprecise. Labels such as *loser, idiot, slob, slut,* or *jerk* are commonly used by clients to describe themselves or others. These labels have tremendous emotional connotations that are usually inaccurate. Labeling tends to be debilitating because its use by the client is emotionally devastating while being devoid of behavioral specifics. There is no clear behavioral response to broad labels, so the client is further discouraged by the fact that he or she cannot even begin to plan a positive behavioral reaction.

7. *Personalization* involves clients blaming themselves for events for which they are not realistically responsible. A client's daughter gets arrested, so the father blames himself; or a factory closes, so a client sees himself or herself as a failure. The facts—that is that the daughter is addicted to drugs in spite of the father's efforts or that the company closed the factory and moved operations overseas—are not realistically considered. The client views this failure or defeat as another example of inadequacy even though the reality is that the "inadequacy" was not the client's.

Summary

There are at least six different major cognitive models. In addition to Aaron Beck's cognitive therapy, a cognitive-behavioral model (CBT), and constructivism, other widely used models include problem-solving or problem-focused interventions, self-instruction training (SIT), and rational-emotive therapy (RET). Most models focus upon the client's thoughts, which directly affect moods and behaviors. Commonalities among the various cognitive models include brevity, a problem focus, problem definition by the client, partnership or a team orientation, activism by both the client and the social worker, and homework assignments. Treatment techniques include questioning, challenging, relaxation, guided thinking or visualization, thought stopping, a three- (or four- or five-) column technique, and the use of journals or logs. Cognitive interventions are particularly effective in treating affective disorders, which include panic disorder, specific phobias, social phobia, acute stress disorder, generalized anxiety, obsessive-compulsive disorder, and post-traumatic stress disorder. Cognitive treatment is also very effective in treating depression, particularly when the client's distorted thoughts are focused upon and challenged. The most common distorted thoughts of depressed individuals include dichotomous thinking, magnification, minimization, emotional reasoning, should and must statements, labeling, and personalization.

BRIEF INTERVENTIONS

Brief therapy or time-sensitive interventions are described separately in this chapter, but they have also been integrated into several preceding chapters. Unlike the psychodynamic, cognitive, or behavioral approaches that have their own specific theories relative to the causes and subsequent treatments of psychosocial problems, brief therapy is relatively atheoretical. Brief therapy is a term used to describe a wide variety of treatments or therapeutic interventions that are both short-term and highly focused. Brief therapy can be cognitive, behavioral, or strategic/structural family based (Wells & Gianetti, 1993) or problem-solving, mixed eclectic, and psychodynamic in its theoretical base (Epstein, 1992). The generally accepted standard is that brief interventions involve fewer sessions, typically anywhere from 6 to 12 sessions but occasionally ranging from one session to as many as 20.

BASES FOR SHIFT TO BRIEF INTERVENTIONS

Brief therapies are emerging as the most common form of practice. Briefer and more focused interventions have become the norm or even the required form of social work practice as managed care systems, employee assistance programs, and increasingly cost-conscious public and private funding sources require greater accountability and quicker results from social workers. The reasons for this shift to brief therapy are based on three factors: (a) economics, (b) research, and (c) cultural/philosophical trends.

Economics

Brief therapy is less costly than long-term therapy. In Austad's (1996) book, *Is Long-Term Psychotherapy Unethical?* the author states that while only 15.7% of current psychotherapy clients have 21 or more sessions, that small percentage of clients account for a full 63% of total mental health expenditures. In brief treatment, the standard eight or ten hourly sessions over as many weeks obviously require far less professional staff hours than previous models.

Several decades ago, some social workers still relied upon the insight-oriented interventions, which required delving into the unconscious, working through the defenses, exploring repressed thoughts and feelings from early childhood, and learning to interpret the symbolic meaning of behaviors or dreams. These processes were long, difficult, and expensive. Publicly funded mental health programs, insurance companies, and managed care organizations are increasingly unwilling to financially support long-term care when there are brief, effective, and affordable alternatives (S. Friedman, 1997).

Research

Second, *research* supports the fact that brief interventions can be as effective and even more efficient than long-term interventions. Brief treatment has been proven to be as effective as long term-treatment for a wide variety of mental health problems (Koss & Shiang, 1994). Research has demonstrated that the vast majority of clinical change happens in the initial, early phase of treatment. In fact, for the cognitive-behavioral treatment of depression, 60% to 80% of symptom reduction occurs within the first four sessions (Ilardi & Craighead, 1994).

Furthermore, a large portion of clients who come to see social workers terminate early while the long-term–oriented practitioner is only beginning to get past initial transference issues. Thirty-four percent of psychotherapy clients attend only one or two sessions; 37% attend 3 to 10 visits; 13.3% attend 11 to 20 sessions; and 15.7% have 21 or more sessions (Austad, 1996). The average number of sessions is four to eight, and a full one-third to one-half of all clients never return after the initial session. By the fifth or sixth session, 60% to 80% of those who began therapy have terminated, and only 8% to 10% of initial patients continue treatment beyond 10 or 15 sessions (Philips, 1985). These data strongly suggest that the vast majority of clients requesting services will stop the treatment after only a few sessions. It is therefore essential that the limited number of sessions be used efficiently and effectively in a clearly focused, organized, and brief manner.

Cultural and Philosophical Shifts

Finally, a number of *cultural and philosophical shifts* have occurred in American culture as well as worldwide. For better or worse, contemporary culture expects change to happen quickly. The pace of life is faster than in the past when social work, counseling, and psychology were developing in the earlier half of the 20th century. The stock market changes more in a single day of trading now than it did in a whole month just a decade ago. Trends in music, art, and fashion change almost overnight; and these changes are spread world-wide on the Internet in seconds. Consequently, today's culture is more result oriented and impatient. Furthermore, there are those in social work who contend that short-term treatment is appropriate and representative of today's fast-paced culture: "[B]rief therapy is symbolic . . . of the modern age in which we do everything intensely and quickly" (Meyer, 1993, p. 571).

Major Models

There are several excellent edited books that describe a variety of different models of brief intervention (Bloom, 1997; Budman, Hoyt, & Friedman, 1992; Wells & Gianetti, 1990). There are also several books that describe a general approach to brief intervention (Friedman, 1997; Garfield, 1989; Wells, 1994). Finally, there are several books that describe specific models of brief intervention in depth such as Davanloo's (1992) approach to short-term dynamic psychotherapy; Dattilio and Freeman's (1994) cognitive-behavioral brief intervention; Parad and Parad's (1990) approach, which deals with crisis intervention; and Hoyt's (1995) book on brief therapy in managed care.

In this section, five major models of brief intervention that are common in social work practice are described. They are crisis intervention, brief cognitive-behavioral, task-centered, solution-focused, and brief psychodynamic models.

Crisis Intervention

Crisis theory originated with the work of Lindemann (1944) and Caplan (1964) but was soon developed for social work interventions by Parad (1971; Parad & Parad, 1990). It was among the first theories to recognize the significance of stress in the environment as a causal factor in dysfunctional behavior. Crisis theory suggests that individuals undergo emotional disequilibrium when confronted by situational stress or hazardous life events. This disequilibrium is not the same as pathology, but, rather, it is a normal life experience that can happen to anyone. As a result of this stress or hazardous event, people attempt to regain emotional balance or equilibrium. While attempting to regain this state of homeostasis, the individual is temporarily in a vulnerable state that allows him or her to be more open to intervention. This state of crisis is characterized by feelings of confusion, anxiety, depression, and anger; and one's usual coping or problem-solving capabilities are diminished (Slaikeu, 1990). Although earlier theorists suggested that this crisis state was limited to 6 to 8 weeks, later practitioners indicate that it varies considerably (Ell, 1995, 1996) and may be a factor in understanding the severity of reactions for some post-traumatic stress disorders (PTSD) (Tomb, 1994).

Crisis-intervention theory tends to support a very positive orientation toward an individual's capacity to grow and adapt. It suggests that crisis intervention gives people opportunities to ultimately reduce the risk of a negative outcome or poor social adaptation later in life. By intervening with individuals who are temporarily vulnerable and psychologically less guarded or defensive, the worker has a window of opportunity to get people to change, grow, and adapt in a short period of time. This constructive response to the change, threat, or loss that previously had overwhelmed the individual becomes a new learned behavior. The client develops a new state of equilibrium in which this new response pattern, learned during the crisis intervention, subsequently becomes the response during similar episodes that follow in life (Parad & Parad, 1990).

Brief Cognitive-Behavioral

Although previous chapters of this book describe both cognitive and behavioral theory and practice, there are also brief models of this approach that should be included in any social worker's repertoire of methods. In relative terms, both cognitive and behavioral treatments are faster in achieving effective outcomes than previous approaches. For depression and anxiety, cognitive therapy is considered to be brief because successful interventions typically require only 12 to 20 sessions and behavioral treatment of phobias rarely uses more than 20 sessions (Sharf, 1996).

However, there are also cognitive-behavioral models that incorporate methods that are specifically designed to make the interventions even briefer than other standard cognitive-behavioral techniques. In Wells and Gianetti's *Handbook of the Brief Psychotherapies* (1990), Lehman and Salovey (1990) describe specific methods of assessment and intervention that place CBT solidly within the brief therapy model. In fact, the methods or techniques they describe, which are essentially highlights from Meichenbaum (1977, 1984), share most of the elements of the common "practice guidelines" for all brief therapies described later in this chapter.

These methods for CBT include encouraging the client to support problem-related cognitions, behaviors, and affects. The worker may use *imagery-based techniques*, asking the client to imagine recent situations in which the problematic thoughts, feelings, or behaviors were experienced. Workers are also encouraged to have clients act out or perform the problematic behavior in a session as a way of improving the *behavior assessment and situational analysis*. The client might be told to focus upon any internal dialogue or thoughts while performing the behavior to conceptualize and evaluate the behavior in a new manner. *Decision-making and problem-solving strategies* are CBT methods that entail helping the client develop the skills necessary to deal with common, everyday problems that have previously been difficult. This method involves discussing new alternative behaviors and exploring practical skills that the client can apply to life situations.

Self-efficacy training is another CBT method (Lehman & Salovey, 1990; Meichenbaum, 1977, 1984) that is based on the observation that one's decision to engage or not engage in any activity is related to that individual's judgment regarding personal self-efficacy. If individuals believe that they are able to cope with a situation, they will engage in that effort whereas they are likely to avoid situations in which failure is believed to be the outcome. CBT social workers therefore create contexts that strengthen self-efficacy expectations through a series of interventions. For instance, once progress is made, the worker helps the client distinguish the past with its associated failures from the present and future, which are associated with new problem-solving skills and a more efficacious belief concerning oneself.

Self-monitoring skills are taught so that the client learns to assess problematic cognitions, behaviors, affects, or environmental circumstances. Self-monitoring sheets include variations of the three-column method described in this text in the chapter on cognitive therapy as well as other behaviorally specific homework assignments that are designed to teach clients to accurately and quantitatively track their cognitions, behaviors, and affects or emotions in a structured manner. By placing the responsibility for objective self-monitoring with the client, the client not only maintains control over the therapeutic process but also develops lifelong skills for independent self-evaluation and monitoring. Finally, *coping skills and stress-inoculation training* methods are utilized so that the skills learned can be generalized to other problems and to the ongoing stressors in life. For instance, *relaxation training and imaging* (see Chapter 9 for specifics) are taught to clients so that they can cope with stress, anxiety, or other problems successfully without the social worker. The importance of *social support systems* and how to develop and maintain them are also integral to most methods of brief CBT (Maguire, 1991).

Task-Centered

The task-centered approach is a social work model developed primarily by Reid and Epstein (1972, 1977), which blended Perlman's (1957) problem-solving methods and the psychodynamic basis of casework into a brief intervention. It is an evolving approach that draws selectively from a wide variety of empirically based theories and methods (Tolson, Reid, & Garvin, 1994). Over the years, it has evolved away from its original reliance upon psychodynamic theory and currently relies upon a combination of practical problem solving, crisis intervention, cognitive restructuring, behavioral techniques, and interventions in the ecosystem (Reid, 1990).

The task-centered approach is characterized by its belief that the client is the primary agent of change and the client must define the problem and take the lead in bringing about change. The targets of this model include problems in family and interpersonal relations, in carrying out social roles, in making decisions and securing resources, and in reactions to situational stress. It views problems as temporary breakdowns in coping strategies that can set in motion forces for change (Reid, 1996).

The task-centered approach was among the first to articulate an empirical basis for brief interventions (Reid & Epstein, 1972) and has consistently supported brief methods by citing three types of research evidence: (a) Clients of brief intervention show as much improvement as clients in long-term treatment. (b) Most of the positive change in long-term treatment occurs in the first few sessions. (c) Most treatment is short in duration, regardless of intent, with very few clients remaining in any type of treatment for more than a dozen sessions (Reid, 1996).

Its *strategy* involves the social worker helping the client to define specific problems that are related to unrealized wants and conditions that can be changed. Change is the result of the client and the worker solving problems, achieving tasks, and carrying out agreed-upon plans. Much of the activity is accomplished outside of the sessions, with the sessions themselves being used primarily to review client accomplishments on each task and to discuss means of overcoming obstacles. Client initiative is valued, although the worker carries out tasks to assist the client, particularly tasks related to securing resources from the system when those are more readily attainable by the worker than the client.

The *worker-client relationship* is designed to stimulate problem solving with the sessions being used to guide subsequent action through which change can develop. The worker holds the client accountable for following through upon the initially agreed-upon contract. Although the tasks tend to be directly oriented to problem solving, contextual change also occurs as a result of the alleviation of a target symptom (e.g., when a client improves his or her grades, the teacher treats that client better or the client's self-image improves) (Reid, 1996).

The *assessment* in the task-centered approach is designed such that the client defines the problems with the assistance and guidance of the worker. If the client cannot concretely define a limited number of problems by the end of the second session, then this approach might not be appropriate. After defining the problems, the worker and the client develop an oral or written contract that typically includes a statement of the client's goals in relation to the problem (i.e., what kind of solution does he or she want to achieve?). The contract usually stipulates the number of anticipated sessions, generally defining 8 to 12 interviews on a weekly or twice-weekly basis extending over a 1- to 3-month period.

Task planning is crucial and involves defining what the client is to do to alleviate his or her problem. The client must agree to try to carry out the task, so it must be both behaviorally clear and reasonably doable. Brainstorming a wide variety of options, presented by both the social worker and the client, is a desirable process, although the social worker's role in this process can vary from the role of pointing out unrealistic tasks to widening the options and encouraging more challenging alternatives. The practitioner never assigns tasks but, rather, proposes ideas for tasks. The tasks can be *general*, such as an agreement to find better child care for a child with autism, or it can be *operational*, such as an agreement to call a specific baby-sitter and make an appointment. At the end of the task-planning session, the worker summarizes the agreed-upon plan and conveys the message that there is an expectation that the client will carry out this plan prior to the next session.

The social worker is expected to establish incentives and a rationale for the task accomplishment to reinforce the client's expectations for positive benefits. The worker also helps the client explore possible obstacles, as well as means of overcoming those obstacles. After the social worker and the client have agreed upon a general task of developing better child care and they have followed through on the operational task of calling a new baby-sitter, the worker and client may need to brainstorm options to transport the baby-sitter to the client's home in a rural setting.

In *contextual analysis,* the practitioner helps the client overcome obstacles and develop needed resources for task achievement. The client's own strengths and resources are particularly focused upon, although unrealistic expectations on the part of the client are also confronted during this phase.

Termination in this approach is relatively straightforward since the contract developed in the first two sessions specifies the approximate time or date of termination. At termination, the worker reviews progress on the problems as well as progress on continuing work on the tasks. Occasionally new tasks are discussed that the client will undertake independently. The client's accomplishments are strongly reinforced with a stress upon the strengths and capabilities that are now evident in relation to independent task achievement (Reid, 1996; Tolson, Reid, & Garvin, 1994).

Solution-Focused

Solution-focused therapy has changed considerably in its relatively short history. It began as a problem-focused alternative to family and marital psychotherapy but evolved into a solution-focused method that is frequently focused upon individuals (Nunnally, 1993). The founder of this approach, Steve de Shazer (1988), takes special note of *exceptions*—those occasions when the problem does not occur—and *reframing* clients' viewpoints and perspectives to become more positive and constructive (Bloom, 1997).

An example of an *exception* is an instance in which a couple indicates that they quarrel too much about finances. The solution-focused worker would ask them if they sometimes discuss money without quarreling. The next step is to identify those elements or conditions that exist in instances in which they do

not quarrel when discussing money so that the couple can explore and incorporate those same conditions and recreate them in the future. The therapist
tries to help clients identify and use behaviors that are already in use by
encouraging those exceptional circumstances. Other *exceptions* include *new
exceptions* that have recently developed, *recurrent exceptions* that occur periodically in the present, and *past exceptions* that no longer occur but have in
the past (Nunnally, 1993).

Another technique identified originally with de Shazer is the *miracle* (de
Shazer, 1988; Sharf, 1996), a rather interesting method in which the therapist
asks the client to consider: "What if there was a miracle and this problem was
solved? What would you be doing differently? What will your life be like when
this misery is over? How would you know that a miracle had occurred?" The
purpose of the *miracle* question is to get the client or clients to concentrate
upon solutions in the future rather than problems in the past.

The term *ecosystem* is used to describe the therapeutic environment,
which includes the individual, family, or group, as well as the therapists. A *conductor* interacts with the family while a team of observers watches the process,
providing feedback and consultation during a planned break. The six stages of
this method are pre-session planning, prelude, data collection, the consulting
break, intervention, and post-session assessment (Bloom, 1997). In the *pre-
session* stage, the *conductor* and the observing team discuss the family's situation and develop a rough guideline for work. The *prelude* includes the first ten
minutes or so, which should be used to casually explore the social context of
the family. At this time, the conductor does not focus on the complaints but,
rather, develops a relationship with the family while learning about the family's environment. During the *data-collection* stage, the conductor noncritically
accepts the observations of various family members. The conductor may also
ask questions concerning which problems the family hopes to change. Questions are also asked concerning family members' observations of each other.
The conductor also helps the family develop goals that are achievable, concrete, and positive. During these stages, the team is observing the family and
conductor through a one-way mirror, making notes regarding family interactions. At the planned *consulting break,* the team provides feedback and suggestions to the conductor and they design an intervention. The *intervention*
always includes two components: a compliment and a homework assignment,
along with a rationale for both. "The purposes of the compliments were to provide a positive context for the therapeutic intervention, highlight the constructive moves already being made by the client by focusing on what seemed
to be working, alleviate anxieties that the client may have had about the therapy experience or the therapist, underline the normal components of what the
client was reporting, give credit to the client for efforts being made to change,
and frame statements with which the client or family could agree so that they

would be more likely to accept suggestions or assignments that followed" (Bloom, 1997, p. 171).

The conductor discusses this feedback to the individual or family during the intervention while the team observes the reaction to the compliment and assignment. The family is allowed to clarify suggestions, but then the session is ended. After the family leaves, the team meets for the *post-session assessment* and discusses the family's reactions and anticipated behavior.

The three objectives of solution-focused practice are helping clients change how they perceive the problem, helping them change what they are doing, and helping them use their strengths as a result of the intervention. Solution-focused treatment is a positive, constructive, strengths-oriented approach that has had a significant impact on family therapy and individual treatment.

Brief Psychodynamic

Psychoanalytically based treatments are inherently relatively long-term. In contemporary social work practice with its focus upon brevity and efficiency, the psychodynamic approaches are, therefore, at a disadvantage as a method of choice. However, as stated in the previous chapter on psychodynamic social work, this approach is still an essential component of practice for many.

In its early developmental years, psychoanalytically oriented therapy was often short-term. Freud and Mahler wrote of cases that consisted of only six or fewer sessions (Marmor, 1992). As early as 1918, Sandor Ferenczi developed "active therapy" as an attempt to make psychoanalytic therapy briefer. His collaborations with Otto Rank on *The Development of Psychoanalysis* (Ferenczi, Rank, & Newton, 1925) emphasized the importance of here-and-now transference interpretations and placed a greater focus upon current events than mainstream analysts (Marmor, 1992).

In the 1920s, social work practice enthusiastically embraced psychoanalysis; but, by the 1930s, major schisms developed within the field. The "functionalists" or Rankians challenged the Freudian "diagnostic" adherents. This struggle abated somewhat in the 1950s with the development of ego psychology, which differed significantly from mainstream psychoanalysis. Ego psychologists focused upon the ego as an autonomous entity that was not simply at the mercy of the id and the unconscious drives (Woods & Robinson, 1996). This practical shift complemented the development of the psychosocial approach within social work that balanced psychoanalytic theory and the social environment.

The *psychosocial* approach has evolved over the years from a psychodynamic approach to a systems-based approach. Although other psychoanalytically based theories such as *self psychology* and *object relations theory* are now accepted among many clinical social workers, the psychosocial approach remains the predominant psychoanalytically based method. It is debatable whether this approach is a "brief therapy" or even if it is psychoanalytically based in its current formulation. However, it is included here since it is a necessary and important method.

There are six procedures that are central to psychosocial practice (Woods & Hollis, 1990; Woods & Robinson, 1996):

1. *Sustainment* refers to communications and procedures that demonstrate interest, acceptance, empathic understanding, reassurance, and encouragement to the client. Occasionally, a nod, a smile, or gentle coaxing to the client to elaborate on some feeling or statement is recommended.
2. *Direct influence* refers to direct advice or suggestions. Although the approach prefers that clients arrive at decisions in their own way, the approach recognizes that, at times, the social worker may need to be quite directive. Statements such as "You may want to consider . . ." or "It might help to . . ." are often recommended.
3. *Exploration, description, and ventilation* include efforts that help the client become more aware of facts relevant to the situation or bring out feelings. "Please tell me more about that incident . . ." or "How did you feel when that happened?" may be appropriate.
4. *Reflection of person-situation configuration* is a hallmark procedure of the psychosocial approach. In this procedure, the worker helps the client to assess his or her current circumstances and interactions with others. This is used to help the client to become more aware of perceptions, thoughts, and feelings as they are experienced in everyday life situations.
5. *Pattern dynamic reflection* refers to a procedure that supports examining patterns of behavior, thinking, or feeling. The social worker points out instances where repetition exists. For instance, a client may have a tendency to argue before listening, to demand perfection from oneself or others, or to put oneself into situations where undesirable behaviors are likely to be exhibited.
6. *Developmental reflection* supports consideration of the family of origin and early developmental circumstances and their impacts upon current thoughts, behaviors, and feelings. The social worker helps the client to recognize how early childhood experiences, such as having a critical, demanding father, might be influencing current anger toward an authority figure, such as one's boss.

PRACTICE GUIDELINES

There is no single method or theoretical base for brief treatment. The major practitioners in this approach describe a blend or eclectic mix of cognitive; behavioral; cognitive-behavioral family (Edwards, 1997); solution-focused

(Campbell, Elder, Gallagher, Simon, & Taylor, 1999; Chang, Hung, & Yeh, 1999); and psychodynamic variations (Daws, 1999).

Bloom (1997) lists five components common to short-term therapy: (a) prompt intervention, (b) a relatively high level of therapist intervention, (c) establishment of limited but specific goals, (d) identification and maintenance of a clear focus, and (e) the setting of a time limit.

Budman, Hoyt, and Friedman (1992) stated in their edited book on brief therapy that there are six generic components of brief treatment: (a) a rapid and generally positive working alliance between the therapist and the patient; (b) focality, the clear specification of achievable treatment goals; (c) clear definition of patient and therapist responsibilities; (d) an expectation of change, the belief that improvement is within the patient's (immediate) grasp; (e) a here-and-now orientation, and (f) time sensitivity.

However, a more detailed listing would include the following eight practice guidelines common to brief interventions:

- *Time limitations.* The client and the worker need to agree to limitations regarding the number of sessions. In the first session, the worker contracts with the client to meet for only eight to twelve sessions (sometimes slightly more or less). If the client's problems are not appropriate for brief treatment or if the client has any reservations, then brief treatment is not pursued.
- *Problem limitations.* A limited number of problems are defined and agreed upon at the onset. In the initial sessions, the worker and the client together develop between two and four problems for intervention. Even though additional and even greater problems sometimes become apparent, the worker and the client stay focused on these initially defined problems and do not add or subtract from that list.
- *Clear behavioral problem statements.* The presenting problems are defined in clear behavioral terms. Brief treatment requires a focus on symptoms, behaviors, and observable or, ideally, quantifiable issues and concerns. Vague thoughts or feelings are not acceptable, nor are non specific, unconscious motivators.
- *Clear goal statements at onset.* Goals are also clearly defined in behavioral terms at the onset. Unlike most interventions, there is a requirement in brief intervention to define clear outcomes as part of the initial agreement. The purpose of this is to maintain a focus on the achievement of those specific goals without wandering or losing focus. Furthermore, it allows the worker and the client to know precisely when to terminate—as soon as those goals have been achieved.
- *Contracts.* The clinician and the client contract or agree to certain prescribed behaviors that are mutually binding. Sometimes these contracts are formally written and signed by both the worker and the client with a conscious and mutually agreed-upon set of expectations for both.

- *Partnerships.* A balanced partnership is accepted by both. In brief treatment, the social worker is generally seen as an advisor, supporter, or helper who encourages the client to work with the social worker or, even better, to lead in the treatment process. The abilities, strengths, support systems, and motivations of the client are all strongly reinforced. The likelihood of a passive dependence on the part of the client is virtually impossible since the client is required to develop ideas in this interactive, working partnership.
- *Flexibility.* In spite of the previous factors and their seemingly cold, quick, and impersonal tone, there is agreement that brief intervention utilizes a wide range of varied behaviors and attitudes on the part of the worker and the client. After the initial treatment phase, which does require an efficient and rather concrete focus, the ensuing process needs to be very open and engaging in order to reach the agreed-upon initial goals within the time frame allowed.
- *Monitoring and evaluating.* Careful monitoring of the process is essential. The brief treatment approach has a premium on efficiently progressing toward the agreed-upon goals. Each session involves a detailed and behaviorally specific discussion of what the client and the worker have accomplished to reach the goal of treatment. If one or the other has failed to perform a certain task, then the reasons for this failure are discussed. Sometimes new behaviors are needed, or the client or worker needs to be given renewed support in his or her efforts. Even though valid, new or different goals not agreed upon initially are generally discouraged.

STAGES OF BRIEF THERAPY

It is not surprising that some of the written work of brief therapists is similar to the approach itself—clear and brief. In Hoyt's (1995) book on brief therapy in managed care, the author recommends five phases: (a) *pretreatment,* wherein the therapist prepares the client for the first session by encouraging the client to think about what her or she would like to accomplish and what he or she expects from therapy; (b) the *beginning phase,* wherein "certain tasks need to be accomplished: developing an alliance; defining the purpose of the meeting; orienting the patient regarding how to use therapy; presenting an opportunity for the expression of thoughts, feelings, and behaviors; mutually formulating a focus and achievable goals; making (initial) treatment interventions and seeing the response; and discussing confidentiality, fees, and future appointments" (p. 4); (c) the *middle phase,* which Hoyt sees as the "working-through" phase (the focus is upon applying whatever is learned in treatment to the patient's life outside); (d) the *end phase*, during which termination is discussed; and, finally, (e) *follow-through*, which can be done by phone, in person, or with questionnaires. Since some therapeutic processes may be set in motion but not fully completed, it is helpful for patients to be assured that follow-up contact is always possible.

Perhaps the best or most clearly articulated description of the stages of this approach comes from Richard A. Wells who has written extensively in this area (Wells & Gianetti, 1993; Wells, 1994; Wells & Giannetti, 1990). Wells (1993) describes three stages of intervention in brief therapy and the techniques and skills required within each stage:

STAGE 1. ENGAGEMENT: TEACHING THE CLIENT ABOUT THERAPY

1. Accept (and refine) the client's problem statement.
2. Start working on the problem immediately.
3. "Diagnoses" through action.
4. Educate clients in their roles.
5. Set up a collaborative relationship with the client.

STAGE 2. INTERVENTION: SETTING THE CLIENT TO WORK

1. Persistently present alternative views of reality.
2. Rearrange or remove obstacles through task assignments.
3. Challenge the client from a novel perspective.
4. Provide the simplest, most immediate intervention.
5. Look for opportunities to teach life skills.
6. Work flexibly across modalities.

STAGE 3. TERMINATION: RELEASING THE CLIENT

1. Let clients know they can return for further help.
2. Avoid attractive detours that can prolong therapy.
3. Connect people to needed resources.
4. Let go, but in a positive way.

By combining, synthesizing, and summarizing the work of several of these brief therapy models, and based upon this author's practice experience and research, the following five stages are those most commonly used in brief treatment.

Stage 1: Define the Problems

This is an extremely important stage in brief intervention because it not only sets the tone for further work but also clearly sets the parameters. In brief treatment, the first two sessions involve a focused effort to behaviorally specify

the reasons for treatment. Furthermore, the worker discusses the other characteristics of this model, which include (a) limitations in the number of presenting problems, (b) a focus on concrete and observable behaviors or symptoms, and (c) a partnership in which the client, not the worker, is expected to
accept the primary responsibility for change and action. See Case 10.1.

Case 10.1: Define the Problems

Maria is a 17-year-old single parent with a 6-month-old daughter. The daughter,
Stacey, has been hospitalized with pneumonia, and the hospital social worker has
been asked to see Maria. Initially, Maria was hostile and uncooperative, but when
the social worker clarified that she was there to help Maria and Stacey, Maria's
attitude changed dramatically. In fact, Maria tearfully blamed herself for her
daughter's poor health and said, "a mother as bad as me doesn't deserve Stacey."

Maria said that her devoutly religious family was embarrassed by Maria's
"illigitimate baby" and had not spoken to her since she became pregnant. They
had warned Maria that her boyfriend would leave her as soon as he could, and
their predictions were accurate. Maria had defended her boyfriend and was now
severely depressed, destitute, and alienated from her parents and two older siblings. She also admitted that she had been neglectful of Stacey, partially due to
the fact that she had no idea how to care for her infant.

The social worker listened at length, occasionally asking for clarification
regarding her parents, siblings, former boyfriend, and past efforts to care for
Stacey. It was apparent that Maria loved her daughter and wanted to care for her
but lacked knowledge and resources necessary for parenting. Furthermore, Maria
was depressed and feeling overwhelmed, culminating in multiple depressive
symptoms.

By the end of the initial session, the worker and Maria had collaboratively
defined the following specific problems: (a) Maria missed her parents and siblings
but was too proud and embarrassed to attempt a new contact with them. (b) Maria
needed help in parenting skills. She was the youngest in her family and had never
had contact with infants until she had her own. (c) Maria needed money to buy
food, clothing, and shelter. There were other concerns such as child care, a job, the
lack of any social life and friends, and a developing problem with alcohol, but Maria
and the worker agreed to limit the focus to only three clearly defined problems.

The worker also supported Maria's many strengths, such as her devotion to
her daughter, and the worker promised that she would make a personal commitment to collaborate and support Maria in every way possible. She even put this in
writing and signed it.

Maria also indicated that she had been quite religious, but now she feared
that her church would also reject her. The social worker reassured Maria that that
was unlikely and encouraged Maria to call a priest who was known to be
extremely supportive and caring. In fact, his parish consisted of many single
young parents who met and socialized regularly and whose spiritual lives were
essential to them.

Stage 2: Define the Goals

The goals or anticipated behavioral outcomes are also clearly and concretely
defined in the first two or three treatment sessions. The goals or outcomes are

specifically matched to each problem and are typically written into a contract with the client. In most clinical records, there is a column for the list of presenting problems and a column next to that list defining the goal to be achieved for that problem. If three problems are listed in *Column 1*, then there are three goals in *Column 2* that specify in behaviorally specific terms precisely how the corresponding problem will be eradicated. See Case 10.2.

Case 10.2: Define the Goals

In the second session, the worker commented that Maria looked a bit more relaxed and that her hair was nicely styled. Maria smiled proudly but quickly changed her affect as she expressed her anxiety that Stacey was now back at home. Maria said that she felt better about herself since their last session, but she was still unsure concerning the problems they had mutually defined the week before.

The worker gave Maria the list of three problems that they had defined the previous week, but they were now typed on a sheet of paper under a column labeled "Column 1: Problems." That column had three numbered statements:

1. Miss family
2. Lack parenting skills
3. Lack money, job, and housing

Next to the three numbered problems was a second column labeled "Column 2: Goals." The worker gave the sheet to Maria and said, "Okay. Let's try to figure out a way to deal with these three problems. Why don't you start by telling me your ideas." After some hesitation followed by reassurances from the worker, Maria started to define her goals.

"This is going to be tough," she said. "My parents go to church all the time, and, when they found out about my pregnancy, my mom just cried and my dad yelled at me and said I had shamed the family."

The worker asked more about Maria's parents and learned that they were both born and raised in Mexico and had developed a comfortable lifestyle and standing in the community. Maria's father was very active in the Mexican American community and his church; and, apparently, Maria had avoided asking her parents for help because she presumed her father would never accept her back. Maria admitted that she may have been wrong in this presumption since one of her sisters had spoken to her several times and suggested that the father was actually upset because he missed Maria and his granddaughter.

After discussing these issues, Maria was able to define her three goals, which she wrote on the same sheet that defined her three problems:

1. Get back together with mother, father, and siblings.
2. Get their help and support with taking care of Stacey and with teaching Maria how to do it.
3. Get short-term financial help and then get a job and a new apartment.

The social worker and Maria added a third column, which specified specific tasks or behaviors associated with the goal achievement. In Column 3, Maria listed three tasks next to the goals. Task 1 was clear—she had to call her family. Task 2 was basically the same since Maria had discussed the fact that she definitely preferred to learn parenting skills from her own mother and one older sister rather than from a course or books. Her third task was to go to the Department of Social Services to get financial aid and possible leads on jobs and new housing.

Stage 3: Collaborate on Tasks, Schedules, and Action Plans

At this stage, the worker and the client have ideally developed a solid, trusting relationship and partnership. If the social worker has modeled an open, positive, and accepting attitude, then the client should feel comfortable in exploring a variety of options relative to tasks. For instance, the client may feel uncomfortable or intimidated about seeking help from formal organizations such as the Department of Social Services or vocational programs. In those instances, the social worker should initiate the contacts or refer the client to a helpful contact person at each of those organizations. Family contacts or linkages with the informal support system of family and friends is generally a task that the client needs to do, with help, support, and guidance from the worker. See Case 10.3.

Case 10.3: Collaborate

Maria and the worker agreed that Maria would call her older sister first. This sister had already spoken with Maria and assured her that their parents were more hurt than angry. In fact, when Maria called her sister, her sister handed the phone to her mother who was visiting. The mother tearfully scolded Maria for not contacting her earlier. When Maria asked her mother whether Maria's father was willing to see her, the mother said, "You leave that to me. Come to dinner with your baby next Sunday after mass. This has gone on long enough. I want to see my baby and her baby, too."

Maria also agreed to go to the Department of Social Services on the following Thursday. Her older sister had enthusiastically offered to come over early with her two children so that they could get to know their new little cousin.

Stage 4: Monitor Progress

In this stage, the worker needs to monitor the client's progress, develop alternatives, support and reinforce gains, assess and overcome barriers, and maintain focus on goal achievement. In practice, the stages rarely move forward without mishaps. Some tasks do not get accomplished because the client has reservations, doubts, or fears or lacks the ability or resources to achieve the tasks. Seemingly simple tasks such as "call mother" or "apply for financial assistance" or "find a job" can all be very difficult.

Obstacles to task achievement for clients tend to be either lack of resources or lack of knowledge, or they can be more psychological in nature. For instance, a client cannot go to apply for aid or a job without knowing how and where to apply. Furthermore, the client may need to find child care before even seeking other needed resources. Psychological obstacles can include guilt, unresolved anger, embarrassment, or a myriad of other common reactions that make seemingly simple tasks difficult. For instance, calling one's parents is a simple task for some. However, for a client who was abused or neglected and subsequently spent years avoiding parents or denying the resultant anger, a "simple" phone call is a monumental task.

Whenever there is hesitation or resistance to performing tasks, the worker needs to probe for the cause. Embarrassment relative to asking for help is common and can usually be overcome by helping the client recognize that he or she deserves and needs the help and that the temporary embarrassment may need to be tolerated in order to achieve goals. In longer-term interventions, the underlying causes would possibly be explored and resolved. For brief interventions, alternative tasks may need to be developed after some open discussion of the basis for the resistance and anger. See Case 10.4.

> **Case 10.4: Monitor Progress**
> Maria was relieved after her discussion with her mother but was very worried about her father's reaction. Maria and her father had been very close, and Maria had always been his "pride and joy." The worker encouraged Maria to discuss her fears about seeing him. Apparently, Maria was her father's favorite child. He had worked hard to achieve a comfortable lifestyle and had expected that Maria would achieve even more. For years, the two of them had talked about her going to law school. As the worker and Maria spoke, it became apparent that the father had never rejected Maria. It was Maria's own feelings of guilt and her belief that she had disappointed her father that had led to this prolonged estrangement. After the worker helped Maria to realize this, the worker further helped her to see that her hopes for law school were still achievable. Having a baby did not preclude the high hopes and ambitions that she and her father shared for her. This knowledge also helped her to feel more comfortable about the upcoming dinner with her family. She realized that she could proceed with her career plans and achieve her ambitions, and she was not accurate in her temporary belief that she would not become a "success" in her own opinion or, once again, in the opinion of her father.

Stage 5: Terminate

Termination in brief treatment involves four distinct tasks: letting go, reviewing, summarizing, and reinforcing behavioral change. *Letting go* refers to the need to say good-bye and to encourage independence. In a positive manner, the worker lets the client know that the client can stop seeing the worker since that client can now solve his or her own problems very successfully. In reviewing the brief treatment process, the worker describes the steps that were taken by both of them to resolve the problems. Obstacles to the achievement of goals or tasks are also reviewed. A summary of what worked or did not work may also be useful so that the client can efficiently overcome problems in the future. Behaviors that were helpful in goal achievement and task accomplishment should be particularly reinforced and discussed at length. The connection between the client's action and the success of treatment is particularly salient. Focusing upon the client's strengths and capabilities increases the likelihood that future encounters with problems in life can be successfully overcome independently by the client. See Case 10.5.

Case 10.5: Terminate

Maria went to her parents' house for dinner and successfully reconciled with her father. The two of them enthusiastically discussed her return to school, and her mother and sister helped her design a child care arrangement that included both of her parents as well as several siblings and cousins. Maria's lack of knowledge about caring for her daughter was dismissed as perfectly normal within her large extended family, and they even joked about how frightened her father had been when he first held his firstborn child.

Maria discussed all of this with her social worker and shared her joy upon reconciling with her family. The social worker also helped Maria in not blaming herself for the long delay before getting help. The worker encouraged Maria to remember to ask others what they are feeling and to not assume that others are angry with her or rejecting her. The worker also summarized Maria's many strengths, including her willingness to seek appropriate help and to use it effectively. Maria's strong ties to her family were also discussed as future sources of support, although her own intelligence and determination to resolve her problems were cited as particularly helpful. Finally, the worker congratulated Maria upon her recent readmission to college. She had decided to move back in with her parents, and she and the worker agreed that, at least temporarily, her return home would help her with her pressing financial, vocational, and housing problems.

SUMMARY

Brief treatment is a term that describes a wide variety of short-term, focused interventions. The focus on brief treatment has increased recently due to economic necessity, research validation, and cultural/philosophical shifts.

The major brief intervention social work models include crisis intervention, brief cognitive-behavioral, task-centered, solution-focused, and brief psychodynamic therapies.

Generally accepted practice guidelines include time limitations; limitations on the number of problems; clear, behavioral problem statements; clear goals stated at onset; contracts; partnerships; flexibility; and monitoring and evaluation.

The stages of brief intervention are (a) define the problems, (b) define the goals, (c) collaborate on tasks and action plans, (d) monitor progress, and (e) terminate.

PUTTING IT ALL TOGETHER

Documentation, Assessments, and Treatment Plans

This last chapter serves four purposes. It will "put it all together" by *reviewing and summarizing* contemporary clinical social work practice with an emphasis upon the *documentation* of that practice in a written format. The last sections describe the process of developing an *assessment* and then a *treatment plan*.

REVIEW AND SUMMARY

Clinical social work is a profession with a long and proud history. It has changed, grown, and adapted considerably over its century of existence. At present, most clinical social workers base practice in a broad, eclectic foundation that recognizes the effects of many systems on clients. As advanced practitioners, clinical social workers move beyond generalist interventions and utilize a research-based mix of relatively brief but effective interventions. In addition to utilizing and incorporating the client's social system, family, community, and relevant groups, clinical social workers integrate advanced methods that include psychodynamic, cognitive, behavioral, and many other related clinical frameworks.

Clinical research is the necessary beginning point for clinical social workers in choosing appropriate interventions. The type of intervention chosen must also meet the specific, culturally appropriate needs of that client. Issues of race, ethnic background, gender, sexual orientation, age, client values, lifestyles, rights, and a wide variety of other relevant clinical considerations must all be assessed as part of an appropriate intervention and treatment plan.

The assessment, treatment plan, and intervention are collaborative efforts that begin with the assessment of the client's problems, strengths, capabilities, and social systems. The clinical social worker's task is to develop and implement a treatment plan that will strengthen and empower the client to overcome problems, concerns, and social-emotional challenges.

Many of the practice methods used by clinical social workers are the same methods used by other practitioners in the helping professions. The various settings in which social workers practice invariably employ other helping professionals such as counselors, psychologists, nurses, psychiatrists, rehabilitation therapists, and many others. The assessments, treatment plans, records, and documentation required in these settings are often inclusive. However, these documents also reflect the specific, idiosyncratic needs and concerns of the agency, its staff, and the client populations served.

The structure and content of contemporary clinical documents are a product of their times. Since the 1980s, there have been significant changes in practice; and these changes are reflected in most contemporary assessments, treatment plans, and case records. During the first half of the 20th century, assessments, treatment plans, and case records reflected the predominant mode of intervention. That mode was psychodynamic; and virtually all case records reflected that orientation and focused upon detailed assessments of early childhood experiences with particular attention toward trauma related to bonding, separation, abuse, or neglect. Case records frequently included speculation regarding significant underlying, subconscious dynamics such as unresolved Oedipal issues, latent hostility, or repressed sexual issues. Although psychodynamically oriented social workers and agencies still include reference to those issues, these clinicians and other contemporary practitioners have also updated and revised their practice interventions and their written treatment plans.

Contemporary documentation in case records reflects a shift toward a focus on observable and behavioral changes in the client. The field is changing; those changes are apparent in the content, structure, and overall significance of the documentation process.

DOCUMENTATION

For the past 25 years, this author has balanced a career that included clinical practice, teaching, and research. As chairman of the clinical concentration for the school, he invited the school's senior, most experienced field instructors and the clinical adjunct faculty to a meeting to discuss contemporary practice issues. He opened the discussion asking for feedback regarding gaps or deficits in the school's clinical curriculum relevant to knowledge, skills, and values. This was actually the fourth meeting of this type, but the other meetings were all composed of full-time faculty members. He thought that he already had a fairly clear understanding of the theoretical areas and developing methods and interventions that the school needed to incorporate into the curriculum to maintain CSWE accreditation

(CSWE, 2001) while staying "ahead of the curve" for new, advanced clinical interventions.

This highly experienced group of full-time clinical social workers clearly indicated that documentation is a primary concern. They emphasized the fact that students do not know how to document their work in assessments and treatment plans that accurately describe the intervention. The specific organization of the case records varies from agency to agency, but there are certain common, generic areas that are invariably included in written documents in contemporary practice. The clinicians at this meeting said that students and clinicians need to be better trained in documenting their assessments and treatment plans.

The documentation of clinical social work interventions is a highly idiosyncratic effort. Case records must be geared to the specific needs of the population served, the agency or program, and the funding sources. The methods of intervention used also partially define the nature and content of the assessments and treatment plans. The treatment plans include statements of goals, objectives, and interventions. As a result of these multiple and wide-ranging demands upon documentation and case recording, it is difficult to describe this process in a manner that is applicable to most clinicians. The clinical social worker, therefore, is encouraged to be diligent to the specific documentation requirements of his or her agency. This brief introduction may help to prepare students and clinicians to understand the broad and basic purposes and terms.

Clinical social work is an art and a science, but it is also increasingly a business. Managed care, insurance companies, government funding sources, and clients themselves are all appropriately demanding accountability and documentation of appropriate services. If services are not documented in a case record, then they do not "count" and the services will not be *reimbursed*. In addition to reimbursement, three other documentation concerns are effectiveness, monitoring, and efficiency. The lack of accurate and thorough documentation hinders *effectiveness* and could result in a negative and inaccurate *monitoring* of the intervention process and poor *efficiency* due to both administrative and clinical causes.

Reimbursement

Reimbursement, or payment for services, is based upon documentation of appropriate services rendered, not upon merely the rendering of appropriate services. The clinical social worker must be able to demonstrate in his or her documented case record that a certain service was rendered at a specific date for a clear, logical reason that was consistent with the treatment plan. If the service is not documented, it will not be reimbursed. Furthermore, if it is documented but is inconsistent with the treatment plan, it may also be disallowed. In the past, clinicians were allowed much more freedom in recording. Reviews of case records were relatively superficial and unrelated to finances. Today, lax recording or inaccurate statements can very often lead to refusal of payments, delays, timely administrative phone calls, and even lawsuits.

Effectiveness

Effectiveness in practice is often a function of adequate recording. A case record improves clinical effectiveness when it clearly, logically, and thoroughly describes the treatment process and includes concise statements of the presenting problems and strengths; short- and long-term goals; and anticipated, measurable objectives. A well-designed treatment plan helps to keep both the client and the social worker "on target." Precise and accurate documentation supports targeted and appropriate interventions and minimizes "straying" from appropriate services and goals. It helps the worker and the client to stay focused on agreed-upon goals, tasks, and ultimate objectives. It graphically demonstrates progress, as well as lack of progress, or instances in which irrelevant or tangential issues were pursued.

Monitoring

Monitoring of the intervention process refers to the overviews and examinations of case records that take place in virtually all practices and agencies. In some instances, records are routinely evaluated during peer-review procedures by fellow clinicians. In other instances, case records are examined by insurance companies or managed care case managers to ensure that proper and effective clinical practices are followed. These assessments are typically made purely on the basis of written records. If the clinical social worker is a brilliant and effective practitioner but a poor recordkeeper, the unfortunate result is a negative assessment of the intervention. This negative assessment leads to wasted clinical and administrative time spent in adding or clarifying missing or inaccurate case related information.

Efficiency

Efficiency in both administrative and clinical practice is the result when documentation is clear, precise, and accurate. Administrative time is often wasted in redoing and reexamining records that are incomplete, out of order, insufficiently behavioral, or otherwise deficient. The cost in both money and time can become overwhelming for case record reviewers, as well as for clinicians. Due to the fact that accurate documentation is now the prerequisite for reimbursement, careful case recording can be a deciding factor in the continued existence of some agencies.

Clinical inefficiency results from imprecise and hazy formulations of problems, strengths, goals, tasks, outcomes, and interventionist techniques. Poor formulations or insufficient precision in behavioral descriptions by the clinician undermine efforts to help the client work through his or her issues quickly and positively. Clear and well-organized assessments and treatment plans minimize the likelihood of engaging in rambling sessions that lack direction or repeat previously resolved issues.

ASSESSMENT

The clinician begins the treatment process by collecting a wide variety of relevant data and listening to the client's perception of the problem. The biopsychosocial data collected usually includes standard demographic data such as date of birth, race, religion, marital status, and birthplace. Most assessments include a history of health or mental health problems for the client and family members. Significant childhood experiences or traumas such as divorce of parents, hospitalizations, accidents, abuse, neglect, and separation from parents are usually noted. Assessments further include psychosocial histories that delve into peer relationships; academic performance; social support systems related to family, friends, and neighbors; and cultural or spiritual affiliations and associations. The strengths and resources of the individual are invariably noted. These may include anything from the existence of a highly supportive extended family to the ability to cook or play an instrument. Standard social work assessments usually include information regarding the referral source and the reason for the referral.

Mental health and psychiatric settings include a history of past treatments, medications, or hospitalizations of the client and family members. In the computerized evaluation performed at the Western Psychiatric Institute and Clinic (WPIC) in Pittsburgh, a checklist of common symptoms is required. A partial list of these symptoms includes sleep disturbance, phobias, anxiety, hallucinations, eating disturbance, alcohol abuse, sexual problems, obsessions/compulsions, suicidal indicators, self-neglect, delusions, poor concentration/distractibility, hyperactivity, and elation. A mental status exam is also a part of the evaluation. It asks for comments regarding the client's appearance and behavior, mood and affect, rate and pattern of speech, thought form, thought content, perception, orientation, and attention and concentration.

Assessments reflect the type of client population, the clinical orientation of the staff, and the agency's mission. For instance, child welfare agencies focus upon the problems of children and their families These staff are clinically oriented toward understanding and modifying family systems and interpersonal behavior, often from a developmental or psychodynamic perspective. The mission of child welfare agencies involves protecting and supporting children and families in relation to social, psychological, academic, health, financial, and housing issues. The assessments therefore include the collection of data relevant to each of these areas, yet specific to the client's personal situation.

A mental health or outpatient clinic treats a population composed of individuals with mental health problems. Diagnoses from the *DSM-IV-TR* (2000) are required. The clinical orientation of the staff may include cognitive and behavioral methods, or it could include a psychodynamic or systems foundation. The agency's mission would be focused upon treating clients who have psychiatric disorders or psychological problems through the use of psychotherapeutic interventions. The assessments, therefore, include data relevant to historical information that support a defined *DSM-IV-TR* diagnosis and an appropriate psychotherapeutic plan.

Assessments often reflect the model of treatment. Although contemporary documentation tends to be oriented toward certain basic, generic data and information, there is also a need for information that is specific to varying treatment approaches. If a clinical social worker decides to choose a psychodynamic intervention, then the assessment necessarily includes data and information relevant to that model. The psychodynamic assessment information differs from the assessment data needed for a cognitive, behavioral, or systems intervention. Each of the major methods described in this text and utilized in contemporary practice has additional assessment information that is specific to that method. In addition to the standard assessment data and demographics included in all generic assessments, there are various "method-specific" assessments that reflect systems approaches, psychodynamic treatment, behavioral interventions, and cognitive therapy. Each is described briefly in the remainder of this section. The case of Ann and her verbally abusive husband John is used as the case example to demonstrate the four different types of assessments.

Systems Assessment

In addition to the standard data collected, a *systems assessment* adds data relevant to the client's social support system, family, community, and other relevant social domains. There are three structured assessment tools frequently used to describe a client's social system. Two of them have been developed from the family systems perspective (Zastrow, 1999) and one from a general systems framework (Maguire, 1991). The two family assessment tools are the *ecomap* (Hartman, 1978) and the *genogram* (Kerr & Bowen, 1988). The third tool is the *social network diagram* (Maguire, 1991).

Typical ecomaps and genograms use symbols, lines and arrows to graphically demonstrate patterns of influence and relationships (see Figure 11.1).

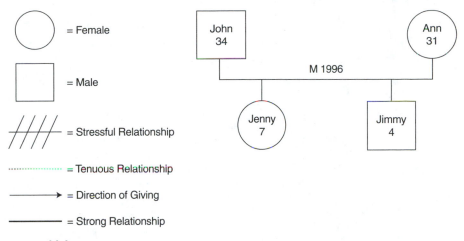

FIGURE **11.1**

A **genogram** uses symbols, lines, and arrows to graphically demonstrate patterns of influence and relationships. John (34) and Ann (31) were married in 1996. They have a son, Jimmy (4) and a daughter, Jenny (7).

A circle symbolizes a female; a square represents a male; straight lines with multiple intersecting small lines indicate a stressful relationship; dashes rather than solid lines symbolize tenuous relationships. Arrows on the lines indicate the direction of giving in a relationship, and solid, thick lines between individuals suggest strong ties. Genograms reflect Bowen's belief (Kerr & Bowen, 1988) that patterns of behavior pass from one generation to the next, so genograms usually include at least three generations of family systems dynamics.

Social network diagrams (Figure 11.2) describe the client's social system graphically through the use of three concentric circles divided into wedge-shaped spheres representing family, friends, and others. See Case 11.1.

Psychodynamic Assessments

A psychodynamically oriented assessment includes additional information regarding early developmental history, divorce, abandonment, school performance, peer relationships, physical or psychological trauma or treatment, hospitalizations, physical and sexual development, sexual experiences, and sexual orientation.

Some psychodynamic practitioners or agencies use projective tests. Three commonly used assessment instruments are the Rorschach or "ink-blot" test; the Minnesota Multiphasic Personality Inventory (MMPI); and the Thematic Apperception Test (TAT), which is a series of pictures that the client is asked to use as a basis for describing possible interactions or events taking place.

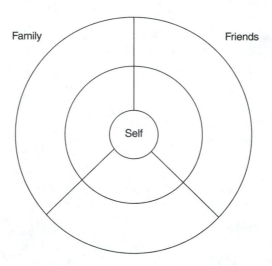

Others (i.e., Clergy, Doctors, Social Workers)

FIGURE 11.2

A **social network diagram** illustrates the client's social system, including family, friends, and others.

These tests assess underlying, subconscious thought processes. They are typically administered and interpreted by clinical psychologists, but the results may be used by social workers as part of an in-depth psychodynamic assessment. See Case 11.2.

Case 11.1: Systems Assessment

Bob Borden, MSW, was assigned to work with Ann. At his agency, the Family Service Center of Toledo, the initial intake assessment is fairly detailed but general. After his first session with Ann, Bob decided that Ann's problems were systems related. She was isolated, had no friends, and was being verbally abused by her husband, John. John deliberately isolated Ann from others, thereby increasing the impact of his negative and intimidating verbal abuse.

Bob instructed Ann to draw her social network diagram as a precursor to developing her social support system. Ann's limited diagram consisted of her two children, Jenny and Jimmy, as the only members of her inner-circle, family network. Her parents were deceased, and she had no siblings. Her husband John was placed outside of the diagram of the family portion, indicating a very distant attachment. Ann listed two friends in the second circle of the "friends" portion of the diagram. These were both neighbors who lived next door and who were aware of Ann's relationship with John. Ann also included Bob in her "other" portion, along with a clergyman who was supportive.

After drawing the diagram, Bob and Ann discussed the fact that she was obviously very isolated. Ann astutely pointed out the fact that she had no friends or relatives available to counteract the effects of John's verbal abuse.

"I know he's just being mean, and he's wrong about me. But he's the only person I ever talk to, so sometimes he makes me believe I really am as bad and stupid as he says," said Ann.

Case 11.2: Psychodynamic Assessment

Jill Johnson, MSW, a social worker with the Counseling Center of Greater San Diego, was assigned to see Ann. After conducting a fairly detailed assessment using the agency's standard format, Jill decided to conduct a more detailed psychodynamic assessment as well. Ann was asked to talk more about her childhood, early experiences, and, particularly, her father. Ann described a history of being criticized by her father, who was a depressed alcoholic. Ann believed that her father loved her and was critical of her because: "He just wanted me to do the best I could. I was never very pretty or smart and he just wanted to protect me from being hurt and disappointed, so he told me to settle for whatever I could get in life."

Ann had two long-term relationships with men before marrying John. Both men were "heavy drinkers," and one was arrested after he physically assaulted Ann, putting her into the hospital for 5 days. At the hospital, a social worker spoke daily with Ann and finally convinced her to file charges against her assailant. The relationship ended when her boyfriend went to jail. Ann said that the hospital social worker told her that Ann should talk to people at the Counseling Center.

Although Ann thought that she was "just talking," Jill probed in depth Ann's self-esteem, sexual history, peer relationships, patterns of relationships with men, and subconscious motivators. Jill even asked Ann to complete various sentences. For instance, Ann was instructed to finish the following sentences without dwelling upon her answers: "When I think about my husband/father, I feel . . ." Or, "When I look in the mirror, I see . . ." Or, "When John calls me names, I'd like to . . . ."

Jill also asked Ann to "play a game" in which Jill said a word and Ann quickly responded with a word that Ann associated with it. They began with "dog" and "house" but eventually associated the words "husband," "children," "good," and "bad."

Behavioral Assessments

A behavioral assessment includes additional data relevant to clear, observable behaviors of the client. Behaviors that can be counted, graphed, or measured are often included in behavioral assessments. Specific and discrete behaviors such as the frequency of eating, weight gain or loss, sleeping, smoking, drinking alcohol, inappropriate sexual acts, violent behavior such as hitting or fights, or various other clear behaviors are all appropriate.

Client problems can be measured in four ways: problem existence, problem magnitude, problem duration, and frequency (Blythe & Tripodi, 1989). For instance, "verbal abuse" is a nominal variable that either exists or does not. Its magnitude can be scaled on a 5-point scale ranging from 1, for *not at all*, to a 5, for *very often*. The problem duration may be "since age 7" or "last 4 months." The frequency can refer to the number of times that the abuse

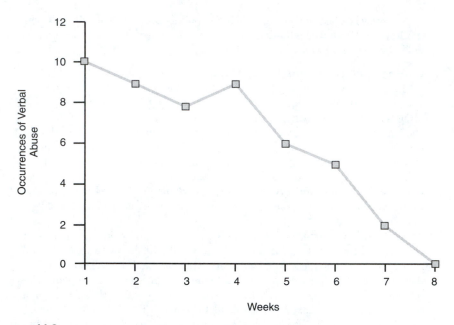

Occurrences of Verbal Abuse / Weeks

FIGURE **11.3**

A behavioral assessment graph can indicate the frequency of a specific behavior.

happens in a specified time frame, such as weekly. A distinct advantage of such a high degree of specificity is that the clinician can accurately assess the effectiveness of the intervention and include a graph of the behavior (see Figure 11.3) and its treatment. A couple is instructed to document each incident. Then they respond in a behaviorally appropriate manner (e.g., the abused spouse tells the partner that the abuse has occurred and is unacceptable) and document it. Over several weeks, the frequency of abuse typically diminishes. See Case 11.3.

Case 11.3: Behavioral Assessment

Ann was referred to the Behavioral Clinic by a police officer who was called to Ann's home by her next-door neighbors during a loud verbal assault from John. Nancy Griffin, MSW, conducted a standard intake assessment and decided to immediately begin collecting a baseline of verbally assaultive behaviors. Nancy initially struggled with the ethics of taking the additional time to collect a baseline of this behavior. However, her supervisor stated that this behavior had been going on for so long and was such an intimate aspect of Ann's history that a thorough and detailed baseline assessment would be essential to ultimately modify this pattern of behavior.

After Ann and Nancy agreed upon a clear, behavioral definition of a "verbal assault," Ann wrote a log that tracked the frequency of the occurrences along with the time, place, antecedent events, and her responses. She was instructed to act the same as she had in the past for a period of 4 weeks. Ann recorded the baseline. There were ten occurrences in the first week, nine in the second, eight in the third, and nine in the fourth. In the fifth week, Ann was instructed to loudly and clearly tell John the following after any verbal assaults: "This is an instance of verbal assault. It is inappropriate and will not be tolerated at any time." The frequency diminished to six instances in the fifth week, five occurrences in the sixth week, and two instances in the seventh week; the behavior was completely extinguished by the eighth week.

Cognitive Assessments

A clinical social worker using a cognitive approach with a client will need additional, cognitively relevant assessment information. The three-column instrument described in Chapter 9 is a helpful cognitively based assessment tool. The Beck Institute also typically suggests a cognitive conceptualization diagram developed by Judith Beck (1995). Essentially, any cognitive assessment includes a statement describing the client's core belief or the cognitive distortion (e.g., "I am stupid") and related assumptions or beliefs. The assessment also includes past responses or compensatory strategies that did *not* work, as well as constructive, alternative responses. See Case 11.4.

The specific format may vary, but basically, a cognitive assessment includes a description of a typical past problem situation, the related automatic thought, the meaning of the automatic thought, the emotion, and the behavior. For instance:

Situation 1. A professor is told that the dean is coming to observe her in the classroom.

Automatic thought: She'll probably think I'm a terrible teacher.

Meaning of automatic thought: I'm incompetent.

Emotion: Anxious.

Behavior: Wastes a great deal of time over-preparing.

Situation 2. Another professor looks angry and ignores the client at work.

Automatic thought: That professor hates me and thinks I'm unable to do this job.

Meaning of automatic thought: Other professors hate me and think I can't do my job.

Emotion: Sad.

Behavior: Gets drunk and angrily calls the dean at home.

Case 11.4: Cognitive Assessment

Ann called the outpatient unit of the Johnstown Hospital after a crisis with John. The crisis worker listened to Ann on the telephone, then assured her that she could be helped. The same worker agreed to see Ann on an emergency basis the next day. After Ann completed several forms, she was relieved to finally meet the supportive social worker she had spoken to on the phone the previous evening. Betty Antonelli, MSW, initially asked Ann about suicide but was assured by Ann that: "I love my children too much to leave them alone with John."

Although Betty's style was obviously caring and supportive, Betty also challenged Ann when Ann defended John's behavior or suggested that perhaps Ann deserved to be treated in an abusive manner. In the second session, Betty asked Ann to describe the assaultive situations, Ann's "automatic thoughts" (A.T.), what those thoughts meant to Ann, her emotions or feelings at the time, and her behavior after the occurrences. She even asked Ann if she had any physical reactions such as sweating. Betty explained that Ann's thoughts have an effect on the way Ann feels emotionally. These thoughts and emotions influence attitudes and behaviors. Ann left the second session with a copy of the following document, which Betty referred to as a *cognitive assessment*.

> Situation: John calls me a lazy, ugly, slob.
> Automatic thought: John is right. I am unable to do anything and I am unattractive and a mess.
> Meaning of A.T.: I'm incompetent and ugly.
> Emotion: Hopeless and sad.
> Behavior: I go to bed and cry.

TREATMENT PLANS

A treatment plan is a written document that includes clear descriptions of the problem or behavior to be addressed, relevant goals and objectives, and a plan for intervention. One widely used text by Jongsma and Peterson (1999) describes six steps in the process of developing a treatment plan. These steps are problem selection, problem definition, goal development, objective construction, intervention creation, and diagnosis determination. That text also includes a list of 39 frequently addressed problems with relevant plans described for each problem.

A broad, basic, general treatment plan that would be acceptable within most agencies that rely upon clinical social workers would minimally contain four steps: define the problems or target behaviors, develop goals, develop objectives, and describe the intervention.

Define the Problem

Problems or target behaviors must be clear, concise, limited in number, and workable. Vague or abstract concepts or concerns are not acceptable as problem statements. Contemporary treatment plans are typically designed or structured to allow for a wide range of interventionist methods. With notable exceptions, funding sources do not dictate the specific method to be used. Instead, treatment plans only require consistency and appropriateness of method. The exceptions include clinics that serve specific disorders (e.g., an eating disorder clinic or a program for clients with obsessive-compulsive disorders) or institutes where the method is a part of the agency's identity, such as psychoanalytic institutes or behavioral programs.

A partial list of the selected problems defined by Jongsma and Peterson (1999) includes: anger management, anxiety, attention-deficit hyperactivity disorder (AD/HD), borderline personality, childhood traumas, chemical dependence, depression, eating disorders, family conflict, grief/loss unresolved, impulse control disorder, low self-esteem, mania or hypomania, paranoid ideation, sexual abuse, and somatization. Many agencies develop their own lists based upon reviews of past caseloads. Often, social workers are simply instructed to be clear, concise, and behavioral in defining problem statements. *DSM-IV-TR* (2000) diagnoses are not the same as problem statements. Since diagnoses tend to be insufficiently behavioral and lack sufficient interrater reliability, most programs prefer behaviorally precise problem statements. However, problem statements and diagnoses are frequently related or overlap, and the Jongsma and Peterson treatment planner includes an index that lists *DSM-IV* diagnoses and frequently associated presenting problems.

Most treatment plans require more than a simple one- or two-word problem statement. Treatment plans usually ask for descriptions or behavioral definitions of the problem. Therefore, in addition to specifying "depression" as the problem, the first part of the treatment plan must also include a behavioral description of the specific problem as it relates to the client. Behavioral definitions might include sleeplessness, social isolation, loss of energy, suicidal ideation, poor self-esteem, hopelessness, or diminished appetite. The problem statement of post-traumatic stress disorder (PTSD) would include behavioral definitions such as nightmares associated with the traumatic event; avoidance of people, places, and objects associated with the trauma; unwanted and obtrusive thoughts that recall the event; inability to concentrate; a sense of detachment; flashbacks; and a fatalistic attitude regarding the future (Jongsma & Peterson, 1999).

In the remainder of this section, depression and post-traumatic stress disorder are used as the defined problems. Appropriate goals, objectives, and interventions are described for both using psychodynamic, cognitive, behavioral, and systems-based approaches.

Develop Goals

Goal statements may be broad, global, and relatively long-term. They do not need to be behaviorally specific, but they do need to describe a desired outcome that will result from treatment. The social worker may develop several goal statements for each problem, although most treatment plans require only one.

Goal statements for the problem of depression for an isolated or angry client could be: "Develop an awareness of the need for a social support system of friends," or "Recognize anger and its effects on self." Goal statements for a problem of post-traumatic stress disorder could be: "Remember and recall the event without becoming overwhelmed with rage," or "Return to the lifestyle and functioning that existed before the trauma."

Define Objectives

Objectives must be clear and specific. In addition to guiding the treatment intervention process, these specific objectives also serve to let the social worker know when the treatment is successfully completed. Objectives are stages in the process of ultimately achieving goals. Most treatment plans suggest two or more objectives for each problem. Anticipated dates for the achievement of objectives should be included, and new objectives can be added as previous objectives are achieved.

Objectives are short-term and are revised and updated during the course of treatment. Examples of objectives for a depressed, angry client could be method-specific. For instance, a psychodynamically oriented clinician may state as an objective: "Describe the underlying sources of the anger/depression," or "Verbalize the association between the feelings of depression and the anger." A cognitively oriented clinician may prefer: "Replace negative automatic thoughts with positive, alternative responses," or "Identify negative thoughts, emotions, or behaviors that support the depression/anger," or "Keep a daily log of negative distortions."

A behaviorally oriented social worker may prefer: "Engage in sports/recreation that increase energy," or "Use anger-management techniques to resolve conflicts." A systems-oriented social worker may choose to use the following objectives: "Increase the frequency of interaction with family/friends," or "Connect with socially/psychologically supportive team sports members/self-help groups."

The worker dealing with a client with PTSD may choose several general objectives, such as: "Clearly describe the initially traumatic event in detail," or "Describe how PTSD has had an impact upon social/psychological/vocational efforts." A psychodynamically oriented social worker may specify: "Sleep without nightmares related to the trauma," or "Verbalize the connection between the trauma and subsequent disassociative feelings."

A cognitively oriented social worker may recommend: "Describe current automatic thoughts that support the anger," or "Develop alternative thoughts, feelings, or behaviors to replace current negative thoughts, feelings, and behaviors." Behaviorally oriented short-term objectives may include: "Interact socially with individuals associated with the initial trauma without stress," or "Verbalize increased comfort while talking about the trauma."

Describe the Intervention

Treatment plans require clear statements describing the treatment intervention or action taken by the social worker. The intervention flows logically from the related objectives. Each objective has one or more interventions. A wide variety of contemporary interventions may be used, but each technique and therapeutic action must further the purpose of achieving the related objective. Cognitive, behavioral, psychodynamic, and systems-based interventions are all acceptable as long as the model is applied appropriately and in a fashion that will meet the objective. Group and family interventions are included in this section of the plan, although this often requires referrals and team efforts.

In the previous three steps of the described treatment plan, the examples of depression and post-traumatic stress disorder were used. Both of these problem statements included behavioral descriptors of symptoms or behaviors. For both problems, related goals and objectives were also described using psychodynamic, cognitive, behavioral, and systems-based options. In Case 11.5, the three previous steps are briefly incorporated into an outline that demonstrates that logical flow. The treatment plan example also demonstrates the use of the various advanced methods applied in contemporary clinical social work.

> **Case 11.5: Treatment Plan for Depression**
> Step 1. Problem: Depression
> > Behavioral descriptors (symptoms): Anger, sleeplessness, social isolation, loss of energy, hopelessness, suicidal ideation, poor self-esteem, and diminished appetite.
> Step 2. Goal: Develop an awareness of the need for a social support system of friends.
> Step 3. Objectives: Verbalize the association between the feelings of depression and the anger. Keep a log of negative distortions.
> Step 4. Interventions: Probe client to discuss past experiences in which she was very sad and the origins of the related anger. Instruct her in the development of a three-column log that includes a brief description of depressing events; her automatic, distorted thought; and possible alternative responses.

Case 11.5 describes the use of psychodynamic and cognitive methods in a treatment plan for depression. In Case 11.6, the clinician uses behavioral and systems methods to treat the problem of PTSD.

> **Case 11.6: Treatment Plan for Post-Traumatic Stress Disorder**
> Step 1. Problem: Post-traumatic stress disorder.
> > Behavioral descriptors (symptoms): Nightmares associated with the traumatic event; avoidance of people, places, and objects related to the event; unwanted and obtrusive thoughts that recall the event; inability to concentrate; a sense of detachment; flashbacks; and a fatalistic attitude regarding the future.
> Step 2. Goals: Return to the lifestyle and functioning that existed before the trauma.

Step 3. Objectives: Engage in sports/recreation. Connect with friends.

Step 4. Interventions: Have client call two members from the soccer club. Have client draw a social network diagram for 2 months ago before the trauma during a soccer game and another diagram of the current, isolated network.

In Case 11.6, the client was severely injured during a soccer game and subsequently became depressed and isolated. The clinical social worker decided to focus behaviorally on the avoidance of people. The clinician's objectives included engaging in sports and connecting with friends. These objectives are consistent with both behavioral and systems methods. Behaviorally, the objective was accomplished in incremental stages and interventions. The clinician instructed the client to call two former, close friends from the team. Later, the objective was modified to rejoin the team. The systems perspective utilized the same objective as the behavioral method. The objective for both methods includes getting the client to reengage in sports activities with her former network of friends.

Treatment plans vary considerably due to the wide range of client problems, agency or programmatic purposes, clinician training, and the requirements of funding sources. Every agency and every social work program design case records that include assessments and treatment plans that attempt to meet the multifaceted and idiosyncratic needs of their own programs. Contemporary clinical social workers are encouraged to appropriately use clear and concise documentation in case records to guide and inform treatment.

SUMMARY

The documentation of practice in clinical social work is an important and necessary skill. Reimbursement for services is based upon accurate, concise, and appropriate recording. Documentation also supports effectiveness and efficiency in the treatment intervention process and allows appropriate case monitoring to take place.

Assessments include a variety of facts and data relevant to the client's presenting problem, as well as his or her biopsychosocial history. General assessments include demographic data and the history of health and mental health issues for the client and the client's family. Assessment requirements vary due to the differential needs and purposes of programs. Psychiatric clinics and mental health programs focus upon defining symptoms related to diagnoses, whereas child welfare agencies are more likely to assess family dynamics and the peer relationships, socialization skills, and academic performance of the children in the family.

Assessments are further differentiated by the method-specific needs of the approach. The theories regarding the causes of biopsychosocial concerns vary by method. The theoretical bases of systems, psychodynamic, behavioral, and cognitive approaches all suggest different causes for problems and behavioral concerns that are seen. Each approach draws upon its specific theoretical base to define the assessment needs. Systems assessments often include ecomaps, genograms, or social network diagrams. Psychodynamic assessments include detailed histories of early childhood experiences and facts relevant to personality development. Occasionally, psychodynamic assessments utilize one of the projective measures that delve into subconscious dynamics, such as the Rorschach, the MMPI, the TAT, or basic word association or sentence completion methods. Behavioral assessments often include graphs or charts that measure the magnitude, duration, or frequency of specific behaviors. Cognitive assessments typically construct diagrams or records that indicate the interconnection of client thoughts or cognitions, attitudes or emotions, and behaviors. These assessments therefore include sequential statements that connect specific problem situations to related automatic thoughts, the meaning of those thoughts, the related emotions, and the behavioral responses.

Treatment plans are written documents that include clear descriptions of the presenting problem or behavior along with related goals, objectives, and intervention plans. The structures and formats vary to meet the specific needs of the agency, the clients, the clinicians, and funding sources. Some programs rely upon predefined lists from treatment planners (Jongsma & Peterson, 1999), whereas others develop their own lists of problems or behaviors that are frequently encountered in their agencies.

After stating the problem, treatment plans also include additional behaviorally specific descriptors or symptoms of that issue or problem in addition to relevant strengths and resources. Goals are stipulated that may be broad or global; but the objectives must be clear, specific, and directly related to the problem descriptors and symptoms. The intervention flows from the objective, and each objective has one or more interventions.

Treatment plans may reflect different treatment methods, and a mix or blend of approaches is acceptable in contemporary practice. However, coherence and consistency are essential in the plan's flow from the defined problem to the goals, objectives, and subsequent intervention.

References

Allen-Meares, P. (1987). Grounding social work practice in theory: Ecosystems. *Journal of Education for Social Work, 89,* 515–521.

American Psychiatric Association. (1994). *Diagnostic and statistical manual of mental disorders* (4th ed.). Washington, DC: Author.

American Psychiatric Association. (2000). *Diagnostic and statistical manual of mental disorders* (4th ed, text revision). Washington, DC: Author.

Andreae, D. (1996). Systems theory and social work treatment. In F. Turner (Ed.), *Social work treatment: Interlocking theoretical approaches* (4th ed., pp. 601–616). New York: Free Press.

Arkowitz, H., & Hannah, M. T. (1989). Cognitive, behavioral, and psychodynamic therapies: Converging or diverging pathways to change? In A. Freeman, K. M. Simon, L. E. Beutler, & H. Arkowitz (Eds.), *Comprehensive handbook of cognitive therapy.* New York: Plenum.

Aronson, J. A. (1996). *Inside managed care: Family therapy in a changing environment.* New York: Brunner/Mazel.

Austad, C. S. (1996). *Is long-term psychotherapy unethical? Toward a social ethic in an era of managed care.* San Francisco: Jossey-Bass.

Austin, D. (1992). Findings of the NIMH task force on social work research. *Social Work Practice, 2,* 311–322.

Austin, D. (1997). The profession of social work: In the second century. In M. Reisch & E. D. Gambrill (Eds.), *Social work in the 21st century* (pp. 396–407). Thousand Oaks, CA: Pine Forge Press.

Baars, B. J. (1986). *The cognitive revolution in psychology.* New York: Guilford Press.

Barbior, S., & Goldman, C. (1990). *Overcoming panic attacks: Strategies to free yourself from the anxiety trap.* Minneapolis: CompCare.

Barker, R. L. (1995). *Social work dictionary* (3rd ed.). Washington, DC: NASW Press.

Barlow, D. J., Hayes, S. C., & Nelson, R. O. (1984). *The scientist practitioner: Research and accountability in clinical and education settings.* New York: Pergamon.

Baucom, D. H., & Epstein, N. (1990). Cognitive-behavioral marital therapy. New York: Brunner/Mazel.

Baum, M., & Twiss, P. (Eds.). (1996). *Social work intervention in an economic crisis: The River Communities Project.* New York: Haworth Press.

Beck, A. T. (1976). *Cognitive therapy and the emotional disorders.* New York: International Universities Press.

Beck, A. T. (1996). *Depression: Causes and treatments.* Philadelphia: University of Pennsylvania Press.

Beck, A. T., Rush, A. J., Shaw, B. F., & Emery, G. (1979). *Cognitive therapy of depression.* New York: Guilford Press.

Beck, J. S. (1995). *Cognitive theory: Basics and beyond.* New York: Guilford Press.

Beitman, B. D., Goldfried, M. R., & Norcross, J. E. (1989). The movement toward integrating the psychotherapies: An overview. *American Journal of Psychiatry, 146,* 136–147.

Belcher, J. R. (1992). Poverty, homelessness, and racial exclusion. *Sociology and Social Welfare, 19,* 41–54.

Belcher, J. R., DeForge, B. R., Thompson, J. W., & Myers, C. P. (1995). Psychiatric hospital care and changes in insurance coverage strategies: A national study. *The Journal of Mental Health Administration, 22,* 377–387.

Benson, H. (1975). *The relaxation response.* New York: Morrow.

Benson, H. (1985). *Beyond the relaxation response: How to harness the healing power of your personal beliefs.* New York: Berkley Books.

Bentley, K. J., & Walsh, J. (1996). *The social worker and psychotropic medication: Toward effective collaboration with mental health clients, families, and providers.* Pacific Grove, CA: Brooks/Cole.

Bentley, K. J., & Walsh, J. F. (2001). *The social worker and psychotropic medication: Toward effective collaboration with mental health clients, families, and providers* (2nd ed.). Pacific Grove, CA: Brooks/Cole.

Bergin, A. E. (1980). Psychotherapy and religious values. *Journal of Counseling and Clinical Psychology, 48,* 95–106.

Bergin, A. E., & Garfield, S. L. (Eds.). (1994a). *Handbook of psychotherapy and behavior change* (4th ed.). New York: John Wiley & Sons.

Bergin, A. E., & Garfield, S. L. (1994b). Overview, trends, and future issues. In A. E. Bergin & S. L. Garfield (Eds.), *Handbook of psychotherapy and behavior change* (4th ed., pp. 821–830). New York: John Wiley & Sons.

Beutler, L. E., & Clark, J. (1990). *Systematic treatment selection: Toward targeted therapeutic interventions.* New York: Brunner/Mazel.

Beutler, L. E., Crago, M., & Arizmendi, T. G. (1986). Therapist variables in psychotherapy process and outcome. In S. L. Garfield & A. Bergin (Eds.), *Handbook of psychotherapy and behavior change* (3rd ed., pp. 257–310). New York: John Wiley & Sons.

Biegel, D. E., McCardle, E., & Mendelson, S. (1985). *Social networks and mental health: An annotated bibliography.* Beverly Hills: Sage.

Bloom, B. L. (1997). *Planned short-term psychotherapy: A clinical handbook* (2nd ed.). Needham Heights, MA: Allyn & Bacon.

Blythe, B. J., & Tripodi, T. (1989). *Measurement in direct social work practice.* Newbury Park, CA: Sage.

Borman, L. (1979, June). *New self-help and support systems for the chronically mentally ill.* Paper presented at the Pittsburgh Conference on Neighborhood Support Systems, Pittsburgh, PA.

Boscolo, L., Cecchin, G., Hoffman, L., & Penn P. (1987). *Milan systemic family therapy: Conversations in theory and practice.* New York: Basic Books.

Bourne, E. J. (1990). *The anxiety and phobia workbook.* Oakland, CA: New Harbinger.

Brandell, J. R. (Ed.). (1997). *Theory and practice in clinical social work.* New York: Free Press.

Brandell, J. R., & Perlman, F. (1997). Psychoanalytic theory. In J. R. Brandell (Ed.), *Theory and practice in clinical social work* (pp. 38–80). New York: Free Press.

Brenner, H. (1984, June). *Estimating the effects of economic change on national health and social well-being.* Testimony before the Joint Economic Committee of Congress. Washington, DC: U.S. Government Printing Office.

Breuer, J., & Freud, S. (1955). Studies on hysteria. In *Standard edition of the complete works of Sigmund Freud* (Vol. 2, pp. 1–305). London: Hogarth Press. (Original work published 1895)

Brieland, D., Costin, L. B., & Atherton, C. R. (1985). *Contemporary social work: An introduction to social work and social welfare* (3rd ed.). New York: McGraw-Hill.

Bromley, D. B. (1986). *The case study method in psychology and related disciplines.* New York: Wiley.

Budman, S. H., Hoyt, M. F., & Friedman, S. (Eds.). (1992). *The first session in brief therapy.* New York: Guilford Press.

Burns, D. D. (1980). *Feeling good: The new mood therapy.* New York: New American Library.

Bush, J. A., Norton, D. G., Sanders, C. L., & Solomon, B. B. (1983). An integrative approach for the inclusion of content on blacks in social work education. In J. C. Chun, P. J. Dunston, & F. Ross-Sheriff (Eds.), *Mental health and people of color: Curriculum development and change* (pp. 97–125). Washington, DC: Howard University Press.

Campbell, A., Converse, D. E., & Rogers, W. L. (1976). *The quality of American life: SSA edition.* Ann Arbor, MI: Institute for Social Research.

Campbell, J., Elder, J., Gallagher, D., Simon, J., & Taylor, A. (1999). Crafting the "tap on the shoulder": Compliment template for solution-focused therapy. *American Journal of Family Therapy, 27*(1), 35–47.

Caplan, G. (1964). *Principles of preventive psychiatry.* New York: Basic Books.

Caplan, G. (1974). *Support systems and community mental health: Lectures on concept development.* New York: Behavioral Publications.

Chang, T., Hung, H., & Yeh, R. (1999). Theoretical framework for therapy with Asian families. In American Counseling Association, *Counseling Asian families from a systems perspective: The family psychology and counseling series* (pp. 3–13). Alexandria, VA: American Counseling Association.

Cheetham, J. (1992). Evaluating social work effectiveness. *Social Work, 2,* 265–287.

Chestang, L. (1972). Character development in a hostile society. (Occasional paper number 3). School of Social Service Administration, University of Chicago, Chicago.

Cohen, I., & Steketee, G. (1998). Obsessive-compulsive disorder. In B. A. Thyer & J. S. Wodarski (Eds.), *Handbook of empirical social work practice: Vol. 1: Mental Disorders* (pp. 343–364). New York: John Wiley & Sons.

Corcoran, K. (Ed.). (1992). *Structuring change and effective practice for common client problems.* Chicago: Lyceum Books.

Corcoran, K., & Fischer, J. (1987). *Measures for clinical practice: A sourcebook.* New York: Free Press.

Corcoran, K., & Fischer, J. (2000). *Measures for clinical practice: A sourcebook* (3rd ed). New York: Free Press.

Corcoran, K., & Videka-Sherman, L. (1992). Some things we know about effective clinical social work. In K. Corcoran (Ed.), *Structuring change: Effective practice for common client problems* (pp. 15–27). Chicago: Lyceum Books.

Corsini, R., & Rosenberg, N. (1955). Mechanisms of group psychotherapy: Processes and dynamics. *Journal of Abnormal Social Psychology, 51,* 406–411.

Coulton, C. J. (1995). Research for initiatives in low-income communities. In P. M. Hess & E. J. Mullen (Eds.), *Practitioner researcher partnerships: Building knowledge from, in, and for practice* (pp. 103–121). Washington, DC: NASW Press.

Council on Social Work Education (CSWE). (2001). *Educational policy and accreditation standards.* Alexandria, VA: Author.

Dattilio, F. M., & Freeman, A. M. (Eds.). (1994). *Cognitive-behavioral strategies in crisis intervention.* New York: Guilford Press.

Davanloo, H. (Ed.). (1992). *Short-term dynamic psychotherapy.* Norvale, NJ: Jason Aronson.

Daws, D. (1999). Parent-infant psychotherapy: Remembering the Oedipus complex. *Psychoanalytic Inquiry, 19* (2), 267–278.

Dean, A., & Linn, N. (1977). The stress buffering role of social support: Problems and prospects for systematic investigation. *Journal of Nervous and Mental Disease, 165,* 403–417.

Dean, R. G. (1993). Constructivism: An approach to clinical practice. *Smith College Studies in Social Work, 63* (2), 127–146.

De Shazer, S. (1988). *Clues: Investigating solutions in brief therapy.* New York: W. W. Norton.

Dulmus, C. N., & Wodarski, J. S. (1998). Major depressive disorder and dysthymic disorder. In B. A. Thyer & J. S. Wodarski (Eds.), *Handbook of empirical social work practice: Vol. 1: Mental disorders* (pp. 273–285). New York: John Wiley & Sons.

D'Zurilla, T. J., & Goldfried, M. R. (1971). Problem solving and behavior modification. *Journal of Abnormal Psychology, 78,* 107–126.

Edwards, J. T. (1997). *Working with families: Guidelines and techniques* (4th ed.). Durham, NC: Foundation Place.

Ehlers, C. L., Frank, E., & Kupfer, D. J. (1988). Social zeitgebers and biological rhythms: A unified approach to understanding the etiology of depression. *Archives of General Psychiatry, 45,* 948–952.

Ell, K. (1995). Crisis intervention: Research needs. In R. L. Edwards (Ed.), *Encyclopedia of social work* (19th ed., Vol. 1, pp. 660–667). Washington, DC: NASW Press.

Ell, K. (1996). Crisis theory and social work practice. In F. J. Turner (Ed.), *Social work treatment: Interlocking theoretical approaches* (4th ed., pp. 168–190). New York: Free Press.

Ellis, A. (1973). *Humanistic psychotherapy: The rational-emotive approach.* New York: McGraw-Hill.

Ellis, A. (1977). The basic clinical theory of rational-emotive therapy. In A. Ellis & R. Grieger (Eds.), *Handbook of rational-emotive therapy.* New York: Springer.

Ellis, A., & Dryden, W. (1987). *The practice of rational-emotive therapy.* New York: Springer.

Epstein, L. (1992). *Brief treatment and a new look at the task-centered approach* (3rd ed.). New York: Macmillan.

Erikson, E. H. (1963). *Childhood and society* (2nd ed.). New York: W. W. Norton & Company.

Eysenck, H. J. (1952). The effects of psychotherapy: An evaluation. *Journal of Consulting Psychology, 16,* 319–324.

Eysenck, H. J. (Ed.). (1960). *Behavior therapy and the neuroses: Readings in modern methods of treatment derived from learning theory.* New York: Pergamon Press.

Feit, M. D., Cuevas, N. M., & Hann-Dowdy, C. A. (1998). The impact of race in social work practice. In J. S. Wodarski & B. A. Thyer (Eds.), *Handbook of empirical social work practice, Vol. 2: Social problems and practice issues* (pp. 241–260). New York: John Wiley & Sons.

Ferenczi, S., Rank, O., & Newton, C. (1925). *The development of psychoanalysis.* New York: Nervous and Mental Disease.

Festinger, L. (1957). *A theory of cognitive dissonance.* Stanford, CA: Stanford University Press.

Fischer, J. (1973). Is casework effective? A review. *Social Work, 18,* 5–20.

Fischer, J. (1976). *The effectiveness of social casework.* Springfield, IL: Charles C. Thomas.

Fischer, J. (1978). *Effective casework practice: An eclectic approach.* New York: McGraw-Hill.

Franklin, C., & Jordan, C. (1999). *Family practice: Brief systems methods for social work.* Pacific Grove, CA: Brooks/Cole.

Franklin, C., & Nurius, P. (1996). Editorial notes: Constructivist therapy: New directions in social work practice. *Journal of Contemporary Human Services, 77,* 323–325.

Freud, A. (1936). *The ego and the mechanisms of defense.* New York: International Universities Press.

Freud, S. (1938a). Psychopathology of everyday life. From A. A. Brill (Ed.), *The basic writings of Sigmund Freud* (pp. 35–180). New York: Random House.

Freud, S. (1938b). The interpretation of dreams. From A. A. Brill (Ed.), *The basic writings of Sigmund Freud* (pp. 181–549). New York: Random House.

Friedman, B. D. (1997). Systems theory. In J. R. Brandell (Ed.), *Theory and practice in clinical social work* (pp. 3–17). New York: Free Press.

Friedman, S. (1997). *Time-effective psychotherapy: Maximizing outcomes in an era of minimized resources.* Boston: Allyn & Bacon.

Gambrill, E. D. (1990). *Critical thinking in clinical practice: Improving the accuracy of judgments and decisions about clients.* San Francisco: Jossey-Bass.

GAO. (1992). *Social security: Racial differences in disability decisions warrants further investigation, report to the ranking minority member, special committee on aging* (U.S. Senate GAO/HRD Publication No. 92-56). Washington, DC: U. S. General Accounting Office.

Garfield, S. L. (1989). *Practice of brief psychotherapy.* New York: Pergamon Press.

Garfield, S. L., & Bergin, A. E. (1986). *Handbook of psychotherapy and behavior change* (3rd ed.). Research, NY: Wiley.

Garland, J. A., Jones, H., & Kilodny, R. (1965). A model for stages of development in social work groups. In L. A. Frey & S. Bernstein (Eds.), *Explorations in group work* (pp. 12–53). Boston: Boston University School of Social Work.

Gerhart, U. C. (1990). *Caring for the chronically mentally ill.* Itasca, IL: F. E. Peacock.

Germain, C. (1970). Casework and science: A historical encounter. In R. W. Roberts & R. H. Nee (Eds.), *Theories of social casework.* Chicago: University of Chicago Press.

Germain, C. (1991). *Human behavior in the social environment: An ecological view.* New York: Columbia University Press.

Germain, C., & Gitterman, A. (1980). *The life model of social work practice.* New York: Columbia University Press.

Germain, C., & Gitterman, A. (1996). *The life model of social work practice: Advances in theory and practice* (2nd ed.). New York: Columbia University Press.

Ginsberg, L. H. (1995). *Social work almanac* (2nd ed.). Washington, DC: NASW Press.

Gitterman, A. (1996). Life model theory and social work practice. In F. J. Turner (Ed.), *Social work treatment: Interlocking theoretical approaches* (4th ed., pp. 389–408). New York: Free Press.

Gore, S. (1978). The effect of social support in moderating the health consequences of unemployment. *Journal of Health and Social Behavior, 19,* 157–165.

Gore, S. (1981). Stress buffering functions of social support: An appraisal and clarification of research models. In B. S. Dowrenwend & B. P. Dowrenwend (Eds.), *Stressful life events and their contexts.* New York: Wiley.

Granvold, D. K. (1994). Concepts and methods of cognitive treatment. In D. K. Granvold (Ed.), *Cognitive and behavioral treatment: Methods and applications.* (pp. 3–33). Pacific Grove, CA: Brooks/Cole.

Granvold, D. K. (1996). Constructivist psychotherapy. *Journal of Contemporary Human Services, 77,* 345–359.

Greene, R. R. (1991). General systems theory. In R. R. Greene & P. H. Ephross, *Human behavior theory and social work practice* (pp. 227–259). New York: Aldine De Gruyter.

Greene, R. R., & Ephros, P. H. (1991). *Human behavior theory and social work practice.* New York: Aldine De Gruyter.

Gross, M. L. (1978). *The psychological society.* New York: Random House.

Grotjahn, M. (1977). *Art and technique of analytic group therapy.* New York: J. Aronson.

Guidano, V. F., & Liotti, G. (1983). *Cognitive processes and emotional disorders: A structured approach to psychotherapy.* New York: Guilford Press.

Gurin, G. J., Veroff, J., & Feld, S. (1960). *Americans view their mental health.* New York: Basic Books.

Haley, J. (Ed.) (1976) *Problem-solving therapy.* San Francisco: Jossey-Bass.

Hanna, S. M., & Brown, J. H. (1995). *The practice of family therapy: Key elements across models*. Pacific Grove, CA: Brooks/Cole.

Hartman, A. (1978). Diagrammatic assessment of family relationships. *Social Casework, 59,* 465–476.

Hartman, A. (1979). The extended family as a resource for change: An ecological approach to family centered practice. In C. Germain (Ed.), *Social work practice: People and environments*. New York: Columbia University Press.

Hartman, A. (1991). Words create worlds. *Social Work, 36,* 275–276.

Hartman, A., & Laird, J. (1983). *Family centered social work practice*. New York: Free Press.

Hearn, G. (1958). *Theory building in social work*. Toronto: University of Toronto Press.

Hearn, G. (1969). *The general systems approach: Contributions toward a holistic conception of social work*. New York: CSWE.

Hearn, G. (1979). General systems theory and social work. In F. J. Turner (Ed.), *Social work treatment: Interlocking theoretical approaches* (2nd ed., pp. 333–359). New York: Free Press.

Henry, S. (1992). *Group skills in social work: A four dimensional approach* (2nd ed.). Pacific Grove, CA: Brooks/Cole.

Hepworth, D. H., & Larsen, J. A. (1993). *Direct social work practice: Theory and skills* (4th ed.). Pacific Grove, CA: Brooks/Cole.

Hill, C. E. (1989). *Therapist techniques and client outcomes: Eight cases of brief psychotherapy*. Newbury Park, CA: Sage.

Himle, J. A. , & Fischer, D. J. (1998). Panic disorder and agoraphobia. In B. A. Thyer & J. S. Wodarski (Eds.), *Handbook of empirical social work practice, Vol. 1: Mental disorders* (pp. 311–326). New York: John Wiley & Sons.

Hirshfeld, R. M. A., & Davidson, L. Risk factors for suicide. In A. J. Frances & R. Hales (Eds.), *Review of psychiatry, 7*. Americ an Psychiatric Press.

Hollis, F. (1964). *Casework: A psychosocial therapy*. New York: Random House.

Hoyt, M. F. (Ed.). (1995). *Brief therapy and managed care: Readings for contemporary practice*. San Francisco: Jossey-Bass.

Ilardi, S. S., & Craighead, W. E. (1994). The role of nonspecific factors in cognitive-behavior therapy for depression. *Clinical Psychology: Science and Practice, 1,* 138–156.

Ivanoff, A., Blythe, B. J., & Briar, S. (1987). The empirical clinical practice debate. *Social Casework, 68,* 290–298.

Jayaratne, S. (1978). A study of clinical eclecticism. *Social Service Review, 52,* 621–631.

Johnson, L. C. (1986). *Social work practice: A generalist approach* (2nd ed.). Needham Heights, MA: Allyn & Bacon.

Johnson, P. J., & Rubin, A. (1983). Case management in mental health: A social work domain? *Social Work, 28,* 49–55.

Joint Commission on Mental Illness and Health. (1961). *Action for mental health: Final report of the Joint Commission on Mental Illness and Health*. New York: John Wiley.

Jongsma, A. E., & Peterson, L. M. (1999). *The complete adult psychotherapy treatment planner* (2nd ed.). New York: John Wiley & Sons.

Kalter, N., Schaefer, M., Lesowitz, M., Alpern, P., & Kickar, J. (1988). School-based support groups for children of divorce: A model of brief intervention. In B. J. Gottlieb (Ed.), *Marshalling social support: Formats, processes, and effects* (pp. 165–186). Newbury Park, CA: Sage.

Karls, J. M., & Wandrei, K. E. (1994). *Person in environment system: The PIE classification system for social functioning problems.* Washington, DC: NASW Press.

Karls, J. M., & Wandrei, K. E. (1995). Person-in-environment. In *Encyclopedia of social work* (19th ed., pp. 1818–1828). Washington, DC: NASW Press.

Kazdin, A. E. (1986). Comparative outcome studies of psychotherapy: Methodological issues and strategies. *Journal of Consulting and Clinical Psychology, 54,* 95–105.

Kazdin, A., & Wilson, G. (1978). *Evaluation of behavioral therapy: Issues, evidence, and research strategies.* Cambridge, MA: Ballinger.

Kelly, G. A. (1955). *The psychology of personal constructs* (Vols. 1–2). New York: Norton.

Kendall, P. C., & Butcher, J. N. (Eds.). (1982). *Handbook of research methods in clinical psychology.* New York: John Wiley & Sons.

Kerr, M. E., & Bowen, M. (1988). *Family evaluation: An approach based on Brown's theory.* New York: Norton.

Kiesler, C. A., & Sibulkin, A. E. (1987). *Mental hospitalization: Myths and facts about a national crisis.* Newbury Park, CA: Sage.

Kirst-Ashman, K. K., & Hull, G. H. (1993). *Understanding generalist practice.* Chicago: Nelson-Hall.

Koss, M. P., & Butcher, J. N. (1986). Research on brief psychotherapy. In S. L. Garfield & A. E. Bergin (Eds.), *Handbook of psychotherapy and behavior change.* New York: Wiley.

Koss, M. P., & Shiang, J. (1994). Research on brief psychotherapy. In A. E. Bergin & S. L. Garfield (Eds.), *Handbook of psychotherapy and behavior change* (pp. 664–700). New York: J. Wiley.

Kramer, P. D. (1993). *Listening to Prozac: A psychiatrist explores antidepressant drugs and the remaking of the self.* New York: Penguin Books.

Lambert, M. J., & Bergin, A. E. (1994). The effectiveness of psychotherapy. In A. E. Bergin & S. L. Garfield (Eds.), *Handbook of psychotherapy and behavior change* (pp. 143–189). New York: John Wiley.

Landon, P. S. (1995). Generalist and advanced generalist practice. In R. L. Edwards (Ed.), *Encyclopedia of social work* (19th ed., pp. 1101–1108). Washington, DC: NASW Press.

Lazarus, A. A. (1981). *The practice of multimodal therapy: Systematic, comprehensive, and effective psychotherapy.* New York: McGraw-Hill.

LeBon, G. (1895). *The crowd.* London: Ernest Benn.

Lee, M. Y. (1996). A constructivist approach to the help-seeking process of clients: A response to cultural diversity. *Clinical Social Work Journal, 24* (2), 187–202.

Lehman, A. K., & Salovey, P. (1990). An introduction to cognitive-behavior therapy. In R. A. Wells & V. J. Gianetti (Eds.), *Handbook of the brief psychotherapies* (pp. 239–259). New York: Plenum Press.

Levine, I. S., & Fleming, M. (1985). *Human resources development: Issues in case management.* Rockville, MD: National Institute of Mental Health.

Lewin, K. (1951). *Field theory in social science: Selected theoretical papers* (D. Cartwright, Ed.). New York: Harper Press.

Lewis, R. (1980). Cultural perspective on treatment modalities with Native Americans. In M. Bloom (Ed.), *Life span development: Bases for preventive and interventive helping* (pp. 411–434). New York: Macmillan.

Lieberman, M. A., Yalom, I., & Miles, M. (1973). *Encounter groups: First facts.* New York: Basic Books.

Light, R. J., & Pillemer, D. B. (1984). *Summing up: The science of reviewing research.* Cambridge, MA: Harvard University Press.

Lindemann, E. (1944). Symptomatology and management of acute grief. *American Journal of Psychiatry, 101,* 141–148.

Locke, B., Garrison, R. J., & Winship, J. (1998). *Generalist social work practice: Context, story, and partnerships.* Pacific Grove, CA: Brooks/Cole.

London, P. (1988). Eclectic psychotherapy gets "uppity." *Contemporary Psychology, 33,* 697–698.

Maguire, L. (1983). *Understanding social networks.* Beverly Hills, CA: Sage.

Maguire, L. (1991). *Social support systems in practice: A generalist approach.* Silver Springs, MD: NASW Press.

Maguire, L. (1992). *Pharmacology in social work education.* Panel presentation at the APM of CSWE, Kansas City, MO.

Maguire, L. (1993). Brief social support interventions with adolescents. In R. A. Wells & V. J. Gianetti (Eds.), *Casebook of the brief psychotherapies* (pp. 91–108). New York: Plenum Press.

Mahoney, M. J. (1991). *Human change processes: The scientific foundations of psychotherapy.* New York: Basic Books.

Marlow, C. (1998). Research methods for generalist social work (2nd ed.). Pacific Grove, CA: Brooks/Cole.

Marmor, J. (1992). Historical roots. In H. Davanloo (Ed.), *Short-term dynamic psychotherapy* (pp. 3–12). Northvale, NJ: Jason Aronson.

Mattaini, M. A. (1995a). Generalist practice: People and programs. In C. H. Meyer & M. A. Mattaini (Eds.), *Foundations of social work practice: A graduate text* (pp. 225–245). Washington, DC: NASW Press.

Mattaini, M. A. (1995b). Knowledge for practice. In C. H. Meyer & M. A. Mattaini (Eds.), *Foundations of social work practice: A graduate text* (pp. 59–85). Washington, DC: NASW Press.

Mattaini, M. A. (1997). *Clinical practice with individuals.* Washington, DC: NASW Press.

McGoldrick, M., Giordano, J., & Pearce, J. K. (Eds.). (1996). *Ethnicity and family therapy* (2nd ed.). New York: Guilford.

McLellarn, R. W., & Rosenzweig, J. M. (1998). Generalized anxiety disorder. In B. A. Thyer & J. S. Wodarski (Eds.), *Handbook of empirical social work practice: Vol. 1: Mental disorders* (pp. 385–398). New York: John Wiley & Sons.

McMahon, M. O. (1996). *The general method of social work practice: A generalist perspective* (3rd ed.). Boston, MA: Allyn & Bacon.

Meichenbaum, D. (1976). A cognitive-behavior modification approach to assessment. In M. Hersen & A. Bellack (Eds.), *Behavioral assessment: A practical handbook* (pp. 143–171). New York: Pergamon Press.

Meichenbaum, D. (1977). *Cognitive-behavior modification: An integrative approach.* New York: Plenum.

Meichenbaum, D. (1984). Fostering generalization: A cognitive-behavioral approach. *The Cognitive Behaviorist, 6,* 9–10.

Meyer, C. H. (1983). Selecting appropriate practice models. In A. Rosenblatt & D. Waldfogel (Eds.), *Handbook of clinical social work* (pp. 731–749). San Francisco: Jossey-Bass.

Meyer, C. H., & Mattaini, M. A. (Eds.). (1995). *The foundations of social work practice: A graduate text.* Washington, DC: NASW Press.

Meyer, C. H., & Palleja, J. (1995). Social work practice with individuals. In C. H. Meyer & M. A. Mattaini (Eds.), *The foundations of social work practice: A graduate text* (pp. 105–125). Washington, DC: NASW Press.

Meyer, W. S. (1993). In defense of long-term treatment: On the vanishing holding environment. *Social Work, 38,* (5), 571–578.

Miller, S. (1981). Reflections on the dual perspective. In E. Mizio & A. J. Delaney (Eds.), *Training for service delivery to minority clients* (pp. 53–61). New York: Family Service Association of America.

Minuchin, S., & Fishman, H. C. (1981). *Family therapy techniques.* Cambridge, MA: Harvard University Press.

Moseley, P. G., & Deweaver, K. L. (1998). Empirical approaches to case management. In J. S. Wodarski & B. A. Thyer (Eds.), *Handbook of empirical social work practice: Vol. 2: Social problems and practice issues* (pp. 393–412). New York: John Wiley & Sons.

Mullen, E. J., & Dumpson, J. R. (1972). *Evaluation of social intervention.* San Francisco: Jossey-Bass.

Munson, C. (1994). Cognitive family therapy. In D. G. Granvold (Ed.), *Cognitive and behavior treatment: Methods and applications* (pp. 202–221). Pacific Grove, CA: Brooks/Cole.

Nuckolls, K. B., Cassell, J., & Kaplan, B. H. (1972). Psychosocial assets, life crises, and the prognosis of pregnancy. *American Journal of Epidemiology, 95,* 431–441.

Nunnally, E. (1993). Solution focused therapy. In R. A. Wells & V. J. Gianetti (Eds.), *Casebook of the brief psychotherapies* (pp. 271–286). New York: Plenum Press.

One on one: Adolph Grunbaum. (1998, October 29). *University Times, 31.*

Orlinsky, D. E., Grawe, K., & Parks, B. K. (1994). Process and outcome in psychotherapy-noch einmal. In A. E. Bergin & S. L. Garfield (Eds.), *Handbook of psychotherapy and behavior change* (4th ed.). New York: John Wiley & Sons.

Othmer, E., & Othmer, S. (1989). *The clinical interview: Using DSM-III-R.* Washington, DC: American Psychiatric Association Press.

Parad, H. J. (1971). Crisis intervention. In R. Morris (Ed.), *Encyclopedia of social work* (16th ed., Vol. 1, pp. 196–202). New York: National Association of Social Workers.

Parad, H. J., & Parad, L. G. (1990). *Crisis intervention, book 2: The practitioner's sourcebook for brief therapy.* Milwaukee: Families International.

Pardeck, J. T., Murphy, J. W., & Choi, J. M. (1994). Some implications of postmodernism for social work practice. *Social Work, 39,* 343–346.

Parsons, T., & Bales, R. F. (1955). *Family, socialization, and interaction process.* Glencoe, IL: Free Press.

Pattison, E. M., Francisco, D., Wood, P., Frazier, H., & Crowder, J. (1975). A psychosocial kinship model for family therapy. *American Journal of Psychiatry, 132,* 1246–1251.

Perlman, H. H. (1957). *Social casework: A problem-solving process.* Chicago: University of Chicago Press.

Philips, E. L. (1985). *Psychotherapy revised: New frontiers in research and practice.* Hillsdale, NJ: Erlbaum.

Piaget, J. (1950). *Psychology of intelligence.* New York: Harcourt Brace. (Original work published in 1947.)

Pine, F. (1990). *Drive, ego, object, and self.* New York: Basic Books.

Plaud, J. J., & Vavrovsky, K. G. (1998). Specific and social phobias. In B. A. Thyer & J. S. Wodarski (Eds.), *Handbook of empirical social work practice: Vol. 1: Mental Disorders* (pp. 327–343). New York: John Wiley & Sons.

President's Commission on Mental Health. (1978). *Task Panel Reports.* Washington, DC: U.S. Government Printing Office.

Rapp, C. A. (1998). *The strengths model: Case management with people suffering from severe and persistent mental illness.* New York: Oxford University Press.

Rapp, C. A., & Chamberlin, R. (1985). Case management services for the chronically mentally ill. *Social Work, 30,* 417–422.

Reamer, F. G. (1982). *Ethical dilemmas in social service.* New York: Columbia University Press.

Regier, D. A., Hirshfeld, R. M., Goodwin, F. K., Burke, J. D., Lazar, J. B., & Judd, L. L. (1988). The NIMH depression awareness, recognition, and treatment program: Structure, aims, and scientific basis. *American Journal of Psychiatry, 145,* 1351–1357.

Reid, K. E. (1991). *Social work practice with groups: A clinical perspective.* Pacific Grove, CA: Brooks/Cole.

Reid, W. J. (1990). An integrative model for short-term treatment. In R. A. Wells & V. J. Gianetti (Eds.), *Handbook of the brief psychotherapies* (pp. 55–78). New York: Plenum Press.

Reid, W. J. (1996). Task-centered social work. In F. J. Turner (Ed.), *Social work treatment: Interlocking theoretical approaches* (4th ed., pp. 617–640). New York: Free Press.

Reid, W. J., & Epstein, L. (1972). *Task-centered casework.* New York: Columbia University Press.

Reid, W. J., & Epstein, L. (Eds.). (1977). *Task-centered practice.* New York: Columbia University Press.

Reid, W. J., & Hanrahan, P. (1981). The effectiveness of social work recent evidence. In E. M. Goldberg & N. Connelly (Eds.), *Evaluative research in social care: Papers from a workshop on recent trends in evaluative research in social work and social services, May, 1980.* London: Heinemann Educational Books.

Richmond, M. (1917). *Social diagnosis.* New York: Free Press.

Rogers, C. R. *Counseling and psychotherapy.* Boston, MA: Houghton Mifflin.

Rose, S. D. (1977). *Group therapy: A behavioral approach.* Englewood Cliffs, NJ: Prentice-Hall.

Rose, S. D. (1990). *Working with adults in groups: Integrating cognitive-behavioral and small group strategies.* San Francisco: Jossey-Bass.

Rothman, J. (1992). *Guidelines for case management: Putting research to professional use.* Itasca, IL: Peacock Publishers.

Rueveni, U. (1979). *Networking families in crisis: Intervention strategies with families and social networks.* New York: Human Science Press.

Salkovskis, P. M. (1996). The cognitive approach to anxiety: Threat beliefs, safety-seeking behavior, and the special case of health anxiety and obsessions. In P. M. Salkovskis (Ed.), *Frontiers of cognitive therapy* (pp. 48–74). New York: Guilford Press.

Saltzman, N., & Norcross, J. C. (Eds.). (1990). *Therapy wars: Contention and convergence in differing clinical approaches.* San Francisco: Jossey-Bass.

Schwartz, A. (1982). *The behavior therapies: Theories and applications.* New York: Free Press.

Seligman, L. (1990). *Selecting effective treatments: A comprehensive, systematic guide to treating adult mental disorders.* San Francisco: Jossey-Bass.

Sharf, R. S. (1996). *Theories of psychotherapy and counseling: Concepts and cases.* Pacific Grove, CA: Brooks/Cole.

Sheafor, B. W., Horejsi, C. R., & Horejsi, G. A. (1991). *Techniques and guidelines for social work practice* (2nd ed.). Needham Heights, MA: Allyn & Bacon.

Sheldon, B. (1986). Social work effectiveness experiments: Review and implications. *British Journal of Social Work, 16,* 223–242.

Skinner, B. F. (1953). *Science and human behavior.* New York: Macmillan.

Skinner, B. F. (1971). *Beyond freedom and dignity.* New York: Knopf.

Skinner, B. F. (1974). *About behaviorism.* New York: Knopf.

Slaikeu, K. A. (1990). *Crisis intervention: A handbook for practice and research* (2nd ed.). Boston: Allyn & Bacon.

Smith, J. C., Mercy, J. A., & Conn, J. M. (1988). Marital status and the risk of suicide. *American Journal of Public Health, 78* (1), 78–80.

Specht, H., & Courtney, M. (1994). *Unfaithful angels: How social work has abandoned its mission.* New York: Free Press.

Specht, R., & Craig, G. J. (1987). *Human development: A social work perspective* (2nd ed.). Englewood Cliffs, NJ: Prentice-Hall.

Spivack, G., & Shure, M. B. (1974). *Social adjustment of young children: A cognitive approach to solving real-life problems.* San Francisco: Jossey-Bass.

Srole, L., Langer, T., Michael, S., Opler, M., & Rennie, T. (1962). *Mental health in the metropolis.* New York: McGraw-Hill.

St. Clair, M. (1996). *Object relations and self psychology: An introduction* (2nd ed.). Pacific Grove, CA: Brooks/Cole.

Stekettee, G. S., & White, K. (1990). *When once is not enough: Help for obsessions and compulsions.* Oakland, CA: New Harbinger.

Strean, H. (1996). Psychoanalytic theory and social work treatment. In F. J. Turner (Ed.), *Social work treatment: Interlocking theoretical approaches* (4th ed., pp. 523–554). New York: Free Press.

Stuart, R. B. (1977). *Behavioral self-management: Strategies, techniques, and outcomes.* New York: Bruner/Mazel.

Sullivan, H. S. (1953). *The interpersonal theory of psychiatry.* New York: Norton.

Sullivan, H. S. (1954). *The psychiatric interview.* New York: Norton.

Sullivan, J. P. (1981). Case management. In J. A. Talbott (Ed.), *The chronically mentally ill: Treatment, programs, systems* (pp. 119–131). New York: Human Sciences Press.

Tannen, D. (1990). *You just don't understand: Women and men in conversation.* New York: Ballantine Books.

Tharp, R. G., & Wetzel, R. J. (1969). *Behavior modification in the natural environment.* New York: Academia Press.

Thomas, E. J. (Ed.). (1974). *Behavior modification procedure: A sourcebook.* Chicago: Aldine.

Thomas, E. J. (1984). *Designing interventions for the helping professions.* Beverly Hills, CA: Sage.

Thyer, B. A. (1983). Treating anxiety disorders with exposure therapy. *Social Casework, 64,* 77–82.

Thyer, B. A. (1984). The treatment of phobias in their natural contexts. *Journal of Applied Social Science, 9* (1), 73–83.

Thyer, B. A. (1987). *Treating anxiety disorders: A guide for human service professionals.* Newbury Park, CA: Sage.

Thyer, B. A., & Birsinger, P. (1994). Treatment of clients with anxiety disorders. In D. K. Granvold (Ed.), *Cognitive and behavioral treatment: Methods and applications* (pp. 272–284). Pacific Grove, CA: Brooks/Cole.

Thyer, B. A., Isaac, E. D., & Larkin, R. (1997). Integrating research and practice: The role of practice-relevant research in social work. In M. Reisch & E. Gambrill (Eds.), *Social work in the 21st century* (pp. 311–316). Thousand Oaks, CA: Pine Forge Press.

Thyer, B. A., & Wodarski, J. S. (1998). First principles of empirical social work practice. In B. A. Thyer & J. S. Wodarski (Eds.), *Handbook of empirical social work practice: Vol. 1: Mental disorders* (pp. 1–22). New York: John Wiley & Sons.

Tischler, G. L., Riedel, D. C., & Myers, J. K. (Eds.). (1974). *Patient care evaluation in mental health programs: Introduction.* Cambridge, MA: Ballinger.

Tolsdorf, C. C. (1976). Social networks, support, and coping: An exploratory study. *Family Process, 15,* 407–417.

Tolson, E. R., Reid, W. J., & Garvin, C. D. (1994). *Generalist practice: A task-centered approach.* New York: Columbia University Press.

Tomb, D. A. (1994). The phenomenology of post-traumatic stress disorder. *Psychiatric Clinics of North America, 17* (2), 237–250.

Tripodi, T. (1994). *A primer on single-subject design for clinical social workers.* Washington, DC: NASW Press.

Tuckman, B. W. (1965). Developmental sequence in small groups. *Psychological Bulletin, 63,* 384–399.

Tuckman, B. W., & Jensen, M. A. (1977). Stages of small group development revisited. *Group and Organizational Studies, 2,* 419–427.

Turner, F. J. (Ed.). (1983). *Differential diagnosis and treatment in social work* (3rd ed.). New York: Free Press.

Turner, F. J. (Ed.). (1986). *Social work treatment: Interlocking theoretical approaches* (3rd ed.). New York: Free Press.

Turner, F. J. (Ed.). (1996). *Social work treatment: Interlocking theoretical approaches* (4th ed.). New York: Free Press.

Van Den Bergh, N. (1992). Feminist treatment for people with depression. In K. Corcoran (Ed.), *Structuring change: Effective practice for common client problems* (pp. 95–109). Chicago: Lyceum Books.

Vinter, R. (1974a). Program activities: An analysis of their effects on participant behavior. In P. H. Glasser, R. C. Sarri, & R. D. Vinter (Eds.), *Individual change through small groups* (pp. 233–243). New York: Free Press.

Vinter, R. (1974b). The essential components of social group work practice. In P. Glasser, R. Sarri, & R. Vinter (Eds.), *Individual change through small groups* (pp. 9–33). New York: Free Press.

Vonk, M. E., & Yegidis, B. L. (1998). Post-traumatic stress disorder. In B. A. Thyer & J. S. Wodarski (Eds.), *Handbook of empirical social work practice: Vol. 1; Mental disorders* (pp. 365–384). New York: John Wiley & Sons.

Walborn, F. S. (1996). *Process variables: Four common elements of counseling and psychotherapy.* Pacific Grove, CA: Brooks/Cole.

Walsh, F. (1997). Family therapy: Systems approaches to clinical practice. In J. R. Brandell (Ed.), *Theory and practice in clinical social work* (pp. 132–163). New York: Free Press.

Waskow, I., & Parloff, M. B. (Eds.). (1974). *Psychotherapy change measures.* Rockville, MD: National Institute of Mental Health.

Wells, R. A. (1992). Planned short-term treatment for persons with social and interpersonal problems. In K. Corcoran (Ed.), *Structuring change: Effective practice for common client problems* (pp. 292–309). Chicago: Lyceum.

Wells, R. A. (1993). Clinical strategies in brief psychotherapy. In R. A. Wells & V. J. Gianetti (Eds.), *Casebook of the brief psychotherapies* (pp. 3–20). New York: Plenum Press.

Wells, R. A. (1994). *Planned short-term treatment* (2nd ed.). New York: Free Press.

Wells, R. A., & Gianetti, V. J. (Eds.). (1990). *Handbook of the brief psychotherapies.* New York: Plenum Press.

Wells, R. A., & Gianetti, V. J. (Eds.). (1993). *Casebook of the brief psychotherapies.* New York: Plenum Press.

Wells, R. A., & Phelps, P. A. (1990). The brief psychotherapies: A selective overview. In R. A. Wells & V. Gianetti (Eds.), *Handbook of brief psychotherapies* (pp. 3–26). New York: Plenum.

Western Psychiatric Institute & Clinic [WPIC]. (1990). Depression/awareness, recognition, and treatment (D/ART), Training for Senior Mental Health Clinicians, March 12–13, 1990.

White, M. (1986). Negative explanation, restraint, and double description: A template for family therapy. *Family Process, 25* (2), 169–184.

Whiteley, J. N. (1984). Counseling psychology: A historical perspective. *The Counseling Psychologist, 12* (1), 3–109.

Whittaker, J. K., Schinke, S. P., & Gilchrist, L. D. (1986). The ecological paradigm in children, youth, and family services: Implications for policy and practice. *Social Service Review, 60* (4), 483–503.

Williamson, E. G. (1939). *How to counsel students.* New York: McGraw-Hill.

Wilson, W. J. (1987). *The truly disadvantaged: The inner city, the underclass and public policy.* Chicago: University of Chicago Press.

Wolfe, B. E., & Goldfried, M. R. (1988). Research on psychotherapy integration: Recommendations and conclusions from an NIMH workshop. *Journal of Consulting and Clinical Psychology, 56,* 448–451.

Wolpe, J. (1958). *Psychotherapy by reciprocal inhibition.* Stanford, CA: Stanford University Press.

Wolpe, J. (1967) The comparative clinical status of conditioning therapies and psychoanalysis. In J. Wolpe, A. Salter, & L. J. Reyna (Eds.), *The conditioning therapies and psychoanalysis.* New York: Holt, Rinehart & Winston.

Wolpe, J., & Lazarus, A. A. (1967). *Behavior therapy techniques: A guide to the treatment of neuroses.* New York: Pergamon Press.

Wood, K. M. (1978). Casework effectiveness: A new look at the research evidence. *Social Work, 23,* 437–458.

Woods, M. E., & Hollis, F. (1990). *Casework, A psychosocial therapy* (4th ed.). New York: McGraw-Hill.

Woods, M. E., & Robinson, H. (1996). Psychosocial theory and social work practice. In F. Turner (Ed.), *Social work treatment: Interlocking theoretical approaches* (4th ed., pp. 555–580). New York: Free Press.

Woodside, M., & McClam, T. (1998). *Generalist case management: A method of human services delivery.* Pacific Grove, CA: Brooks/Cole.

Yalom, I. (1985). *The theory and practice of group psychotherapy* (3rd ed.). New York: Basic Books.

Yalom, I. (1995). *The theory and practice of group psychotherapy* (4th ed.). New York: Basic Books.

Yamatani, H., Maguire, L., Rogers, R. K., & O'Kennedy, M. L. (1996). Battered households. In M. Baum & P. Twiss (Eds.), *Social work intervention in an economic crisis: The River Communities Project* (pp. 65–74). New York: Haworth Press.

Zastrow, C. H. (1989). *The practice of social work* (3rd ed.). Belmont, CA: Wadsworth.

Zastrow, C. H. (1999). *The practice of social work* (6th ed.). Pacific Grove, CA: Brooks/Cole.

Zastrow, C. H., & Kirst-Ashman, K. K. (1997). *Understanding human behavior and the social environment* (4th ed.). Chicago: Nelson-Hall.

Name Index

Ackerman, N., 161, 163–164
Addams, J., 11, 59
Ahola, T., 161
Allen-Meares, P., 69
Alpern, P., 150
American Psychiatric Association, 3, 18, 20, 67–68, 83, 124, 238, 268, 300
Anderson, C., 161
Apponte, H., 161
Arizmindi, T. G., 52, 53
Aronson, J. A., 159
Atherton, C. R., 79
Attneave, C., 161
Austad, C. S., 277
Austin, D., 2, 9, 20, 29

Baars, B. J., 249
Bales, R. F., 69
Barbior, S., 270
Barker, R. L., 16, 27, 79, 129
Bateson, G., 161
Baucom, D. H., 274
Baum, M., 71
Beck, A. T., 124, 161, 250, 251, 255, 258, 271, 274
Beck, J., 305
Belcher, J. R., 23, 31
Bell, J., 161
Benson, H., 260, 263
Bently, K. J., 38, 40, 43, 50, 51, 114
Berg, I. K., 161
Bergin, A. E., 3, 10, 13, 20, 22, 35, 39, 52, 57, 78
Beutler, L. E., 52, 53
Biegel, D.E., 74–75
Birsinger, P., 269
Bloom, M., 83, 279, 284, 285, 287
Blythe, B. J., 18, 59, 60, 303
Borman, L., 148
Boscolo, L., 166

Boszormenyi-Nagy, I., 161
Bourne, E. J., 257, 263, 264, 270
Bowen, M., 161, 260, 300, 301
Brandell, J. R., 43, 62
Briar, S., 59
Brieland, D., 79
Bromley, D. B., 56
Brown, J. H., 165, 166, 167, 169
Budman, S. H., 279, 287
Burns, D. B., 39, 112, 260, 268, 271, 274
Bush, J. A., 75
Butcher, J. N., 15

Campbell, A., 74
Campbell, J., 287
Caplan, G., 12
Carter, E., 161
Cassell, J., 74
Cecchin, G., 166
Chamberlin, R., 95, 102
Chang, T., 287
Cheetham, J., 13–14
Chestang, L., 75
Choi, J. M., 17
Cohen, I., 269
Converse, D. E., 74
Corcoran, K., 36, 59, 60, 88
Corsini, R., 147–148
Costin, L. B., 79
Coulton, C. J., 68
Courtney, M., 38
Crago, M., 52, 53
Craig, G. J., 41
Craighead, W.E., 278
Crowder, J., 74
CSWE, 27, 28, 39, 79, 83, 93, 297
Cuevas, N. M., 53

Datillio, F. M., 279
Davanloo, H., 279

327

Subject Index